COMING A

11-6-2012
Happy 21st Lex!
Remember to spend
time exploring things
you love.
    -Sarah

TEXAS FILM AND MEDIA SERIES
Thomas Schatz, Series Editor

Coming Attractions

Reading American Movie Trailers

LISA KERNAN

UNIVERSITY OF TEXAS PRESS, AUSTIN

Kernan, Lisa.
    Coming attractions : reading American movie trailers / Lisa Kernan.— 1st ed.
        p.   cm. — (Texas film and media series)
    Filmography of trailers viewed: p.
    Includes bibliographical references and index.
    ISBN 0-292-70558-1
  1. Motion picture trailers—United States.   I. Title.   II. Series.
    PN1995.9.T68K47   2004
    791.43'75'0973—dc22
                                                        2004007809

IN MEMORIAM:

George Custen
Jeannine Ivy
Nina Leibman
Beverly Robinson
Christine Saxton

A few in my scholarly orbit whose legacies remind me to keep it real.

Contents

Acknowledgments

I have been blessed with the generosity of many friends, colleagues, teachers and institutions during the long process of bringing this book to press. The insight of Texas Film and Media Series editor Tom Schatz was much appreciated in the process of transforming a dissertation into a book, and my editor, Jim Burr, has intelligently and cheerfully made doing a book seem like a friendly, easygoing enterprise. Lynne Chapman, ace copyeditor Bob Fullilove, and two anonymous readers also helped make it a better book.

I want to acknowledge Jeff Joseph of Sabucat Productions, whose love of trailers has borne fruit in the form of an unsurpassed private collection, which he was generous enough to share with me for the creation of the illustrations as well as for my presentation at the Vienna conference "You Can Have It." Our discussions over the years were helpful in many ways, and Jeff's passion for seeing and sharing films and trailers is a gift that the Los Angeles area is lucky to have. Marilyn Frisbee of Sabucat cheerfully helped me not once but twice to obtain clips for illustrations. I also want to thank the Librarians Association of UCLA for two LAUC-LA minigrants that enabled me to provide Sabucat with at least a gesture of remuneration.

I have been fortunate to be inspired and taught by generous mentors whose approaches to teaching and writing about film have reminded me of the potential for such work to be more than just a product of an academic career. The adage "When the student is ready, the teacher appears" certainly applies in my case to both Bill Nichols and Vivian Sobchack, whose works moreover offer examples of film writing that successfully aspires at once to be an art form and to raise consciousness. Besides Vivian, without whose encouragement and critique this book might not exist, the committee of Nick Browne, Meg Campbell, Douglas

Kellner and Bob Rosen provided support and guidance through the dissertation process, and Doug in particular continued to guide me as the book took shape. The UCLA Film, Television and Digital Media faculty have guided and influenced me in countless ways, as did San Francisco State University's Cinema faculty during my MA. Thank you also to my first film teachers, David Pini and Jake Shearer.

I am grateful to other colleagues who influenced the work and/or offered encouragement, especially Jane Gaines, Rhonda Hammer and Susan Ohmer. Noël Burch, Jill Casid, Sumiko Higashi, Arthur Knight, Katie Mills and Lutz Nitsche offered valuable feedback on portions of the manuscript. Vinzenz Hediger, my Swiss trailer-scholar counterpart, found me during his dissertation research. We shared findings, presented at conferences together, and became friends, although not reading German has impeded my understanding of his work. He also gave me the honor to participate with him for a brief presentation on trailers for the Winterthur (Switzerland) Short Film Festival in 2000. We hope our respective approaches are complementary.

Students in the doctoral program at UCLA have been invaluable colleagues, including my original Ph.D. classmates, Peter Bloom, Bernard Cook, Colin Gardner, Hyun-ock Im and Lael Loewenstein; and a dissertation reading group of Gilberto Blasini, Jim Friedman, Bambi Haggins and Kristen Hatch. Other UCLA dissertators also inspired me along the way, particularly Luisela Alvaray, Vicki Callahan, Victoria Duckett, Susan Englander, Rita Gonzalez, Haden Guest, Jennifer Holt and Maja Manojlovic.

The work was significantly assisted by two scholarships from the Plitt Theatre Southern Employees, to whom I am very grateful. My employers and colleagues at the UCLA Library have been extremely supportive. I especially want to thank the head of the Arts Library, Gordon Theil, for his advocacy, as well as Janice Koyama and Rita Scherrei. Thanks also to my archival education colleague Steven Ricci, as well as my mentor in librarianship, Maurice J. (Mitch) Freedman, whose example helps me keep the faith that library work constitutes the front lines of democracy in education.

Thank you to Dietmar Schwärzler and Tanja Widmann, organizers of the conference "You Can Have It: Kinorituale" at the Wien Kunsthalle's "Projektor" lecture series at Vienna's Depot, as well as to Julia Ezergailis for her simultaneous translations. The UCLA Department of Film, Television and Digital Media has a dedicated support staff, and I particularly want to thank Zareh Arevshatian, Brian Clark, Julius Lopez and

Cecilia Wilmott for their help. Thank you to the staff of the UCLA Film and Television Archive for facilitating my trailer viewing and providing information, especially Dan Einstein, Charles Hopkins, Eddie Richmond and Martha Yee; and of course again to Bob Rosen, for his mentorship during my archival fellowship year. Thanks also to the Margaret Herrick Library at the Academy of Motion Picture Arts and Sciences, especially Barbara Hall and Linda Mehr. I am grateful as well to Jo Donaldson and Debbie Fine, former colleagues at Lucasfilm Ltd., where the seeds of my interest in promotional film paratexts were planted in the 1980s. My friends Olaf Kallstrom and Smitty gave me insight into contemporary trailer production practices. Other friends and mentors, including Norma Barzman, Joe Brenner, Michele Benzamin-Miki, Barbara Clare, Glenn Farr, A. P. Gonzalez, Ray Greenfield, Harry Kelley, Linda Moakes, Charlotte Norris, Janet Patterson, Caitrióna Reed, Stan Rowett, Kay Salz and Douw Smith inspired me every day. And finally, my gratitude to my family—and my shining parents, Margot Starr and Michael Kernan—only deepens as time goes by.

Coming Attractions

1

Trailers: A Cinema
of (Coming) Attractions

railers, or previews of coming attractions, are both praised
and reviled by film scholars and regular moviegoers alike.
"They give away too much of the movie." "They're better than
the films." "They only show the spectacular parts." "All the best jokes
are in the trailer." "They lie." "They're the best part of going to the
movies." "They're too loud." At the same time, they are used by both
groups precisely as they're meant to be used, as free samples to aid in
moviegoing decision making. And in the contemporary market, trailers'
reach is ever expanding, with their inclusion on videotapes, DVDs, and
on the Internet, where they are an increasingly popular and influential
marketing tool. Yet very little scholarly attention has been paid to the
way trailers characterize films, and thus presume audience desire, in
order to sell them.[1]

While trailers are a form of advertising, they are also a unique form
of narrative film exhibition, wherein promotional discourse and narrative pleasure are conjoined (whether happily or not). Thus this book is
not a study of film advertising as a whole, and will not treat television
advertising for films, nor key art such as posters. I am defining a movie
trailer as a brief film text that usually displays images from a specific
feature film while asserting its excellence, and that is created for the
purpose of projecting in theaters to promote a film's theatrical release.
Trailers are film paratexts that are especially important to study in an era
when promotion and visual narrative have become increasingly difficult
to disentangle in all kinds of popular media, whether music television,
children's cartoons, "infotainment," or films themselves. Indeed, as Jane
Gaines noted as early as 1990, "Today, the analysis of culture as commodity may have lost its explanatory potency since we are left with so
few examples of uncommodified relations."[2] And more recently, scholars

are finding that global capitalism's pervasive systems of cultural marketing necessitate a rethinking and re-visioning of the role of "screen studies" in contemporary media analysis.[3] Neither advertising theory nor
narrative film theories adequately address what consequences the current ubiquity of the promotional message might hold for contemporary
definitions and understandings of moving-image narrative forms. The
study of trailers, a long-standing popular form of promotional narrative
(which both sells and tells a reconfigured version of a film narrative),
may shed historical light on the emergence of this particular convergence of spectator and consumer address, and the project of this book
is to further that investigation.[4]

By offering audiences concise, direct-address cinematic texts that
serve as both attractions and as a form of persuasion, trailers allow
audiences to read the phenomenon of promotional narrative in a particularly dramatic way. Trailers *are* a cinema—of (coming) attractions.
Analysis of trailers as a unique cinematic form can bring a greater critical awareness to audiences' readings not only of trailers themselves,
but of the variety of marketing-laden texts comprising the contemporary visual culture industry as a whole. Trailers' unique status as cinematic promotions of narrative—and narrativizations of promotion—
enables a treatment that transcends a mere marketing critique and has
the potential to contribute to a social history of desire.

Generally present in popular film, the processes of filmic narration
that ensure that audiences are caught up in identifying with fictional
film worlds and suspending disbelief result in a familiar relationship
(analyzed by countless film theorists)[5] between audiences and the films
unreeling before them. Shot-reverse-shot structures and other framing
conventions ordinarily keep viewers from looking directly into the eyes
of characters, and even voice-over narrations, while addressed to viewers, generally tell their part of the story without directly invoking the
audience. Trailers, on the other hand, have often spoken to us directly,
frequently telling us to SEE! COME! JOIN IN! THRILL TO! . . . , even at
times using characters or actors shown looking directly into the camera
and at the audience (although contemporary trailers usually display such
injunctions more obliquely).

The actual identity of this "us" that trailers and other promotional
discourses address—the historical, gendered, racially and class-specific
spectator of American popular film—is now a prime object of film
reception studies. Indeed, the recent and widespread "return to history" within the field of film studies addresses this historical spectator in

two important ways. First, many ethnographic investigations of the consumption behavior of film spectators attempt to ground the field on a more material basis from which to make claims about the cultural contexts of film reception; and second, a number of archival investigations of the extratextual discourses (such as posters, pressbooks, reviews, exhibition documents and fan magazines) surrounding films themselves are being performed that shed new light on the industrial, institutional and cultural influences that shape both audiences' interpretations of films and the ideological underpinnings of Hollywood production practices. A study of trailers seems a logical fit that would continue both these approaches. But my interest in trailers and audiences lies more in the process by which audiences are implicitly defined by promotional discourses, as the studios attempt to know what "the audience" wants. Rather than exploring the actual spectator, I am interested in the hypothetical spectator that can be read within trailer texts themselves: an "audience study" through the looking glass of the Hollywood film industry.[6]

My project of reading trailers to discern who the film industry *thinks* it is addressing within trailer texts is designed to invite a more critical approach to spectatorship itself—for the benefit not only of scholars but also of "rank and file" spectators. People watching films need not do in-depth primary research on film reception to get a handle on the ideological implications of the commodity relations of film spectatorship. Trailers provide unique and specific rhetorical structures that fold visual and auditory evidence of the film production industry's assessment of its actual audience (as well as its desires for a potential audience) into a one- to three-minute cinematic experience. Film studies has explored various models for considering those who watch films: among these, semiotic and psychoanalytic theories treat them as (ideal, implied, constructed or historical) *spectators*; in commodity theories they're considered *consumers*; in historical reception studies they tend to be called the *audience*. While my perspective draws on all three models and each of these words may be called into service depending on whether the aspect under consideration is semiotic, economic or historical, trailers are most interesting to me for the ways they can vividly illuminate (more than merely measure or document) how the motion picture audience was imagined by the film industry—a historical fact in its own right.

This approach comes from an urge to resist the current trend in film historiography to eschew textual analysis of films in favor of archival document research, to the degree that it sometimes seems film historians aren't writing about movies anymore. I suggest that the (understandable) reaction against the totalizing forms of textual analysis favored by earlier structuralist approaches has resulted in scholars occasionally "throwing the baby out with the bath water,"[7] as film studies valorizes certain styles of industrial and institutional historiography while at times minimizing the importance (indeed, inevitability) of grounding film history within a *point of view* about our actual historical object, the cinematic text. Regardless of its occasional lapses into historical relativism, the advances of poststructuralist theory still apply. "History" is not written by a unified, centered historical subject who stands apart from the object of study and can freely consider "facts" and documents as objective—to the contrary, history often "writes us." Analysis of film texts is as crucial to the historian as visits to the archive, although of course any analysis must be couched within as much acknowledgment as possible of his or her own subject position. This book represents an effort to posit nontotalizing, accessible, yet theoretically informed methods for analyzing film texts and paratexts *as* primary archival documents. As ecologists can analyze a tree to determine facts about its entire ecosystem, a rhetorical textual analysis of trailers can facilitate a cognitive mapping of where we stand in relation to the cultural and historical "ecosystem" of the commodity relations of Hollywood film.

My own subject position as a middle-class WASP second-generation film scholar coming of age in the United States in the second half of the twentieth century has obviously influenced my interest in trailers. During an informal seminar at UCLA in 1992, historian Hayden White encouraged film and television students to "privilege your neurosis to tell you what interests you," and expressed interest in theories "based on unease, on what embarrasses." Coming from my particular class and family background, it embarrassed me how easily I can be seduced by all kinds of promotional texts. While I have always imagined that I am not drawn to select brand-name products on the basis of advertising, trailers, as ads for watching, are the perfect seduction for me because movies are a "product" I "consume" extensively and (almost) without shame. Yet contradictorily, the impulse to resist the pull of images has been with me almost as long as their seductiveness, thanks to a film scholar mother who would "bare the device" of movie scenes that scared me as a child and who introduced me to the films and theories of Jean-Luc Godard as a teenager. At times my resulting tendency to survey and examine, more than participate in, film and media culture has also been a source of unease, given my (also class-based) desire not to set myself apart from or above "the masses." I have pursued this work on trailers partly as an attempt to model the kind of critical spectatorship I would like to be able to experience naturally: a reconciliation of critical distance and emotional engagement.

This positioning results in my research emerging from an inevitable point of view, or in Kenneth Burke's terminology, a "terministic screen."[8] One reason I have been drawn to rhetoric as a methodology is precisely its acknowledgment of vantage point in the context of scholarly research. Indeed, David Blakesley's anthology of recent work on film and rhetoric takes Burke's concept as its title. And while "rhetoric's function as a filter or screen, enabling some things to pass through clearly, obscuring or repressing others" requires of rhetorical film scholars a vigilance to avoid allowing pet theories to determine, a priori, our analyses, we must acknowledge that "what theory 'produces' . . . is in part a consequence of its terministic screen," that is, the speaking position of the theorist.[9]

I rely on classical rhetoric, the art of persuasion, to analyze trailers because they are quintessentially persuasive cinematic texts. While looking to rhetoric is a move that places my work strongly within a structuralist/semiotic tradition, my overall methodology and purpose is that of ideological critique within a social-historical framework. The recent re-visioning of the uses of rhetoric for film studies—and specifically for ideological critique—is surveyed in Blakesley's anthology, which attempts to "map the emergent field of rhetorical studies of film."[10] By integrating a rhetorical method within a social history of trailers I participate in this re-visioning and thereby hope to demonstrate the ongoing use value of textual analysis for film historiographic investigation. Aristotelian rhetoric offers a method by which one can pinpoint textual evidence of trailer producers' assumptions about their audience(s). The enthymeme, Aristotle's word for those figures of speech wherein commonplaces shared by the listener are incorporated into a speaker's assertions, is key to locating this evidence. I identify enthymemes as components of trailers' promotion of three principal textual features of films: genres, stories and stars, in the process assessing some of the broader ideological implications of the industry's assumptions about its audiences' interest in these features.

Trailers, of course, are not the only film texts that demonstrate the extent to which spectatorship is institutionalized within cinema practice as a term of the text: this is a historical condition of Hollywood film.[11] Theatrical trailer spectatorship is, however, a heightened spectatorial mode, an arena where spectators tend to evince greater awareness of themselves as a collectivity, even as they are subjected to a more pointed ideological thrust by trailers' specifically promotional forms of address than they may be in the general experience of film spectatorship. There is a carnivalesque atmosphere to the trailer segment of the theatrical exhibition experience that contradicts trailers' supposedly disciplinary or instructional function.

In quoting from the films they promote and giving spectators "free samples" of them, trailers can be seen to reframe their original fictional film narratives into a (window) shopper's world. Much recent film scholarship has called attention to the relationships between film spectatorship and shopping, and specifically to the "shop window" analogy.[12] Trailer spectatorship increases the implied distance of the speculative consumer contemplation involved in cinematic window shopping;[13] it also removes the commitment to enter the familiar contract of "suspension of disbelief" entailed in the process of watching a complete narrative film (we aren't "buying it"), doubly distancing spectators from either a lived-world agency or an imaginary one. At the same time, trailer spectatorship is one of the primary sites where audiences are pointedly "shopping" for films. Contemporary audiences sometimes express awareness of the greater distance entailed in the theatrical trailer viewing experience by manifesting interactivity among themselves—as when hisses, cheers and other editorial comments punctuate the exhibition of trailers or fill the silences between them.

The distance from the source text's narrative pull entailed in trailers' *quoting* from the films they promote thus enables a greater closeness to other spectators *as* consumers and critics. Susan Stewart's phenomenological study of narratives of exaggeration and nostalgia comments on the transformative aspect of quotation:

> *In quotation we find the context of production transformed and the utterance detached from the authority of that context. . . . As Bateson has explained in his studies of the message "This is play," the play message signifies a transformation of interpretive procedures, a transformation partaken of by members of the situation and which they understand as a device for entering into an abstract and metaphorical play world.*[14]

One sometimes experiences such "an abstract and metaphorical play world" in the movie theater when trailers are screened, and editorial comments exchanged among strangers during the trailers are perhaps less likely to be "shushed" than talking that occurs during the film itself, at least in the contemporary era (and I have found no evidence indicating this was any different earlier). The recent popularity of repertory trailer compilation screenings as nostalgic, camp, and/or ironic spectatorial experiences underscores the appeal of the sort of detachment Stewart characterizes. Whether "bought" or not, the transformed narrative coherence of this quotational "world" inhabited by spectators of trailers constitutes the diegesis of the promotional film text.

In this aspect, trailers resemble a prenarrative system of filmmaking that evokes Tom Gunning's influential work on early cinema. Gunning uses Eisenstein's notion of a "montage of attractions" to characterize pre-1906 cinema as "a cinema of attractions," which he describes as "less . . . a way of telling stories than . . . a way of presenting a series of views to an audience, fascinating because of their illusory power . . . and exoticism; . . . a cinema that displays its visibility, willing to rupture a self-enclosed fictional world for a chance to solicit the attention of the spectator."[15] In trailers, images are selected and combined in ways that privilege attracting the spectator's attention over sustaining narrative coherence. Yet trailers also maintain a relationship to the narrative they promote, and in this relationship between promotional images of attraction and coherent cinematic narrative lie the unique characteristics that constitute the rhetoric of trailers.

To be precise, trailers are film paratexts. As Gérard Genette has characterized them, paratexts are those textual elements that emerge from and impart significance to a (literary) text but aren't considered integral to the text itself, such as all prefatory material, dust jacket blurbs, advertisements and reviews. Specifically, trailers can be seen as instances of a film's "public epitext."[16] Because of their heavily quotational aspect and the way they rhetorically reconfigure scenes from the film, endowing them with persuasive content, I would suggest moreover that trailers are both para- and metatexts. Communication theorists remind us that to analyze metacommunication is to "look for the abstract structural frameworks and systemic processes, the codes and constraints, which allow only certain messages to be transmitted in the system."[17] Thus an analysis of trailers' promotional rhetoric speaks to the ideological and cultural conditions of, or constraints within, Hollywood cinematic narrative itself in specific historical moments.

As both narrative and promotional texts, trailers themselves can be seen as a hybrid *genre* within the canon of Hollywood film. They offer film viewers an italicized, alluringly reconfigured narrative space of ellipsis and enigma, where features such as characters' gestures and gazes, spatial relations, character and camera movement, dialogue, narration, music, and evocations of film's narrative structure have particular signifying characteristics, as will be explored in these pages. Considering trailers as a genre of film practice—and this book as a genre study—helps us look at these particularities as partaking of more than merely a type of advertising: to see trailers as cinematic textual practices among others. This in turn reminds us that the intersection of selling and telling in these little pieces of film varies perhaps only in a matter of degree from that of Hollywood films themselves.[18] It also reminds us to consider trailers' place in the cultural imaginary of Hollywood film reception: that is, as more than a mere reflection of their industrial role as a marketing practice constituting one facet of a promotional campaign. Trailers are at once ads and more than ads. People who are incensed to see product advertising on the big screen (a phenomenon that is on the increase) rush to be in their seats in time for the trailers. During the course of my research I have repeatedly heard "I *love* trailers" in reaction to my topic, and invariably, what's meant is not just "I love being shown ads for new movies so I can decide which ones to go to," but rather an appreciation of the unique visual and narrative/promotional qualities of these short film texts.

Like many film scholars, I often find viewing films a divided experience. As mentioned, I can feel the detachment of retaining an awareness of the artifice of filmmaking[19] while simultaneously losing myself in the seductive qualities of projected celluloid, "going along with" the mechanisms of spectator-construction that I know are operating in most narrative feature films. The two modes of viewing are inscribed in each other in that any attempt to describe the one relies on a knowledge of the other, yet their coexistence in my experience of movie spectatorship seems irreconcilable, impossible.

Trailer spectatorship heightens the presence of this doubleness. The contradictoriness of trailers is perhaps their salient feature, and for me at once their greatest source of pleasure and the point where they most incisively display Hollywood's view of its audience(s). In fact, trailers operate as a unique sort of cinematic gyroscope in which a host of contradictions are briefly (for one to three minutes) sustained in balance—not the least of which is the quality of nostalgia for a film we haven't even seen yet.[20] Because they are anticipatory texts, they need no resolution. For all the weightiness of their narratorial pronouncements and the booming sound effects of their cataclysmic imagery, they are breath-less, liminal and ephemeral. They are fun because they play (or *trail . . .*) at the edges of narrative cinematic sense. Like the brief moment in which the cloaked Klingon "bird of prey" warships in *Star Trek* must become visible (and thus vulnerable) in order to have enough power to discharge their weapons, trailers are where Hollywood displays its con-tradictions right at the point where its promotional message is most direct. Describing the play of rhetorical features in this zone of contra-diction and potential dialectic within and among trailer texts comes as close as anything to satisfying my desire to understand some of the con-tradictions of my own relationship to spectatorship.

GENERIC FEATURES OF TRAILERS

As suggested earlier, there are common features among trailers from all eras as well as historical transformations within the genre. Most trailers have in common a few generic features: some sort of introductory or concluding address to the audience about the film either through titles or narration, selected scenes from the film, mon-tages of quick-cut action scenes, and identifications of significant cast members or characters. The genre of trailers also has much in common with other kinds of advertising. Audiences for advertisements are con-stantly re-creating meanings as they read or watch them. They mediate between particular ads and "referent systems"—or the body of social knowledge on which advertisers and audiences alike draw and rely—and in this process audiences co-constitute the meanings of ads.[21]

Yet film as a product differs from most other advertised goods in that the referent systems that trailers use and audiences transform in the process of constructing meaning are more than a body of social knowledge. They are that, plus a body of specific cinematic conventions, a body of expectations about what films can offer narratively, and a set of desires. These desires are not to consume an object, but to engage in an experience, in a process of meaning-production through narrative film, a "free sample" of which the trailer constructs. If a trailer can "pig-gyback" the captive and willing movie audience's desire to see a given film (the one they've come to presently see) onto, first, a desire to see another film (the one being promoted), and next, to *other* desires the audience is believed to hold, the audience is more likely "sold" on the promoted film. This principle is the basis of the film industry's exploita-tion practices as a whole, which owe as much to the historical precedent of P. T. Barnum as to other advertising. Through trailers, the use value of narrative (enjoying a film) is subsumed to its exchange value (wanting to see another film) by a process of transforming the codes of narrative fiction into the codes of promotional rhetoric. In this process, new narrative (or more precisely, narrative/promotional) codes or rhetorical devices are produced.

Trailers construct a narrative time-space that differs from (and creates desire for) the fictive world of the film itself. The fast pace of most trailers accentuates the film's surface of cinematic spectacle, displaying the film's shiniest wares, or most *attractive* images, positioning it as a commodity for sale. Narrative, however, does not disappear in this process. Trailers are themselves little stories constructed within the anticipatory dimension of capitalist realism in which carefully selected individual cinematic images, dynamically combined in highly teleological editing structures, shine with a surface gloss of exaggerated spectacularity.[22]

In particular, as I will explore, trailers commonly utilize codes of voice-over narration, sound and sound overlapping, music, graphics, and most importantly, editing, or montage. A system of discontinuous continuity editing—which I call *dis*continuity editing—operates through alternation, combination and abbreviation of scenes to construct a new, *trailer* logic, differing from (yet, obviously, related to) the narrative logic of the film. One shot in a two-minute trailer is called upon to stand in for a number of narrative elements, such as character subjectivity and relations, plot development and suspense. Of course, this can be true of film in general, but since in trailers each of these abbreviated stand-in images is part of an ad for an as-yet-unseen film, they become charged with excess signification. Faces, for example, bear tremendous weight as carriers of various emotional signifieds and enigmas. The Bazinian emphasis on the capacity of human facial physiognomy to reveal interior life[23] is endowed with a promotional kick: in trailers the intensity of facial expressions acts as a window not onto the world or the interior spiritual state of a human being, but onto a sort of imagined narrative plenitude of whatever film is being promoted. Images of faces also draw upon a large cultural lexicon of photographic portraiture, endowing shots such as one of Denzel Washington as Malcolm X staring at the camera from behind prison bars with extra emotional punch (in trailers, photographic cliché can work to advantage).

Similarly, gestures and movements create impressions of narrative thrust, whether compatible or not with their actual narrative function in

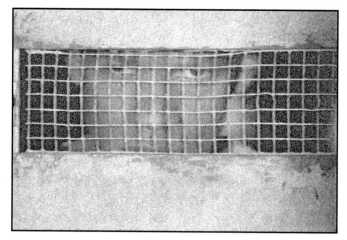

Figure 1.1. Denzel Washington as Malcolm X
behind prison bars in the *Malcolm X* trailer.

the film. Indeed, the "Kuleshov effect" gets fresh validation in the occasional repositionings of the meanings of shots from a film to better fit a trailer's narrative trajectory.[24] Thus, a shot of Meg Ryan falling on her bed in the trailer for *You've Got Mail* (1998), which in the film is a gesture of sadness and frustration after the character is stood up by her cyber-date, appears in the trailer to be a swoon, thus better contributing to the film's overall generic positioning as a romantic comedy. Moreover, a trailer can imply plot developments that are false (such as Kurt Russell apparently dying in the trailer for *Unlawful Entry*, 1992); can contain conversations that never happen (juxtaposing two lines of dialogue unconnected in the film so that the second appears to reply to the first); or provide false narration (in which spoken lines of dialogue are abstracted from the drama and inserted as trailer voice-overs). Additionally, shots are sometimes included in trailers that do not appear in the finished film (such as a "silly walk" Jack Nicholson does in the trailer for *As Good As It Gets*, 1997). Trailers get away with numerous falsifications in the interests of promotion, just as other ads do, but because these advertisements are for a product that is a longer form of the same type of cinematic text, a trailer's truth claims "claim" different kinds of "truth" about the films they promote than other ads do, thus potentially creating a range of responses in audiences that may vary from their responses to ordinary advertising rhetoric.

In these "montages of (coming) attractions," spectacular features such as explosions and car crashes are often emphasized, with a frequent

Figure 1.2. Meg Ryan's apparent swoon in the *You've Got Mail* trailer.

result that trailers are the loudest part of moviegoing.[25] Trailers' less cataclysmic imagery, such as the requisite star identifications and expository dialogue, are thus dynamically punctuated with an excess of affective cues that assure audiences of action films, for example, that there will indeed be action. Shots of nature and other scene-setting devices are endowed with a graphic and textural "feel" that emphasizes the travelogue aspect of locations, and the experience of seeing the full film is often equated with travel by voice-over narrators or titles enjoining spectators to "come" or "voyage to . . ." An intriguing contemporary variation on this invitation is an evocation of the film's time and/or space as different from "ours" by narrations that begin "In a time when . . ." or "In a world where . . ."[26] Christian Metz's "Grande Syntagmatique," an early exploration of rhetoric as an analytic tool for identifying significant units of film, offers a singularly apt term for these types of texturizing sequences of generalizing scenes so common to trailers: the "bracket syntagma," a nonchronological set of scenes that serve as successive examples.[27]

Indeed, many codes of shot combination in trailers can be seen as variations on Metz's categories of the bracket and parallel syntagmas.[28] Metz's parallel syntagmas, which are *alternating* series of shots without any spatial or temporal relation to each other, are often called into play in trailers, wherein elaborate systems of counterpoint are constructed between two or more different scenes, sometimes attenuating dialogue scenes by insertion of parallel shots of some kind; or presenting a variety of scenes crosscut with a recurrent graphic element such as a title (for example, the big "X" in the *Malcolm X* trailer). This very common convention of trailer crosscutting is known in industry parlance as a "grid."[29]

Wipes, seen primarily in trailers of the classical and transitional eras, can serve different purposes, but their overall effect is to endow the trailer with a graphic surface that prohibits our ordinary cinematic relation to the screen (the suspension of disbelief required of narrative film spectatorship). Like graphic elements in magazine ads, they also keep us more aware of the promotional message than of the photographic image per se. Contemporary trailers often utilize sound effects and title graphics for the same purpose (while they too use wipes, if less frequently). Regardless of which type of (historically specific) transitional device is used, the montage structure of trailers is key to their production of meaning, and transitions other than straightforward cuts are generally utilized to participate in a trailer's "hype," calling attention to the advertising function of these short film texts. In the process, they also can function to promote genre (such as heart-shaped wipes in the classical era or the slamming sound effects which cue action-adventure in the contemporary era) and story features (such as a mirror-cracking wipe in the *Casablanca* trailer).

The narrational component of trailers is also key to their production of meaning. Early trailers of course relied on intertitles, but beginning in the 1930s titles would work in conjunction with voice-over narration. Both modes were sustained throughout trailers' history, although contemporary titles are more sparse and schematized. Many trailers have experimented with minimal narration, but the persistence of the (nearly always male) narratorial voice is overall a striking feature of trailers, again functioning to maintain viewers' awareness of the promotional message.

Trailers offer figurations of felicitous spaces so as to make audiences wish to be there or, conversely, horrific or suspenseful spaces to create audience desire to experience the "safe" fear and terror of the movies. The restriction of trailers to a few minutes of carefully selected and edited shots and scenes endows what we do see, from faces to car crashes, with a kind of pregnancy or underdeterminacy that allows audiences to create an imaginary (as-yet-unseen) film out of these fragments—we desire not the real film but the film we want to see.[30] This filling-in of trailer enigmas with an idealized film thus heightens trailers' promotional value, as well as the visibility of the production industry's assumptions about what its hypothetical audience desires.

In addition to being a genre of sorts of their own, trailers (along with other promotional discourses) have been instrumental in the formation or legitimation of Hollywood genres, steering our interests in a given film into established or emerging generic categorizations and heightening our interest in the genre as a whole, facilitating the film's positioning as a commodity. Trailer producers' rhetorical appeal to spectators' familiarity (or desire for familiarity) with a genre or genres is one of several primary rhetorical tropes that inform trailers. In their efforts to persuade viewers to see a film, trailers may also appeal to spectators' desire for story, emphasizing a film's plot and characters, or to the spectators' attraction to well-known stars (or alternatively, directors or authors as stars). Often, the rhetoric of trailers combines all three appeals—genre, story, and stars—each of which has its own conventions. (These three are not the only types of appeal, but are trailers' primary *rhetorical* appeals, as will be explained. Other, extratextual appeals are occasionally invoked as well: notably reviews, awards, and box-office figures.)

The rhetorical appeals in turn rely on certain affective expectations, or qualities of experience that the viewer brings to the trailer. These affective expectations are what reception theorist Wolfgang Iser calls textual "gaps," or what Judith Williamson calls the "transformational spaces"[31] the text leaves open for spectators' expected emotional, physical, aesthetic or other responses.[32] In effect, as trailer producers have variously described,[33] the industry assumes these gaps will be filled in by the spectator in habitual ways. For example, within any one of the above three primary categories of appeal, a trailer's rhetoric might privilege a film's heartwarming qualities, its verisimilitude, or heightened spectacle. However, the realization (or not) of affective cues dwells in the experience of the spectator, not within the rhetorical tropes of the trailer itself. This distinction is important to clarify in ensuring that this analysis is indeed a *textual* analysis, treating the trailer's visible textual features (appeals to interest in genres, stories and stars) in order to discern underlying assumptions that can be read therein, rather than generalizing from the analyst's subjective responses to a trailer's affective cues. This summary of the way rhetoric is being brought to bear on my analysis of trailers will be detailed in the following chapter, wherein I characterize and describe the operations of the three primary types of rhetorical appeals under discussion—the rhetorics of genre, story and stardom.

Demographics has an impact on trailer rhetoric, as quantified by market research and/or as imagined by trailer makers.[34] Different markets are made visible in trailers by textual evidence of "targeting," or appeals to specific genders, age groups, or other categories of subjectivity within trailers' overall mission to expand the audience. Comparisons of a film's theatrical trailer with other facets of its promotional campaign, such as pressbooks, print advertising, or TV spots, affirm the trailer's role as a sort of coalition of the campaign's various demographic strategies. The semiotic density of trailers allows for many buttons to be pushed at once, making the trailer operate as a nucleus, or "navel," of the promotional campaign.[35] Television ads are an important subject in their own right, as are presskits, posters, key art, and in the classical era, exhibitor ballyhoo. But while I do refer to other elements of a film's promotional campaign, this study of the implied audiences rhetorically inscribed within Hollywood promotional texts limits itself to the original theatrical trailer.[36]

As the nuclei of the promotional effort, trailers resemble a larger cinematic unit—not only the film they promote, but the entire film bill of which they are a part (here I am thinking specifically of the classical-era film bill). The first-run theater film bill in the classical Hollywood era was an ideological smorgasbord that offered to the public commodified views of all things visible, as Eric Smoodin has pointed out.[37] Smoodin argues that the film bill's visual cornucopia of different modes, genres, lengths and styles of film within the theatrical exhibition space (which, although unavailable for his study, prominently featured previews of coming attractions) also contributed to social control by communicating acceptable cultural norms and marking out a zone where sights and sounds were assembled for the purpose of commodification.[38] The variety and diversity of the bill came to signify the peaceful coexistence of potentially conflicting ideas or values, and became "part of the mythology of pluralism."[39] Trailers themselves contribute to such a mythology, I would suggest, by their concatenation of promises to fulfill the diverse narrative and generic desires of a variety of demographic groups. "Something for everyone," as will be seen, is a primary ideological underpinning of much trailer rhetoric, begging the questions this book asks: who are they calling "everyone" (and how do they know what we all want)? Throughout their history, trailers have contributed to the naturalization of a variety of social desires that will supposedly be fulfilled by going to the movies. "All the emotions of a lifetime!" proclaims the trailer for Disney's *Pollyanna* (1960)—"For years to come, you'll remember. You'll remember this girl and this motion picture."

Trailers' unique temporal status as, paradoxically, nostalgic structures of feeling for a film we haven't seen yet cues us to their status as

Figure 1.3. Nostalgia for the future:
the *Pollyanna* trailer.

fundamentally contradictory texts.[40] Their rhetorical appeals reify not only (fictionalized) past experience but also the future—the anticipated experience of future moviegoing, and even future memories of past moviegoing.[41] Examples of this are rife throughout the trailer corpus. Yet if all trailers did was reify cinematic experience, I suggest that they would not hold such powerful appeal. Many kinds of feelings are in play as we watch them. At their most provocative, they can also evoke what Ernst Bloch, in his Frankfurt school–era Marxist study of daydreams and utopian hope, attempted to formulate as a historical consciousness of a collectively hoped-for future, an "anticipatory consciousness,"[42] as we invest them with our fondest hopes for a movie to come—and at times, for a world to come. Again contradictorily, the mythological aspect of trailers is thickened by the unique capacity of their montage structures to evoke real hopes.

While today's feature film exhibition experience no longer contains the range of types of film texts that it did in the classical era, today's trailer "supertext"—that is, the total "set" of trailers preceding a given film—offers its own metasignifying properties, often indicating to audiences the assumptions studios and/or exhibitors have made about the demographics to which the particular film will appeal.[43] These "supertexts" are of particular critical interest when the film that follows the set of trailers in question is one that studios assume is of interest to a certain race, gender or age group. Research into which trailers accompany "chick flicks" or "black-themed" films, for example, might reveal studio assumptions about demographics in ways that the individual trailers alone cannot.[44]

Of course, trailers don't necessarily "work" in the ways they are intended to. In the contemporary market, we can all cite anecdotal examples of the antipromotional capacities of trailers. The most common remark I tend to hear is that today's trailers give too much away—"if you see the trailer you don't need to see the film." (Since I began my research, this has been the most frequent response to my subject.) Thus, although this is not an audience study per se, it is important to acknowledge that trailers can be received in oppositional ways by audiences, yet as will be seen, viewing trailers oppositionally is not necessarily incompatible with trailers' promotional effect "working" on audiences.

ATTRACTIONS AND COMING: TRAILERS AND TEMPORALITY

The model proposed by Tom Gunning of the "cinema of attractions," which he uses to distinguish spectacle-driven early cinema texts from those that exemplify the emergence of cinematic narrative, has become a popular concept to apply more widely to nonnarrative moments or modes within Hollywood cinema of any era. Gunning himself points to the contemporary persistence of the cinema of attractions "in the interaction between spectacle and narrative so frequently observed in Hollywood genres,"[45] and another scholar has pointed specifically to trailers, as texts that foreground cinematic attractions in the process of promoting various features of a film without giving the story away.[46] Regardless of the specific rhetorical appeals they exemplify, trailers themselves are cinematic attractions par excellence, and like other sorts of attractions, they possess a unique temporality that sets them apart from narrative cinema.

Elaborating on his formulation, Gunning characterized the temporality of attractions as fundamentally different from that of narrative: "In effect, attractions have one basic temporality, that of the alternation of presence/absence which is embodied in the act of display. In this intense form of present tense the attraction is displayed with the immediacy of a 'Here it is! Look at it.'"[47] However, attractions are often augmented by an "announcing gesture," such as the sweep of the hand or bow of the magician designed to call the audience's attention to a transformation about to take place, and that such announcements,

> beyond enframing (and therefore calling attention to) the act of display, . . . also perform . . . the important temporal role of announcing the event to come, focusing not only the attention but the anticipation of the audience. The temporality of the attraction itself, then, is limited to the pure present tense of its appearance, but the announcing gesture creates a temporal frame of expectation and even suspense.[48]

Trailers, I would argue, are attractions that combine and/or alternate these two temporal modes, offering an intensified present tense into which is woven the anticipatory dimension of the "announcing gesture." Trailers are a specific, persuasive kind of attraction: while they continually invoke a heightened presence through their display of spectacular images, essentially the announcement (of a not-yet-seen film) *is* the event. Thus, the temporality of trailers comprises a present that is thoroughly imbricated in an anticipated future: truly *a cinema* of (coming) attractions. Trailers are a unique cinematic form that embodies a unique temporal mode.[49]

Trailers are both like and unlike the precinematic attractions to which Gunning compares early cinema. But their overall ideological function to promote the experience of cinematic spectacle, naturalizing cinema as spectacle and creating expectations for it, has obvious echoes in precinematic attractions and their "announcing gestures." The notion of spectacle, or "the show" as experience or attractions rather than narrative content, precedes film, in such forms of entertainment as vaudeville (and other popular theatrical forms) and the circus, which exemplify different ways of combining attractions with an anticipatory promotional address to audiences.

I would suggest that there is a "vaudeville mode" and a "circus mode" of audience address in trailers, and while the individual models become less distinguishable within actual trailer promotional practices, they can be seen to utilize these strategies. In trailers, the vaudeville mode appears to be the source of the representation of a given film as having "something for everyone," participating in the rhetoric of generalization and inclusiveness, and thus incorporating a given film's attractions within the broader context of promoting the film narrative as a whole. The circus mode more directly encourages or invites audience participation (like the circus barker) and emerges from a rhetoric of hyperbole (like the circus poster), usually singling out the film's attractions as the phenomenon or event that will draw audiences to the theater.[50]

Early cinema borrowed much from the tradition of vaudeville, including, as Miriam Hansen has pointed out, differentiation between genres.[51] Just as early film genres emerged from vaudeville roots, their promotion in trailers often relied on a vaudeville or popular theatrical model to sell cinematic spectacle. Early sound trailers often contain literal vaudeville echoes, such as stars standing in front of stage curtains and directly addressing audiences (as in the trailer for *The Jazz Singer*, 1927), introductory titles that set up subsequent film scenes like vaudeville placards (and like silent cinema intertitles), or smorgasbord samplings of the variety of the film's features (as exemplified by the *Day at the Races* case study to follow). And just as contemporary trailer graphics can be seen as echoes of silent-era intertitles, trailers' salesmanship of the varieties of cinematic experience still resonates with a vaudeville model of audience address.[52]

Trailers that exemplify the vaudeville mode of promoting spectacle tend to address the audience as if talking to them in front of a stage curtain (which some trailers literalize), an approach resembling less hype than the straightforward address of a lecture hall setting, or at times even of an informal conversation or a comedic interaction with the implied audience. They present the film as a variety show or cornucopia of generic and narrative features as well as attractions, announcing a range of different kinds of pleasures the film will offer, implying that whatever "you" want, the film will provide it, in the process acknowledging audiences and acknowledging that audiences have a choice and have preferences. They may specifically (through direct address or, more commonly in the contemporary era, through montage structures) offer the audience a range of reasons to choose the film, assuring them that no matter who they are, the movie's "variety show" is for them. This invoking of audience discrimination as a feature of film promotion is more direct in the vaudeville model than the circus model's hyperbolic assumptions that spectacle is universally appealing.

The rhetoric of "something for everyone" is usually posited within the generalized framework of an individual genre. By quantifying or encapsulating aspects of the films' generic appeals in this way, such trailers construct genre at the same time as they construct genre-transcending commodity-units of spectacle (or attractions), aiming to land as broad an audience as possible to see a genre film by emphasizing the range of different aspects that might appeal to audiences within the specific genre.[53] Thus, the vaudeville mode of trailer address emphasizes the role of attractions along with narrative and generic elements, all considered as equally desirable aspects of commodified spectacle.

In the contemporary era, this mode persists particularly within trailers for films that rely more on human interaction than dazzling visual effects: a range of star types, story situations, and/or genre signifiers is often offered up in order to appeal to the broadest possible audience by emphasizing the film's variety. If spectacle is emphasized in this type of trailer, it is presented as one element among many, interspersed within rapid-cut montages of clips of differing dramatic, spectacular or comedic registers. By privileging accumulations of dialogue scenes removed from their narrative context, vaudeville-mode trailers posit them as attractions too: in the realm of trailers, anything that can be promoted as stirring any sort of emotion in spectators tends to be on some level reconfigured as an attraction. Again, trailers promote these attractions within their own particular, anticipatory yet present, mode of temporality.

Another precinematic mode of spectacle is the circus. Early cinema publicity borrowed much from P. T. Barnum's brand of showmanship and the rhetoric or "hyperbolic discourse" of the circus.[54] Trailer hyperbole often contains distinct circus echoes. While the model of promoting film spectacle as variety relies more on generalization than hyperbole, perhaps prefiguring the strategy of selling spectacle by emphasizing inclusiveness rather than targeting segmented audiences, the circus mode relies more on hyperbole than generalization. Trailers frequently offer literal hyperbolic statements such as the *Brigadoon* (1954) trailer's claim that it is "the most spectacular singing-dancing entertainment ever produced!" The commanding injunctions to audiences to experience film spectacle rely on strategies drawn from a long American tradition of blatant exaggeration made famous by P. T. Barnum. Jane Gaines compares early film publicists' exploitation stunts to Barnum's "promotional antics," characterizing their use of a rhetoric of excess in a manner that holds true for trailers as well:

> By definition, hyperbole is always more than the literal meaning. The pleasure afforded by hyperbolic representation is actually in this going beyond the literal or going "overboard," yet the hyperbolic mode is straightforward and unmistakable. Knowing this, motion-picture showmen following Barnum have conceived of their craft as the attempt to construct the perfectly hewn blatant message. . . . American culture, to a certain degree, equates hyperbole with value. . . . In a culture that depends upon notions of "bigger" and "better" to evaluate all aspects of life, verbal exaggeration itself may be seen as a measure of worth. Puffery must be proportionate to the excellence of the product.[55]

The hyperbolic pole of the circus mode of trailer rhetoric in the promotion of spectacle differs from the pole of generalization exemplified by the vaudeville mode in its manner of audience address. Where the vaudeville mode chatted with or lectured to an implied audience who was assumed to desire a range of choices among a variety of spectacular features, evoking individual genres, stars and stories as vehicles for expressing the full and generalized variety of consumer choice, the circus mode exhorts an undifferentiated audience that the spectacles it offers, regardless of their particularities, will provide unqualified pleasure and undisputed excitement to all. This mode more blatantly emphasizes the promotion of cinematic attractions in Gunning's sense, over the vaudeville mode's broader conception of spectacle.

The circus mode does evoke a range of possible relationships between the attractions and the spectator beyond that of a seated audience facing a curtained stage at a distance—as does the circus itself. Posters heralding a coming circus as well as shouting barkers invite audiences to See! Hear! and Feel! the circus's many features. The sideshow barker invites the audience to "step right up" to experience sideshow attractions. The circus comes to the audience when it comes to town, with the circus parade's arrival as much a part of the show as the circus itself. The circus mode of trailer rhetoric similarly invites audiences to experience features of the promoted film and to join in the fun. It also alerts audiences that the film spectacle—or, particularly in the contemporary era, event—will in some way come to them.

The "see/hear/feel" imperative hyperbolically touts the sensory appeal of the film's spectacular elements, often including an announcement of special technical features enabling this appeal, and often (in classical trailers and later ones that satirize them) actually hailing spectators with the words ("See!" "Hear!" or "Feel!") in spoken narrations or titles. The THX and other sound system trailers that often precede coming attractions trailers in contemporary theaters are a good example of the persistence of the hyperbolic "hear!" rhetoric into the contemporary era, while earlier examples of "hear!" are most frequently found in trailers for musicals, which list and sample the songs from the film that audiences are assumed to desire to hear in full.[56]

In the "see!" vein, trailers for musicals or comedies hyperbolically evoke visual pleasure, alliteratively announcing the movies' spectacular sights in titles or narration. Musical trailers of the classical era often add to this emphasis on glitter and shimmer with sparkling letters and graphic borders surrounding trailer imagery. The "see!" motif is also called upon in trailers for adventure films or thrillers to emphasize visual oddity or unusual sights, like the circus's presentation of wild animals, foreigners or "freaks." Thus a strange or mysterious visual (generic) atmosphere is enlisted to sell audiences on a barely described story. Or the "see!" motif can make an adventure film resemble a travelogue, emphasizing exotic locales as spectacles. Another use of "see!" is to promote a film version of a steamy or controversial work of literature that formerly could "not be seen."

The "feel!" motif abounds in horror and adventure trailers in which various kinds of attractions are promoted as sensory assault. A hyperbolic form of "feel!" is the exploitation gimmicks pioneered by William Castle in the fifties and continued by Samuel Z. Arkoff and American International Pictures (AIP) in the seventies, in which audiences were reminded of the power of horror films to assault them physically (such as ambulances parked outside theaters or vomit bags issued as audiences purchase tickets). Again, wild animals and exotic geography can be "felt" as well as seen in trailers for adventure films. Contemporary variants of "feel!" include trailers that choose lines from the film that indirectly address audiences in addition to their diegetic function, such as "Ready everybody? Here we go again!" (*Return of the Jedi* trailer, 1983) or "Fasten your seatbelts!" (*Men in Black* trailer, 1997). The physical effects of spectacle and attractions on audiences are assumed across genres to be desired as part of the moviegoing experience, and such trailers promote spectacle by rhetorically implying that the boundary between the screen and the audience might be crossed through spectatorship.

This boundary is also crossed via the circus mode's "join in" or "step right up" motif, which lures audiences to see the film by inviting them inside the screen as if they are stepping into a sideshow tent, to participate in the film's discourse in some way. Related to the "join in" motif is the "everybody's talking" motif, which piques audience interest by assuming that interest is already there, in the case of well-known presold properties, in which case a book's readers or a play's audience become the film's assumed audience (as in the trailer for *Peyton Place*,

Figure 1.4. Promoting presold
properties: the *Peyton Place* trailer.

Figures 1.5, 1.6, and 1.7. The movies come to you: the trailer for *The Vikings*.

which announces, "At last! It's on the screen!"). Trailers also tell audiences that the film they promote will come to them, just as the circus comes to town, both in graphic or narrated tags announcing (some variation of) "coming soon to this theater" and by metaphorically demonstrating that the film will enter audiences' physical or psychic environment in some way (". . . Across the screen come The Vikings").

The circus mode thus overwhelmingly promotes spectacle by emphasizing attractions as cinematic events that transcend narrative—that indeed come to, or *at*, you. This feature is seen repeatedly in contemporary trailers for blockbusters or "event films," a term that emphasizes the increased importance of the initial release as the moment during which a film has a heightened "event" status (a moment that can even be seen as a sort of "prepublicity" for films' now attenuated lifespans in a range of formats).[57] Indeed, one critic calls attention to the extent to which the anticipation of films as events pervades not only trailers but film content itself, such that by the latter half of the 1990s, a sort of generalized cinematic imminence is deeply felt and overdetermined. The "event" is both the film and the expectation of the film: "advent and event become indistinguishable."[58] Many nineties films incorporate scenes of expectation or anticipation within their narratives (*Dante's Peak*, *Volcano*, *Armageddon*, *Deep Impact*, *Independence Day*), and there is a general prevalence of weather and war narratives evoking global destruction surrounding the promotion of "blockbuster" films, from the general notion of a "media blitz" to specific visual motifs like the hurricane or tornado.[59] Moreover, today the role of trailers is ever broader, as they proliferate in new types of exhibition formats in the consumer market (on DVDs, in store displays, on the Internet), and they are increasingly necessary to the assimilation, regeneration and replication of the film event. The pure cinema event is thus sensed as *never* present, but always coming—the attraction of the contemporary event film is "an attraction of coming."[60] Trailers do, however, retain their particular function of withholding the fullness of the cinema event, even as they display a unique sense of heightened presence.[61]

Regardless of the historical moment in which trailers are produced, the circus mode and the vaudeville mode exemplify ways in which trailers embody a temporal zone that both emerges from earlier forms of attractions and possesses its own unique features (combining a heightened present tense with an "announcing gesture"). The anticipatory nature of this zone, whether comprising an anticipation of boundless variety and abundance or of an intensity of imminent sensation, is both a feature of reification and commodification, as we have seen, and simultaneously speaks to audiences' broader and deeper hopes (and fears) for the future.

TRAILERS AND/IN HISTORY

Trailers are thus also interesting as evidence of Hollywood's expression of a historical consciousness in twentieth-century popular culture that occasionally gives us glimpses of ideology's utopian dimension. As Jane Gaines points out in her recent resurrection of Ernst Bloch's work for film studies, Bloch has tended to be neglected in past appropriations of Frankfurt school critiques of media culture, wherein utopianism has for the most part been discarded in favor of a paradigm of resistance.[62] But when it comes to Hollywood's industrial-strength film production and its attendant marketing regimes, the idea of consumers/spectators effectively resisting the influence of commodity culture through "reading against the grain" has limited use value in an era when even oppositional cultural forms can contribute to commodification. For some time now, the old sacred cows of left filmmaking practice—self-reflexivity and Brechtian distanciation—have been subject to recuperation within a cultural climate in which even ads display their own conditions of production, and popular culture encourages consumer behavior *by way of* ironic attitudes toward consumption.[63] New critical relationships to commodified culture are needed beyond the ironic, in order for both scholars and consumers/spectators to navigate new levels of corporate dominance while sustaining, as much as might still be possible, a sense of connection to the human community through culture.

What is especially interesting about applying Bloch's incorporation of hope into historical consciousness is that his theory is, according to Gaines,

> a purely socialist dream, not a theory of dreams or wishes in general[.] . . . [A]lthough it is about the anticipation of materially better lives, it is not about the achievement of more in capitalist terms. Ironically, in this theory of the good dream factory, capitalism gives us glimpses of the socialism we have never known and may never know in our lifetime. Bloch's theory is a theory of the longing for change, for world-transforming revolution, and therefore it is a theory for the mass audience without whom the theory is incomplete.[64]

In other words, Gaines sees Bloch's theory as potentially empowering for movie audiences in that it expands the notion of popular historical representation to include a hopeful future. Trailers, the quintessential anticipatory cinematic texts, can occasionally evoke this type of audience empowerment even while, contradictorily, their assumptions about audience interests reify their source films specifically, and cinema and the social world in general—their anticipatory dimension more often than not restricted to the commodifying parameters of capitalist realism. While the hopeful dimension of trailers often lies in the spaces between the montage of promotional images (the ideal film we create out of the trailer's fragments), thus belonging not so much to the texts as to an often amorphous anticipatory potentiality available in the trailer spectatorship experience, they are thus enriched as metatexts where Hollywood history can fruitfully be interrogated—both in the sense of the history of Hollywood and Hollywood's view of history—in ways that do not necessarily *merely* reduce this view to that of a consumer.

The history of trailers themselves is only now beginning to be explored.[65] Attempts were made to advertise films with trailers as early as 1912, and beginning in 1919, a company called National Screen Service (NSS) made crude 35 mm film ads from transferred film stills (without the studios' permission) and sold them to exhibitors to run following feature films—hence the term "trailers." The studios soon realized the potential of trailers and began supplying NSS with film footage. Early trailers are simply scenes spliced together in a "long-running newsreel format," but they quickly demonstrated increasingly sophisticated editing and graphic techniques.[66] By the early 1930s trailers had already begun to look very much the way they would continue to look until the end of the old studio system in the late 1940s. That is, as a "genre," they utilized somewhat routinized structures of address emphasizing the studio star machinery and other characteristics of studio-era publicity familiar to anyone who has seen old trailers: hyperbolic titles and narrations enjoining audiences not to miss the film, visual and graphic linkages between romantic storylines and exotic settings, and identifications of cast members reminding audiences of stars' previous successes. At various times many of the major studios produced their own trailers, although Warner Bros. was the only studio to do so throughout the early sound era.

Beginning in the 1950s, trailers broke away from prior formulas, and while they retained their unifying function of attempting to bring as many different kinds of audiences as possible into the theater, trailers displayed a great deal of variety and experimentation up until the emergence of new promotional formulas in the mid-seventies. Trailers and other film advertising come under the jurisdiction of the same regulatory bodies as feature films (the Production Code in the classical era, the MPAA in the contemporary era), although in the classical era, as Mary Beth Haralovich argues, ads tended to get away with more than the films did (she points to posters for Warner Brothers' 1943 film *The Outlaw*), because the industry acknowledged the importance of heightened sensationalism in the selling of films.[67]

There is usually only one final theatrical trailer made per film, and it has generally been designed to draw as large an audience as possible to see the film.[68] (This has begun to change, in conjunction with the increased importance of the Internet, as will be discussed.) Throughout the period of time I treat, this single trailer's job has been to lay out all the advertising campaign's major elements (which in other media may be broken down to appeal to specific audiences). Thus, unlike television advertising for films (which market studies suggest currently ranks first, above trailers, second, and newspaper advertising, third, among sources for audience awareness of upcoming films),[69] most theatrical trailers through the end of the twentieth century have not placed great emphasis on the targeting of particular demographic groups. Indeed, according to one trailer producer, the job of the trailer is not so much to appeal to a specific audience as to avoid alienating *any* potential audience.[70] Trailers are thus a unique site where the film production industry "talks" to its audience in the broadest possible terms, in the process displaying— through its rhetoric of address—its own notion of who that audience is.

The precursors to trailers were magic lantern slides resembling posters, each film identified with titles and images of its stars or significant elements of its iconography. These were projected between features much like today's slides of local restaurant advertising and movie trivia quizzes. According to Lou Harris, head of Paramount's trailer division in the 1960s,

> *The first trailer was shown in 1912 at Rye Beach, New York, which was an amusement zone like Coney Island. One of the concessions hung up a white sheet and showed the serial "The Adventures of Kathlyn." At the end of the reel Kathlyn was thrown in the lion's den. After this "trailed" a piece of film asking Does she escape the lion's pit? See next week's thrilling chapter! Hence, the word "trailer," an advertisement for an upcoming picture. They've tried calling them Previews or Prevues of Coming Attractions, but everybody in the trade calls them trailers.*[71]

Harris notes that trailers weren't much beyond assemblies of scenes cut from the film until the coming of sound. But by 1935 optical wipes and superimposed graphics were used, and by 1938 trailers had their own scores and material written especially for them.[72] As mentioned, most trailers in the classical era were made by National Screen Service, which had exclusive contracts with all the major studios for use of footage from their films from 1922 through 1928. In 1928 Warner Bros. opened its own in-house trailer operation, and Metro-Goldwyn-Mayer did the same in 1934. In turn, NSS brought its trailer production to the West Coast and assigned producers to the studios still under contract. In 1960 Columbia broke away, in an attempt to remake the studio as a self-sufficient marketing and distribution concern.[73] Setting aside subtle differences marked by studio imprimaturs or signifiers, the look and structure of NSS trailers and the in-house studio-produced trailers are very comparable during the classical era. As the classical-era case studies will detail, they are characterized by lots of wipes; dazzling titles that move and grow and shrink to interact with the image; frequent use of a narrator to augment title information; and the elaboration of formulaic rhetorical appeals to audience interest in stars, genres and story.

The periodization of Hollywood movie marketing is inseparable from the familiar landmarks of the broader history of American film. The well-defined period of the classical Hollywood cinema—an industry-based classification of the time between the invention of sound and the post–World War II antitrust legislation, a time when the "big five and little three" major studios dominated production (along with distribution and exhibition) to a degree never matched in American film history—also produced "classical" trailers. The term "classical Hollywood cinema" has recently been problematized by Miriam Hansen, whose salutary concept of "vernacular modernism" is useful in conjunction with trailers, which can be seen as significant contributors to the emergence during this era of "something like the first global vernacular,"[74] to which I will return. Although I have viewed trailers from throughout their history, I am forgoing close analysis of silent trailers, since the first trailers to demonstrate a coherent and consistent rhetoric emerge largely in the early sound era, when interactions among diegetic sound, music and narratorial voice become elements. Silent trailers tend to present longer clips and less dynamic montage structures.

While the classical era is generally considered to have ended with the Paramount divestiture decrees of 1948, Hollywood continued to turn out films and trailers whose aesthetics and economies were more or less reflective of the studio-era mode of production up to the end of the 1940s (and even, in many ways, into the 1950s, as will be seen). Another industrial factor affecting changes in film promotion at the end of the classical era was the emergence of television, which, while ultimately enabling an economically auspicious reconfiguration of the studio system, contributed (along with suburbanization) to a crisis at the box office and sent Hollywood producers in search of new means of ensuring the biggest possible audiences for feature films. Both Hollywood filmmaking as a whole and movie marketing underwent an "identity crisis" during these years that in many ways paralleled broader problems facing American cultural identity/ies. The postclassical pre–New Hollywood era of trailer production falls roughly into two periods: the 1950s, and the era from 1960 to the early 1970s. This distinction does not coincide with precise industrial benchmarks, but rather reflects the fact that the fifties and sixties are important intervals in the American cultural imaginary. The break between those two periods does fall in about 1960, with the end of the Blacklist and the beginning of the Kennedy "Camelot" era.

The gradual loss of studio-era production mechanisms during the fifties was reflected in many by-now familiar compensatory gestures in the film industry, such as the proliferation of widescreen formats, new sound systems and new paradigms of "realism," reflected in increased location shooting, shifts in performance styles (exemplified by method acting) and increased use of unknown faces. All of these efforts were strongly foregrounded in trailers of the time. During the fifties, the need to reinscribe faith in Hollywood films was a clear mandate for the industry and its promotional mechanisms at a time when television was captivating audiences, most of whom had moved to suburbs and away from the city center's traditional site of movie spectatorship; and when sociopolitical events such as the HUAC and Kefauver hearings had rendered the industry insecure about its role in society. One ideological function of fifties trailers was thus to promote the cinematic institution as a whole (much as films themselves were made to do in the early days of cinema), along with new features such as widescreen formats. Studios can also be seen to more pointedly aim at specific market segments, notably the teenage audience, a strategy that went hand in hand with the industry's first serious interest in market research, although it wouldn't be until the 1970s that studios figured out how to systematically use it.[75]

The era that fell between classical Hollywood's formulaic trailers and New Hollywood's formulaic blockbuster-driven trailers thus stands out as a transitional period when no formulas seemed to work. While echoes of studio-era formulas abound in the trailers of the fifties, there is also a great degree of variety and experimentation, with both NSS and studio-produced trailers exhibiting comparable confusions and concerns about what to promote and how to bring flagging film audiences back into theaters.[76] The trailers that, as a group, follow most closely the formulas of the studio era are those for lower-budget exploitation films such as the works of William Castle, Sam Arkoff and, later, American International Pictures. These trailers often reference classical trailer formulas in ways that can be seen as self-parody.

When austerity measures hit the studios in the 1960s, many in-house trailer departments were scrapped and independent trailer producers flourished (many from the ranks of former studio "trailer men"), and the era of "boutique" trailer production took shape. Whereas during the fifties and well into the sixties, a large percentage of trailers were still produced by NSS or studio trailer departments, by the late sixties "the current system began to emerge, with each studio running a more or less important in-house operation which more often than not has to compete with vendors (depending on the wishes of the producers)."[77] National Screen Service continued to produce trailers up to the early eighties, but its importance to the industry was increasingly relegated to its role as the primary trailer distributor.[78]

The sixties expanded the trend toward both big-budget "road-show" set pieces from the major studios (mostly widescreen spectacles, presented limited showings with reserved seating) and smaller-scale and independent productions, with a corresponding shift in trailer hyperbole. Furthermore, the influence of foreign films on domestic product was evident in trailers' increased reference to prestige signifiers such as directors' names, film festival awards and critics' quotes. With the discovery of the potential impact of youth-oriented films like *Bonnie and Clyde* (1967), *The Graduate* (1967) and *Easy Rider* (1969), different "buttons" start to be pushed in trailers, with appeals to audience interest in story elements increasing in importance (to rival genres and stars). New film genres are explored—and increasingly during this time trailers can be observed to contribute to the formation of genres by positing them as such, whether successfully or not. While the industry continued to have difficulty bringing audiences into the theater, the sixties thus saw more pronounced efforts to redefine Hollywood cinema. As sixties trailers illustrate, promoting the cinematic institution became even more about promoting difference and novelty (as much in order to reinvent itself as to court the counterculture) than about celebrating new ways to enjoy Hollywood's traditional fare.

In response to the trend toward smaller-scale youth-oriented filmmaking, the early seventies became "an incredibly rich period of American film history; in many ways, the years 1969–1975 can be characterized as a period of extensive experimentation in industrial practice, film form, and content."[79] Yet trailers from this time still exhibit confusion as to who their films' audiences are and how to appeal to them.[80] As market returns for "the iconoclastic, antimyth films"[81] began to wane in the mid-seventies and the New Hollywood blockbuster era emerged, trailers reasserted tried-and-true appeals to the elements of genre, stardom and more formularized story appeals designed to bring a number of different types of audiences into the theater; but the formulas that emerged in the blockbuster era were very different from earlier studio-driven ones, as will be seen.

The year 1975 is significant as the year Hollywood moved into the contemporary blockbuster economy, as a result of the success of new levels of saturation booking and advertising for the opening weeks of release of the film *Jaws*.[82] Thomas Schatz has argued for consideration of the release of *Jaws* as a marker for the beginning of the New Hollywood era:

If any single film marked the arrival of the New Hollywood, it was Jaws, the Spielberg-directed thriller that recalibrated the profit potential of the Hollywood hit, and redefined its status as a marketable commodity and cultural phenomenon as well. The film brought an emphatic end to Hollywood's five-year recession, while ushering in an era of high-cost, high-tech, high-speed thrillers. Jaws' release also happened to coincide with developments both inside and outside the movie industry in the mid-1970s which, while having little or nothing to do with that particular film, were equally important to the emergent New Hollywood.[83]

Those developments, according to Schatz, are the rise of mall movie exhibition and of a post–baby boom mall-wandering and repeat-viewing audience; the waning of the "Hollywood renaissance" of the art cinema movement; the growth of the "star director" phenomenon and increased influence of the Hollywood talent agency; and three major changes in the relationship between cinema and television: greater emphasis on television advertising for motion pictures, the emergence of pay cable channels, and the home video revolution.[84]

In conjunction with these changes in exhibition practices, a number of financial changes begun in the sixties were being felt in the industry, characterized by Timothy Corrigan as "an age of inflation and conglomeration" that enabled many of the new production structures Schatz details, and as a result of which, audience address changed as well. Corrigan writes:

The studios transformed the fundamental nature of the film product by forcing massive alterations in the relation of a film to an audience, since to return . . . massive investments meant appealing to and aiming at not just the largest possible audience (the more modest strategy of classical films or the alternative art-house audiences of early auteur film culture) but all audiences. No longer is investment capital directed at differentiating one audience, however dominant, from another. Instead, those investments must aim to "undifferentiate" the character and desires of different audiences, usually by emphasizing the importance of that investment as a universal value in and of itself. . . . [I]t becomes the only methodology that makes sense to a conglomerate's bottom line.[85]

This era's trailers, from the mid-seventies to the present day, demonstrate a consolidation of marketing strategies developed during the formation of the blockbuster era. The prevalence of "high concept" films and their marketing fulfills the corporate methodology cited above—where product is now differentiated by way of an "undifferentiation" of audiences. "High concept," defined in Justin Wyatt's pithy phrase as, "the look, the hook and the book," delineates those contemporary films characterized by "the emphasis on style in production and . . . the integration of the film with its marketing."[86] The increased embeddedness of marketing within film production practices results in a contemporary body of trailers that is at once highly formulaic and predictable—at times almost neoclassical—and visually dynamic and arresting.

Contemporary trailers are now big business, their production costing anywhere from $40,000 to $100,000 and up. With the increased importance of television advertising for films, market research has proliferated for film promotion and is utilized from the earliest preproduction stages of most film productions. Again, the theatrical trailer is but a single facet of a larger promotional network.[87] But, as Vinzenz Hediger notes, in the contemporary market, trailers are very cost-effective since they utilize approximately 4.5 percent of the advertising budget of a given film, while generating at least 20 percent of the film's box-office revenue.[88] They are also increasingly available for sustained study, as one of the most frequent components of ancillary "value-added" features that are included in DVD versions of films.

For all the changes in trailer production practice, one of the striking things about viewing a lot of trailers from throughout film history over a short period of time is the sense one gets of continuity of trailer technique in certain respects. For example, trailers are where intertitles "went" after the arrival of talkies. The interspersal of a graphic title card with a film scene was a familiar cinematic rhythm for audiences of silent films, and one that disappeared with the sound film. This silent film convention, however, helped naturalize trailers' continuation of a graphic regime that used titles to connect—and simultaneously hype—the disjointed scenes.

In early trailers, graphics resemble silent film intertitles (or at times their precursors in vaudeville placards), but titles soon come to dominate the visual impact of classical-era trailers in familiar and oft-parodied ways. And the graphic element is still evident in many contemporary trailers, where, for example, words or phrases from the title are intermittently formed letter by letter or word by word in a bold or colorful typeface, intercut with or laid over scenes, with the entire film title then flashed as an element of the trailer's denouement. Or less frequently, a promotional "tagline" will be graphically presented. In each era of trailer production, graphics are an important aspect of rhetoric. Like the presence of a narrator (also significant to trailer rhetoric throughout the sound era), they serve to distance viewers from ordinary spectatorial involvement with the scenes presented and remind them of the film's status as a package. They also present a graphic "look" that is often consistent with other features of the film's promotional campaign or title graphics, such as the repetition of the animated snake-and-apple motif in both the credits and the trailer for *The Lady Eve* (1941), or the baby carriage image with its tagline "Pray for Rosemary's Baby," seen in both posters and the trailer for the 1968 film.

The case studies in this book break down trailer practice along the lines of the periodization I have traced here, examining those from the classical era (approximately 1927 to 1950), the transitional era (1950 to 1975) and the contemporary era (1975 to the present).[89] Over seven hundred trailers were viewed for this examination of trailer rhetoric. I used the rich and comprehensive collection of trailers at the UCLA Film and Television Archive, and at first viewed as many as possible, taking only brief notes to assess their typical characteristics.

The next step was to determine an appropriate sampling method that would both suit this book's focus on trailer *rhetoric* (beyond just a history of trailers per se), illuminating the special features of audience address that I argue make trailers a unique form of cinema, and at the same time provide adequate evidence of the *range* of typical characteristics of trailers. I first rated the main corpus of viewed trailers in two ways. I selected out trailers that clearly and interestingly demonstrated the rhetorical inscription of assumptions about the film's audience and its desires in one way or another; and I selected a group of trailers that were representative of the larger group—whether of their era's trailers in general, or of specific aspects of trailer rhetoric. My goal was to include in these smaller groups enough trailers that the entire corpus of viewed trailers was fairly represented—both by calling attention to the prevalence of interesting forms of audience address in trailers and without omitting any major typical trailer characteristics (although many anomalous ones inevitably got left out). The smaller group of about eighty trailers were viewed again and rough shot analyses were performed.[90]

The twenty-seven case studies in this book were selected to present a range of genres, story types, studios, budget and popularity levels and years within each era, while sticking to trailers for films that are fairly well known. At best, these analyses are imperfect and partial, both because they are filtered through a selection process that privileges trailers that foreground their own address to audiences in one way or another and because any selection by an individual is evidence of that individual's own speaking position. My purpose here is not so much to draw an accurate picture of the universe of sound-era trailers as to vivify for the benefit of *real* movie audiences the ways trailers' rhetorical tropes construct imaginary ones. While this selection process demonstrates my "terministic screen," or the ways in which my research is inevitably influenced by the questions I am asking of the material, I present a range of trailers that I feel can fairly stand in for the larger group in the sense of both typifying trailer rhetoric and highlighting the unique capacities for audience address that I argue make trailers qualify as a "cinema of (coming) attractions."

Theatrical trailers, central components of any film's promotional campaign, make assumptions about their audiences. Displaying the variety of these assumptions through rhetorical analysis of trailers throughout the history of Hollywood film adds to our understanding of the way narrative film is promoted, thus enhancing the use value of trailers by encouraging a more conscious critical spectatorship. Trailers, of course, are a prime site for a *less* conscious sort of critical spectatorship by virtue of their conventional function, wherein audiences are encouraged to turn their critical eye on a trailer solely for the purpose of a thumbs-up or thumbs-down (will they spend money on the film it promotes?). Popular critical spectatorship thus tends to be reduced to a *consumer* critical spectatorship by the trailer exhibition experience.

Once we are in the movie theater with our popcorn and our heightened spectatorial readiness, we often allow ourselves to be tucked into the rhetoric of "previews of coming attractions" and their appealing mininarratives in ways that haven't yet been analyzed either by media scholarship or by the literature on advertising. Increasing our knowledge of trailers' patterns of address allows us greater critical awareness of these packaged assumptions about our desires, which in turn can help clarify how our own real hopes and desires are brought into play in the contradictory experience of trailer spectatorship. Thus a critical trailer spectatorship can help accustom us to distinguishing between the two (assumptions about our desires versus real desires) as we watch other popular media as well—particularly those corporate/commercial media texts with a stake in managing our desires. Rhetorically mapping Hollywood studios' ideas of how they broadly conceived of their audience(s) enables us to more effectively place such assigned spectatorial positions in perspective, as a historically determined industry imaginary, while potentially allowing trailers themselves to contribute to the awakening of audiences to their own role in the commodity relations of Hollywood film.

2

Trailer Rhetoric

The case studies in this book are analyses of specific trailers wherein I provide readings of their address to audiences. As I have pointed out, trailers are similar to, yet different from, other advertising, and the purpose of this chapter is to introduce the guiding principles of the analytic method I use in the case studies, by breaking down and describing key textual features and conventions of trailers' persuasive techniques throughout the sound era, following a brief discussion of Aristotelian rhetoric and its value for film studies. Taking time to parse out trailers' principal rhetorical appeals to audiences is important in order to clarify the workings of trailer rhetoric in the specific case studies that follow, wherein the appeals are often interwoven with one another and/or integrated within broader structures of meaning.

The book approaches the subject of trailers in an attempt to answer the question, Who do they think they're talking to? The "who" of this question refers to the implied audience as a basically imaginary construct, which I seek within the trailers' texts through rhetorical analysis, in order to learn more not about who audiences *really* were, but about changing Hollywood studio *assumptions* about audiences.[1] The "they" in my question refers to the Hollywood film production industry, which can be seen at once as an imaginary cultural construct in its own right, and as the actual historical producers and industrial determinants of trailer practice. The "talking to" in the question refers to a combination of industrial and cultural/ideological processes— including trailer producers' readings of actual audience behaviors—that inform trailers' unique rhetorical address to this implied audience. The interaction of historical and cultural/mythological determinants implied in the "dialogue" I thus characterize is key to my method, which is neither a "reception studies" approach proper, nor an industrial history,

nor a strictly formalist textual analysis. I have argued that earlier cinema studies paradigms of textual resistance and reading against the
grain do not adequately take into account the realities of cinematic representation in an era of culture as corporate commodity, indeed an era
when marketing heavily dictates what films get produced in the global
film industry.[2] Still, by using rhetorical analysis to investigate
Hollywood trailers' implied audience(s) through readings of trailers
selected to illuminate their unique forms of audience address, a more
conscious trailer spectatorship becomes possible. Gaining a greater
awareness of the roles or positions audiences are encouraged to inhabit may enable these same roles or positions to be sidestepped or
experienced critically, without necessarily interfering with the potential pleasures of the utopian dimensions of these anticipatory texts.

Until recently, rhetorical analysis was surprisingly underutilized in
approaching the film industry's promotional discourses, or indeed film
in general.[3] But as David Blakesley has pointed out, rhetorical studies of
film generally are an "emergent field," responding to current debates
about the ongoing value of film theory by means of work that valorizes
"a dialectic of competing perspectives."[4] Bill Nichols also calls on rhetoric as a way through the impasse of recent film theory debates when he
highlights it, along with the concepts of visual culture and representation in general, for its "centrality to theorizing about film in materialist,
situated ways still capable of confronting the work of desire and the
unconscious, conflict and class struggle, value and symbolic exchange in
both theory and practice."[5]

Specifically, I find Aristotelian rhetoric fruitful in treating trailers
because of its focus on persuasion. Trailers both tell and sell a film story,
and as the art of persuasion, rhetoric comprises both the means by
which trailers sell films and an analytic method to examine the persuasive strategies and appeals to audiences within the trailers themselves.
Rhetorical analysis makes possible a more precise delineation of the
"spectator-in-the-trailer" that Cathy Klaprat and Mary Beth Haralovich
posited over twenty years ago.[6] The various ways rhetorical components
and assumptions of audience affect are combined within trailer texts are
linked to historical changes in industrial practice and, I argue, can also
inform us as to the film industry's changing ideas about its audience.

Trailers are ripe for rhetorical analysis because they are among the
film industry's most overtly persuasive texts. As mentioned, they
address us fairly directly, and the fact that they propose an imaginary
address for us, with which we may or may not identify, is a rhetorical

issue. As I watch trailers I am even more acutely aware than I am with other film texts of that slippage in the communicational process wherein the real social subjects in this exchange are missing on both sides—where, as poststructuralist theory reminds us, neither "we" nor "they" can ever be experienced in a prelinguistic fullness of identity where we are truly "known," but can only be made out as shifting signifiers. That is, audiences come to trailers with (imaginary) notions of what Hollywood is, while trailer producers present images, usually developed with the help of market research, of those elements of a film they feel will capture and maximize their (imaginary) audience. Trailers attempt to position spectators within the imaginary, in an illusory security of unitary identities constructed for us as audiences by the film industry (of which, in turn, we construct an imaginary identity).[7]

In fact, perhaps we can see trailers as the imaginary of movies just as movies have been characterized as the imaginary of everyday life.[8] As hyperbolic narratives that celebrate not themselves but a longer, more nuanced narrative, trailers rely on the binaries and stereotypes of the imaginary to *promote* the riches of symbolic difference.[9] Only by viewing the film in question can we to a certain degree break out of this imaginary relationship between the cinematic institution and ourselves as spectators, and enter (again, to a degree) the symbolic realm at the level of the complexities of the film narrative, as we watch cinematic stories unfold that existed in the trailer only as hyperbolic montages. This points to a potentially progressive aspect of trailer spectatorship—where the act of viewing a film after having seen its trailer enables spectators to "learn after the event" (Freud's *nachträglichkeit*) that trailers were an illusory unity; in the process reminding us that the unitary worlds presented by film and television images and narratives themselves are illusory.[10]

Watching the aforementioned *You've Got Mail*, for example, and experiencing Meg Ryan's fall onto the bed as a component of her character's emotional state in the film reminds us that the trailer's positioning of the gesture as a swoon was a lie;[11] perhaps contributing consequently to our questioning the truth of the characterization as a whole (if we haven't already). This formulation might point as well to a regressive aspect of trailer spectatorship—where the fact that we keep seeing trailers every time we go to the movies can reinforce our acceptance of the imaginary identities that trailers assume for us as audiences, since these identities are ever renewed again with each trailer we see. In any event, an analysis of trailers that investigates the positions of address proposed for us in the audience by the movie industry can enhance our understanding of how these assumptions about us relate to our actual experiences as spectators and social subjects. And rhetoric offers tools for such an analysis.

In the last decade scholars have become increasingly aware of the importance of the surrounding promotional discourses for the study of films as both cultural texts and commodities.[12] Yet while trailers constitute important cinematic epitexts like other promotional discourses, they are also film texts themselves. As Barbara Klinger argues, analysis of films should incorporate discussion of this extratextual network of industrial practices, but additionally, I contend that the commodifying features of trailers—plural film texts in their own right—are illuminated by *their* textual analysis, over and above considering their place in the larger network of promotional discourses. Trailers are texts *and* contexts, and need to be addressed in ways that acknowledge both their stature as specific cinematic signifying systems and their promotional persuasiveness. I posit rhetorical analysis as a form of textual analysis that can be compatible with both semiotic and commodity theories.

Rhetoric, never popular in film studies "proper,"[13] has additionally had a bad rap among those cultural theorists inclined toward politically engaged writing, some of whom have seen it as a signifier of the post-modernist tendency toward cultural relativism.[14] I would argue that rhetoric does not constitute a signifier of textuality's dominance, but rather of ideology.[15] While rhetoric does bracket decisions about the ultimate truth of an argument in its concern with the pragmatics of persuasion, the fact that it calls attention to questions and positions of address encourages me to consider its use to further the goals of an ideological criticism with the potential to contribute to political transformation through the development of a conscious critical spectatorship. Specifically, a rhetorical analysis of trailers, in conjunction with an understanding of their historical moment and attention to how they display historical contradictions, can facilitate a critical contemporary trailer spectatorship whereby we can read in trailers some of the contradictions of our own age (perhaps more quickly and accessibly than we can in films themselves).

Rhetoric is a communicational tool, and as such it has the capacity to move people, whether to reinforce dominant social practice *or* to transform it, as Bill Nichols has pointed out.[16] Nichols asserts cinematic rhetoric's value "as a vehicle through which we experience and affirm connection to various forms of community," while taking into account that often—and I would argue certainly in the case of promotional discourses—this "community" is an imaginary, ideological or mythical one.[17] Rhetoric is the means by which movie trailers appeal to spectators' assumed desires and interests, displaying industrial assumptions about our lives and our identities as individuals within (imaginary, ideological or mythical) communities. By calling attention to trailers' rhetoric as an institutional expression of the social relations of their time, I hope to theorize one of the ways such imaginary communities are articulated or constituted in the public sphere.

A rhetorical perspective on film, as characterized by David Blakesley, "usually focuses on problems of appeal in the broadest sense, as symbolic gestures involving the familiar components of any communicative act: an address with a variety of means for a purpose in a context and situation that ranges from the internal world of the film to the external world of the viewer and critic."[18] Aristotle characterized the process by which assumptions about an audience become structured into a rhetorical argument in his description of the *enthymeme*, a component of what he termed "epideictic rhetoric" (wherein rhetorical arguments are constructed for the purpose of praise or blame).[19] Usually thought of as an abbreviated syllogism, an enthymeme omits one of the logical steps within a syllogism, allowing it to remain as an implicit assumption within the logic of the remaining terms.[20] Enthymemes are usually seen as unproblematic shortcuts for stating a conclusion that has already been made by syllogistic reasoning. But their incorporation of assumptions about audiences makes enthymemes central to my textual analyses of trailers. They can be (and have been)[21] seen as the essence of rhetorical persuasion and, indeed, are a key component of the means by which rhetoric signifies ideology.

The recognition of enthymemes in trailers thus allows for a characterization of a literal "audience in the text," flagging, or in effect problematizing, the seemingly unproblematic assumptions trailer producers make about audiences. Treating trailers as rhetorical enthymemes puts the focus on the audience as filtered through the texts of trailers themselves. The film industry attempts to know its audience both through increasingly sophisticated market research and through tried-and-true "seat-of-the-pants" techniques,[22] and trailers display the nature and extent of this knowledge enthymemically. That is, trailers utilize enthymemes, or deliberately incomplete syllogisms, which rely on *implicit* assumptions that the audience is enjoined to "fill in," thus becoming *complicit* with the advertising argument to the degree that they do so. For example, in the well-known Pablo Ferro trailer for Stanley Kubrick's *Lolita* (1962), a narrator asks incredulously, "How did they ever make a movie of *Lolita*?" The shared commonplace of this statement is the assumption that Nabokov's novel is racy, perhaps too racy to film, and that its raciness is its principal appeal. The novel's other qualities are assumed to be of lesser importance as viewers are drawn into the logic of the trailer for its film version.

These rhetorical structures are generally spelled out in trailer titles or voice-over narration, and their logic is backed up by selections of particular images in the promotion of a given film, through a "discontinuity editing" that makes connections between scenes, demonstrating the enthymeme's assumptions about emphases the audience may want to see in the film, and through further titles and narration that posit what the audience will want to see as well as other ideas and assumptions about the social world. The trailer for *The Greatest* (Columbia, 1977) opens with a narrator announcing it as "a story you only *think* you know." The assumption here is that audiences are acquainted with the persona of Muhammad Ali as that of a boxer, a knowledge that the trailer then proceeds to assert is inferior to the film's view, beginning with the unusual feature that the film presents "a powerful drama of a remarkable life, starring the man who lived it." The story's presumed emotional truth is thus promoted by juxtaposing it to audiences' assumed partial knowledge (and assumed desire to see Ali as more than just a boxer). By analyzing specific rhetorical appeals such as this, along with their interactions within trailers, we can discuss various parameters of this implied movie audience or ideal consumer at particular historical moments.

The principal rhetorical appeals by which Hollywood attempts to reach audiences through trailers have been identified by Janet Staiger in one of the first scholarly articles to interrogate the history of film advertising. While she treats advertising discourse as a whole, her rhetorical categories have been borne out in my research on trailers. Early film advertising, according to Staiger, followed a conscious choice to eschew "brand-name" or studio-identified advertising for promotion of individual "product features"—of which she identifies genre, stars, plots, spectacle and realism as primary—in the belief that each film presents a separate promotional challenge.[23] Three of the features she names—genres, stories and stars—constitute the three principal rhetorical appeals I have identified as central to trailers. The other two, spectacle and realism, are affective cues that trailers often enlist in the service of these three rhetorical appeals. This is an important distinction: while all of Staiger's "product features" are indeed elements that are promoted to audiences, only the former three are wholly *textual* elements,[24] hence accessible as a basis for true rhetorical analysis. Appeals to audience interest in a film's realistic or spectacular features rely on questions of degree and magnitude that depend largely on the subjective experience of the spectator, and are not necessarily objectively determinable in themselves. But genres, stories and stars are undeniable textual features of films that trailers promote. It is rare that any of these primary rhetorical appeals is found in isolation, since virtually all Hollywood films can be said to have stories, stars and some relationship to existing genres. Thus, most successful trailers usually tend to invoke an interaction of the three. Nevertheless, in each era a dominant rhetorical appeal is discernible within most trailers.

These rhetorical appeals operate in trailers on several levels, which deserve further explanation. At this point I am prompted to cite a question posed by a reader of this book: Can an image be an enthymeme?[25] In other words, if an image is either present or not, how can it structure an argument or contain a missing term?[26] This question can best be addressed in relation to trailers by invoking the similarity between enthymemic structures and Eisenstein's concept of intellectual montage. By definition, according to Eisenstein, montage incorporates the associative capacities of the film spectator as a component of its process of signifying through visual conflict.[27] The final of his five types of montage (following or building on metric, rhythmic, tonal, and overtonal montage) is that of intellectual montage, or "conflict-juxtaposition of accompanying intellectual affects."[28] The term has come to be used to distinguish within cinematic texts "editorial relationships of a particular kind whose aesthetic (based on discontinuity) and rhetorical aim (to awaken cognitive processes and ideological awareness) is quite opposite from those of 'classical' Hollywood montage (based on continuity editing and psychological motivations.)"[29] This categorization, while usually pointing to film texts with overtly political or at least nonfictional aims, holds true for trailers as well, which elicit from spectators on some level an intellectual awareness of the films they promote, each time attempting to construct a persuasive argument that we should see the film. Essentially, *any* montage creates assumptions about audience associations. But when a montage structure is created for the purpose of persuasion, these associations can be categorized as enthymemes, and fall within the domain of rhetoric.[30]

Trailer enthymemes operate on several levels. At the broadest level, trailers implicate audiences within their persuasive regimes just as other forms of advertising do. As Judith Williamson characterizes this process, we (ad audiences) are drawn "into the transformational space between the units of the ad. Its meaning only exists in this space; the field of transaction; and it is here that we operate—*we are this space*."[31] The missing (yet blatant) term of the large-scale enthymeme of the category of trailers as a whole (defined, again, as brief promotional film texts that usually display images from specific feature films while asserting their excellence) could be expressed as "You're going to want to see these films!"

Next, within the category of trailers, there are enthymemes that are structured to promote each of the three principal rhetorical appeals (genre, story, stardom), as will be detailed below. Briefly, they operate as follows. Trailers' appeals to audience interest in genres assert that, regardless of the specific genre, genre films are at once "more of what you know and love," and "all new and different." The missing term in this enthymeme of genre could be expressed as: "You want familiarity *and* novelty." Trailers' appeals to audience interest in stories assert that, regardless of the type of story, film stories present at once universal elements or features, knowable by reference to the audiences' (assumed) experiences, and yet have highly specific narrative elements that are particular only to the film being promoted (and of which the trailer may reveal only hints). The missing term here could be expressed as: "Film stories offer experiences and knowledge you want to have (even if only in the safety of the movie theater)." Trailers' appeals to audience interest in stars assert that, regardless of the individual star(s) being promoted, stars are at once *like* audiences, possessing familiar and identifiable characteristics, and *unlike* them, in their celestial distance and dazzling unattainability. The missing term here could be expressed as: "You can be these stars *or* have them, at the movies." Again, while I parse out the three principal appeals separately for the purposes of analysis, they usually operate in combination.

Finally, enthymemes operate at the level of individual trailers as discrete montage structures combining enframed images, sound and editing. Like the examples cited above, these elaborate and expand on the more general appeals to audience interests in genres, stories or stars, in the process displaying assumptions about movie audiences. These various assumptions can provide a vantage point—perhaps more incisively than the films themselves—from which to read some of the ideological substrata of the Hollywood film production industry's pro-motional impulse beneath individual films, such as specific notions of Americanism, individualism, sexuality, race, class, historical change, or other issues.

Although the ways the interactions among the three appeals play out are specific to the individual trailers, a general relationship does exist among them. The three appeals are not symmetrical in the logical hierarchy of their respective positions in the rhetorical signifying system of trailers: the rhetoric of genre is of a higher logical type (and thus a lower level of organization) than that of story, which is of a higher logi-cal type (and lower level of organization) than that of stardom.[32] In other words, within the system of Hollywood film production, on some level each narrative story belongs to (or invents, resists or is in some way emplaced within the parameters of) a genre (or genres). And each star—each individual iteration of the star system in a Hollywood film—belongs to a narrative story. Thus the rhetorical appeals to each of these aspects of films in trailers are likewise imbricated within one another. This is not to ascribe any sort of hierarchical importance to any of the three categories, but when looked at as elements of trailer rhetoric, the *logical* relationships between these three parameters are more comple-mentary than symmetrical. So the analysis of star appeals builds on the conventions of story appeals, which builds on those of genre appeals.[33] This imbrication is useful to bear in mind in reading this book's case studies, which are presented chronologically yet were selected to exem-plify the workings of each of these rhetorical appeals. In many cases they demonstrate the logical relationships I have traced. Moreover, viewed chronologically, the trailers point to shifts in Hollywood's con-ception of its audience over time.

THE RHETORIC OF GENRE: TRAILER SPACE

Genres have long been called on to differentiate artworks within a framework of similarities, and have proven to be an effective means for the film industry to encapsulate and promote the particular type of experience a given film will provide. At the same time, one of the principal goals of Hollywood film promotion, as emphasized by Rick Altman, Janet Staiger and others, is product differentiation.[34] Promoting films on the basis of a rhetoric of genre would appear to contradict this goal—in its emphasis, literally, on the generic. It is this apparent con-tradiction that informs and animates appeals to audience interest in genre in Hollywood trailers. In those trailers where the rhetoric of genre is dominant, product differentiation is mediated by a comforting familiarity in representations of those elements of a film that producers are assuming the audience will want to see.

The promotional appeal of genre as a whole rests heavily on familiarity, on the lure and comfort of the known. Generic worlds are instances of a particular kind of cinematic place where we want to go again and again, whether by re-viewing favorite genre films or by revisiting such a place via a new film of the same genre. The decision to attend, rent or buy a film is at times determined by the kind of (known) generic place we may desire to inhabit or revisit, and it is this oneiric and/or ritual aspect of moviegoing that the rhetoric of genre exploits.[35] At the same time, the promotional category of genre is a key method by which films are efficiently packaged as commodities.[36]

Recognizing this process of ideological containment or boundary-policing is key to the discernment of Hollywood's implied audiences through trailers' rhetoric of genre. Like all systems of communication, rhetoric, and particularly rhetoric's figure of the enthymeme (where assumptions about the listener or audience are structured into an argument), relies on the setting and recognition of boundaries between self and other, or in this case producer and audience (the trailer producers' assumptions of where the audience's shared understandings of a given topic are likely to start and stop). Protecting the industry's investments in its control of these boundaries is the domain of ideology. Trailers highlight such attempts at boundary-policing through their formal properties. As perhaps the most montage-driven signifying system in the regime of popular cinema, their discontinuity editing comprising a sort of "metamontage," the rhetoric of trailers trades heavily in boundaries, edges, and the spaces between where meaning happens (or is assumed to happen). Looking in particular at how generic boundaries are policed, whether by containment or expansion, gives us an idea of the parameters of trailers' assumptions about audiences.

Even as the lure of familiarity in the rhetoric of genre in trailers can be seen as a strategy of ideological containment, it strikes a chord with real audience desires for certain kinds of generic "spatial" containment—the feeling of being "in the mood" for film noir, for a romantic comedy, or for fifties science fiction, for example. Trailers do things to generic space. While the "metamontage" structure of most trailers makes their temporality arguably more important to their signification than their spatiality (since they do not generally provide spatial continuity), trailers still enable a reading of the forces at work in the Hollywood culture system in relation to social space. The conceptual generic "spaces" that movie audiences crave and that the industry attempts to configure or contain are at once *products* of a social imaginary and material industrial *products,* and we can conceive of trailers as a "production" of space that encompasses both of these aspects of the word.[37] By analyzing the ways that trailers' discontinuous representations of generic space rhetorically display industry assumptions about audiences' desires for these spaces, we can think these "representations of space" dialectically, neither reducing them to *just* an "effect" of capitalist marketing tactics nor treating them as an unproblematic fulfillment of real audience desires. In turn, analysis of the promotion of generic space can begin to illuminate other features of actual social space in each of the three eras of trailer production.

Spatial analogies are also explored in relation to movie marketing by Janet Harbord, to characterize the role of genre in the "reconfigured landscape" of the contemporary market-driven film industry. She points out that genre is a key means by which the industry attempts to manage the "tangential paths, alleyways and flights of passage" that contemporary film texts take during the course of their construction as commodities. "In effect, genre creates the unifying principle of the hyper-text" (Harbord uses this term to refer to the contemporary film text's no longer unitary identity as a constellation incorporating promotional and ancillary texts as well as the film proper), "facilitating the role of marketing in pre-selling audiences to a film; genre presents overarching continuity for the audience and the historically proven formula for the production company."[38] This perspective is consistent with my argument that trailers' appeals to audience interest in genres are the highest logical type of the three rhetorical appeals.

Genre has become an increasingly problematic and nuanced category of film analysis in recent years, as critical discourse has begun to make a stronger attempt to take into account both reception practices and the studio production discourse in the process of genre formation. As Rick Altman and Steve Neale (among others) point out, genre is a multiply and historically determined category, and often what critics define as one genre, the studios might define as another.[39] Altman, moreover, has also argued that movie posters demonstrate that classical-era films were often promoted by invoking multiple genres. Altman offers the example of two generic promotional hooks frequently utilized for classical adventure films besides that of the adventure genre itself: these are "romance" and "travel." Characterizing a poster for *Only Angels Have Wings* (1939), Altman argues,

> *Hollywood has no interest, as this poster clearly suggests, in explicitly identifying a film with a single genre. On the contrary, the industry's publicity purposes are much better served by implying that a film offers "Everything the Screen can give you." Typically, this means offering something for the men ("EACH DAY a Rendezvous with Peril!"), something for the women ("EACH NIGHT a Meeting with Romance!"), and an added something for that tertium quid audience that prefers travel to adventure or romance ("the mighty tapestry of the FOG-SHROUDED ANDES").*[40]

In trailers, however, this multiplicity tends to play out more as an inclusiveness *within* genres. Once we look at trailers, elements that might appear as divisive or segmented appeals to different markets in print promotions can contribute to a perception that studios are offering audiences a more inclusive construction of individual genres by virtue of the trailer's inevitably more "holistic" presentation of these same diverse filmic elements within a single cinematic text—one that apes and reproduces (small portions of) the film itself.

The trailer for *Only Angels Have Wings*, for example, repeats the poster's "each day" and "each night" lines in its titles, and appeases the tourist faction in its introduction, where a narrator states, "This is Barranca, a South American banana port where men live by their daring, and women by their charm." Overall, the trailer functions within the rhetoric of stardom, folding all three of the generic elements the poster calls to our attention into a text that keeps returning to images, scenes and titles promoting stars Cary Grant and Jean Arthur, as well as the "return to the screen" of Richard Barthelmess. While genre is not the principal focus of the trailer's rhetoric, the film is promoted as an adventure film, and the titles (which in the poster, Altman felt, appeared to fragment generic coherence) here function as assumptions that audiences want romance and exotic locations to be *incorporated into* the adventure genre.

The most obvious way that many trailers invoke specific genres is through *iconography*. Most trailers show live-action clips from the film, so it is hard to avoid presenting genre iconography in any trailer, but those with strong genre appeals will often underline familiar generic iconography by presenting it in hyperbolic fashion, such as opening a Western trailer with dynamically intercut shots from a horseback chase scene over picturesque Western terrain, or by allowing an iconographically significant but narratively insignificant scene, such as an extreme long shot of a group of people—for example, a chorus line dancing on stage in a musical—to play under the trailer's titles. This is a frequent trailer trope used to create visual generalizations and place locations generically.[41]

Hyperbole and *generalization* work together in genre appeals to differentiate each film within an overall fabric of familiarity. Their interaction is also evident in trailer graphics. Titles may announce the film as "the most spectacular singing-dancing entertainment ever produced" (*Brigadoon*, 1954), or tell us that "It has the burning brand of greatness on it!" (*The Big Country*, 1958), often in letters that themselves evoke generalized generic associations, such as sparkling title lettering for classical musical trailers; wavy, jagged or soft-focus lettering for horror film trailers; or big square early printing press fonts that connote "Wanted" posters for Western trailers. Graphic genre generalization in classical and transitional-era trailers also takes the form of generically cued drawings accompanying titles, such as musical instruments or musical notes, lassos or cacti, skeletons or gravestones, flowers and birds or other "feminine" motifs (for romantic comedy or melodrama trailers). Contemporary trailers also use graphics, heavily interwoven with sound effects, to signal genre, such as the flashing titles and percussive sounds punctuating trailers for action films.

Another pervasive trailer convention often marshaled for the rhetoric of genre is *repetition*. Frequent repetition within narration, titles and visual motifs connotes both sameness (again and again) and newness (unprecedented abundance). Repetition also generates rhythm, and rhythm is an important structural feature of trailers' sensory appeal. Examples of rhyming, alliteration, visual doubling and other refrains of return and repetition abound in the case studies that follow, even when the trailers are not for sequels or cycle films (which of course capitalize on repetition in numerous ways).[42] Repetition is at the heart of the concept of genre in mass culture, a point emphasized by Fredric Jameson: "The atomized or serial 'public' of mass culture wants to see the same thing over and over again, hence the urgency of the generic structure and the generic signal."[43] The fact that repetition functions within trailers' rhetoric of genre in overdetermined ways redoubles and reinforces

Figures 2.1 and 2.2. "The day you count on for terror is not over!" The counting segment in the *Friday the 13th Part 2* trailer (murder victim number 16 is caught by a rope).

a conception of audiences as craving repetition and familiarity in genre films. Strong figures of repetition also remind audiences of their own attachment to this kind of repetitive and ritualized spectatorship.

Within trailer rhetoric, repetition generally functions to reinforce existing genres. This is most obviously demonstrated in trailers for sequels, films that belong to cycles, and double-bill trailers, or the more frequent rerelease double-bill trailers. Trailers for sequels (and sequels themselves) emphasize repetition throughout the sound era but become more prevalent in the contemporary era, and their use of repetition continues to draw audiences in with a promise of familiarity and novelty.

The prevalence of sequels in genre films of the late seventies and eighties enables even a trailer sequel, elucidating the importance of repetition. The trailer for *Friday the 13th Part 2* (1981) is a sequel to the trailer for *Friday the 13th* (1980). The first film's trailer establishes a graphic motif of counting days, with screen-filling titles that list the numbers 1 to 12, each followed by a clip from the film, the clips building in suspense to the final title, "Friday, the 13th," followed by an announcement, "You may only see it once, but that will be enough." The sequel's trailer announces, "On a June night in 1980, Friday the 13th . . . ," followed by a clip from the original film, then, "Why should Friday the 13th, 1981, be any different? The body count continues." The numbering motif is reprised (14 to 23). The clips following each number decrease in length as the numbers ascend, then the trailer's tagline announces: "The day you count on for terror is not over!" The idea of repetition and the notion of sequel are overdetermined in this trailer series in a clever way that links repetition with terror (and thus with genre appeals)—and manages to create anticipation for the next film out of dread of the next murder. Even the first trailer's remark about seeing the film only once can be read in this context as a challenge to see it, and its sequel(s), more than once. (The film ultimately spawned six sequels.)

The *Friday the 13th* trailers hyperbolically illustrate the way in which sequels reinforce audience viewing of genre films by linking the repetition of production with the repetition of reception (repeat viewing). The rhetorical logic of sequel and cycle trailers entails a textual demonstration of the producers' knowledge that audiences liked the original film by asserting in the sequel trailer their desire to make another one like it, which in turn creates an assumption that audiences will want to come see the latest episode or version since they are assumed to have liked the first one. However, this logic can only succeed if novelty is asserted along with the original film's proven likability. The rhetoric of sequel and cycle trailers dovetails with the rhetoric of genre in part because sequels tend to be genre films, but also because genre, as previously mentioned, is the packaging of a circumscribed generic world, as opposed to story elements or stars in situations. Sequels and cycles thus duplicate the precise generic worlds of their predecessors more consistently than they do their story elements or stars—thus, trailers that assert the rhetoric of genre reinforce existing genres almost as if genres were sequels on a grander scale.

"Generic sequels" are posited in trailers that capitalize on generic "sameness" by explicitly reminding audiences of similar successful films within the same genre that have preceded the film being promoted, a strategy common to trailers throughout the sound era (as exemplified by the frequent classical-era trope of "From the studio which gave you . . ." In *The Last Outpost* [1935] trailer, for example, a title proclaims "Produced by the studio which gave you 'The Lives of a Bengal Lancer'" [also 1935], another empire-building war drama).[44] Trailers can refer even more obliquely to earlier films and thus assert genre by using the earlier films' music, such as the *Sliver* (1993) trailer's use of the *Basic Instinct* (1992) score.[45]

Repetition is related to another convention common to the rhetoric of genre, *the equation*. Through narration or titles and at times visual linking, trailers often assert an equation between the film and its generic subject matter, or between the spectator's (assumed) experience and the characters' experiences.[46] Puns might link characters' desires or actions to assumptions about audience desires to view the film, such as the reference to "Dangerous curves ahead for . . . [cast members]" followed by the tagline "It's the entertainment 'pick-up' of the year!" in the

Figure 2.3. Equating sex, hitchhiking, and
spectatorship: the trailer for *They Drive by Night*.

trailer for *They Drive by Night* (1940). In this case both the reference to "dangerous curves," which at once equates driving with sex and sex with danger, and that to an "entertainment 'pick-up,'" which equates hitchhiking with sex and both with spectatorship, assume spectators' interest in the perilous sexuality of film noir. Trailers utilize such equations to allow audiences to link particular generic features with their anticipated spectatorial experience.

Beyond merely invoking genres, trailers also contribute to genre definition. Much has been made in recent work on genre of the hybridity of contemporary genres in the pervasive postmodern media climate of pastiche and recombination of earlier popular narratives and myths. Trailers are a historical precedent for generic recombination and quotation, even as they illustrate the industry's attempts to force unusual or anomalous films into familiar generic molds. In addition to repetition, which allows genres to be reinforced in close continuity with audience expectations based on prior experiences, trailers reinforce genres by bringing in "new blood" while making comparisons with earlier generic models. The reconfiguring of established genres to accommodate new kinds of filmmaking usually takes the form of associating new elements with a genre, fitting odd films or smaller market films such as "art films" into established genres, or even positing a new subgenre to consolidate audience familiarity with something new. Trailers for many 1980s films characterized by nostalgia and quotation maximized the appeal of the old genre *and* the film's revisions of it, such as a trailer for *One from the Heart* (1982), which opens with citations of Coppola's credits and calls the film "a new kind of old-fashioned romance."

Another way trailers reinforce genre is to promote anomalous or one-of-a-kind films under familiar generic rubrics. A type of anomalous film that became institutionalized as such within the Hollywood film market after the demise of the studio system was the "art film." These films are occasionally promoted within the rhetorical terms of established genres, but more prevalent is the emergence of new generic conventions in the attempt to promote the art film as a genre in the late fifties and early sixties, such as the *Pawnbroker* (1965) trailer's innovative stylized graphics and use of a dissonant jazz soundtrack. Moreover, artistry itself becomes a selling point for such films, as exemplified by the frequent citation of critics and references to the film's director as an artist, such that certain ways of flagging the director mark the film as an art film and thus as belonging to a genre.

Trailers also differentiate films with regard to genre by labeling a new cycle within a genre, or at least helping a cycle to become familiar to audiences. This latter aspect backs up Rick Altman's argument that studios employed promotional discourses in the service of their project to "initiate film cycles that [would] provide successful, easily exploitable models associated with a single studio."[47] A cycle, of course, is a group of films within a genre that possess strong plot and/or star continuities, such as the Dead End Kids or *Star Wars* films. In the more commodity-oriented contemporary market these have come to be called "franchises."

From the 1950s onward, trailers have demonstrated a self-awareness of their status as a genre, and many evidence a *self-referentiality* generally thought to be prevalent only in later postmodern popular media texts. This self-awareness of trailers as a genre is illustrated by numerous examples that parody classical trailer rhetoric, such as the self-conscious tabloid-style block titles in the trailer for Kubrick's *The Killing* (1956), which start as pseudonews headlines: "Daring hold-up nets $2 million! / Police baffled by fantastic crime! / Masked bandit escapes with race track loot! / Suspense! / Terror! / Violence! / Will grip you as no other picture since Scarface and Little Caesar!" Other trailers that overtly satirize classical trailer form include those for *Fritz the Cat* (1972), *Young Frankenstein* (1974), *The Wanderers* (1978) and *Tag: The Assassination Game* (1982). More recently, trailers also demonstrate awareness of their own generic status by presenting self-contained "minimovies"—such as the dialogue-free montage trailers for *Cliffhanger* (1993), *Desperado* (1995) or *Eyes Wide Shut* (1999)—or using extra footage and telling their own "story" to promote their source films. These latter cases are examples of a recent trend in trailer production, where two factors—increased interest in promotional discourses, reflected in popular and trade press articles and in awards such as the Hollywood Reporter Key Art Awards; and the generally increased "buzz" factor of contemporary Hollywood—combine to encourage a newly self-aware artistry in trailermaking, along with a greater competitiveness among the various ad agencies that produce trailers. As promotional budgets have become a higher percentage of a film's total budget, and as technology has enabled cost-effective electronic editing, studios have responded to the higher stakes by at times hiring competing ad agencies to produce more than one trailer campaign for a film, increasing the mandate to dazzle and attract.[48]

Through iconography, hyperbole and generalization, repetition, equations (or other comparisons) and self-referentiality, the rhetoric of genre utilizes assumptions about audience desires for familiar generic spaces to enhance their desires for something new. The conventions of the rhetoric of genre demonstrate that, allowing for some historical variation, this balancing act took place throughout the three periods of the sound era in Hollywood. Indeed, the similarities of the promotional message in trailers of different eras are, paradoxically, almost as striking as their differences.

THE RHETORIC OF STORY: TRAILER TIME

Unlike the rhetoric of genre's concerns with promoting overall generic categories that evoke promises about the space or "feel" of a film, the rhetoric of story deals with specific, not-yet-seen story elements. But just as Hollywood films fit into genres, their stories can fit into story types—and even when they don't, story elements can be enthymemically linked to *experiences* that are assumed to be desired narratively by audiences. The rhetoric of story deals with assumptions trailers make about what kinds of experiences audiences want to watch unfold in narrative time, and what kinds of knowledge they desire to gain at the movies.

As mentioned previously, the overall message of the rhetoric of story could be expressed thus: "You would like to experience these events—*at the movies*." Movies, in other words, aren't just like ordinary experience (although verisimilitude is often assumed to be a desired feature of certain types of narratives), but at times provide safe opportunities to experience events narratively that audiences might avoid, fear or for other reasons *not* experience outside the movie theater. In addition, the rhetoric of story withholds the actual experiencing of these narrative events in their fullness, obviously in order to promote the film effectively and, to one degree or another, "not to give away the product."

Along these lines, Vinzenz Hediger has identified what he calls a "narrative turn" in the development of trailer practice. He argues that studio trailermakers started out in the classical era emphasizing the withholding of story elements as much as possible (on the assumption that the story *is* the product). Trailers would lay out instead a bundle of questions that the viewing of the film would answer. Later, he argues, trailers move to a "two-thirds formula," whereby two-thirds of the film's story arc is revealed by the trailer (on the assumption that contemporary marketing practices, along with the phenomenon of repeat viewing, have lessened the necessity to withhold story elements). Hediger's research shows that this "turn" began during the transitional era but was not fully in place until the mid-seventies.[49] His findings raise the question: What is "the product" when it ceases to be the story? I argue that in the contemporary era, the product becomes the movie event (an event that is itself, as previously argued, weighted with anticipatory significance and suspense regardless of how much of the story is known). Nonetheless, the idea of *knowledge* of the story—withheld as well as given—is an important aspect of trailers' rhetoric of story throughout the sound era. In the process of making assumptions about what kinds of experiences and types of stories audiences want, and through providing as well as withholding knowledge about film stories, broader assumptions about relationships between audiences, experience, knowledge and the historical world in the three eras of trailer production can be discerned.

Within trailers' persuasive metatextual system, the rhetoric of story operates at a metanarrative level. Narrative theory's concern with "who tells" a film story is here reconfigured as "what sells" a film story. Tom Gunning's idea of a discursive filmic "narrator"[50] resolves the "who tells" question at the level of films themselves. In trailers, in addition to inscribing the image of the story's "author" (often a different image than that gained from the narrators of films themselves), the trailer's filmic narrator rhetorically inscribes an image of whom that "author" is addressing—or more specifically, persuading to see the film—a hypothetical addressee who helps us relate trailer form to broader social and ideological contexts. The rhetoric of story utilizes such a trailer "narrator"—and often a flesh-and-blood voice-over narrator as well—to promote filmic narrative. Trailers typically redouble the phenomena of narrator and narrative (a trailer narrator tells the trailer's *own* narrative *about* the film narrative) resulting in condensed layers of storytelling about storytelling that inevitably withhold more than they reveal—and the withholding can be just as revealing as what's shown or told.

Specifically, I find that the aspects of narrative that tend to be invoked in order to sell a film within trailers' rhetoric of story throughout the sound era coincide with the four aspects delineated by Roland Barthes in his pioneering work on narrative structure, *S/Z*: characterization, causality (Barthes's "proairetic code"), narrative suspense (Barthes's chain of enigmas) and the creation of a consistent fictional world.[51] Indeed, the four principal rhetorical "hooks" identified by Barthes guide most trailer enthymemes where story is the principal appeal: characterization, causality, suspense, and narrative worlds. In other words, appeals to audiences' interest in a film's story might assert, for example, the fascination of the film's characterizations or the excitement of following the film's causal plot elements, all within a reconfigured and discontinuous trailer rhetoric (which I consider a metanarrative).

Like the rhetoric of genre, which performs the inherently contradictory task of product differentiation within a framework of promoting familiarity, the rhetoric of story operates within a contradictory framework. By appealing to audiences' desires to experience events, watching them play out through narrative time in ways they can only do at the movies, the rhetoric of story makes the assumption that narratives present experiences that are familiar to audiences, while also assuming that narratives fulfill their desires for events never experienced. In the process, trailers both satisfy and withhold satisfaction of audience desire to know about a film's story. Both the rhetorical appeal to known and unknown experiences and the rhetorical appeal to story knowledge in general operate within the textual domain of what Bill Nichols refers to in his study of documentary film as "epistephilia," or desire to know.[52] Of course, all trailers assume that audiences desire to know what happens in the films they promote, but by analyzing the trailers' persuasive strategies in order to examine the industry's assumptions about that desire, we can thematize industry assumptions about other desires for knowledge and experience in the audience. Again, the two other rhetorical appeals (to genre and to stardom) can be present at the same time (increasingly so with contemporary trailers). Nonetheless, the operations of the rhetoric of story—the promotion of narrative characterizations, causality, suspense, and narrative worlds (and their interactions)—can still be described on their own in order to investigate the narrative "desires" of implied audiences for Hollywood film.

The salient feature of trailers where the rhetoric of story is dominant is a reliance on commentary and exposition to a greater degree than when genre or stardom is dominant. This commentary need not only be voice-over narration or titles (although in classical-era and early transitional-era trailers these forms are preeminent), but also can be in the form of a series of nuggets of dialogue selected for their expository semiotic density, or even a series of action scenes with minimal dialogue, but in which the visual imagery and its editing serves an expository function.

In trailers in which narrative is promoted primarily through a film's *characterizations,* several conventions prevail across the three eras. The trailer may use its cast identification segment to introduce a number of characters, describing the film's story by delineating their narrative identities, as exemplified by the voice-over narration for the *Doctor Zhivago* (1966) trailer: "Geraldine Chaplin as Tonya, tender child. Delicate woman. Loving wife of Zhivago. Julie Christie as Lara, the violent, sensual, sensitive girl, Zhivago's great love, and mistress. The dedicated young revolutionary leader (Tom Courtenay). And Omar Sharif as Zhivago, a man of peace, forced into war. A man who will love deeply, tenderly, passionately. Zhivago—a man in love—with life." Often such trailers use the film's principal character to introduce an enumeration of the film's narrative virtues, such as *Tip on a Dead Jockey* (1957): "He'd take a chance on anything / anywhere / with anyone / he'd even take a "tip on a dead jockey"; or *F.I.S.T.* (1977): "His name was Johnny Kovac. He was born in central Europe. He grew up in the slums of Cleveland. [. . .] In the '30s, he fought company goons and Pinkertons. And he built a union. A union that became—a fist."

Sometimes characters are introduced but despecified narratorially through the use of personal pronouns, describing their actions or roles more in terms of function than character, which enables the trailer to better place the audience enthymemically within its discourse. For example, using titles, the trailer for *Undercover Man* (1942) spells out story premises while showing scenes of the principals and introducing them: "He smiled in the face of death! / . . . He pitted himself against the craftiest brains of the upper-Underworld / with a girl who flung aside *convention* / risked honor and love / . . . braved *death* / for the sake of *vengeance!*" Here the missing term in the enthymeme could be expressed as: "He/she could be you!" One contemporary trailer, for *Running* (1979), expands on this trope by linking the second person with the third in its address to audiences: "The one thing he's good at is the one thing nobody understands. He's finally decided to do it his way. It's about having the courage to be what you are." Some trailers allow the principal actors to narrate the trailer in character or in their star personae or both, often conflating character and star. Generally, such characterization-based narrations open the trailer, which then proceeds to use a combination of narration (or titles) and scenes to elaborate on or back up the characterization.

These appeals to interest in narrative characterization draw audiences to films on the basis of identification with the character, as does the rhetoric of stardom, but more specifically, audiences are invited to identify with the character's situation or motivation in the particular film, and to want to participate or share in its narrative resolution. These trailers create cinematic meanings that circulate around questions dealing with identity and relationships, both within the film they promote and hypothetically treating such issues as they apply to the film's assumed audience, through enthymemes. For example, a typical trailer syllogism might express the following: "This is quite a character and quite a situation he/she's in." And the missing term or enthymeme could be expressed as: "You would like to experience his/her situation—at the movies, and find out how he/she resolves it."

Trailers that promote films by assuming audience interest in watching the film's *narrative causality* play out often do so utilizing some kind of list format, enumerating the film's key plot points. For example, the *Thunderbolt and Lightfoot* (1974) trailer narration breathlessly lists plot elements: "A preacher, a killer, a car thief . . . a chase, a getaway, a gang, a bank, a gun, a plan . . . a team, a caper, a movie—*the* movie, a knockout," as we see illustrative quick-cut clips from action scenes. In the trailer for *True Confessions* (1981), titles and then a narrator similarly extol, "Two brothers / a priest / a cop / brought together / torn apart . . . The questions. The answers. The secrets. The truth . . . The past. The present. The memories. The sins." Such segments can also combine emphasis on characterization with an enumeration of causality, as in the narrated trailer for *The Good, the Bad, and the Ugly* (1966), a film that promotes its characterizations in its very title. The trailer presents a barrage of quick-cut scenes, each accompanying a narrated phrase:

Figures 2.4, 2.5, and 2.6. "The good . . . the bad . . . the ugly."

"The blue . . . the grey . . . the Civil War . . . the good . . . the bad . . . the ugly . . . the questions [a bloody interrogation scene] . . . the answers [two men fall off a train] . . . the showdown [a graveyard] . . . the reason . . . the gold."

Many trailers give minimal or no introductory narration, but rather clips edited to privilege the film's narrative causality (visual lists). The contemporary "minimovie" trailer format, as exemplified by the famous *Cliffhanger* (1993) trailer (which delineates the film's most spectacular action set pieces, sans dialogue, choreographed to Mozart), also privileges narrative causality, although by altering the sequence of some of the film's images, it can in addition (as previously discussed) create trailer-specific narrative trajectories that diverge from that of the film.

Another way causality is promoted in trailers within the rhetoric of story is when the film's historical premise is promoted as the basis of its story, placing the audience within a historical as well as a narrative discourse of cause-and-effect. This is seen frequently in trailers for films made during World War II, as well as trailers for historical epics made in any period. Such trailers assume, again, that audiences would like to experience these events and watch their narrative trajectories play out at the movies: the enthymeme could be summarized as "You are there!"

Whether narrative flow or causality per se is the focus or whether the trailer promotes its film on the basis of a historical causality, these conventions posit an audience who wants both to *experience* the film's events and to *know* what happens in a film story. Trailers operating in this register address the viewer as a discriminating consumer, and while they are easily as likely to deceive about a film's narrative focus and trajectory as they are to inform in their brief, discontinuous montages, the impression they create is one of straightforwardness, sampling the film's experiences and informing about the film's events—it's the "just the facts, ma'am" tradition of trailermaking. The lists or series of clips they give audiences are carefully edited to satisfy certain aspects of epistephilia, while the omissions and "spaces between" are designed simultaneously to create it. Cinematic causality is treated by this rhetoric somewhat like a journey on which the audience is invited along, and for which the trailer serves as a sort of travelogue. Trailer narration in the contemporary era can be very formulaic in the way it expresses such causal elements. For example, "Now" is a familiar trope: after the film's basic premises are laid out, trailers may introduce core plot points with this word, as in "Now, in order to . . . he must . . ."

Trailers for films involving substantial *suspense* elements—including but obviously not limited to those for films in suspense-driven genres such as mysteries, espionage adventures or thrillers—frequently hang the promotion of the film on teasing hints of the film's core enigma. Within an enigmatic syllogism—that is, a trailer that presents a film's suspenseful narrative premise yet withholds key elements, the enthymeme consists of clips and/or narration that explicate some plot developments while leaving out others, sometimes literally asking the question that comprises the enigma, and the missing term is the assumption that audiences will want to guess the rest, and that their guess might well be wrong. Unlike appeals to causality, where we get the sense of a film as a journey not yet taken, of which we see travelogue-like excerpts in the trailer, appeals to interest in suspense promote the film more along the lines of an amusement park attraction; the trailer informs us that by seeing the film we will get a number of shocks or revelations that the trailer cannot divulge—and encourages us to let our imaginations run wild. Often the suspense-building narrations and titles for these trailers are backed up by teasing visual clips, such as someone pointing a gun at an unseen party, someone opening a door or entering a dark place, or hints of impending monster attacks. On the soundtrack, sound overlaps (giving an auditory hint of the trailer's next narrative feature) are increasingly heard in the transitional era and are all but ubiquitous in contemporary trailers. Trailers for films made from other works (of which, it is assumed, many in the audience must "know the outcome") can also be promoted in enigmatic terms. In these cases, a film's controversial or sexually explicit story might be treated teasingly, as apparently (until now) unfilmable.

Such suspense-based trailers attempt to create strong desire in the audience to resolve the enigma by seeing the film, thereby experiencing the emotional exhilaration of suspense (coupled with its resolution) that the trailer offers. Thus, they display assumptions about what kinds of mysteries, shocks or suspenseful experiences trailer producers believe audiences will find thrilling and desirable. Withholding the resolution of a film's enigma entails a display of assumptions about what kinds of cinematic narrative experiences will satisfy audiences' desires for knowledge, both of story outcomes and more broadly, of social and historical unknowns.

The most frequent convention of the rhetoric of story is the promotion of a film's *narrative world*. The contemporary cliché of trailer narration "In a world where . . ." evidences the extent to which such a formulation is considered effective, whether on its own or in combination with other appeals. Narrative worlds are depicted throughout the two hours of a feature film, and a majority of trailers address the challenge to draw their viewers, who are still settling in their seats, talking and rustling candy wrappers, into experiencing this world (and wanting to experience more of it) in two minutes. Trailers' frequent use of the bracket syntagma (again, Christian Metz's term for shots that relate to each other as a series of examples) contributes to the promotion of narrative worlds, where a trailer minimontage offers up an atmospheric sampling of the story's environment, rather than a linear sampling of story causality. Often a film's narrative world is the principal feature promoted in trailers when the film is based on a "presold" property or story. Trailers rarely let an opportunity pass to mention if a film is based on a best-selling novel or a successful play, and many emphasize that entity's narrative world as a place the audience has been to and is assumed to want to go again, often literally picturing the book from which the film was made, its pages fluttering or its words magnified as they come to life in clips from the film. Narrative worlds are also promoted in trailers that succinctly characterize a film's high concept (or its equivalent in pre-high-concept eras) by delivering a tagline.

Some trailers promote a narrative world beyond that of their film, which I have come to call "the narrative of Hollywood." In these, significant trailer time is devoted to describing innovations in technology, showing footage of the film's premiere, or representing some other aspect of the institution of Hollywood, which is seen in these trailers as belonging to a coherent narrative world important enough to the audience for the trailer to step outside the strict promotion of its film's story.[53] The trailer for *The Jazz Singer* (1927) presents a man in front of a stage curtain announcing the arrival of sound on film. *Carousel*'s (1955) trailer begins with a long sequence promoting Cinemascope '55, in which Darryl Zanuck himself does a minilecture on the format. The narrative of Hollywood serves to place the film being promoted within its institutional context, both naturalizing and celebrating the activity of going to the movies. While this is an activity in which trailer spectators are obviously already engaged, such "metatrailers" provide evidence that Hollywood promoters have felt this message needed reinforcement, and/or that this is a world (of information, technology, art and celebrity) to which the audience wants entry.[54] Contemporary trailers evoke the narrative of Hollywood less directly—primarily by occasional intertrailer referentiality.

Promoting narrative worlds serves similar functions to the promotion of genres, including the presentation of a particular (in this case, narrative) space evoked by the film. However, whereas the rhetoric of genre reminded audiences of the similarity of such spaces to ones experienced previously, the rhetoric of story promotes narrative worlds that tend to be unique to the film being promoted. Often the evocation of the film's narrative world is a key means by which the trailer differentiates its product, yet trailers that center on this appeal can deliver a great deal of information about their narrative worlds while still withholding enough information about the film's characters, events and suspense elements to sustain the film's appeal. These trailers also display assumptions about what kinds of spectatorial experiences—that is, what kinds of narrative worlds—audiences will embrace. By offering these worlds as desirable, they draw a perimeter around them, implicitly communicating norms or ideas as to what kinds of (narrative) worlds or experiences might be *un*desirable within the parameters of Hollywood film.

Through the conventions of the rhetoric of story, trailers generate promotional metanarratives that display assumptions about the implied audiences for the films they promote. By playing at the edges of the audience's assumed desires to experience a film's events and know its narrative trajectory, and at the same time, *not* to know too much of the film's narrative (to save it for the viewing experience)—whether promoting elements of characterization, narrative causality, enigma and/or the film's narrative world, these metanarratives begin to assert rhetorical boundaries as to what constitutes appropriate cinematic narrative for the audiences of their time.

THE RHETORIC OF STARDOM: TRAILER SELVES

Stars function differently in trailers than they do in most other facets of film promotional campaigns (with the partial exception of television spots), and of course differently than they do in the film itself. The rhetoric of stardom in trailers is the most ubiquitous of the three rhetorical appeals, since the mere representation of a star's image in a trailer constitutes a strong promotional message about that star, so almost all trailers draw on the rhetoric of stardom. At the same time it is the most particularized of the appeals, since promoters appealing to audience interest in a film's stars are banking on their very specific characteristics to draw audiences back into the theater. The ubiquity of stars and their centrality to film promotional discourses of all kinds problematizes their analysis as indicators of trailer audience address. Do stars function primarily as signifiers of sexuality and/or provokers of sexual desire in trailer audiences? Or is their promotional status as commodities linked more to their particular capacity to evoke intertextual associations as signifiers of genre, of fashion, or simply of their own offscreen personae? The specific goal of my analyses of trailers that appeal to audience interest in stardom is to interrogate the commodity status of stars, along with their facticity as historical and eroticized subjects, in relation to trailer-makers' rhetorical constructions of movie audiences.

There have been many attempts to reconcile the role of stars with respect to Hollywood genres and story types in the production and dissemination of popular film, following Richard Dyer's characterization of the star system as a "structured polysemy."[55] Discussions have explored, for example, the relationship between the star "vehicle" and genres; the roles of stars in the constitution of stories during the classical era; stars, stories and genres as different "regimes of verisimilitude"; the shift away from stars as draws for studio product in the postclassical years and the renewed importance of star personae in the marketing of film stories increasingly by way of "character typing rather than character exposition" in the high-concept era.[56]

Such complexities of the "structured polysemy" of the star system within Hollywood film as a whole are duplicated within the general rhetoric of stardom in trailers. But since the theatrical trailer is a specific, self-contained type of cinematic/promotional text, we can return to Anthony Wilden's communicational model of logical typing to somewhat clarify the rhetoric of stardom's operations with respect to the other two rhetorical appeals. Again, since Hollywood trailers virtually always represent stars as part of cinematic narratives, which in turn are virtually always represented as belonging to genres, the rhetoric of stardom in trailers is of the lowest logical type of the three appeals. And the lower the logical type a communicational category belongs to, the higher the level of organization it contains—the more systematization and semiotic freedom within the classification.[57] This characterization is borne out by the Hollywood star system's greater level of individualization and specificity than the other two rhetorical appeals under discussion: the rhetoric of stardom is the only one of the three forms of appeal that relies on a feature of the film that possesses an indexical relationship to the social world.

Furthermore, stars implicitly bring to their representation in trailers an association not only with the corpus of their prior films and the typologies of all the characters they've played, but also with all of the extratextual knowledge that Hollywood promotional and publicity mechanisms have imparted about them.[58] This is a more systematized and semiotically dense kind of information than a trailer's invocation (in two minutes) of either story types and details, or generic features— hence the rhetoric of stardom receives the most extended treatment of the three in this chapter. The conventions of the rhetoric of stardom are nonetheless folded into the conventions of the other two rhetorical appeals: particular qualities of stars may be promoted, for example, in a trailer that also promotes a film's narrative enigmas within a framework of familiarity with the film's genre. This tiered relationship is crucial to analyzing phenomena that are of lower logical types.[59]

Like the rhetorics of genre and story, the rhetoric of stardom within trailers is founded on a core contradiction. Here, the contradiction is the need to bring stars closer to audiences so that they seem real and accessible for audience identification (enhancing audience desire to *be* the star), and conversely the need to keep stars magically and mythically distant from audiences' everyday lives in order to perpetuate their allure and aura (enhancing audience desire to *desire* the star). In specific trailers, this plays out in various ways and with varying intensities, but generally, stars are promoted either as desirable or as accessible for audiences to identify with (or both). Because the eroticized desires often invoked within the rhetoric of stardom are inflected by sexual difference, this contradiction is moreover built upon all the extracinematic contradictions of the representation of sexual desire and gendered identities in twentieth-century popular culture.[60]

Christine Gledhill treats the contradictions of stardom in a provocative characterization of the interrelationship between the star system and genres, positing that the star system *itself* works on a register akin to a cinematic genre, and, more particularly, that "stars function as signs in a rhetorical system which works as melodrama."[61] She elaborates:

> *Melodramatic excess exists in paradoxical relation to the form's commitment to the real world. The star system works with similar paradoxes. If the excessive moment in melodrama infuses ordinary characters and relationships with excitement and significance, stars represent ordinary people whose ordinary joys and sorrows become extraordinary in the intensity stardom imparts to them. If melodrama, while confirming the boundaries of social convention, derives its energy through the villain's willingness to break them, the star system promotes model domestic lives irradiated by exciting hints of scandal.[62]*

Indeed, Gledhill writes, "[t]he first promise of the star is access to the personality itself. At the same time the visibility of the star system and the operation of fictional and generic structures emphasize the economic, social and cultural forces that make such access an illusion. The excess of stardom represents a melodramatic response in the face of this dilemma."[63] We might ask, then, whether a trailer's reliance on the rhetoric of stardom results in a melodramatic trailer, regardless of the genre of the film itself. The melodramatic features of star-oriented trailers will be explored further in the case studies that follow.

The indexical basis of star images is key to understanding the contradictions of stardom within trailers. Richard Dyer characterizes this indexical relation, a form of "authenticity" that contains a "built-in instability" due to the questionable veracity of the behind-the-scenes star discourse on which it is based, "a *rhetoric* of authenticity."[64] This rhetoric of authenticity ensures that when stars are displayed, the dynamics of the screen's surface (which include an implied "beneath-the-surface") are visible by virtue of stars' known indexical ties to the world external to the film. The visible fact of the star's existence in the world, however much we think we know or don't know about him or her, can invoke an awareness of both the cinematic apparatus and the extratextual world of the specific film.

In trailers, again, even as stars can be seen in terms of typologies and stereotypes, they possess a greater level of textual specificity than any of the features of the other rhetorical appeals. As we watch a trailer, the images we see of the star are endowed with all our past associations of him or her, perhaps more significantly than our apprehension of what the star is doing in this film that we haven't yet seen. In the trailer, the star is distanced from his or her character within this individual (still hypothetical) film, and is understood in large part on the basis of our intertextual knowledge. Yet while trailers remove the stars' images from the film's story continuity (albeit not from the film's genre), they generally also don't provide audiences with much extratextual information about their lives; thus the stars exist in a kind of limbo, suspended between their past star personae (and roles) and their present characterological one. This limbo is a space of tension and oscillation. Since the trailer gives us a sumptuous widescreen, Dolby-ized and THX'd image of the star yet denies us much of the pleasure in identifying with him or her "in character" in the present film, which we haven't yet seen, *and* also the pleasure of insider knowledge that other forms of star publicity provide, our desire to see "more" of the star intensifies: trailers are indeed teasers. And the locus of their "tease" within the rhetoric of stardom is precisely this play at the edge of indexicality that separates and joins the cinematic apparatus and the social world.

The indexical linkage between the cinematic image and its subject matter has often been discussed in film studies as the (albeit always problematic) bottom line of film's truth claims. Thus Bill Nichols, in his study of documentary, points to the Hollywood star system as evidence that indexicality alone "is not enough to produce the impression of a unique historical referent reproduced as image."[65] While this is true of the level to which the star's indexicality is discounted in the spectator's experience of the feature film, with promotional discourses the phenomenon is a bit different. The promotional world of which trailers are a part is a realm that relies on the "rhetoric of authenticity" that Dyer characterizes—appealing neither to true authenticity nor to the centripetal pull of the fiction film. What results is a demimonde, another zone between the storied world of the film and the historical world. It constitutes the world of "Hollywood"—that promotional realm where audiences, stars and filmmakers alike play roles, and where there is a different set of expectations as to truth claims than either fiction or documentary engender. This promotional world is a known entity, yet it has no geographic or even conceptual boundaries. It's a culturally determined site, a shared commonplace: everyone knows what you mean when you say "Hollywood." And wherever stars physically reside, they are the denizens of Hollywood along with the invisible technical crews and semivisible above-the-line production personnel such as directors and writers (who also sometimes appear in trailers).

Like "the narrative of Hollywood," which the rhetoric of story exploits, shared knowledge of the promotional "*world* of Hollywood"—considered as the dwelling place of the stars—is a hook trailers use to enhance the audience appeal of films on the basis of the rhetoric of stardom. Trailers usually don't give us more information about the actual world of Hollywood; rather, they rely on our preexisting knowledge of it to amplify the indexical connection of the stars to the social world—here mythologized and naturalized as this promotional world of Hollywood wherein audiences too are called upon to play their part by patronizing the movies. Thus, in trailers, the industry relies on the audience's sense of stars' indexical relation to the historical world *stopping* at this demimonde and not going further—to knowledge of the stars' real working conditions or alienation within the industry, for example (unless such details fit the category of scandal, which Dyer sees as enhancing the rhetoric of authenticity).[66] Like the kingdom of Oz, Hollywood is a place where ordinary people who might otherwise work and live right alongside us are endowed with spectacular, fantastic characteristics. And because of trailers' positioning in the aforementioned limbo between the fullness of the film text and its extratextual star publicity, they are perhaps more embedded than any other cinematic texts in the contradictory pulls of this promotional world of Hollywood, a "place" where closeness and distance fold into each other like some impossible Escher puzzle.

Of the three rhetorical appeals in trailers, it is thus the rhetoric of stardom that potentially has the most power to invoke audiences' desire to be physically close to what's on the screen, even as this rhetorical appeal provides the most vivid reminders of audiences' distance from what's on the screen. And the rhetoric of stardom's core contradiction is built on its oscillation, which in specific instances is in turn inflected by gender and sexuality. This contradiction can be expressed in terms of such oppositions as closeness/distance, identity/difference, and identification/desire; and it forms the basis of my analysis of how the rhetoric of stardom communicates Hollywood's assumptions about audience desires within trailer texts, and promotes certain ideologies of desire and identification. Thus, in relation to trailers, I would agree with Gledhill, who suggests that the "genuine paradox" of the star-audience relation is the way these contradictions play out more often than not along melodramatic registers:

> . . . [P]aradoxically, the star, more overwhelmingly present than any actor can be to a theatre audience, is also not, and never can be, there for the audience to cinema. This poignant "presence in absence" lies at the heart of the desires stimulated by stardom. But it is a genuine paradox in which presence can be understood not as simple mystification but as an assertion by the melodramatic imagination in the face of absence.[67]

Of course, romantic and sexual desires are not the only kind that Hollywood ascribes to audiences. But star images more often than not connote the realm of eroticism in trailers. And since not everyone in the audience is "supposed" to be erotically attracted to all of the stars, other kinds of attraction are also called upon, particularly identification. As trailers demonstrate, assumptions are made as to culturally appropriate forms of desire and identification, while "inappropriate" sexual desires or cultural identifications are implicitly rejected. Even while addressing the largest possible audience, the rhetoric of stardom assumes that audiences *desire* stars who represent *sexual* difference (male/female), while they *identify with* stars' representations of *cultural* sameness ("Even though they're beautiful, famous and rich, they're like you"). This is an ideological complement that conceals the more culturally threatening possibilities of stardom's appeal for audiences: sexual desire for stars of the same gender, or identification with stars who represent cultural difference (apart from the homogeneous "differences" available within the promotional world of Hollywood).[68]

The ideological function of the promotion of desire for and identification with stars feeds into the rhetoric of stardom's maintenance of a contradictory balance between inviting audiences to feel close to stars and sustaining the mystique and allure of their distance from everyday life. With their powerful indexical ties to the promotional world of Hollywood, stars are thus the industry's most effective salespeople, and beyond the immediate assumption that audiences will desire or identify with particular stars in particular films, the rhetoric of stardom in trailers demonstrates the industry's assumptions that stars can stand in for the pleasures of moviegoing itself.

Audience interest in stars is usually assumed to take the following three forms, each of which has its own conventions: stars in their mythic or spectacular aspect (that is, stars in relation to their own image and star quality); stars in intertextual relation to other stars or to their appearance in other films; and stars in relation to the institution of cinema (that is, as guides to or exemplars of the workings of the star system and the moviemaking apparatus). Trailers that appeal primarily to audience interest in *star quality* generally make assumptions about audience desires relating to questions of self and identity; those appealing to interest in stars and *relationality* tend to assume things about audience interactions with the other; and those that appeal to interest in the *star system* make assumptions about the role of the individual within social institutions. And, within each of these frameworks, stars are called into service to promote moviegoing as a whole.

The common denominator of those trailers that promote stars in mythic or spectacular terms (the first principal convention of the rhetoric of stardom) is the trailer's focus on a *quality* with which the star is associated in him or herself: the star as icon—or in the more precise terms offered by S. Paige Baty, as potential icon or "mediapheme."[69] The overriding assumption of trailers that promote star quality is that audiences go to movies in order to derive pleasure from individual stars. They emphasize either the visual or aural pleasures associated with the star as spectacle, or the narrative pleasure of recognizing a beloved star's familiar personality or qualities in a new but familiar film story. The pleasures of seeing movies for the sake of stars, such trailers imply, lie in the opportunity for audiences to experience either dazzlement by the star's spectacular presence, or the pleasure of increased knowledge of (and thus closeness to) the star that the film will provide—or both.

Stars are often assumed to draw audiences for their sheer spectacular appeal, whether as signifiers of glamour, action, musical performance, high art, or other cinematic elements. Sex appeal and glamour are obvious selling features within the rhetoric of stardom throughout Hollywood history. Here, as with the rhetoric of story, a dynamic of revealing/not revealing images of the star (or parts of the star's body)

Figures 2.7 and 2.8. Star quality *and* relationality are enhanced
by widescreen: the *River of No Return* trailer.

often contributes to the trailer's promotional value (and the star's
appearance of unattainability). Sometimes glamour is even called into
service to help promote cinematic processes, calling attention to star
quality and image quality in the same breath and cementing stars even
more to the unattainable realm of the screen. Thus, a *Cobra Woman*
(1944) trailer narrates, "[Maria] Montez, Queen of Technicolor!" while a
trailer for *River of No Return* (1954) announces that Marilyn Monroe "celebrates Cinemascope," offering a final title that proclaims, "Made for
each other! / Mitchum and Monroe in Cinemascope."

Trailers for musicals tend to feature their stars as musical icons or
mediaphemes (within the rhetoric of genre), sampling their singing (and
dancing) appeal during a long portion of the trailer. Musical trailers
literalize the crossing of the two promotional axes of distance and closeness: while the singing segments enhance the stars' allure and separate-
ness from everyday life, the trailers repeatedly insert and alternate clips
from dialogue scenes that tend to contradict this emphasis by presenting the stars "off their pedestals"—regular folks available for identification, whether as figures of romance or action.[70] Like the unattainable
beauty featured in the glamour trailers, male action-hero qualities are
likewise held up as untouchable—their bodies dazzlingly omnipotent,
their exploits beyond the normal human range of activity.

Star quality is associated with prestige in films that are promoted
as high art. In the classical era, stars were endowed with extra prestige
by the prior prestige of the film property, as in the trailer for *Alice in
Wonderland* (1933), which visually emphasizes the film's innovative set
design as it touts "the world's greatest story with the world's greatest
cast." Trailers for "art films" similarly link their stars to various prestige
signifiers such as Academy Awards, names of prestigious directors
or classic book titles. The *Trojan Women* trailer (1971) showcases the

theatricality of its cast, sampling performances by Katherine Hepburn, Vanessa Redgrave, Genevieve Bujold and Irene Pappas, and setting it apart from the spectacle-driven Hollywood epic by noting that it is a "Cacoyannis film."

Star quality is especially important to trailers for the many films that deal with stardom as a story element on some level (whether movie stardom or any other type of fame), such as the trailers for *Jolson Sings Again* (1949), *Man of a Thousand Faces* (1957), *Lenny* (1974), *A Star Is Born* (1976) or *The Greatest* (1977). Such metastar rhetoric often layers assumptions about audience interest in stars onto the hyperbole of "biopic" trailer conventions within the rhetoric of genre, at times giving the trailer an opportunity to remind audiences of their own prior participation in a star's success. These overdetermined appeals to (proven) audience interest in star quality serve to emphasize the power of (certain types of) individual personality and identity—especially those associated with showmanship—to draw audiences, who are assumed to want to see shows about stars that earlier audiences enjoyed.

Conflating stars with their characters is a fairly common convention of trailers that posit a quality or qualities of the star(s) as a film's primary appeal. ("The system gave Schwarzenegger a raw deal. Nobody gives Schwarzenegger a raw deal."—*Raw Deal* trailer, 1986.) The conflation of star and character serves to enhance the larger-than-life quality of the characters, emphasizing the overarching star personae above either a star's actual real-life identity *or* his or her character in this particular film, and endowing the fictional characters with a surplus sheen of star quality and unreachability that reminds audiences of the pleasures of stars, and thus moviegoing, as spectacles.

In trailers that focus on star quality, assumptions that audiences will want to be or desire the star enable a direct promotional link between a star image and the lure of the movies. Thus through spectatorship, the rhetoric of stardom asserts, audiences can at once have their own familiar experiences validated and experience the impossible, through the figure of the star, whose iconic (or sometimes just "mediaphemic") characteristics often stand in for historicized questions or concerns about identity. For example, the Schwarzenegger trailer's assertion (above) assumes audiences can identify with the star's hyperbolic masculinity and its imperative to go up against "the system," here connoting (given the star's extratextual conservatism) a notion of excess government congruent with mid-eighties Republican ideology.

The second principal appeal and set of conventions of trailers where the rhetoric of stardom is dominant is a focus on star *relationality*. The common denominator here is that other stars or other star texts participate strongly in the trailer's appeals to audience interest in an individual star. By emphasizing relationality as a value, these trailers make assumptions both about how or where audiences assign the relative value of a promoted star(s) with respect to other stars, and about the kinds of relationships audiences want to have with others in general. These trailers name names, juxtapose faces with others and at times create their own imaginary dialogues between stars, in the process positing notions about how relationships happen in real life as well as offering representations of perfected relationships that avoid all the messiness of real-life ones.

Pairings, whether of the romantic or "buddy" variety, are often promoted. Star juxtapositions are presented graphically, such as positioning stills of a romantic pair within hearts, as well as narratorially, such as equating star pairings with explosions, conflagrations, or other types of momentous *events*. Trailers may offer narrations that imply that the whole is greater than the sum of its parts (once these two stars get together, watch out . . .). The trailer for *The Paleface* (1948) announces in titles, "The news is spreading like wildfire! / Paramount matches two terrific stars / and when they meet / it's dynamite!" A narrator then amplifies, "Lamour was lovely, Goddard was glorious. But when Bob starts to nestle up to Russell, something new has been added. He's the dizziest dentist that ever yanked molar. She's the deadliest shot who ever stalked an outlaw. When they ride the Indian trail together, there's howls-a-poppin'." The trailer spells out that "something new has been added," implying an exponential increase in your moviegoing pleasure due to the screen union of these two stars, and trading on the "opposites attract" ideology of heterosexual romance.

Contemporary trailers heavily emphasize star pairings. The rampantly quotational and intertextual star system of today's global Hollywood appears to rely on relational cues and the interconnection of multiple stars more than was the case in the studio era, when stars were the property of individual studios. The trailer for *The Siege* (1998) intersperses clips of Denzel Washington's FBI good guy with Bruce Willis's protofascistic military bad guy in ways that invite audiences to enjoy the confrontation of two very different star personae. Younger stars are promoted through their pairing with older-guard megastars (and/or vice versa) in trailers for *Meet Joe Black* (1998), pairing Brad Pitt with Anthony Hopkins; and *Stepmom* (1999), pairing Julia Roberts with Susan Sarandon—in both cases the relationship in question is presented as a (pseudo)familial one, with a strong component of rivalry. Repeat pairings are heavily promoted as cinematic events—such as 1998's *You've Got Mail*, which pairs 1993's *Sleepless in Seattle* stars Meg Ryan and Tom Hanks; and *Runaway Bride* (1999), which pairs 1990's *Pretty Woman* stars Julia Roberts and Richard Gere—even without directly referencing the former pairing.

Promoting pairs of stars by considering the romantic, adversarial and/or familial screen relationships between them as cinematic events serves to naturalize relationships as events that *happen* to individuals, rather than as ongoing components of people's lives, reinforcing ideologies of individualism. And whether the relationships the trailers promote are assumed to be "true-to-life," idealized or dramatized, these trailers assume that audiences desire to experience relationships at the movies in ways that heighten the appeal of individual stars. Relationships are thus intensified and simplified: stars are lovers, enemies, work partners or family (occasionally, stars are friends); regardless, the rhetoric of stardom in this instance asserts that a major reason audiences go to the movies is to watch relationships "happen."

Beyond dualistic pairings, ensembles and groups are also promoted as such, in trailers that imply that as the number of stars increases, so do the odds of the audience's cinematic pleasure: quantity (lots of stars and lots of story) equals quality. Early trailers use graphics to communicate this, from the common celestial motif to decks of cards with stars' faces on them, or later we see the hyperbolic confluence of numerous stars characterized by trailer narration as a spectacular element, such as the familiar campaigns for seventies disaster films that emphasized their accumulated star power with star-driven clips (these films were usually accompanied by posters that incorporated a lineup of a number of stars' pictures, along with characterological captions). Most contemporary trailers for ensemble films use the editing of identification segments, as do the trailers for *Paradise Road* (1997) and *Mystery Men* (1999), to juxtapose familiar stars in rapid succession in ways that underscore the appeal of seeing multiple stars together (All those strong actresses in one movie! All those cool Gen-X stars in one movie!).

Like trailers that emphasize pairings, those that promote films on the basis of star ensembles make assumptions about audiences' interest in seeing stars in relationship to one another. With larger ensembles, these relationships border on representations of collectivities. Like pro-filmic spectators, collective groups of stars are sometimes shown as mass groupings engaged in the same activity, such as walking, singing, or conversing. But trailers promoting films on the basis of the rhetoric of stardom set groups of stars apart from other collective groups they may figure by emphasizing their individual star identities at least as much as the mass character of their activities as an ensemble, through the convention of the star identification segment wherein the major stars are inevitably singled out. The ensemble provides both additional purchase for audiences' assumed closeness to stars ("somewhere in this group you can find yourself") and additional emphasis for the lure of stars' distance ("this is a privileged group you may watch but never join"). Again, the rhetoric of stardom tends to naturalize the primacy of individualism even as it promotes relationality or collectivity.

Relationships between the film being promoted and other films in which the star has appeared are another form the relational rhetoric of stardom can take. Such references are usually narratorial, although trailers are also endowed with intertextual richness when a film's visual quotations of other films get included in the trailer. These appeals to audiences' cinematic memories operate so as to balance familiarity with product differentiation (an operation shared by the rhetoric of genre). Classical- and transitional-era trailers may state the title of the star's prior film directly, collapse titles familiarly in a trailer's narration, such as Brando being referred to as "That 'Streetcar' man" in a trailer for *The Wild One* (1955), or include the audience in an in-joke, such as Barbra Streisand chiding Ryan O'Neal in a scene included within the trailer for *What's Up, Doc?* (1972), "Love means never having to say you're sorry"— a reference to O'Neal's prior appearance in *Love Story* (1970).

Intertextual references to stars' other performances in contempo-rary trailers are often less overt, although there are increased intertrail-er references as a whole (especially, but not always, within trailers for comedies). Due to the higher levels of media saturation that obtain in the marketing-driven contemporary market, where well-known stars' faces and celebrity are an endlessly circulated feature of the cultural landscape outside the movie theater (such as on billboards, in maga-zines and within numerous television contexts), the showing of a star's face in a trailer may be said to connote that star's iconic image (and thus his or her prior roles) to a degree beyond that possible in the studio era. Regardless of whether intertextual star references are explicit or implic-it, they serve throughout sound-era trailers as reminders of and appeals to the audience's assumed knowledge of the star's qualities and/or relational dynamics in past films. Thus, they reinforce trailers' assumptions that audiences will want to either identify with or desire the star— by demonstrating that audiences already have. Through intertextuality, such trailers also remind audiences that moviegoing itself is a relational activity (in which audiences too are enjoined to take part), that no film stands alone and that movies are interdependent in the Hollywood firmament. Such a reminder helps reinforce moviegoing as a frequently repeated activity by implying that the next film will more than likely be just as good as any films audiences liked in the past, as well as implicitly patting audiences on the back for recognizing the references (i.e., for their past moviegoing).

Relationships are thus promoted within the rhetoric of stardom in trailers as a means of singling out particular assumptions about the kinds of relationships audiences desire to watch take place on the screen, in ways that tend to result in a naturalization of individualism. They are also promoted as a means of reinforcing the repetition of moviegoing, reminding audiences that other movies also feature these stars, and that the relational dynamics of the particular film being promoted are but one facet or iteration of the stars' potential relational positioning in other films.

The third principal convention of the rhetoric of stardom in trailers is the promotion of stars in relation to the *star system*. During the studio and transitional eras, frequent explicit references were made to the "star system" itself, with trailers incorporating assumptions of audiences' understanding of and participation in the making of stars. For the most part, this convention is specific to trailers from the two earlier eras, perhaps due to the greater media visibility of most stars in the contemporary era and to their increasingly diffuse "provenance" in contrast to the earlier studio contract system. There are many examples in the classical and transitional eras of trailers that invite and take audiences along with stars to go behind the scenes of the making of the movie or in which the star addresses the audience directly. Other examples promote the movie by explicitly characterizing its participation in the Hollywood star-making discourse, such as a trailer for *Night after Night* (1932) that even includes a graphic of a finger pointing at the audience as titles announce, "YOU! The makers of stars, have made him a star!" All these trailers assume a shared understanding of Hollywood as a place where stars are made and where audiences help make them (just by going to the movies, audiences are thus "in" Hollywood). Such blatant

Figures 2.9, 2.10, 2.11, and 2.12. Hailing the audience as
"makers of stars": The trailer for *Night after Night*.

assumptions of prior audience interest in stars (indeed often employing
direct-address documentary imagery) serve to remind audiences of their
own role in the operations of stardom, and act as polite solicitations of
the audiences' continued participation through moviegoing.

By reminding audiences of the mechanism of star-making, these
trailers associate their films with celebrity and success, implying that
since their stars have already made it, the film must be a success as well;
and perhaps additionally implying that the stars' success might rub off
on the audience. Stars' success narratives are the principal subject of the
massive extracinematic publicity discourses that grew up around the
Hollywood star system prior to and during the sound era. I would suggest that the convergence of the development of trailer rhetoric in the
early sound era with the Great Depression, during which time movies
held a special appeal to audiences for whom success seemed a remote
dream, had some impact on trailers' audience address throughout the
classical era and into the transitional era, furthering an ideology of luck,
rather than hard work, as the primary reason for success (since, in the
depression, hard work didn't pay off). The rhetoric of stardom seems to
be addressing an audience that (it is assumed) both needs stars to be
emblems of unimaginable success and wants to feel that, with luck, their
success is within the audience's own reach.

While the star system is rarely overtly represented like this in trailers of the contemporary era, celebrity and stardom are nonetheless

embedded into many contemporary trailers in ways that tend to under-score the trailers' appeals to audience interest in stars. In examples such as the trailers for *Air Force One* (1997), *Any Given Sunday* (1999), and *The Hurricane* (1999), the buildup of the protagonist's celebrity *within* the story is an allegorical mobilizing force of much of the trailer's montage. In popular film franchises of the contemporary era, trailers foreground the star and the franchise in ways that are mutually enhancing. Without actually referring to the star system, these trailers' centering of the stars within the overall film package can contribute to audience awareness of stars' importance to contemporary promotional discourse. The trailer for *Wild Wild West* (1999), whose producers hoped to achieve summer blockbuster status on the basis of Will Smith's star turn (popular press references to Smith as king of the Fourth of July movie openings, allud-ing to his former hits *Independence Day* and *Men in Black*, abounded), priv-ileged Smith's wisecracking persona in ways that made the film resem-ble an oblique sequel to *Men in Black*, and the trailer for *Batman & Robin* (1997), which introduces new stars to an existing franchise, positions them centrally as well. Whether it is the star or the story that is new this time around, continuity is emphasized in trailers for franchise (or de facto franchise) films in ways that foreground stars.

In the contemporary era, the mythological place that is Hollywood seems less rhetorically circumscribed within trailers than in earlier eras. Stardom still "happens" in Hollywood, regardless of whether trailers overtly represent the process, and since a characteristic of the contem-porary era's massive media saturation is a "Hollywoodization" of other public discourses into which celebrity enters, contemporary trailers' assumptions about audience involvement in the discourses of celebrity are broader than ever. It is assumed that audiences hear the latest star "buzz" to such an extent now (whether on television shows such as *Entertainment Tonight* or increasingly celebrity-dominated popular jour-nalism) that trailers need not remind them of it. In the contemporary environment of image-glut, keeping the stars' images in frequent view seems to be more important to trailermakers—on the assumption that seeing is desiring. Contemporary trailers thus naturalize the star system and celebrity as a desirable institution that goes without saying, there-by creating assumptions about audiences' emplacement within social institutions and systems, naturalizing the inseparability of human beings from commodified relations of production and distribution.

These three primary conventions related to the rhetoric of stardom (appeals to interest in star quality, relationality and the star system) point to the principal foci that trailers tend to take in relation to the types of textual evidence they provide of the implied audiences to which they are addressed. Trailers' appeals to audience interest in stars assume things about the kinds of selves spectators want to be (or desire), the kinds of social relationships that are important to moviegoers, and the ways audiences want to relate to social institutions. Within Hollywood trailers, these assumptions are articulated within the broader terms of a shared imaginary space, the promotional world of Hollywood (the presumed dwelling place of the stars), to which audiences are invited[71] yet from which they're simultaneously excluded. More often than not, trailers express assumptions about audience interest in stars through a melodrama of inclusion and exclusion that the industry hopes will work as intermittent reinforcement, keeping audiences coming back to the movies again and again—for a "more" they don't always get.[72]

Whether from the vantage point of the classical era's more systematically "typed" stars, the transitional era's declarations of star independence, or the contemporary era's chimerical star-commodities, Hollywood trailers appeal to audience interest in stars primarily by acknowledging that stars provoke many contradictory feelings in audiences, but always exert fascination. Throughout the sound era, promoters have evidently aimed to maximize the potential audiences for their films by utilizing the rhetoric of stardom to express or literalize such contradictions within trailer texts. Thus within the melodramatic realm of the rhetoric of stardom, we can even read in trailers references to features of a film's star that might be considered negative or antipromotional: we often see implications or figurations of failure, grossness, scandal, abjection, incapacitation or the decadence or backbiting of the world of movie stardom itself (as in two of the case studies that follow). But within the promotional realm there always seems to be room for such representations to be incorporated and recuperated so that in the end stars always shine—endlessly available for the Hollywood film industry as sites where assumptions about the desires and identities of audiences can be made flesh.

The three rhetorical appeals, and their imbrication within one another, are highlighted in the following case studies in an attempt to read in selected trailers of the three sound-era periods I treat (the classical, transitional and contemporary eras) key assumptions that Hollywood trailer producers make about audiences during each era.

3

The Classical Era: The "Mythic Universal American"

From early in the classical era, trailers can be seen as contradictory in their address to audiences. Motion picture attendance reached its all-time high in 1946, and the conventional wisdom about the period is that studios did not yet need strategies to bring different kinds of "niche" audiences into the theater. But as Richard Maltby has pointed out, the classical era's "undifferentiated audience," while "a rhetorical trope vital to the industry's claims to practice a form of cultural democracy," was in practice understood as a hierarchy of differentiated groups that were implicitly addressed separately by the workings of the distribution system. According to Maltby:

> Distributors classified theatres hierarchically from first-run picture palaces to neighbourhood double-bill houses, allocating each theatre a position in a movie's commercial life-span on the basis of their potential audience. By this process, audience tastes were categorized implicitly by income and class as well as explicitly by gender and age.[1]

Thus, while trailers were apparently addressed during this era to an audience that was assumed to include everyone, implicit segmentation was taking place at the level of exhibition. The question of audience address in classical trailers, which followed films throughout their runs, becomes an intriguing one of interrogating them as single texts that were designed to appeal at once universally and sequentially, to audiences of different economic strata—again, as contradictory texts.

The use of sequential appeals to various audiences was also designed as a way to bring new audiences to the moviegoing experience, according to Maltby. "The Classical Hollywood industry was engaged in a periodic process of reinventing and reconfiguring its audience. . . . The strategy of reconfiguration . . . sought to unite the existing audience with [the] new audience," comprised of "highbrows" and middle-class families who had formerly considered cinema as "lowbrow stuff." Thus, Maltby argues, the audience reconfiguration that classical Hollywood undertook in the 1930s engaged a strategy of additivity that resulted in the prevalence of a "bourgeois cinema of prestigious uplift."[2]

The classical era's "mythic universal American,"[3] was not fabricated from a synchronic, blanket conception of the audience, but rather sequentially and additively universalized by production strategies. Looking at classical trailers, we can thus consider the textual evidence of multipronged appeals to the assumed undifferentiated audience, such as the vaudeville mode's rhetoric of "something for everyone" and the circus mode's rhetoric of "everything for everyone," as ways trailers served to draw different audiences in, creating in the process representations of an imaginary plurality consonant with the "bourgeois cinema of prestigious uplift."

The case studies that follow were chosen because they in some way point up problems of, or approaches to, audience address in the classical era. Although for the most part they promote well-known films, these movies represent a variety of genres and story types, and thus divergent potential audience appeals. I do not attempt here to represent all types of trailers of this era, nor do I claim that the chosen examples accurately "stand for" the history of classical trailers, but I have chosen texts that illuminate key features of the era's promotional rhetoric as a way of demonstrating its operations. Because they are presented in chronological order, I hope these cases can also offer examples of how trailers can reveal some of Hollywood's changing assumptions about popular historical consciousness.

The job of the rhetoric of genre in the classical era was primarily to promote familiarity by assuming unanimity within a discourse that also acknowledged consumer taste and allowed variety. Genre appeals, the lure of familiar generic worlds or spaces coupled with the lure of the new, were promoted as felicitous and familiar places where any and all audiences would want to go, while simultaneously offering new elements every time. Trailers demonstrate how the boundaries of traditional genres are expanded to assert their universal appeal, and in the process they posit a mythic universal American spectator who inhabited these familiar generic spaces right along with the stars on the screen. Such representations of generic spaces in turn imply a social space that is constructed as familiar and shared by all—an assumption that correlates with ideologies of unanimity that were promoted in the American public sphere in conjunction with both depression recovery and World War II.

Trailers also help delineate the kinds of stories that were assumed to be desired by the hypothetical mythic universal American who constituted the classical Hollywood audience. Through the rhetoric of story, trailers both impart and withhold story knowledge, performing a balancing act that both provides enough information and holds back enough information to maximize interest in seeing the film (i.e., not "give away the product"). In the classical era, the process is complicated by actual regulation against, literally, telling certain stories or including plot elements that the Production Code had deemed inappropriate, as detailed in the famous list of "Don'ts and Be Carefuls" and the various strictures that subsequently governed film production during these years.[4] Overall, the rhetoric of story in the classical era works similarly to the rhetoric of genre in that its address to audiences tends to assume that there is something for (a mythical) everyone in each story type. The case studies chosen to exemplify this rhetorical appeal demonstrate a boundary-policing around story interest typical during this era, whether necessitated by the Production Code or other ideological pressures.

The star system in the classical era had clear parameters. Under contract to individual studios (but "loanable" to others), stars participated in fairly formulaic publicity efforts, of which the trailer was but one example. Pressbooks in this era often amplified how individual stars were promoted for each film, presenting studio-sanctioned interviews and suggesting promotional tie-ins and exhibitor ballyhoo. From the time movies became big business in the silent era, when stars were discovered to be "the surefire box-office money-makers," as Robert Sklar put it, a mystique built up around just what it was that made a star:

> Stage success apparently had nothing to do with it. . . . Natural movement, the glow of a vital personality, perhaps one's resemblance to a type, were what seemed to count on the screen. . . . Not even the professionals could always tell; the ultimate judge was the mysterious collective choice made by moviegoers in the dark. Potentially anyone, anywhere, possessed the special quality that made one out of thousands a star.[5]

By the early sound era, each studio's "stable" of featured and star players was well established, with the emergence of new ones an ongoing aspect of promoting stars. Trailers, as one of the prime sites where this "mysterious collective choice" of stars took place, had a large stake in making them look good. The mythic universal American who, as we've seen, was assumed to want both novel and familiar genres along with clearly circumscribed types of stories during the classical era was also assumed to want certain types of stars and certain narratives of stardom—indeed, the job of trailers during this era was often to sell stardom itself.

Regardless of which rhetorical appeal (to interest in genres, stories or stars) is preeminent in each of the following trailers, the assumptions about audiences that each trailer expresses display some of the contradictions of Hollywood's idea and image of its audiences and their desires in each particular historical moment, allowing us to read another kind of cinematic (meta)fiction across the classical era through these brief texts. These trailers demonstrate moreover an overall assumption on the part of the Hollywood production industry that the historical contradictions of the times could be resolved by consumer behaviors, and that consumption was *the* way all audiences might best participate in culture and become historical agents. Thus classical trailers are a "cinema of (coming) attractions" wherein representations of human agency and activity are often transformed into prefigurations of the activity of going to the movies.

DINNER AT EIGHT
(Classical Star Rhetoric)

The trailer for *Dinner at Eight* (1933) lays out in clear terms the ways relationality is invoked through the rhetoric of stardom in the early sound era, providing a strongly overdetermined emphasis on stardom by incorporating story appeals into star appeals. It is interesting inasmuch as it displays more distinctly than most trailers of its time the push-pull dynamics of the melodrama of stardom, demonstrating some of the contradictions of addressing audiences through star appeals in the classical era. Each member of the film's ensemble cast is introduced both as a star and as the character he/she plays; the stars are presented sequentially and linked narratively to one another. Typically of trailers made in the early thirties, these linkages are laid out without attempting to create a seamless narrative or dramatic structure internal to the trailer itself (this would wait for more sophisticated trailer rhetoric to develop toward the mid-thirties). The star introductions function rather like diachronically presented poster elements, spotlighting the draw of the film's star ensemble as a sequentially built aggregate while integrating discrete nuggets of story information and creating enigmas.

The sequential introduction of this film's ensemble cast and of its characters' interrelationships is in line with reviewers' perceptions of the film as more a "star-studded" variety show than a unified story. The film is referred to as "a fascinating mosaic," which "offers a greater variety of characterizations than have been witnessed in any other picture,"[6] and two reviewers note that the film could hardly be anything but a hit, since "veteran players of the stage, who have since been won over to talking pictures, are the principal assets"; with *Variety* gushing, "Marquee speaks for itself. Spells money and couldn't very well be otherwise."[7] That said, the trailer still generates its own melodramatic narrative, building its posterlike star segments into a teasing appeal to classical audiences' assumed ambivalent desires to be (identify with) or to have (desire sexually) stars.

The trailer opens with a title card, unaccompanied by music. We then see a still of Marie Dressler with her name in cursive (her implied autograph) diagonally scrawled across the screen, which cuts to another still of Dressler's face juxtaposed to a full shot of her in character, with a title, ". . . as the musical comedy star—living in the glories of the past!" A new line flashes into the title: "among them . . ." (flash) "her playboy memory . . . Lionel Barrymore." The still of Dressler's face is replaced with Barrymore's, while the full shot of Dressler remains next to it. This replacement of her close-up with his, while her full shot remains, creates a dynamic graphic linkage signifying that he's the one she's dreaming of. In terms of the conventions of the rhetoric of stardom, this also graphically establishes the idea that in this film, relationality is as important as individual identity or star quality, while the trailer does assume some audience awareness of these stars' qualities (such as Billie Burke's matriarchal purity, the younger Barrymore's reputation as a rake and Jean Harlow's femme fatale status). The trailer then cuts to a clip from the film of Barrymore and Dressler seated on a sofa, as Dressler says, "I was very fond of you, Arthur," and Barrymore replies, "I was very much *in love* with you, Carlotta. You were the most entrancing creature in the world." Neatly encapsulating the relationship between the two, this clip exemplifies early trailermakers' efforts to use clips that lay out as clearly as

Figures 3.1 and 3.2. Identification titles
for Lionel Barrymore and Billie Burke (her
autograph is in the process of fading out)
in the *Dinner at Eight* trailer.

possible expositional elements, and initiates a use of clips that show the
stars' narrative interactions in order to integrate story aspects into an
appeal to interest in stardom.

The trailer continues in this vein, with identificatory stills of stars
with their autographs serving as title graphics, interspersed with clips.
Each star's photograph is linked through fades to another star with titles
explaining the ties between the two characters: "a successful business-
man" (Lionel Barrymore) "now . . . on the brink of failure!" "Married
to . . ." (Billie Burke) "who would sacrifice everything to give a society
dinner!" Madge Evans, "her daughter / recklessly worshipping a forbidden lover." The trailer flashes a pair of stills of John Barrymore looking
dissolute, "as the fallen screen idol / who has outlived everything but his
vanity!" The trailer cuts to a typical clinch scene on a divan, with Madge
Evans on top of Barrymore (the younger), as they kiss and she expresses
longing for him. The titles' implicit judgments of these two characters
are visually contradicted by the clinch scene's implicit assumption of
audience desire to participate in the characters' romance nonetheless.

Stills of Lee Tracy are seen, with a title, "as the theatrical agent / who tells actors *the truth* about themselves!" followed by a scene between him and John Barrymore: "All right, if you think I've been lying to you all this time, you're gonna get the truth now." The audience is privy to this "truth" (but is assumed to enjoy watching him get his comeuppance from this character's voice of sobriety). The trailer's rhetoric of stardom feeds into the fact that the film is *about* stardom and its effects in the lives of those connected to it, and like the narratives of stars' personal lives provided by film publicity discourses, those effects are assumed to be at once unappealing and appealing—yet both their scandals and successes are equally watchable.[8]

Stills of Wallace Beery follow: "as the financial tyrant / who rules everyone but his wife." The title stays on the screen as his face is replaced with Harlow's face and title below. Again, the bigger (this time, female) star moves in on the other's identification shot, here signifying a narrative control over him as well as the star's dominance. A dialogue scene between Beery and Harlow is followed by more stills of Harlow with her autograph, and a title: "who couldn't get enough of anything / including love! . . . and . . ." We then see stills and signature of Edmund Lowe, and the title ". . . as the society physician / specializing in the bedside manner!" There is a kissing scene with Harlow in bed and Lowe seated next to her. The voyeuristic yet superior attitude the trailer has thus far assumed of the audience is here given a gossipy edge, the clip again offering risqué romantic action as the titles nudge the audience in the ribs.

The trailer then cuts to a long shot of all eleven stars dressed for dinner. A title reads, "All of them" (as they start walking together into the dining room), "covering up enough secrets to make a dozen sensational dramas . . . / *together* in the most glamorous production of all time." Servants close the dining room doors—teasingly, on "us," and a rapid horizontal wipe up the screen leaves a star field graphic on which the stars' names come forward one by one in a title crawl, accompanied by stills. Orchestral music swells, and the trailer ends with a brief shot of the title graphic. The finale shuts us out of the dinner party both verbally and visually (we have to see the film to get invited in), yet the trailer has already let us in on many of the characters' secrets. This simultaneous exclusion and inclusion plays into the rhetoric of stardom's contradictory appeals to audience desires to be close to stars yet to perceive them as unattainably distant. The trailer spells out the core relationships, but how the ingredients mix together is the enigma that we must see the film to apprehend. But we do know that the *number* of stars in this ensemble—all *"together"*—will hyperbolically enlarge the film's appeal, since among them they have "enough secrets to make a dozen sensational dramas." The trailer thus illustrates the star relationality rhetoric of quantity equaling quality.

The promotion of the film's *narrative* preoccupation with stars and ex-stars, the pedigree of its ensemble "marquee" and status as a theatrical adaptation, and the trailer's star field graphic all contribute to an overdetermined focus on the melodramatic discourse of *stardom,* thus reinforcing the ideology of stardom as seduction and deception, as an irresistible corrupter of relationships. The titles, which evoke scandal far more than glitter ("glories of the past . . ." "brink of failure . . ." "sacrifice everything . . ." "recklessly worshipping . . ." "vanity . . ." "tells actors the *truth* . . ." "couldn't get enough . . ." "bedside manner . . ." "enough secrets to make a dozen sensational dramas . . .") form one side of this ideological coin, cautioning audiences of the pitfalls of stardom, while the literally sparkling imagery of a glamorous dinner party held during the depths of the Great Depression (that audiences are assumed to wish to attend) forms the other. The trailer assumes an audience at once longing for and disdainful of the glamour and profligacy of stardom—and simultaneously of Hollywood and the medium of film itself, which likewise during this time was still considered by many as both irresistibly glamorous and corrupt. Thus audiences are offered a melodrama of seduction and rejection not dissimilar to that occurring between characters in the film, but one that works as promotion precisely because within the generic terms of melodrama, dystopic elements of stardom such as scandal and corruption are themselves irresistible.

FURY (Classical Story Rhetoric)

The trailer for *Fury* (1936), Fritz Lang's film about mob violence, is in some ways typical of earlier thirties trailers, which generally display both nascent forms of familiar classical Hollywood trailer conventions and a more rudimentary language of film promotion. Since it relies on the rhetoric of story more than that of either genre or stardom, it serves as an early example of the promotion of interest in withheld knowledge. As was conventional for classical-era trailers, it opens with bold, brief expository titles (it uses no voice-over narration, which appears to have become more prevalent toward the latter part of the thirties). Wipes are used for transitions, and there are many short scenes contextualized by titles. Major and some minor cast members are introduced in short identifying scenes. The *Fury* trailer offers oblique and tantalizing hints of the story that lay out the barest of premises.

Although the film was touted by reviewers as an "antilynch picture" for example,[9] the generalized mob scenes of the trailer despecify this historical thematic even more than does the film's deliberate deracialization of the lynching issue.[10] Not only are we removed from the discourse of race relations, but the trailer obscures even the nature of the accusations against Spencer Tracy's character. The audience is enjoined by the trailer's very incomprehensibility to see the film in order to make sense of this "fury" (which the trailer ascribes to the mob alone, omitting all scenes of Tracy's vengeful excesses). The fact that the *Fury* trailer attempts to promote this film that "dropped all the formulas" within *promotionally* formulaic terms—albeit at a time when classical promotional formulas were still being determined—makes it an interesting case study. Even in this early and rather crude example of the appeal to audience interest in film stories, there are clear textual assertions of the promotional value of enigma going hand in hand with ideologically determined absences.

While the rhetorical appeals are not as clearly lined up for audiences as they tend to be in later trailers, the trailer still relies on commonplaces that are assumed to be shared by audiences. The principal rhetorical appeals displayed in the trailer entail assumptions about the value of character identification, inviting the audience immediately into a hypothetical experience of the film's (sketchily presented) premises from the point of view of the wronged couple, as well as assumptions about audience interest in the workings of mobs and the justice system. The trailer opens with the title "It might happen to anyone," over a shot of Spencer Tracy and Sylvia Sidney talking intimately in profile, followed by another title, "It did happen to them!" over a shot of Tracy yelling from a jail cell. The missing term of this enthymeme, clearly, is "It could happen to you!"

This image is erased by a wipe matching the vertical bars of the cell and replaced with a shot of a mob accompanied by the title "The Fury of a hate-driven mob," followed by another shot of the mob advancing with clubs. A title follows, "Innocent of any crime. . . . They were victims of mob violence." A wipe shaped like two hearts transitions the trailer from a shot of men trying to fend off the mob to the next shot, of Spencer Tracy looking out through a barred window. The heart wipe at first seems incongruous, but serves to demonstrate the occasionally narrative function of wipes: here, an anticipatory one, for the next title reads: "Two lovers tossed into the inferno of men's maddest Passions." As flames start licking the prison wall, a slow fade takes us to Sylvia Sidney's horrified face, followed by a title with the (so enigmatic it's baffling) question: "What could they do to bring vengeance to the 22 accused of one murder?" The couple is not only united by this discourse into one dramatic unit with which audiences can identify regardless of gender (belying the fact that the couple is both physically and motivationally separated throughout the actual film's central dramatic portion), but their couplehood is also linked by the heart wipes and the title's wording ("lovers/passions") to the mob's fury, firmly cementing drama to romance in keeping with the inclusive conception of genres we saw as common to classical Hollywood trailers.

This is the extent of the plot description, and ensuing clips of scenes from the film are then laid out with no apparent narrative bridges. After this opening, shots follow in rapid succession: two men, whose roles and allegiances we do not yet understand, vowing revenge on "them skunks"; Sylvia Sidney flanked by two men and crying, "I know he's alive!"; a tense courtroom outburst in which an unknown woman begs someone's forgiveness for her testimony. Through a selection that emphasizes tense dialogue and dramatic outbursts over exposition, the audience's interest in dramatic action is assumed to be piqued by watching intense emotion on the screen.

The trailer moves into its actor (and director) identification segment with a shot of the mob seen through prison bars superimposed with "FURY, directed by Fritz Lang" and the MGM logo.[11] Supporting actors are then introduced with short scenes—the identifications of Bruce Cabot, Edward Ellis and Walter Brennan form a virtual courtroom interrogation scene, as each responds to an unseen character, asking, respectively: "What are you trying to do, Hummell?" "Where did you say you spent the night before last?" "I ain't answering the questions, buddy, you are. C'mon, get out." Rapid repetition of similar types of shots or scenes is a familiar convention throughout Hollywood trailer history, and when repetition is utilized in terms of the rhetoric of story, the accumulation can underline the trailermakers' assumptions about audiences' interests in knowing more, or here, in getting to "the truth." The final identification shot, of George Walcott, has him speak the line "She must love you an awful lot," followed by a cut to Sylvia Sidney walking to Spencer Tracy in the courtroom and embracing him. The words "Two great stars, in their greatest roles. The year's strangest . . . most powerful dramatic surprise" are superimposed over their kiss, followed by the title and the MGM lion superimposed over a high shot of the mob rushing the jail building, as the music crescendos.

Although we can assume the two main stars are the "innocent victims of mob violence," we understand neither why they are nor what they do about it. The trailer's disjointed depiction of the film's causality and its emphasis on high emotion (largely textured by fear of an unidentified mob), on the discourse of legal justice and on the triumph of heterosexual romance present an argument that what is most important to audiences is not Spencer Tracy's moral rectitude or course of action, of which the trailer gives us little idea, so much as the couple's fear of the mob, with which we are invited to identify ("It could happen to anyone"), and its ultimate resolution through the justice system's interrogatory discourse, with the woman's courtroom embrace as final reward. The other reward the trailer proffers, "the year's strangest . . . most powerful dramatic surprise," is an interesting example of the way some early trailers promoted enigma by announcement—here, reinforcing the suspense the trailer has attempted to build—it's a hyperbole that still, contradictorily, withholds more than it reveals. The spectators in this trailer's courtroom scenes, its profilmic audience, stand in for the trailer spectators, here serving the function of reminding us of the inherent "watchability" or spectacular value of getting to "the truth," solving the film's mystery in the courtroom.

The trailer demonstrates an assumption that audiences find the cinematic experience of mob fear and its narrative resolution in the courtroom unusual, interesting and thus desirable, and that this is the aspect of the film about which they will be most curious. The embrace is shown as the trailer's climax without revealing its prior motivation, figuring a juridical and a romantic resolution—of what, we don't quite know. The assumption that audiences share the characters' fears and believe in the possibility of resolving conflict in the courtroom is held out by the trailer as a resolution both for the characters and for the audience, whose real resolution can be achieved only by seeing the film.

This trailer thus ascribes to audiences, both by its representations of the film and by the information it withholds, a desire for knowledge—perhaps even beyond the narrative knowledge the film will impart—while at the same time contradictorily withholding even more than just the story's enigma, in the way it builds on the film's whitewashing of the lynching issue by obscuring core plot elements. In the prewar social world of a country that welcomed this film's émigré director when he fled the Nazi "mob," the possibility of gaining knowledge of "the truth" (a term that today can rarely be used without quotation marks) was still embraced as a reality. Yet the exigencies of the Production Code rigidly determined and circumscribed the parameters of how much and what kinds of knowledge were appropriate to go on movie screens, and this trailer's attempts to appeal to audiences' interest in its story display evidence of Hollywood's contradictory role in fulfilling, yet not fulfilling this interest. The trailer's "shell game"— of hyperbolic dramatic cues without a real drama in evidence, and hints of a "surprise" that must be announced yet cannot be disclosed— reveals some of the conflicted assumptions made by classical promoters as to what audiences really wanted out of film stories.

A DAY AT THE RACES
(Classical Genre Rhetoric)

The trailer for the Marx Brothers' comedy *A Day at the Races* (MGM, 1937) demonstrates how comedies were promoted in the classical era, and since this trailer promotes both a genre and a cycle (Marx Brothers movies), its appeals to audience interest in genre are overdetermined. The trailer is also an example of how the vaudeville mode is invoked to sell genres through inclusiveness. At the same time, the trailer's unusually vivid inclusion of implied audience anarchy and its figuration of a significantly multiracial and cross-class profilmic audience make it an interesting example of a utopian impulse in the promotion of genres in the classical era.

The vaudeville mode's chat motif, frequently seen in classical trailers, incorporates comedic interaction with an implied audience. This trailer opens with a man in front of a curtain announcing, "Ladies and gentlemen, may I request your absolute silence. I have a message of great importance for everyone in the audience—remember, absolute silence," this followed by a pie thrown at him from the offscreen vicinity of the audience, followed by two more pies, then by a rapid barrage of clips of scenes from the film. The trailer then follows a common classical-era trailer structure, opening with a bracket syntagma (Metz's term for a sequence of nonchronologically edited shots that give examples of an overall theme or idea) to characterize the film, next identifying the film's title and cast members, followed by slightly longer dialogue scenes, and winding up with rousing visual summaries of the film's generic (and cycle) appeal using titles and musical/comedic scenes.

The rhetoric of the trailer's framing device comprises an assumption of the audience's interest in taking the pompous man in front of the curtain down a peg. The missing term in this trailer syllogism (in which a man speaks formally to an implied audience, signifying "You are here to be educated"; followed by the throwing of a pie at him by someone in the implied audience, signifying "We are not!") is the assumption that such a formal address is inappropriate to a movie audience and deserves to be ridiculed. The trailer thus asserts, "This is comedy," working on the register of genre appeals, as well as making an interesting class-based assumption about movie audiences—or at least comedy audiences. (The "bourgeois cinema of prestigious uplift" is taken down.) The fact that the pie originates from the direction of the implied audience sets up the subsequent visual barrage of slapstick clips connected by an assortment of wipes as a cornucopia of delights not only desired by the audience but also imaginatively instigated by them. The clips culminate with a punch line as Groucho takes a horse's temperature and remarks, "Either he's dead or my watch has stopped."

The trailer's cast identification segment begins with a cut to the film title, followed by visual identifications of the Marx Brothers (close-ups with their names in title overlays), accompanied by antic music. This segment promotes the film on the basis of an appeal to audience interest in its cycle within the comedy genre. Titles continue to introduce the film with quick cuts and varied wipes: a long shot of the racetrack is papered over with a title, "in the spectacular successor to 'A Night at the Opera,' 'A Day at the Races.'" Other cast members are then identified via quick-cut visuals and titles after which the trailer slows to longer musical and dialogue scenes (including a 12-second shot of Harpo playing the harp and an 18-second shot of Chico playing the piano), still linked by varied wipes. These are interspersed with slapstick dance scenes along with a sampling of Groucho's one-liners, and are followed by another punch line, Groucho telling his dance partner, "If I hold you any closer I'll be in back of you!"

There is a double diamond wipe to an extreme long shot of the main characters and couples in the foreground after the assumed titular race (interspersed with cutaway shots to individual stars within the group), with Harpo on the winning horse and a crowd of people (many of them black) all walking and dancing with them as everyone sings a familiar African-American spiritual. This "generalization" shot is characteristically overlaid with typically alliterative summary titles that flop onto the

Figure 3.3. Alliteration in the final generalization
shot of the trailer for *A Day at the Races*.

screen from left to right: "Gags and Girls! / Romance and Rhythm! / Stars
and Songs!" The trailer then ends with the same medium shot of the
man from the beginning, wiping pie out of his eye with his mouth agape.

In addition to the vaudeville mode's use here as a framing device to
insert the audience's assumed desire for irreverence into the trailer text,
the foregrounding of Harpo's harp and Chico's piano via long solos is a
vaudeville echo, in its assumption that audiences will want to pause to
sample their musical talents in the middle of the slapstick trailer (as well
as during the film itself). The trailer thus posits an inclusive notion of
comedy, which it does also by assuming audiences want a little romance
as well as music (even the "high culture" connotation that Harpo's solo
provides) in their comedies, as the shots of romantic couples in the final
crowd scene (and several romantic dialogue exchanges during the
course of the trailer) attest. Groucho's singing is the emotional center of
this finale, so the trailer's summation of the film's comedy elements contains signifiers of romantic resolution as well,[12] positing the appeal of
(this) comedy as a utopia in which appropriately coupled people and
racehorses all dance together in the end.

Bringing together the slapstick, musical, romance and comedy elements of this trailer's "variety show" notion of comedy is its emphasis on
all these elements as a spectacle we can (and should) consume—and that
the package it comes in is that of comedy. This generic emphasis is visually inscribed repeatedly by a variety of different wipes connecting the

short scenes: an x wipe, a spiral wipe, a version of the curtain-dropping wipe, vertical stripe wipes, a circular wipe with spikes on it, a plain horizontal wipe and the double diamond wipe. They remind us not to expect narrative causality from the trailer's editing (and possibly even from the film as an anarchic comedy), serving the function of highlighting these scenes instead as quotations from the film that signify "this is fun." The wipes remind us by their variety of the many different types of pleasures the film will give us within the genre of comedy, almost in effect literally wrapping each little scene in paper and ribbon as a consumable for our consideration. Anarchy, the Marx Brothers' stock in trade, is in a sense recuperated by this rhetoric that corrals it into the familiar domain of the comedy genre.

Yet contradictorily, the zany fun of having so many types of wipes is also related to the trailer's main rhetorical assumption of inscribing the audience in the trailer on the side of the pie-throwers—our implied assault on the assumed seriousness can be seen as extended throughout the trailer by these highly foregrounded wipes, which continually rub and bother the film (in our stead). Thus, the comic utopia, literalized by the final happy mass gathering singing about "all God's children," invites and includes us, and the "us" it includes is a democratic, populist group.

As scholars have shown, classical Hollywood's cinematic address to the audience in films tended to pay significant attention to questions of individuality and collectivism. Thomas Cripps points out that early in the New Deal thirties, more collectivized heroism was emphasized, and although by the time of *A Day at the Races* there was a "shift from collective to individual heroism"[13] that accompanied American economic recovery after the depression, as well as a concurrent taming of the Marx Brothers' subversive comedic gifts in the wake of the arrival of the Production Code,[14] this trailer emphatically figures the profilmic audience as a populist (multiclass, interracial) collective. Its finale constructs a utopian exterior social space of happy coexistence and unbridled self-expression—which the trailer moreover has constructed as the product of a *generic* space, that of comedy. The superimposed titles then brand this scene with the legitimacy of finality, endowing its massive (and mass) quality with significance beyond the scene's assumed presence in the actual film's happy ending.

As a representation of the social space of the late depression, this trailer's summary scene figures the Marx Brothers as harbingers of redemption within the chaos of the era's cross-class hardship (winning big at the racetrack being, moreover, a cross-class fantasy). The trailer's novel rhetorical inclusion of mass audience irreverence in the service of laughs, that is, of comedy, can perhaps be thought of as a compensatory gesture that assumes that all strata of the audience (even harp aficionados), if not the Production Code–hobbled films themselves, would rather still be throwing pies at the cultural status quo—and that consumption of comedy films is the way to do it.

HISTORY IS MADE AT NIGHT (Classical Star Rhetoric)

In the trailer for *History Is Made at Night* (1937), a romantic shipwreck drama starring Jean Arthur and Charles Boyer, the rhetoric of stardom is once more the key appeal, and audiences are not only invoked, but represented as a vital component of the promotional world of Hollywood. Here, the downside of celebrity is nowhere to be seen. Like many from the classical era, the trailer is split between an evocation of the narrative world of Hollywood and more familiar kinds of promotional imagery that utilize clips from the film. The first third of the trailer addresses audiences directly, taking them behind the scenes and informing them about the film's production. This has the effect of establishing the later clip portion (during which there is no narration and very few titles) as the desired and desirable product resulting from the narrative of moviemaking labors depicted in the first part, confidently offered up for audience approval, as it were, without need for further commentary. The trailer evokes equally the rhetoric of stardom and of story, but it focalizes the story strongly through its star in ways that both call attention to the star system and highlight relationships within the film. Moreover, the interaction between the two sections (the promotional world of Hollywood and the promotion of star appeals within the film) creates an unusually direct interpellation of audiences.

It opens with an establishing extreme long shot of a Hollywood landscape, the camera panning left under a title, "Hollywood, California," offering the localizing rhetorical mode of a newswire or press release (familiar to classical-era moviegoers from newsreels). There is a newsreel-like montage of camera setups and lighting crews and a narrator announces, "The crucial moment in the making of all motion pictures, the final scene. Here we see the studio crew shooting the last bit of action in Walter Wanger's production, History Is Made at Night."[15]

A large camera and cameraman dolly toward us, all business. The implied audience is positioned amidst the production goings-on casually, as if we were also involved in them.

The trailer next dramatizes the preview process: we see men putting film cans into a car. "Secretly the producer, director and cutter steal away to some outlying theater, where the film is shown to the public for the first time." The trailer cuts to a marquee with Charles Boyer and Jean Arthur listed, but no film title, emphasizing the centrality of star popularity as *the* draw for the preview audience. The narrator extols suspensefully, "Preview! The banner is raised. Preview! The crowds pour in!" We see the audience (which appears to be composed primarily of men) looking at the screen, from a side angle. Narration continues: "The picture is screened. The producers await the verdict of this mighty jury. *and* . . ." (the crowd applauds) "it's a hit!!" The trailer presents audience response as one of the suspenseful factors of the film's promotion.

Like many trailer (and narrative) representations of (actual or implied) profilmic audiences, this introductory segment makes the assumption that if audiences see other audiences enjoying something they're watching, they will want to see it too. In this case, the mythic universal American and "mighty jury" represented by the preview audience is more male than female, and apparently exclusively white. Having been let into the behind-the-scenes process, and having been privy to the suspense and gratified hopes of the producers that the film is a hit, audiences then see "themselves" represented, the seated figures an

Figure 3.4. A movie preview audience, the "mighty jury,"
applauding from the *History Is Made at Night* trailer.

extension of their own seatedness as they watch the trailer. They are hailed as a vital link in the chain—indeed flattered as the "happy ending" of the production narrative, perhaps as consumers and consumption could be seen as the imagined "happy ending" to the depression during these prewar years. Seeing an audience applaud the film may have been no more convincing to audiences of the time than any other sort of hyperbolic trailer rhetoric, such as quotes of reviews or box-office figures (or today's technique of interviewing spectators emerging from the theater for TV spots), but it is a clear textual example of the fact that trailermakers are addressing a social entity that is considered (and considers itself) a vital component of the industry and of the film's success.

A star-shaped wipe then reveals the film's title, superimposed over a shot of Charles Boyer and Jean Arthur. After the prolonged behind-the-scenes segment, stars are the first element we see of the film proper, their human forms thus effectively juxtaposed to those usually invisible ones of both the production crew and the audience, yet exalted by their positioning alongside the title graphics: these human forms are more than human. The stars' bodies are thus at once associated with and separated from the production and reception of the film. We next see them in close-up, identificatory titles underneath. Like the marquee seen earlier, this front-and-center positioning of the two main stars signals their centrality to the promotional campaign for the film. Reviews of the film from the time validate this approach—while both *Variety* and the *New York Times* are lukewarm about the film's prospects, they do cite the film's "good names" and "extremely clever cast" as redeeming features.[16]

The trailer cuts to Boyer instructing his staff of women and signaling the chef, who says, "OK, everybody take your stations. Scram." The film's dialogue thus contributes to the trailer's fanfare for the film: the audience is thus also instructed to "take their stations" in readiness for the film's romantic adventure, and fittingly, the shot is followed by a wipe (shaped like two hearts) to a clip from a love scene, and the transition from behind-the-scenes to "the show" is complete as we see a two-shot of Boyer and Arthur in profile, and she brings her head to touch his. Two scenes are excerpted delineating the love triangle of Jean Arthur, Charles Boyer and Colin Clive, with wistful dialogue clueing us in to the fact that Clive knows about Arthur's affair with Boyer.

This is the trailer's emotional center, and it calls attention to the ways male and female stars are promoted in the era before films were clearly targeted to male or female audiences. There is a striking image of Jean Arthur looking at herself in a double mirror as Clive asks if she would like to transform him into her lover, which strongly promotes audience identification with Arthur's character—the memorable image tends to reverberate throughout the rest of the trailer, which loosely presents plot elements other than the romance. The double image literalizes her apparent position as torn between two men, centering the trailer's rhetoric of stardom on Jean Arthur as a romantic/dramatic figure. Although Arthur's star persona had previously embraced the element of tragic romance (in the form of close calls with spinsterdom and unrequited love), she was primarily a comedienne.[17] This trailer's presentation of her somewhat against type contributes to her differentiation as well as potentially drawing her fans to see a film of a different genre.

The juxtaposition of a behind-the-scenes narrative (which strongly addresses audiences and asserts their role in the ultimate shape of the film) to the questioning mirror shot invites audiences to participate likewise in Arthur's choice between the two men. This trailer assumes an audience that is actively engaged in forming opinions about what choice Jean Arthur should make just as they will be/should be active in choosing the film itself. The melodrama of stardom within which audiences are positioned is thus weighted toward *including* the audience, inviting them within the circle of the star's specialness as fellow agents of choice, and the female lead's choice is assumed to be of equal interest to men in the audience (who were previously seen flocking to the theater and choosing the film) as to women. The incorporation of down-to-earth comedienne Jean Arthur as a romantic lead also implies a class-based inclusivity.

There is a brief comic interlude, followed by a clip in which Clive remarks that he feels like he's seen Boyer before, which Boyer denies as we see Arthur in close-up watching Clive, horrified. Even this somewhat enigmatic clip retains the trailer's focalization through Jean Arthur's character, heightening the melodramatic import of the scene: it's obvious that there is something at stake for her romantically in this exchange, yet in this case, the audience is excluded from knowledge of what it is, and must see the film to find out.

The shipwreck drama is then introduced, and we see a brief montage: a smokestack toots, hands operate telegraph equipment jotting out an SOS, a shot up the telegraph antenna double-exposed with another man receiving the message: "It's Princess Irene!" A sailor rings an emergency bell. Men run upstairs on the ship. A big gate closes, and we see Jean Arthur get back on the ship from a lifeboat as Boyer protests, "This is the *last* boat! Darling, it's not worth it! We would only have a moment together!" The trailer wraps up with a generalizing long shot of a lifeboat leaving the ship, with a title superimposed: "'Brilliant! Shipwreck sequence takes rank with the famed earthquake in "San Francisco,"' says Time The Weekly Newsmagazine. / You will never forget / the year's most outstanding entertainment." Typically, the trailer here announces its assumption that the film will stand out in audiences' future memories—not only will they choose to see it, but its images will remain permanently emblazoned in their minds.

It is interesting that a shipwreck drama the likes of which would inspire *Titanic* promoters fifty years later to make a trailer almost twice the usual length in order to properly hype its enormity is here treated in a brief montage comprising a small proportion of the trailer's overall content.[18] Instead, the audience is first shown its own importance in the film's success, then is invited to weigh in on a star-centered melodramatic plot point from the female character's point of view, but ultimately, the dramatic payoff of a shipwreck and the implication of a much more serious choice the same character must make is largely withheld. In other words, the participatory hailing of the audience that includes us in Jean Arthur's focalization at one point later excludes us teasingly from participating in her greatest choice: we must see the movie to continue our involvement with this character and star.

This trailer thus encourages audiences to come see *History Is Made at Night* in order to be involved with its stars: specifically, to perform an activity (choosing a film) that will align it with the female star's melodramatic choice—inserting the audience into the melodrama. It addresses a cross-gendered, multiclass audience whose choice-making capacity is vital to the survival of the film and of the film industry just as, in the trailer's narrative of stardom, Jean Arthur's romantic choices are linked to survival choices. Audiences' role as spectators and consumers in the promotional world of Hollywood is thus constructed as a significant one, and the trailer's withholding of the character's ultimate choices contributes to audiences making the "right" consumer choice— to actively make their own history at night, with and through stars, in a darkened theater. The idea of movie audiences' primary means of cultural agency (making history) comprising their choice to see a film can be seen as Hollywood's acknowledgment of audiences' vital role in re-stimulating the late-depression economy.

THE GRAPES OF WRATH
(Classical Story Rhetoric)

lassical trailers also depict profilmic audiences in the interests of promoting film stories, such as that for *The Grapes of Wrath* (1940), John Ford's classic film based on the Steinbeck novel of 1939, which privileges the popular novel's narrative world. The trailer both assumes and represents this world as being well known to American audiences—so well known, apparently, that an assumption is made that we don't need to see it or be told what it's about. Indeed, the cast identification segment of the trailer and one other shot are all we see of the film itself. One might have expected the trailer to promote the film's reconfiguration of the book's indictment of class-based injustice into a cinematic reinforcement of "Ma's values . . . the small-town ethos of self-help and good neighborliness"[19]—which, in fact, it doesn't address.

Instead, the trailer couches the film (and novel) within a text exemplary of classical-era trailers' treatments of that phenomenon I have identified in trailer discourse as the narrative of Hollywood. That is, the narrative world of *The Grapes of Wrath* is promoted with very little description, while its treatment at the hands of the "narrative world of Hollywood" is shown in surprising detail, down to revealing how much money the studio paid for the novel. Newsreel conventions, such as music typical of newsreels of the time and a voice-over narrator familiar to newsreel audiences, are utilized. The trailer raises the question, Whom do they think they're talking to? by virtue of its unusually frequent invocation and representation of audiences and their reactions to this narrative world, foregrounding classical trailer address to implied audiences in a particularly vivid way.[20]

It opens with a map of the United States papered with multiple covers of the book. The narrator extols this ". . . human, revealing, soul-searching story, that instantly becomes the most discussed novel of modern literature." The combination of the brief, blurblike adjectival clause with the hyperbolic mapping that indicates the book's "takeover" of the country establishes the trailer's rhetorical approach, the assumption being that audiences will go see *The Grapes of Wrath* because of the *popularity* of its story, not its (sketchily described) content. (The syllogism here: "Everyone's talking about the book; everyone's bought it. Now there's a film." The missing term: "Because the book is popular, the film must be good!") The cover fades to a double exposure of another angle on the book cover superimposed with a series of shots of people asking for the book at libraries and bookstores, and a bookseller ordering more. We next see a shot of people looking in a bookstore window as the double-exposed image of the book opens and its pages are turned. We hear; "grapes of wrath, grapes of wrath . . ." in a verbal collage of different (male) voices. The bookstore image fades to a montage of newspapers (still over the double-exposed image of the opened book). Headlines are legible: "WRATH HITS 300,000 MARK," and the narrator states, "As sales skyrocket, *The Grapes of Wrath* becomes the book of the nation. Everyone, everywhere, joins in the discussion of its social problems." Another headline reads: "*GRAPES* BREAKS ALL RECORDS! CRITICS ACCLAIM STEINBECK'S HIT!" This remarkable series of accumulated shots of people clamoring for the book (rare trailer images of classical-era "mythic universal Americans"), layered voices, and even print superimposed upon print is a cinematic palimpsest promoting the popularity of the Steinbeck novel—about which all we are told is that it's a "human, revealing, soul-searching story" about "social problems." The trailer is a visual ode to reading (consuming stories) as a marker of the formation of national community, which is then built upon by promoting, naturally, the *film* made from the book.

The narrator announces: "Due to this unprecedented popularity, producers vie for the motion picture rights." We see trade journal headlines in the *Hollywood Reporter*: "FILM STUDIOS BID FOR GRAPES OF WRATH—PRODUCERS OFFER FABULOUS SUMS FOR SENSATIONAL NOVEL." In *Variety*: "HOLLYWOOD BATTLES OVER GRAPES OF WRATH." The narrator goes on, "Finally, 20th Century Fox announces the purchase of the book, and plans for its immediate production." A *Motion Picture Daily* headline reads: "ZANUCK GETS GRAPES OF WRATH—20TH CENTURY FOX PAYS $70,000 FOR BEST-SELLING NOVEL," followed by a *Variety* headline: "MILLIONS DEMAND 'WRATH'—STEINBECK'S READERS

Figures 3.5 and 3.6. A palimpsest of reading and spectatorship: the trailer for *The Grapes of Wrath*.

ASK HOLLYWOOD TO GO AHEAD WITH FILMING." This last headline stays on the screen and is then double-exposed with a montage of people (studio bosses in an office, a cook and a waitress in a kitchen, a priest in a pulpit) talking about a film that doesn't exist yet. The narrator comments, "A storm of discussion arouses the nation. Speculation and rumor are rife to the effect that no producer will venture to film this great, dramatic masterpiece of human hearts." Another headline (from an unidentified newspaper) is seen: "ZANUCK ASKED TO SHELVE BOOK—OBJECT TO DARING ATTACK IN GRAPES OF WRATH," superimposed with more shots of regular folk (a delivery man, farmers) talking. (Here, the promotion of an extracinematic enigma—what "daring attack"?) The narrator goes on, "Darryl F. Zanuck, production head of 20th Century Fox, emphatically announces that *The Grapes of Wrath will be* [filmed]. All of the resources of this vast studio are marshalled for the production." We see an aerial pan over studio lots double-exposed with a montage of production scenes. "John Ford, Academy Award winner, is given the directorial assignment. The cast is carefully chosen to make John Steinbeck's unforgettable characters come to life." More production and postproduction activities are shown (researchers, a mechanical shop, a sound truck, an editor).

This series of bracket syntagmas of studio activity overlaid on, first, headlines, and then the aerial pan of the studio, continues the palimpsest effect of the book montage, creating a paean to *cinematic* writing, an avalanche of discourse, all devoted to bringing (the still unglimpsed) *Grapes of Wrath* to the screen. As the images accumulate (both on top of one another and in our minds), the success of the film becomes a foregone conclusion as the film's visual treatment is equated to the success of the book, and "we" are inscribed rhetorically as influential in that success, since our on-screen counterparts have been so busy buying the book—the assumption being that we will continue such behavior by flocking to the movie.

The trailer finally cuts to a single image of Henry Fonda in costume, smiling, walking forward screen left. The major cast members are identified, with fades between each, and wider shots of minor actors, some standing against tents. The trailer then fades to a shot of the road, an Arizona state sign to the right of a bridge, as the camera travels onto the bridge and the narrator says, "and now, at last, *The Grapes of Wrath*," and the trailer tantalizingly ends. Stars and the road are all we see of the film, and none of these images stimulates much thought about

America's "social problems." The most important thing for audiences to know in advance about the narrative world containing these "problems," the trailer asserts, is that—through the elaborate and complicated agency of the narrative world of Hollywood—it sells.

Our assumed desire here is to be a spectatorial version of the hungry readers (as seen in the trailer) who already know the world of *The Grapes of Wrath*'s story, which is all but withheld from us. The narrative world the trailer wants us to want to know constitutes not so much the book's world itself, or its controversial images of and ideas about America, as it does the cultural capital of being in the know *about* those controversies. The book is a downer, but its success isn't—a success that appears to contradict the book's message about the failure of the American dream and its economic causes. These assumptions about audiences' desires to "be in the know" are conjoined with a withholding of knowledge of the narrative world of the film itself. Thus is set in motion a play of knowing/not knowing (and desire/apathy) that displays the fundamentally contradictory character of a trailer that attempts to engage audiences to participate in the success of a film about the failures of capitalism. It posits an audience that while comprised of average American working folks, neither has experienced nor perhaps even cares to experience narratively the rigors of the Dustbowl on the eve of a world war. Other hungers are assumed to preoccupy them. Breadlines are magically transformed into bookstore lines and, by implication, theatrical box-office lines.

CASABLANCA (Classical Story Rhetoric)

The *Casablanca* (1942)[21] trailer is a good example from the classical era of the interweaving of appeals to audience interest in a film's narrative causality with interest in historical causality within an overall emphasis on the film's narrative world.[22] This trailer displays assumptions about how audiences will respond to the film's narrative and its relationships to history, while also demonstrating some typical ways classical trailers integrated genre and story appeals.

The trailer's opening evokes the narrative world of the film's geographically framed premise, that of the waiting zone of Casablanca in wartime North Africa. An iris opens up to clips from the police chase scene in the street market, interspersed with superimposed titles, "If you are looking for adventure / you will find it / in Casablanca." In a shortened version of the film's prologue, we see a series of long shots of the street scene, connected by a variety of wipes. "You," here, is an amalgam of the implied audience for a film, and a hypothetical seeker of "adventure" who is being informed, travelogue-style, about a city—the audience is addressed at once as spectator and historical agent.

A narrator begins, "Casablanca, city of hope and despair. Located in French Morocco in North Africa." A brief montage of people on the street moves into a more sustained sequence of a pickpocket being grabbed and police giving chase. Narration continues, "the meeting place of adventurers, fugitives, criminals, refugees, lured into this danger-swept oasis by the hope of escape to the Americas." We see Peter Lorre escaping police and closing an ornate door behind him as the narrator continues, "But they're all trapped." Lorre shoots behind him at the door as policemen push through it. "For there *is* no escape." Here, causal story elements (Lorre's predicament) are swept up into the trailer's evocation of the film's narrative world, which is rhetorically linked to the adventure genre (the trailer assumes audiences "are looking for adventure," and that the film's world of "adventurers, fugitives, criminals [and] refugees" trapped in a "city of hope and despair" constitutes the specific adventure they seek and will find in *Casablanca*). The trailer at once draws on audience interest in its present historical moment and yet elides the historical conditions of the vast majority of fugitives and refugees victimized by World War II, repositioning these historical subjects as ideal protagonists for an adventure story.

As the narrator says, "Against this fascinating background is woven . . . ," a pinwheel-like wipe serves to punctuate, moving the trailer into more directly story-based clips, beginning with a shot of Germans entering Rick's Café Americaine and crossing the room. Wipes of many shapes continue to serve as transitions and we see shots of Humphrey Bogart and Ingrid Bergman embracing, then Bergman seated, flanked by Paul Henreid and Sydney Greenstreet, as the narrator continues, ". . . the story of an imperishable love. And the enthralling saga of six desperate people, each in Casablanca to keep an appointment with destiny." The trailer wipes to a medium shot of Bergman in her room, in which a mirror reflects her face on the right side of the screen. This splits apart with an unusual wipe like a mirror cracking in pieces (visually problematizing the narration's assertion of "imperishable love"), to a medium long shot of Bogart at the airport in the fog. The narration's characterization of the story with summary clichés ("imperishable love," "enthralling saga," "appointment with destiny") emphasizes the film's overall narrative world, and its collapsing of a historical fact (massive

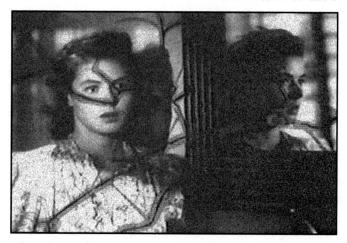

Figure 3.7. Ingrid Bergman seen along with her reflection in a mirror, as the image cracks apart in a wipe, in the *Casablanca* trailer.

wartime displacement) into a focus on a few fictional characters ("six desperate people") integrates the historical world with the narrative world. The narration also continues the trailer's couching of its story appeals within terms compatible with the adventure genre.

Clips from dialogue scenes follow, backed by a score that evokes the film's key diegetic song, "As Time Goes By": Bogart, at the airport, threatens Major Strasser; a shot rings out and the trailer wipes to a shot of Bogart running into Rick's with his cast identification title superimposed, which spins around to become another title, as he accosts a man at the bar: "The most dangerous man in the world's most dangerous city!" Ingrid Bergman's identification shot follows, a close-up of her teary face, with the title (on the flip side of her name) "Fighting the strange fascination that draws her closer and closer to him!" These cast identification segments use characterizations to cement the trailer's story appeals. In another shot, Bergman walks toward Bogart, and the trailer then cuts to their famous profile clinch wherein Bergman declares her love, followed by a kiss. Paul Henreid's identification close-up wipes to a two-shot of him with Bogart, in which he tells Bogart he knows they are both in love with the same woman. Sydney Greenstreet's identification shot is also followed by a two-shot of him with Bogart, as he asks, "What do you want for Sam?" "I don't buy and sell human beings." "That's too bad, that's Casablanca's leading commodity." These introductions also serve to impart elements of story information through characterization.

The trailer then uses a more emphatic diamond wipe, again to punctuate the end of the identification segment, as the trailer returns to clips that sample the film's plot, now focused more on story causality, beginning with a scene that gives indications of the film's "macguffin," the letters of transit—in a two-shot of Bogart and Bergman. Bergman bargains with him, then pulls a gun on him. As Bogart walks toward her the shot has an iris-ed edge, and the title, "Casablanca," is superimposed, then wipes to a street scene, with another title: "Where every burning moment brings a new danger." Police arrive at Rick's, rush out, and a scalloped, jawlike wipe opens up to a two-shot of Bergman and Henreid. "Where every kiss may be the last!" He kisses her forehead, and a curtain-wipe reveals a long shot of Bogart standing with Claude Rains and a young couple, serving as a generalization shot over which the names of the three main stars are superimposed. Over another generalizing extreme long shot of Rick's, the four other stars' names are then superimposed, with orchestra music that has the flavor of a Hollywood "exotic" version of North African music. The trailer's final image is a track left and forward in the interior of Rick's Café, with anonymous shadowed figures in the foreground, and the studio credit superimposed.

The summary ("Casablanca, where every burning moment brings a new danger") neatly folds the trailer's primary rhetorical appeal—story causality ("every burning moment") within a narrative world (the trapped waiting zone of Casablanca)—into the context of a simultaneous appeal to the interest in the adventure genre assumed at the outset. (Again, the trailer serves as an effective example of the logical imbrication of the three appeals within classical trailer rhetoric.) It is interesting to compare this trailer's heavy use of elaborate wipes to that of the trailer for *A Day at the Races*, where the wipes could be seen as both contributing to an implied audience-originated anarchic impulse and as a packaging or co-opting of anarchy within the acceptable terms of the comedy genre. Here, the wipes actually contribute to the imparting of story information (the splits and shatterings) in addition to generic signals, but as in the comedy trailer they have a "packaging" effect, essentially reminding the assumed escape-seeking wartime movie audience that this is a (safe) story, in spite of the undeniable appeal of its drawing on the reality of their historical moment.

The transformation of the representation of historical *facts* (which like many trailers this one assumes will pique audience interest) into an appeal to interest in a narrative specificity that in the trailer (more than the film) digresses from historical *truth* is typical of the ways current events were reconfigured as entertainment in classical-era trailers, in a time when audiences spent an evening being entertained at the movies not just by features but by newsreels as well. The film's wartime audiences are assumed to want an "enthralling saga" filled with dangerous, "burning moments." They are assumed to want all these moments emplaced within the arguably enthralling, dangerous and burning historical setting of the audience's own present-day situation—and thus to desire their diffuse wartime angst soothed by distilling and individualizing it into the satisfyingly finite and emplotted dimensions of a story of adventure and love. Contradictorily, audiences are thus encouraged to escape by enjoying the trailer's narrative of entrapment.

YANKEE DOODLE DANDY
(Classical Genre Rhetoric)

ankee Doodle Dandy (1942)[23] is both a musical and a biopic (of showman George M. Cohan), and its trailer illustrates the way classical trailers promoted multiple genres (or what Rick Altman would call "hyphenates") smoothly within an overall single generic rubric—in this case, the musical.[24] The trailer utilizes numerous clips that offer signifiers of the show musical, opening with behind-the-scenes banter such as people yelling "curtain going up," and "places, please, stand by," as chorus girls dash about and people go to their seats, followed by a shot of a

Figure 3.8. James Cagney invites the (trailer) audience
to sing in the *Yankee Doodle Dandy* trailer.

closed curtain superimposed with a title reading: "Up with the curtain and on with the show of the century!" Strikingly shimmery with sparkle effects typical of musical trailers of the era, this hyperbolic title creates an equation between George M. Cohan's show and the film being promoted. We see James Cagney (as Cohan) singing the title song, interspersed with title graphics (using unrelenting flag iconography) and curtain-wipes to different angles on the song. Unlike the *Casablanca* trailer's narrative of escape, this wartime film is promoted by way of an engaged patriotism, with the trailer's greater emphasis on the rhetoric of genre resulting in a more participatory address and appeal.

The film's songs are introduced with a title invoking trailers' typical nostalgia for future moviegoing: "The world will always remember . . ." (in this case layered with real memories of Cohan's songs). Also typically, we see a clip of a singer or singers performing the title phrase from each song, with the song titles superimposed. These are connected by vertical wipes. After the film's costars are identified, the trailer moves predictably to brief clips from dialogue scenes. We glimpse a few narrative elements, such as family problems and a paean to female domesticity behind the scenes ("Here was a little boy who needed a lot of looking after, so I gave myself a job. There are a lot of singers, . . . but very few good looker-afters"), but the trailer's inclusion of these serves less to create desire to solve enigmas or sort out story elements than to sample the different elements of appeal within this genre film, employing the "variety show" mode seen earlier in the trailer for *A Day at the Races*. The trailer's long finale begins as a woman in uniform sings "Over There," addressing the screen. Cohan/Cagney addresses the (profilmic and movie) audience yelling, "Everybody sing!" We see a high shot of crowds singing the song at a USO-type show, superimposed with a title: "It's really something to sing about!" Over soldiers marching, a title delivers the trailer's ultimate generic promotional address, offering at once hyperbole, generalization, and strong signifiers of repetition linked to patriotism: "Every great entertainment thrill of the past 50 years / rolled into one unforgettable motion picture. . . . With a song for every star, and a star for every stripe!"

The trailer directly exhorts its wartime audience to sing along with Cohan and the trailer's profilmic audience of soldiers and paradegoers. The rhetoric serves to redouble the promotional impact of the trailer. We've all got to do our patriotic duty to win this war; and just as it's patriotic to entertain the troops (or to be a "looker-after" of someone

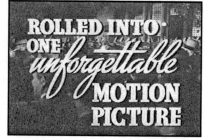

Figures 3.9 and 3.10. Trailer title hyperbole in the *Yankee Doodle Dandy* trailer.

who does), it's patriotic to go see this musical. Moreover, the fact that this trailer too, as a biopic of a showman integral to vaudeville's history, self-referentially evokes cinema's precursor as a signifier of "show biz" by way of both its "variety show" vaudeville mode rhetoric and its stage curtain iconography (mingled with the flags), extends the central rhetorical appeal further: it's patriotic to go see *any* show—that is, any movie.

Thomas Schatz has written about Hollywood war films made during World War II, in which "war themes" were prevalent in genres other than the war film proper, and in the musical in particular.[25] He asserts a wartime conversion of the classical Hollywood paradigm briefly away from the dominance of an "individual goal-oriented protagonist and the formation of the couple. During the war . . . these two qualities had to be radically adjusted: the individual yielded to the will and the activity of the collective. . . ."[26] Collectivity has a brief historical moment alongside the larger ideological pull of individualism in the cinematic discourse's representation of social agency, which is reflected in this trailer's assumptions about audiences.

Yet this collective audience, in addition to being physically represented by the trailer's parade-watchers, is also distilled into the individual heroic figure of the generic biopic hero, Cagney/Cohan, whom the trailer offers as a synecdoche of a universal American via both narration ("He took the heartbeat of a nation, and set it to music") and dialogue excerpts ("Because he's the whole darn country squeezed into one pair of pants"). The trailer's invocation of the audience as a collective participates in the rhetoric of genre by assuming audience desire for the familiar, interwoven with signifiers of individual-centered patriotism and an assertion of product differentiation (via the rhetoric of stardom) in the novelty of watching James Cagney, previously associated with the gangster film, dance.

George Custen's study of the "biopic" genre discusses at length the ways in which this particular genre contains and polices the boundaries of social agency. Films such as *Yankee Doodle Dandy*, he argues, "assured us that we had not lost our communities, and that the redefinition of the self from producer to consumer still left room for a greatness that had individual contours. . . . [They] convince[d] moviegoers that the self was constructed in relation to great figures fit to lead us in times of peril."[27] The trailer's patriotic address emphatically equates the "great man" and the community (that can, through film spectatorship, at once follow him and *be* him). It uses iconography, music (the sing-along) and the force of James Cagney's presence to reinforce the universality of appeal of musicals, biopics and the grand old flag, all at once. The representation of social space that defines and sums up this trailer is a martial thrust of patriotism, producing the individual as part of a larger, coherent social good. Patriotism, the trailer asserts through this equation, is entertaining, and entertainment is patriotic. In mobilizing the audience this way, the trailer makes clear Hollywood's wartime faith in the patriotism of its undifferentiated American audience, here figured as implicitly male, white and middle class, since "everyone" is squeezed into Cohan's/ Cagney's pants. The trailer's rousing appeal to the democratic spirit along with its implicit assumptions about who leads and who follows in this particular democratic space encapsulate the inherent contradictions in the classical era's appeals to a mythic universal American, which the trailer attempts to resolve by reminding all audiences that moviegoing is patriotic.

DUEL IN THE SUN (Classical Genre Rhetoric)

A trailer for *Duel in the Sun* (1947)[28] offers an example of how classical trailers attempted to promote a film that recent scholars have considered generically hybrid or problematic to a "universal" audience within the rhetoric of genre. The film itself has been seen as a female-centered melodrama.[29] It concerns a love triangle between Jennifer Jones, a half-Indian foundling raised by a wealthy ranch owner (Lionel Barrymore), and the ranch owner's good and bad sons, Joseph Cotten and Gregory Peck. Viewing the trailer, one would not contest the film as a Western.[30] The "mythic universal American" is constructed as neither anarchic nor patriotic (as in the other examples of genre rhetoric), but still the audience is assumed primarily to comprise consumers of genre films.

In typical fashion, the trailer opens with a rhetorical assumption that the rest of the trailer will serve to back up, in this case through a series of visual images combined with narration, which together form a generic appeal. A shot of the Selznick Studios logo (a shingle with the "Tara" building that served as studio headquarters in the background) is first seen, accompanied by an epic trombone fanfare. Then a narrator announces, "The studio that made *Gone with the Wind* brings you . . . ," after which there is a cut to a graphic of the sun with jagged brown lettering inside it that zooms slowly into the foreground until "Duel in the Sun!" can be read. Visually, the graphic (on the heels of a picture of Tara) echoes the famous *Gone with the Wind* title silhouette of Scarlett O'Hara on the hill at Tara with the sun behind her (which was also a key image in the *GWTW* trailer). The image/sound combination rhetorically and intertextually asserts that *Duel in the Sun* is similar (but not identical) to *Gone with the Wind*, and that the earlier film was popular and memorable. The missing term of this enthymeme could be expressed as "You will like this one even better!" The assumption that audiences want a movie like *Gone with the Wind* guides the rest of the trailer.[31]

The next shot is a generalizing high-angle shot of a party with lots of people dancing, and the narrator continues, ". . . a spectacular, adventurous love story [i.e., like *Gone with the Wind*] of the Old West." The party shot also echoes *GWTW* iconography, and the narration states the trailer's genre rhetoric clearly: this film is a Western, yet not *just* a Western, but an epic spectacle and a love story (an adventurous one)—like its famous predecessor. The visual and narratorial generalizations combine with the opening to construct *Duel in the Sun* as an *epic* Western—in Rick Altman's terms, positioning the epic as an "adjectival" cycle within the genre of the Western.[32] This enables an undifferentiated (but specific and gendered) universal audience (the men, women and children who loved *Gone with the Wind*—and hopefully others like them) to be addressed to promote a film utilizing the heavily "masculine" genre iconography of the Western yet appealing to women by virtue of its female protagonist and a romance-driven story (i.e., its similarity to *Gone with the Wind*).

The trailer's identification segment follows, which in the process of introducing the stars presents visual elements exemplifying the description the narration has just spelled out ("spectacular, adventurous love story of the Old West"). Each of the three principal stars—Jennifer Jones, Joseph Cotten, and Gregory Peck—is introduced with a close-up or medium shot as he or she looks offscreen intensely. A romantic triangle is suggested. We then see a wide shot of about thirty men riding on horseback together, and are told of ". . . the unparalleled thrill-packed spectacle that was two years in the making!" The trailer cuts to a long shot of railroad workers laying track in the foreground with men riding over a hill in the background, the narration and subsequent shot constituting an equation common to later promotional campaigns for historical epics, linking the monumentality of the building of the West with that of the making of the film.[33] This is followed by a provocative shot of Jennifer Jones lying in the grass with Gregory Peck standing above her as two men ride toward them and clouds mass above brown, scrubby hills, and the identification segment goes on to present shots of Lionel Barrymore, Herbert Marshall, Walter Huston, Lillian Gish, and Charles Bickford in Western settings.

The trailer's main segment further elaborates the principal rhetorical assumption ("you want more *Gone with the Wind*") by breaking it down into discrete units. A title appears over a sunset horizon (no further narration is heard): "*Duel in the Sun*—the picture of a thousand memorable *moments*" (italicized words in this segment are in big craggy block letters). The music changes to suit the mood of the "moments" as we see a series of short dialogue scenes designed to illustrate them. The title "moments of *romance*" is followed by a love scene with Jennifer Jones and Gregory Peck. The trailer then cuts to the title "moments of *adventure*," which is followed by a clip from a confrontation on horseback featuring Barrymore. Next it cuts to a long shot of Gish, Huston and Jones—"moments of *comedy*"—with antic woodwind music as Huston teases Jones; then "moments of *tenderness*" as an interior shot shows Joseph Cotten packing and declaring his love to Jones; followed by "moments of *heartbreak*" with Barrymore in a wheelchair by a fire upbraiding Lillian Gish for bringing "that Indian baggage" into the house and ordering Gish to get her out. A summary title in craggy letters reads "*Moments never to be forgotten!*" as we see a high-angle interior shot of people in a dance hall cheering as they watch a Native American woman dance. Then in medium shot, her skirts twirl up and around the titles: "David O. Selznick's spectacular production of . . ." followed by a cut (accompanied by a gunshot sound) to the trailer's opening title against the sun with the title looming in and another trombone fanfare.

This section of the trailer demonstrates one of the persistent ways the rhetoric of genre utilizes the vaudeville mode's "something for everyone" rhetoric. The variety show promoted in this trailer atomizes and packages experience—here, the feature film moviegoing experience—into structures of feeling called "moments" in order to construct

Figures 3.11 and 3.12. The "MOMENTS" motif from the *Duel in the Sun* trailer.

the experience as a generic one. That is, the enumeration of what these moments contain (romance, adventure, comedy, tenderness, heartbreak) both displays industry assumptions about what kinds of emotions audiences might desire to experience in an epic Western and in doing so *equates* specific emotions with a specific genre, thus commodifying and attempting to manage spectator emotions by linking them with genre appeals. In the process, this segment backs up the trailer's core assumption ("You want more *Gone with the Wind*") and posits the Western as a genre of epic scope, containing a variety of subcategories that will appeal to everyone—an "everyone," that is, who could relate to *Gone with the Wind*.

The rhetoric of genre here provides a perfect fit for appeals to the mythic universal audience in the classical era, eliding complexities of the film's cross-generic plot under the rubric of the vaudeville mode's variety show motif. While the trailer appeals to all of "us" to see the film, we can choose which of these "moments" will most make us want to. What doesn't get promoted by this trailer's strategy of appealing to the rhetoric of genre rather than story is the woman's point of view and identity, a novel feature for films of the time that merely remains on the screen as excess. Is Jennifer Jones's character an "Indian"? What are the choices she faces with regard to the two men? What does she have to do with Barrymore and Gish's ranch? These questions are not raised as story enigmas by the trailer, but are instead avoided in the trailer's overwhelming emphasis on familiarity over novelty within the rhetoric of genre. Unlike many classical trailers for films that deal with a woman choosing between two men, her focalization is ignored, as is (virtually) the issue of race—except for the "moment of heartbreak" and the implicit assumption that the film would treat the issue similarly to *Gone with the Wind*. Linking Jennifer Jones's character with the willful Scarlett O'Hara belies the trailer's apparent treatment of her as currency exchanged among the male characters.[34] The marginalization of female subjectivity to which these "moments" of epic Western-dom call attention, moreover, is appropriate to the social space of the immediate postwar period in which this film was released, a period renowned for pulling out all the ideological stops to bring newly independent women back into the domestic arena.

ROPE (Classical Story Rhetoric)

The trailer for Hitchcock's *Rope* (1948),[35] a film of Patrick Hamilton's play that presented a thinly disguised dramatization of the Leopold and Loeb thrill murder case, offers an example of the use of the rhetoric of story to promote interest in narrative causality as well as enigma. Like many trailers for Hitchcock films, this one departs from typical trailer formulas in many ways, while utilizing a number of familiar conventions.[36] It begins with an unusual sequence of specially shot footage that actually provides additional scenes for the film, presenting audiences with a backstory that those who haven't seen this trailer never get.[37] The trailer plays with questions of visibility and invisibility, of disclosure and withholding, in ways that are typical of classical trailers and yet depart from them: since the film itself plays with these same elements within its narrative, the trailer is in a way more accurate than most in representing its film's narrative concerns. It thus warrants a detailed description.

It opens with a title, "New York, One Spring Afternoon," over an aerial long shot of Central Park, followed by an idyllic dialogue scene between the murder victim, David Kentley, and his potential fiancée, Janet Walker. They are seated on a park bench as he tries to convince her to say yes to his marriage proposal. She resists because she wants to wait until after he graduates, but he won't have it—"Sorry, I personally consider us engaged as of now. Congratulations." He glances at the camera, leans in, and kisses her briefly. She protests, looking around to see if they were seen. More words and a kiss are exchanged as they part without having resolved the issue, followed by a shot from her POV as she watches him walk away, then followed by a medium close-up of her waving, and James Stewart's voice-over begins, "That's the last time she ever saw him alive."

The trailer cuts to Stewart (in character), standing in the domestic interior in which the film takes place, who continues (facing the camera): "And that's the last time *you'll* ever see him alive. What happened to

Figures 3.13, 3.14, 3.15, and 3.16. Missing scenes from *Rope*: the engaged couple in a city park (3.13); the film's murder victim walking away (3.14); his fiancée watching him (3.15); James Stewart (in character) explaining: "And that's the last time *you'll* ever see him alive!" (3.16) in the *Rope* trailer.

David Kentley changed my life completely. And the lives of seven others. . . ." The semi-intradiegetic voice-over (he's in character but he addresses the trailer audience directly) is meant to jar audiences out of the happy mood of the preceding scene with its direct, almost accusatory address, as if we've seen something we weren't supposed to. This audience address serves to promote *Rope* on the basis of Stewart's characterization, since we are assumed both to "get" that he is talking to us in character and to want to trust in this character's apparent authority (the character is not named—we haven't even been "properly introduced") as he expresses the film's core narrative premise ("what happened to David Kentley").

Stewart continues as he lists the characters and we see harsh *Dragnet*-like close-ups of each looking around with serious, worried, or sad expressions against a blue studio backdrop, wearing the dinner party clothing they wear in the film. Stewart's narration gives each character (other than Janet Walker, who was in the park scene) a brief characterization as he or she is named ("Henry Kentley, the boy's father. His aunt, Mrs. Atwater. His best friend, Kenneth Lawrence. A housekeeper, named Mrs. Wilson. And the two who were responsible for everything . . ."). The descriptions in no way amplify the harsh facticity of the images—other than Stewart's, the trailer does not promote this film's narrative on the basis of its characterizations, but rather the close-ups seem to victimize all the characters, scrutinizing them with a morbid curiosity. The music returns as we see a medium shot of the two men standing as if in a line-up, in the suits they wear at the party, their shoulders touching. Both first look screen right, then Brandon (John Dall) looks at Philip (Farley Granger) as Philip looks at the camera, then Philip looks at Brandon. A big crescendo on the music track accompanies a cut to a close-up of Brandon with his mouth open and a rather menacing look, slightly to screen right, as Stewart says, "Brandon Shaw . . . and Philip Morgan." We see a close-up of Philip looking worried, slightly screen left. Music swells.

There is a vertical wipe (like curtains closing) to a shot of the apartment window exterior with closed curtains, and the sound of a man screaming, as distinctively Hitchcockian orchestral music is heard. The trailer then begins a segment of dialogue scenes combined with generalized views over which titles are superimposed. The wipe opens back up to a medium shot of James Stewart, looking down and screen right, and his identificatory title then falls forward (like a calendar page dropping) onto the screen. The trailer fades to a long shot of the three men, Stewart talking inaudibly, the wooden chest in the foreground with books on it. A big yellow title appears, "Alfred Hitchcock's ROPE!" The title recedes and Philip throws a glass down violently, saying "Cat and mouse, cat and mouse." Brandon: "That's enough of that." Philip (angrily): "Which is the cat, and which is the mouse?" With another wipe the scene switches to a long shot of the party showing the penthouse setting with its New York skyline, the aunt and Janet seated listening to Philip play the piano, with the rest of the cast identifications sequentially superimposed. The camera pulls back so that we see the chest, now set up as a buffet table with food, candlesticks and a tablecloth. A diagonal wipe takes us to a long shot of Stewart and Brandon in the living room later, and both look at the chest, which now has piles of books on it and no tablecloth. The film title swells out to big yellow letters. Stewart walks toward the chest. Title: "Alfred Hitchcock's most startling adventure in suspense . . ." He lifts the lid violently in the foreground, books falling toward "us," the lid concealing our view of the chest's contents. The trailer's emphasis on murder and suspense has led us to believe we know what is in the chest, yet the party setting and other benign elements such as the opening, with its "One Spring Morning" title and happy conversation, have the effect of making our suspicions themselves seem morbid and unclean. We *know*, yet we can't quite believe—until we see the film.

An iris opens out from black to an extreme close-up of Stewart's hand in his pocket, and he pulls out the rope. There is a cut to a medium close-up of Brandon and Philip watching, and Philip yells, "He's got it! He knows, he knows!" The camera travels with him as Philip crosses the room, grabs something, and Brandon tries to placate him ("Easy, I'll take care of it") as we see that Philip has a gun pointed at Brandon: "No you won't! I'd just as soon kill you as kill him!" Stewart lunges for the gun as the title appears again in big yellow letters. He grabs the gun and wrestles with Philip, his hand on Philip's wrist, and the camera moves in closer as the final title sequence appears: "Alfred Hitchcock tells a story you will never forget! / ROPE!" (below the final title are studio credits). The two men still wrestle as the gun goes off harmlessly into the floor near the piano in a smoky blur, then the music crescendos and the trailer cuts off abruptly.

Although the suspenseful elements of the film are highlighted in the titles, the trailer emphasizes the promotion of the suspense of finding out "what happened" in the story (the process) over appeals to interest in actual story enigmas (such as who did it). It both shows us who gets murdered and names the murderers by introducing Brandon and Philip as "the two who were responsible for everything," even obliquely showing the murder victim being revealed to Stewart, as he is seen opening the chest where the body is kept throughout the film. Yet rather than promote "what happened" within the terms of the usual promotion of narrative causality (as a journey audiences will go on when they see the film), causality is promoted as *itself* an enigma: the shock of the trailer's opening, with its unusual direct address to the audience and its special footage only to be seen by trailer spectators, creates interest in the suspenseful workings of the basically known story primarily by evoking its transgressive elements and heightening the story's shock value. In a very real way, we're seeing something we're not supposed to see—a piece of the film that's not part of the film. Janet's surreptitiousness as the couple kisses contributes to this effect, as do the trailer's subsequent voyeuristic close-ups of the characters affected by the murder.

This is a fitting approach in a trailer for a film story that is in a sense about something that it's not supposed to say it's about—"the homosexual element," a strong subtext in the film and an important part of the Leopold and Loeb case on which the film (and play) are based. Homosexuality was obviously an unacceptable plot element in classical Hollywood film. Yet in *Rope* it could be said to be at once everywhere and nowhere, "hiding in plain sight." As happens in other areas of social discourse, it "went without saying" that forbidden interest in homosexuality was an integral aspect of the film's appeal.[38] Even reviews of the film at the time, one indicator of its contemporaneous reception, are full of intimations of transgressions of various kinds, hinting at but not naming homosexuality as one of them.[39] The trailer's greater focus on the more specifically gay-coded of the two men, Farley Granger/Philip, puts this unmentionable aspect of the film's story at least virtually on the screen, as does the trailer's culminating emphasis on the crotch-level shots of Stewart and Granger tussling with a gun, which is eventually fired at the trailer's climax.

The rhetoric of story's core contradiction—appealing to interest in audience knowledge about (here) what happens and why while at the same time withholding it—is thickened within this trailer by another level of contradiction between visibility and invisibility that was overtly operating to draw boundaries between appropriate and inappropriate narrative stories or subjects in Hollywood film during the classical era. The trailer thus manages to appeal to audiences' transgressive interest in something they're not supposed to be interested in (indeed, knowing something they're not supposed to know), while simultaneously performing a recuperation of that unmentionability into socially acceptable dimensions of plotted mystery and suspense. In this way, the *Rope* trailer fittingly serves as the final classical-era trailer example, hinting at things to come.

SUMMARY

The trailers selected from the classical-era sample all offer complex and contradictory images of some of the ways studios viewed the "mythic universal American" spectator and his/her relationships to social space, knowledge, and identity. Through the rhetoric of genre, a surprisingly multiracial and cross-class audience is represented and interpellated in a trailer for *A Day at the Races* that configures comedy as a consumable utopian generic space where cross-class redemption is possible (as the Great Depression recedes into recovery), encouraging a view of generic comedy as an outlet for populist, anarchic impulses at the same time as it packages those impulses. Later, in the trailer for

Yankee Doodle Dandy, the "mythic universal American" spectator is marshaled into a wartime unanimity in the service of promoting musicals by a rhetoric that glorifies democracy through an emphasis on the appeal of one great man. The trailer assures audiences that the individual can still affect society as part of a larger social body by performing his or her patriotic duty: to go to the movies. And the postwar spectator is encouraged in the *Duel in the Sun* trailer to subsume any potentially complex social dimensions of a film within a simplified construction of spectatorship as consumption, recuperating the female agency its film figures into discretely consumable generic "moments" through appeals to audience interests in the Western genre. Generic space in these classical-era examples thus seems to figure a social terrain where questions about the role of individual agency in the modern world are played out, and where the individual is both invited and assumed to play a participatory role in cultural discourse—yet already overwhelmingly that of a consumer.

All the trailer examples promoting their films on the basis of story assume audience interest in both the represented and withheld elements of the films' narratives. The *Fury* trailer's withholding of plot causality configures the appeal of the film as one of getting to the truth, even as the trailer, like the film, whitewashes its own racial subtext. The withholding of *The Grapes of Wrath*'s narrative world in its trailer heightens interest in experiencing the broader narrative world that made it into a movie—that world where, the trailer shows us, "everybody" is either reading the book or seeing the film—rather than attempting to draw audiences into the story's bleaker world. The trailer emphasizes success and winning, drawing on audiences' assumed desires to join in the production's success narrative: in direct contradiction to its source film's narrative of the failures of capitalism, success is equated with consumption. The withholding of the enigma in the *Casablanca* trailer assumes that a story addressing the contemporary historical moment in which they are involved is desired by audiences, yet the trailer promotes the film contradictorily as a narrative of escape, by packaging historical specificity into familiar story dimensions of adventure and romance. This mirrors the 1942 audiences' historical positioning as not knowing how the war will turn out, while reassuring audiences by presenting their social reality within the familiar emplotted temporality of a suspense story. The withholding of causal information in the *Rope* trailer heightens curiosity about the film's crime and its transgressive subtext, presenting a promotional rhetoric of enigma that hides more than just the film's surprises: deeper taboos and unmentionable cultural knowledge are reconfigured as a suspense plot, the resolution of which can be found at the movies. The trailer also gives audiences that pleasantly squirmy feeling of complicity for which Hitchcock was famous, by virtue of our very desire to see what's withheld. These classical trailers that exemplify the rhetoric of story display the rather strict boundary-policing of social knowledge available in film texts during this Production Code era, while contradictorily backing up the participatory rhetoric of genre appeals of the period with their strongly inviting direct address. The withheld knowledge that each of these classical trailers evokes is at once a problem and a promise, to which moviegoing is rhetorically inscribed as *the* solution and fulfillment.

Classical trailers can offer stars to audiences seemingly without needing to individualize them—even when the film being promoted isn't "about" stardom, often it is the *idea* of stars that is being promoted, with specific individuals and their conventional types plugged into the templates. Stardom, the supposedly desirable human embodiment of the tinsel-draped world of Hollywood, can itself be assumed to be the object of desire and identification as much as the gendered individuals inhabiting it. Early in the depression, a trailer for *Dinner at Eight* asserts that the scandals of stardom are equally appealing as its success narratives when considered as product features and promoted to audiences assumed to be ambivalent about the value of glamour in an age of poverty. For promoters in an era in which audiences experienced unprecedented economic hardships while the movie industry experienced its apex of popularity, assumptions that audiences held contradictory attitudes toward these human embodiments of success and glamour was perhaps an effective way to forestall wholesale envy and resentment and keep people coming to the movies. Later, the *History Is Made at Night* trailer offers an interpellation of audiences as the stars' ultimate choice-makers—where choice is also the choice to consume (movies) and where consumption can thus serve as the depression's happy ending. Classical trailers often reflect studio assumptions that the safest ways to make audiences want stars were to remind audiences that while they could identify with them, they couldn't *really* have them. What they could have, over and over again, was an ongoing melodrama in which these stars' qualities, relationships, and/or places within a star system served to embody the ever-changing yet enduring pulse of desire itself.

Regardless of which rhetorical appeal is paramount, classical trailers tend to demonstrate that trailer producers thought they were addressing an undifferentiated audience that was accessible and present in the movie theater, ready to consume any type of film Hollywood had to offer, a group whose primary form of agency in the social world is constructed by this "cinema of (coming) attractions" as moviegoing. Yet as contradictory texts, trailers also do more than construct this "mythic universal" audience as consumers. Their unique present/future temporality enables classical trailers to figure a sense of promise in the process. For example, by promoting audience involvement in cinematic moments such as a liberatory victory dance, a democratically shared pleasure in reading, a fervent parade of warriors, or the collective choice-making of this "mighty jury" itself, they also occasionally offer us hopeful images of a new world that might be viewed, and made, through spectatorship.

4

The Transitional Era: Chasing the Elusive Audience

The era I identify as transitional is that period from the beginning of the 1950s through 1975, the watershed year associated with the release of *Jaws* and the emergence of blockbuster marketing. Market research was utilized increasingly during this time, with a correspondingly greater acknowledgment that there might be different audiences for different films, even as the theatrical trailer's job remained to cast as wide a net as possible and maximize a film's potential appeal. Trailers in the transitional era vary widely in style. The era encompassed two distinct periods of trailer production—the still National Screen Service–dominated fifties and the roadshow/experimental sixties period (which overlapped with the early seventies). Interestingly, television advertising for films was not widely explored until the 1970s, a consequence of the industry's massive efforts in the early postclassical era to differentiate film from television. There was a corresponding increase in the degree to which the film industry utilized market research. The era of conglomeration, wherein the major studios were bought by large multinational firms with interests in numerous media forms and other products, began to open vast new areas for synergy and cross-promotion in the 1970s.[1] In a broader sense, the era as a whole saw many concurrent stylistic and historical shifts in American film culture during those tumultuous times spanning from the immediate postwar era through Watergate. The era's trailers, stranded between the certitudes of classical Hollywood promotional discourses and the new formulas of the contemporary era, share in common a confusion and questioning of who their changing audiences are and how to reach them, mirroring larger confusions and splits in the culture.

Trailers promoting films on the basis of genres became a prime site where the industry acknowledged and courted new kinds of audience interests—at first to chase after dwindling film audiences by drawing them to spectacular or gritty generic features that could not be experienced on television. Science fiction trailers of the fifties highlight some of these shifts, and have been invoked in both critical discourse and the popular press to characterize the move toward audience targeting and the cultivation of the teenage audience (along with the new feature film venue, the drive-in).[2] Classical-era trailer conventions such as stentorious narrators, sweeping titles and booming music reached baroque proportions in trailers for science fiction films by the latter half of the fifties. This itself can be interpreted as a sign that, at least later in the fifties, the rhetoric no longer addressed an implied universal audience— by virtually quoting their own conventions, the trailers enter a realm of the playful that functions slightly differently in terms of audience address than earlier trailers. The 1960s, in which the industry moved from the economic reliance of the Hollywood studios on their major big-budget "roadshow" films to a smaller-budget "renaissance" inspired by the success of films such as *Bonnie and Clyde* and *Easy Rider*, demonstrated a deeper questioning of how to appeal to increasingly segmented audiences. Audiences' growing awareness of film authorship becomes more prevalent as a means to promote genres in the 1970s (in cases where directors were associated with genres), and the much-cited emergence of nostalgia and quotation brings with it to promotional discourses new dimensions of the familiarity/novelty appeal, as novel elements of old genres are directly promoted.

A questioning of how stories should be promoted is also evident, accompanied by a confusion about the nature and the interests of audiences and their desires to gain experience and knowledge through the unfolding of cinematic narrative. New kinds of stories opened up as potential subjects for Hollywood film in the transitional era. From the emphasis on more "adult" themes that accompanied the economic and ideological shifts and the breakdown of Production Code Administration enforcement practices during the fifties and early sixties, to the stylistic experimentation and thematic liberalism of the later sixties and early seventies, film stories differed in many ways from those of the classical era. Trailer production also went through marked shifts during this period, but not always in sync with the changes that were taking place in film practice. The rhetoric of story in trailers of this period demonstrates that trailermakers were unsure how to promote new kinds of stories to the transitional era's fragmenting audience. A mismatch is often evident in the rhetoric of story in trailers: throughout this era, the assumptions of trailer producers as to what audiences want in a story and what a film is "about" test new ground, and appear to miss the mark more frequently than in the classical era. Doubting the former certitude about whom they thought they were talking to, promoters experimented with the kinds of story information they provided and/or withheld in trailers, often falling back on genre terms to define stories.

Following the Paramount antitrust decrees, the studio contract system was called into question as stars and other top production personnel gained greater degrees of independence and uncertainty, and by the 1950s, the studios were both looking for new stars and making efforts to configure new ways stars could draw audiences (lured away from moviegoing by television and the appeals of suburban life) to films. Furthermore, the period's trend away from studio formulas and toward more adult themes was complemented by changes in performance styles and an increased interest in "gritty realism," influenced by the rise of method acting and the popularity of stars like Marlon Brando and James Dean. But the extent to which stars could overwhelm story or generic considerations in Hollywood films had diminished by the end of the studio era, as Hortense Powdermaker notes, citing two articles in *Variety* that indicated a new trend away from star-driven formulas, under the headlines "Stars Ain't What They Used to Be" and "Hot Stars with Cold Yarns Give Hollywood Lukewarm Profits."[3] Transitional-era trailers indeed evidence confusion as to how stars fit into the selling of films: while innovations in performance and other shifts in the discourse of stardom were acknowledged in trailers' address to audiences, many characteristics of classical-era trailers, such as the reliance on the appeal of stars based on their past performances, were still operative. However, the melodrama of stardom is now increasingly focused on the individual characteristics and ideological significance of specific stars, on whom rests a greater responsibility for a film's success than in the more heavily systematized studio era.

While the era's trailers are therefore extremely varied in style and approach (as are the films), the conventions of the three rhetorical appeals remain in force, with interesting results. The case studies have in common with the wider sample both a nostalgic tendency to try to make older forms fit new texts and a pull toward new forms. Despite their variation among themselves, transitional-era trailers embody more evocatively than either earlier or later ones the unique and contradictory temporality of this "cinema of (coming) attractions." Their insecurity about the nature of the audience they address results in trailers that display the cinematic attraction's heightened present tense without really knowing where they are, and that invoke the future promise of seeing new kinds of films without having language with which to promote them.

ALL ABOUT EVE (Transitional Star Rhetoric)

A *ll About Eve* (1950)[4] was made on the cusp of the transitional era, and its trailer's address to audiences bears evidence of new appeals as well as those of classical trailers, in the service of the rhetoric of stardom. The version I saw is a post–Academy Awards rerelease trailer that promotes the film's success at the Oscars, but like most rerelease trailers, it appears to have merely inserted the award information into the original theatrical trailer. Like the trailer for *Dinner at Eight*, it promotes an ensemble cast and has an overdetermined focus on stardom (promoting both its stars and stardom as the film's subject matter). And like the *History Is Made at Night* trailer, it steps outside the usual clip-with-commentary mode to appeal to audience interest in going "behind the scenes" to the promotional world of Hollywood in ways that illuminate some of the many contradictions of this type of address. However, the clips selected to promote the film and its stars give evidence that the trailer attempts to address a different audience than in the earlier era.

The trailer opens with a shot of a collage of *Newsweek* magazine covers with a woman's picture, as a title fades in over it, growing until we can read: "Scoop! Bette Davis tells Newsweek Magazine *All About Eve*." Over a long shot of Davis and a man seated on a sofa, a title reads "Reporter Leonard Slater interviews famous actress on the set." The reporter asks, "Miss Davis, ever since I've been on the set I've heard nothing but discussion of Eve. May I have your opinion of her?" Davis responds, "The golden girl, the cover girl, the girl next door, the girl on the move. Time's been very good to Eve, life goes where she goes. She's been profiled, covered, revealed, reported. What she wears, and where and when, whom she knows, where she was, and when and where she's going. Eve has insatiable ambition and talent. An improbable person with a contempt for humanity, an inability to love or be loved." The reporter retorts, "But how can such a woman fool so many?" Davis replies, "How does *any* Eve do it?"

This specially shot scene inhabits a peculiar position in that while positioned as a behind-the-scenes vignette, with "Miss Davis" clearly

Figures 4.1 and 4.2. A collage of *Newsweek* magazines
and Bette Davis with reporter, in the *All About Eve* trailer.

represented in her own star persona rather than that of her actress
character Margo Channing, the *Newsweek* interview is a fictional promotional ruse, and Davis speaks of the fictional character Eve as if she
were a real person—discussing her more or less as Davis's Margo
Channing would speak of her. The scene deliberately plays with the
"edge" the rhetoric of stardom inhabits between fictional narrative and
the promotional world of Hollywood, and it makes a clear assumption
that audiences are comfortable slipping back and forth between seeing
stars in character and in their star personae.[5]

Moreover, when Davis says, "She's been profiled, covered, revealed,
reported," the line applies to the activity being filmed for the trailer as
well, creating a reverberating commentary about stardom as it applies
to both the film diegesis and the main star, Davis herself. The desirability of such exposure and the negative consequences of ambition are
assumed in this pseudointerview to be understood to go hand in hand,
and are linked to an inevitability that is defined as feminine by Davis's
rhetorical question, "How does any Eve do it?" ("Eve," this rhetoric
asserts, signifies biblical Eve, and the line implies that there are many
like her. The enthymeme's missing term is that the movie's Eve, like her
Edenic ancestor, is a temptress.) The line thus disavows Davis's own
"Eve-ness" while asserting the ubiquity of this type of woman. The multilayered referentiality of this scene's commentary on stardom makes
the trailer—like the film itself—a limit case of Hollywood's image of its
own operations, and a fitting paradigm of how transitional-era studios
saw audiences' interest in stars.

The trailer follows this segment with intense moments from dialogue scenes designed as a series of examples to back up Davis's statements, and answer her final question ("How does any Eve do it?"). The

first is a clip of Davis with Gary Merrill, in which she mocks his praise of Eve. Next, dialogue from a scene with Davis and George Sanders spells out Eve's understudy status. Another clip from a scene with Anne Baxter (Eve) and Merrill makes clear that he is rejecting her advances. These three clips serve primarily expository functions, communicating to audiences through the rhetoric of story that Bette Davis is jealous of Eve/Anne Baxter's apparent hold on Merrill, the implication being that Baxter is machinating to replace her in a role, and that Baxter's attempt to ply her feminine wiles on Merrill doesn't seem to work. At the same time, the inclusion of emotionally rich dialogue scenes featuring Davis emphatically asserts her star power by highlighting her performance as complex. (In the process, these clips provide evidence to back up Davis's claim in the trailer's framing structure that Eve is an "Eve.")

We next see Davis in the now-famous party scene standing at the stairway addressing Baxter as the rest watch, culminating in Davis's line, "You're in a beehive, pal, didn't you know? We're all busy little bees, full of sting and making honey day and night, aren't we, honey." Then, in a clip from a different scene, Celeste Holm appears to give a pseudocritique of Davis's foregoing speech as she remarks to one of the men in a two-shot in front of a fireplace, "Very touching, very Academy-of-Dramatic-Art." There is another wipe to a shot of Davis, who says, "I admit, I've had better days, but I'm still not to be had for the price of a cocktail, like a salted peanut." Holm is next seen laughing at a dinner table where four are seated. "What's so funny?" "Nothing . . . Everything. Everything's so funny."

This group of clips, sequenced in a bracket syntagma that displays the film's sophisticated dialogue without significant expository value, functions primarily as evidence of the intensity and fire of the film's performances. The sarcastic, "adult" flavor of the performances and dialogue glimpsed in the clips differentiates the film from classical-era treatments of the subject matter (such as the dialogue excerpted in the *Dinner at Eight* trailer). If stars, as this trailer implies, no longer command audience loyalty by virtue of their earlier successes alone (both extra-textually, because they are no longer "branded" by individual studios, and intratextually, where, as the trailer demonstrates, the predicament of aging stars is an element of the plot of *All About Eve*), they do so by the virtuosity of their edgy performances. Central to this trailer, of course, is Bette Davis's multilayered commentary on stardom. Her ultimately victorious battles with Jack Warner for the control of her acting choices inevitably reverberate in the trailer's inclusion of the "salted peanut" line. Ringing in the method-heavy fifties, the film and the trailer pave the way for new assumptions about what audiences want from their stars.

The trailer's final title sequence incorporates a number of rapidly juxtaposed graphic signifiers of stardom and success (Eve's acting award plaque, congratulatory flowers and champagne bottle, a poster of Margo), adding to the trailer's melodramatic flair—like the frequently piquant use of objective correlatives in the melodramas of Douglas Sirk; such markers here, on the heels of the trailer's intimations of the problems stardom brings, are doubly weighted as signifiers not only of the prizes of fame but of its price. Cast titles are then superimposed over an unusual shot of the star ensemble out of character—the three couples, smiling and walking confidently arm in arm on an unidentified and otherwise unpopulated film lot—an image perhaps resonant of stars' new status as independent producers untethered to studios. In conjunction with the earlier framing sequence, this shot helps create an impression of star omnipotence, of movies as the product of stars alone. The film title is superimposed over the staircase scene, followed by a dinner table shot as the music crescendos and titles are superimposed: "All About Eve is all about women . . . and their MEN!" In the final medium shot, we watch Celeste Holm laugh again, this time without sound.

Aside from the public relations shot of the cast, the final, dialogueless clips in the trailer all exemplify the film's principal settings, delineating its dominant generic register of drawing-room melodrama while keeping the focus more on stars than on genre. The trailer's offering of a film that is "all about women . . . and their men" implies that, through virtuoso star performances, we learn things about both stardom and human nature (and the visual coda reprising Celeste Holm's cynical laugh tells us that what we're going to learn won't be pretty). Nonetheless, having been introduced to the film by Bette Davis's own commentary on it, the trailer assumes audiences still want to venerate stars, no matter how ruthlessly the film critiques their ambitions.[6] The contradictory attitude toward stardom assumed of audiences in the *Dinner at Eight* trailer still obtains, yet Hollywood's shifting power dynamics are acknowledged as stars themselves are celebrated as participants in the making of their own performances and images.

This trailer can be seen as a melodramatic text representing the promotional world of Hollywood as one that excites and repels audiences. Acting in front of audiences is, again, an overdetermined feature of the trailer, from the framing sequence in which Bette Davis is mock-interviewed for an implied audience of *Newsweek* readers, to the clips of flamboyantly delivered dialogue that, as characters themselves remark, often seems designed for a theatrical audience even when it's ostensibly not. This self-awareness attributes to audiences an insider's perspective on theatrical performance yet at the same time represents that world as one from which they might be just as happy to be excluded. The trailer thus addresses an audience who wants stars to be more than just servants of studios, and who, more like theater audiences, craves virtuoso performances. Stars, it would seem, have more to prove to such an audience than in the classical era—indeed, at a time when stars and other film workers crossed the line into the public sphere to a new degree, becoming newsmakers and political spokespeople in response to the congressional witch hunts that resulted in the Blacklist.[7] The trailer's compensatory attempts to explain the film's characters by way of a pseudojournalistic interview, adding at once more glamour *and* more drawing away of the tinseled veil (with its nonfictional conceit and Davis's jaundiced view), appear to acknowledge 1950 audiences' increased desire to know "all about" stars as historical subjects.

THE WAR OF THE WORLDS
(Transitional Genre Rhetoric)

Perhaps the genre most frequently evoked in the popular media in relation to the historical epoch of the 1950s in America is science fiction. It is by now a truism that the proliferation of alien invasion films in the fifties (at both A and B budget levels) hit a nerve in their veiled expressions of the cultural anxieties of the country with regard to the Cold War. In the forefront of the fifties science fiction genre is the A-level work of producer George Pal, whose use of special effects was considered exemplary at the time, inspiring special mention in reviews of their virtuosity, their maker and their great expense.[8] *When Worlds Collide* (1951) and *The War of the Worlds* (1953), two A-budget Paramount releases of Pal's, are promoted through the rhetoric of genre in two similar trailers that draw heavily on classical-era conventions yet anticipate the camp appeal of later sci-fi trailers. The later one, for the better-known film, is interesting for the way it introduces such modes in the early fifties—indeed prefiguring many of the motifs of trailers to come. The film's dual emphases (typical of the emerging fifties science fiction film) on the sober discourses of science and the military and on the magical visual spectacle of spaceships and star fields are consolidated in the trailer's brief montage in such a way that the serious is counterbalanced by the spectacular, and hyperbolic appeals to audience interest in the latter have the (perhaps still) unintended effect of making the former appear not quite so weighty.

The trailer for *The War of the Worlds* opens and closes with dramatic titles but, like many fifties trailers, minimizes their use (titles were usually relegated to openings and closings) along with that of other graphics such as wipes, in favor of allowing dialogue scenes, supported by narration, to move the trailer. The opening titles appear over a shot of an animated cloudy, starry sky with distant comets speeding across it. Successive titles read, "It's Coming! / The BIGGEST STORY that could ever happen to our world / filling the screen with a MIGHTY PANORAMA OF EARTH-SHAKING FURY! / (as a large meteor falls to earth) Paramount's The War of the Worlds." The meteor lands outside a town in extreme long shot as the narrator begins: "This could be the beginning of the end of the human race. For what men first thought were meteors, or the often-ridiculed flying saucers" (the "meteor" explodes in a bright light) "are in reality the flaming vanguard of the invasion from Mars!" A big saucer-shaped craft slides into a farmhouse and wrecks it.

This opening establishes a rhetorical appeal of a different logical type than those of classical-era trailers. The juxtaposition of the title ("the BIGGEST STORY that could ever happen to our world") with the narration ("This could be the beginning of the end of the human race") constitutes a level of hyperbolic excess that assumes an audience that does not take the narrator's words completely seriously. The opening title's labeling of the film as a fiction (albeit one that "could" happen) combines with the narration's heretofore rare use as a means to state an intradiegetic premise as if it applied to the world outside the movie theater ("the beginning of the end of the human race"), forming a metacommunication akin to Gregory Bateson's nip that is not a bite: "this is play."[9] The assumed audience for this film might or might not be a young (i.e., playful) one, but this trailer's address to its audience appears to break new ground in enlisting the audience into the film's diegesis, inviting them to play along in this way. The precedent for this trailer is the film's precursor, Orson Welles's Mercury Theater radio production of "The War of the Worlds" (1939), which actually masqueraded as news reports of a real Martian invasion, and whose broadcast itself became a story as audiences ignored the disclaimers and believed Martians were indeed invading Earth. It is interesting that the trailer echoes the pseudodocumentary conceit of the radio show while the film does not.[10]

The rest of the trailer backs up this assumption of audience desire to "play along," presenting a series of military-industrial dialogue and action scenes overlaid by pseudonews narration. Following the spaceship-wreck we see a scene with Gene Barry (a scientist) discussing battle plans with a helmeted soldier as they crouch in a trench, then a brief extreme long shot of the spaceship glowing and rising, accompanied by ominous music. (This and the earlier wreck are the only actual shots of the alien ships in the trailer.)[11] With a sound overlap of dialogue that appears at first to be narration (continuing the blurring of the diegetic and extradiegetic trailer discourse), the trailer fades to a scene in which scientists and military men crowd around a blackboard, discussing the impenetrability of their defenses. The narrator interjects, "The nations of the world mobilize their armed might, rushing to defend the earth against the unknown weapons of the super-race from the red planet," over a battle scene. Trailer narration utilizes the film's dialogue to complete its points, querying, "Is there *nothing* that can stop the Martian death machines?" as we watch tanks shoot off charges, followed by a response from a general in the battle, "Guns, tanks, bombs, they're like toys against them!" Gene Barry expands from his foxhole, "We know now that we can't beat their machines. We've got to beat *them*!" Even setting aside or bracketing the hindsight of subsequent decades of viewing camp science fiction trailers and their parodies, it is hard to imagine that the strained seriousness of this exchange between the trailer's narrator and the film's dialogue was not meant to invite a playful, genre-based response from audiences—indeed perhaps, given its thinly disguised figuration of Cold War fears, one designed to appease public anxieties.

The next segment of the trailer is a bracket syntagma of shots summing up the havoc wreaked by these still unseen aliens as the narrator announces, "From all over the world, human beings cower before the onslaught of these unearthly enemies who no one has ever seen." A newsstand with catastrophic newspaper headlines is displayed, followed by shots of urban chaos and looting. The narrator links the preceding shots, continuing, "Panic that sweeps around the globe as the great masses of mankind flee blindly in a headlong stampede of hysteria." The idea and/or image of masses cowering is an iconographic staple of the science fiction genre of this time, as is the use of newspaper headlines

Figure 4.3. A mob scene exemplifies "human beings cowering" in the trailer for *The War of the Worlds*.

or multilingual news reports to signify their international stature. Frequently, as in this early trailer, such images are juxtaposed against the vain but heroic efforts of scientists and the military to protect these masses. The masses also serve as the science fiction genre's stand-ins for the film viewer, and although in this trailer they do not actually *watch* the action as literal profilmic spectators would (indeed they "flee blindly"), their foregrounding in the trailer's summary scene underscores their importance to the genre (and the trailer's appeals to interest in genre).

The final titles echo the graphics from the opening, superimposed over a long shot of a ruined landscape with a fire raging in the background. "NOW after TWO YEARS IN THE MAKING! / H. G. Wells's most famous and fantastic story comes to the screen. / Produced by George Pal, who gave you Destination Moon and When Worlds Collide. / In color by Technicolor. / Paramount's The War of the Worlds." (Smaller titles below cite director Byron Haskin.) The hyperbolic exclamation "two years in the making" fairly precisely dates this as a trailer from the early fifties—even a few years later, two years would not seem that long. It also emphasizes the promotional value of the complexity and artistry of special effects filmmaking (and specifically that of George Pal), later to become a key element in the selling of science fiction films. The evocations of *Destination Moon* and *When Worlds Collide* provide authorial as well as generic appeals to audience interest in familiarity.

As a precursor of many subsequent fifties sci-fi trailers, this one lays out key generic elements that appeal to audience interest in the (here newly) familiar, while providing the oblique hints of novel special effects that ensure product differentiation. The heavy emphasis on the military-scientific side of the genre in its selection of dialogue scenes along with its teasingly brief glimpses (and hyperbolic descriptions) of the film's beautiful otherworldly element (spaceships and creatures) privilege audience interest in authenticity, a paradoxically crucial feature of this most fantastical genre.[12] The trailer also invokes the generic feature of the "group protagonist" in its melding of the military general's dialogue with Gene Barry's and with the trailer narration, while its concluding emphasis on worldwide mass terror underscores the typically public concerns of the genre.[13]

Although the one-second shot of the Martian spaceship constitutes the trailer's most effective product differentiation in the sense of literal presentation of new images, the hyperbolic appeals to audience identification with a scared mob and the trailer's dominance by the publicly familiar sci-tech discourse combine with the trailer's overall assumption of audiences' desire to enjoy its fantastical generic premises, to produce a basically paranoid representation of the social space of the early 1950s. This trailer addresses an audience that wants its Cold War anxieties quelled, one eager to view the military-industrial complex as something capable of being folded into a fictional sphere of fantastical adventure (generic space) instead of an intrusive part of the increasingly corporatized space of (nonfiction) daily life in the early 1950s. By both playfully quoting classical-era trailer discourse and prefiguring many conventions of the science fiction trailers of the decade to come, this trailer innovates through a nostalgic retrogression (as does the earlier George Pal *When Worlds Collide* trailer), making it a standout example of the paradoxical quality of the rhetoric of genre's strategy of tying product differentiation to familiarity, and of trailers' uniquely contradictory temporal mode.

BAD DAY AT BLACK ROCK (Transitional Story Rhetoric)

Another example from the fifties, the trailer for *Bad Day at Black Rock* (1955),[14] resembles classical-era trailers but demonstrates a more restrained use of titles and an emphasis on promoting the widescreen format in the process of appealing to audience interest in its story. It also demonstrates some changes in trailer practice typical of the early transitional era—most prominent, an effort to shift the rhetoric of story away from an actual narrator's voice to an intradiegetic narratorial one (characters serving as de facto narrators in sound overlaps). It is structured around the promotional appeal of withheld plot information, while integrating appeals as well to Spencer Tracy's star persona and the genre of the Western, and the interaction of appeals to star and genre with that of story demonstrate their increasingly seamless interweavings during the transitional era. However, the trailer's dominant appeal is to audience interest in the suspense generated by the withheld narrative enigma.

Bad Day at Black Rock's trailer opens with a series of shots of a train arriving in a town and Spencer Tracy getting off the train and walking into the town, accompanied by superimposed titles ("From MGM's world-famous studios comes a provocative drama of suspense"). The length of the sequence emphasizes both the narrative importance of Tracy's arrival[15] and the stylistic importance of the widescreen format, nicely displayed in the train shots. Cast identifications follow, along with enigmatic titles that utilize the rhetorical convention of asking questions: "What shocking secret did this unwelcome stranger expose at Black Rock—a desert town in the southwest[?]").

As Tracy walks away from the train station, we hear his voice and assume it is a low-key voice-over narration: "There aren't many towns like this in America. But one town like it is enough. Because I think something kinda bad happened here, something they can't quite seem to find a handle to." But as the trailer cuts away from Tracy walking through the town to a clip of him with Anne Francis, what seemed to be voice-over is revealed to be sound overlap of Tracy's dialogue with Francis, who responds, "You don't know what you're talking about." This technique is repeated in the next scene when, as we see Tracy poking around an oil derrick, we hear Robert Ryan's voice sounding similarly narratorial: "Somebody's always looking for something in this part of the west. This place is our west, and I wish they'd leave us alone!" The trailer cuts to a dialogue scene between Ryan and Tracy as Tracy responds to Ryan's apparent voice-over, "This is where you're beginning to make me mad." A later sequence again repeats the technique when Walter Brennan's dialogue, "Four years ago something terrible happened here. We did nothing about it, nothing!" begins as voice-over and is completed in on-screen dialogue.

This implicit narration has an odd effect—as trailer spectators, we give the voices the authority of narration, expectantly attending to their words for additional information about the stark images we see, yet

Figures 4.4 and 4.5. Enigmatic title rhetoric
in the *Bad Day at Black Rock* trailer.

because the voices have the low-key timbre of dialogue (instead of the
booming voice-of-God effect typical of earlier trailer narration), they
seem intimate, personal, conspiratorial, and inform us only partially. The
classical-era "trailer narrator"—in both the institutional sense and the
aural sense—has been dethroned: instead of booming certitudes and
hyperbole, this opening has offered audiences questions (in title form)
and conversational dialogue, displaying, perhaps, an assumption that
audiences no longer want to be told what to think. The technique invites
different characters (even antagonists) to contribute to the trailer's textual authority. The audience derives knowledge from these multivocal
sources, as well as from the trailer's somewhat less authoritative (than
in the classical era) titles.

The technique also shifts the terms of the trailer's audience address,
at least superficially, away from the institutional to the personal.
Narrators, even semi-intradiegetic ones such as James Stewart in *Rope,*
stand in for the institution that wants us to go see the film; they speak to
us from a place somewhere between the film's diegesis and the narrative
of Hollywood. But narrators after the fact—characters speaking the film's
dialogue, which is transformed by trailer producers through sound overlaps into a de facto narration—insert audiences virtually within the film's
story. We listen as if *we* were the person being talked to, only afterward
realizing the character was talking to somebody within the film. In the
context of a trailer that still utilizes many classical-era conventions, this
personalization creates a disjuncture in the trailer's address to audiences.

Cryptic clips from several scenes follow, all of which contribute to an accumulation of narrative question marks and suspenseful moments: Tracy's interrogation of townspeople; Tracy being threatened; four men discussing Macreedy (Tracy) and plotting to get rid of him; Anne Francis mysteriously confronted by Robert Ryan ("This is liable to be the hardest ten dollars you ever earned in your life"); Tracy yelling more pointedly at townspeople to tell him what happened; a chase scene; Tracy and Francis being shot at; and finally, concluding titles (which fall back on classical rhetorical modes): "Caught in a crossfire of emotion from which there is no escape! The MGM thrill drama that will hold you in suspense!" followed by familiar fifties titles promoting Cinemascope, "with the added wonder of stereophonic sound." The final generalizing shots under the titles hint tantalizingly that an unspecified denouement has happened, in which justice has prevailed. We see the jail and the town in long shot, and a group of police cars pulls away as Tracy and Dean Jagger watch, followed by a long shot of the train (reprising the trailer opening) pulling up to the station to take Tracy away.[16]

The rhetoric of genre is also mobilized here. The thematic of the lone gunman who comes to an isolationist town to straighten out a corrupt law-enforcement system (the generic trope of the "town-taming Western")[17] is backed up by the film's title and the trailer's strongly Western iconography, with its frequent selection of exterior low-angle shots of men in lanky cowboy poses against mountains and its association of the one woman in the film with money, echoing the Western archetype of the prostitute. This theme is also underscored by the trailer's selection of dialogue ("The rule of law has left here, and the gorillas have taken over," "This place is our west . . .") and the early title describing Black Rock as "a desert town in the southwest." In assuming audience interest in the answer to its question—"What shocking secret did this unwelcome stranger expose? . . ."—this title's geographic reference links the genre of the Western with the plot's withheld mystery.

The mystery is that the Japanese-American farmer whom Tracy has come to visit was murdered by the townspeople the day after Pearl Harbor. The town's sinister secret is its racism. By omitting any indication of this aspect of the film, the trailer emphasizes the film's connections to its film-historical genre over its connections to its own historical moment and specific story. The trailer's iconography and odd, conspiratorial pseudonarration link its Western cues to a figuration of the generally repressive climate of the fifties without promoting interest in the film's highly topical theme of the evils of guilt by association.[18]

The interaction between the generic cues and the trailer's primary hook ("What shocking secret did this unwelcome stranger expose?") creates a rhetoric of enigma and suspense firmly grounded in the Western's discourse of spatial conquest, wherein the secrets of the other can be uncovered by moving in on the other's territory. But beyond the withheld plot information, this trailer assumes of its audience a more generalized desire for knowledge: a desire to know the secrets of the other—here coded as an isolationist town populated mainly by retrograde modern cowboys. As many historians have recently pointed out, the value of knowledge shifts after World War II, and the search for the "truth" becomes problematized by recognition of the human potential for atrocity. The trailer reflects this shift in its deflection of textual authority to intradiegetic "narrators."

Knowing the secrets of the other in one's own backyard can be seen as a prime goal in the paranoid Cold War cultural environment, and this trailer's rhetorical appeals to an audience assumed to prefer to trust its own authority (or more precisely, that of its surrogates in the film's characters) over the institutional authority of a narrator to guide it to discovering this town's "shocking secret" suggest that seeing the film can fulfill this desire—but that at the same time, such a multivocal knowledge might not be so clear-cut. The intradiegetic narrators indicate the trailer's assumption that audiences would like to *participate* in the conspiratorial mode of the isolationist townspeople and their appealing Western environment almost as much as they are assumed to root for Spencer Tracy's one-man investigation. The key assumption of the rhetoric of story, "You would like to have these (novel) experiences—at the movies," here interacts with the rhetoric of genre's invocation of the desire for (familiar) Western iconography and dynamics, complicating and problematizing audience interest in having the specific protagonist's experiences (which are moreover unclear, even given the enigmatic terms of the rhetoric).

As in classical-era promotions of controversial stories, the trailer hints that the film contains subject matter that it still doesn't quite dare promote (here, the exposure of a community's racism), resulting in an ambiguity about the film's appeal that ultimately dilutes the impact of the rhetoric of story, its principal appeal, in favor of that of genre. The trailer seems to be addressing an audience assumed to be able to handle the film's racial angle (along with other more "adult" subject matter newly deemed appropriate during the fifties), but still an audience that race might not bring into the theater, whereas a good old-fashioned

Western will.[19] The trailer's hedging in this regard thus interestingly displays some of the contradictions visible in trailer rhetoric during the 1950s, an era when the prevalence of issues of visibility, secrecy and paranoia foreground the elusiveness of the truth.

THE MAN WHO SHOT LIBERTY VALANCE (Transitional Genre Rhetoric)

The trailer for *The Man Who Shot Liberty Valance* (1962)[20] draws on the rhetoric of genre in that although the trailer also strongly invokes the rhetorics of stardom and story, it reads primarily as a canonization of the Western, hyperbolically promoting its film as an artistic apotheosis of the genre. The film itself has been cited as central to the Western's transition from a genre that celebrated an idealized cultural self-image to one that "deconstructs and critiques that image, finally acknowledging the necessary role of myth and legend in the development of history and civilization."[21] However, the trailer's contemporaneous assumptions about what's interesting in the film tell another story about its place in the culture of its time, emphasizing its continuity with past Westerns.

The trailer reprises classical-era trailer tropes, such as its familiar structure. It opens with a hyperbolic achronological sequence of typical shots exemplifying the film (a bracket syntagma) with overlay titles, then moves into a narrated segment that offers longer dialogue scenes and presents story premises, followed by an identification segment utilizing titles and shorter dialogue scenes to introduce the characters and stars, and reaches a dynamic crescendo (consisting of tantalizing fragments of the Western's ritual shoot-out scene) framed by the film's title and credits. Iconographically too, we are again in the familiar territory of the "town-taming Western,"[22] with its (and thus the trailer's) visual emphasis on the peopled spaces of the genre's familiar saloon and storefront.

But the classical era's wipes and title swells have been replaced by subtler cuts and fades, and the trailer's choice of shots and scenes evidences not only the familiar assumptions that audiences are interested in generic iconography, stars and story, but also a sense that the film's cinematic artistry, trumpeted in the promotion of its auteur John Ford, is equally important to audiences (strong master-shot compositions and shots exemplifying an exaggerated chiaroscuro effect common to sixties films that chose anachronistically to film in black and white are prevalent). Although rhetorical appeals to stardom and story are central to this trailer, neither is dominant. The roles of John Wayne and James Stewart are obliquely presented (we never even hear Stewart speak); and although the trailer sustains its core enigma—"who shot Liberty Valance?"—expository elements are very jumbled and confused in its presentation of the story. The film's draw as a Western, however, is promoted in every shot.

The trailer opens with a sampling of nondialogue scenes with overlay titles introducing hyperbolic equations to promote the three principal hooks the trailer assumes will draw audiences: "As *Mighty* / as its cast . . . / The two great stars / it brings together for the first time!" as we see a long shot of a rider intercepting a carriage. A closer shot reveals John Wayne and James Stewart, and the trailer cuts to a shot of Stewart aiming his gun, and identificatory titles for each of the two stars. This scene fades to a generalizing long shot of a melee at the newspaper office, with a title: "As *Powerful* as its direction by the four-time Academy Award winner / John Ford." Then there is a fade to an exterior fight scene, with Stewart being socked as a couple watches: "As *Explosive* as its characters who bring America's frontier to heroic life again . . ." A shot of a man on a horse shooting in the street as townspeople watch is seen under the film title.

The trailer's assertion that stars, director and characters (more than story) are the film's most appealing features introduces its key assumptions: that audiences in 1962 will want their A-budget Westerns canonized with the imprimatur of the genre's paramount storyteller, and that the film centers on people and identity (i.e., that Ford's direction is character-centered). The trailer thus assumes that audiences want a new kind of Western. The opening also demonstrates an assumption that Westerns as a genre are associated with might, power and explosiveness. The three opening titles thus attempt to court audiences interested at once in character-driven stories (increasingly typical of Hollywood fare in the fifties and early sixties) and in spectacle.

As we see a series of shots (linked by fades) of the principals (and various gawking townspeople) moving dramatically in and around the saloon, a narrator begins alliteratively and generically, "Out of the flame and fury of the frontier, the Old West lives again, as only John Ford can re-create it. Peopled with wonderful characters, who have become legends in their own time." This narration asserts the film's continuity with past Westerns, and in particular with past John Ford Westerns. The trailer then presents most of the scene in which Wayne, Stewart and Lee Marvin have a confrontation, as the voice-over continues, "Of them all, two are the most memorable. Liberty Valance and the man who shot him. And the man who shot him was destined to become a hero." The dramatic impact of the scene is obscured by the trailer's extraction of it from its context, for we know neither the stakes nor the outcome of the confrontation, just that it reprises a familiar Western genre convention, the showdown.

The trailer's subsequent clips and narration sustain and heighten the mystery of who shot Liberty Valance by deliberate obscurity about both the characters' identities and the relationships between the men, even as it touts the three characters as "legends." The trailer's identification sequence is next, followed by more pointed dialogue scenes: in the bar, Marvin looks around and speaks to the crowd: "You all heard him say he had a gun in his hand, didn't ya?" Men respond ("That ain't murder, Marshal, that's a clean-cut case of self-defense"), and another angle on the scene shows the setting to be a quintessential Western saloon, with card table in foreground, men standing around, a bartender in the center of the shot, a mirror behind, and people seen in the mirror—a classic Fordian master shot that organizes the space of the saloon in a particularly orderly way. Given the trailer's foregrounding of this scene, the master shot can be seen as comprising a signifier of "frontier justice" (the trailer assumes audience knowledge of the generic convention equating barroom and courtroom). The subsequent fade to a crowd scene—with campaigners, placards, top hats and ribbons, and titles proclaiming, "It has a great cast, great performances, in a picture about a man's greatness!"—visually links the men's barroom witnessing to the more formal institutional regime of electoral politics.

Again, there are profilmic spectators who serve as correlates to the hypothetical trailer spectator. The prevalence of these profilmic spectators and the iconographic dominance of the proscenium of the Western saloon setting enable us to make out in the trailer a representation of space appropriate to the historical moment of the film's production. The juxtaposition of Marvin's call to the townspeople to be witnesses, with the subsequent campaign scene, links an overdetermined "greatness" (great cast, great performances, great man) to signifiers of electoral politics. Through this juxtaposition, the trailer thus valorizes spectatorship as citizenship, an appropriate equation to an era in which Hollywood is anxiously recruiting spectators following the tremendous drops in feature film viewing at the end of the studio era, while being accustomed to the linking of film spectators (and the Hollywood institution in general) to their role in the public sphere following the political dramas of the HUAC years.

The simultaneous appeals to audience interest in Western grandeur, character-centered drama, and cinematic artistry make apparent this trailer's address to an audience that sees the John Ford Western as superlative filmmaking. With a couple of significant exceptions (including Lang, Hitchcock and Capra), trailers' appeals to audience awareness of the director's role in film production postdate the classical era, and their more frequent appearance during the transitional era in association with the rhetoric of genre is interesting. Promoting even a familiar director such as Ford seems to serve primarily as an effort to align Ford with Westerns and thus at once to democratize interest in cinematic artistry by aligning it with its expression through genre and to valorize the Western as worthy of interest by audiences who want "art films."[23]

The rhetoric of genre's mission to highlight product differentiation through familiarity here effectively utilizes the Hollywood auteur: even as the promotion of Ford serves to *differentiate* the film from the run-of-the-mill Western, the trailer celebrates this film's similarity by linking it to *other* Ford Westerns (rather than noting its thematic and ideological departure from them), thus corralling and containing Ford's oeuvre to the Western genre. The convoluted efforts to highlight the enigma of identity in the film while promoting it as a typical Western (rather than using the rhetoric of story to call attention to its emotional complexity or to assert that it stands apart from other Westerns) perhaps bespeak a confusion about identity that extends to a confusion about the identity of its audience. Gone is the *Yankee Doodle Dandy* trailer's sense that "a man's greatness" could stand in for "our" own. In its place is not so much product differentiation as a narrative cipher, bolstered by assumptions that audiences will be drawn in by the familiar conventions of the Western, along with an appeal to assumed auteur-conscious audiences to trust veteran movie wrangler John Ford to work it all out.

THE GREAT ESCAPE
(Transitional Story Rhetoric)

The trailer for *The Great Escape* (1963),[24] the story of a group of Allied soldiers in World War II who plan an escape from a Nazi prison camp, represents a transitional-era example of a rhetorical appeal to story that assumes audiences are primarily interested in sampling the film's narrative causality. It illustrates the tendency of trailers for the big-budget widescreen "roadshow" productions of the early sixties to minimize trailer narration and titles, privileging dynamic action clips and expository montage structures, supplemented by brief explanatory dialogue scenes.[25] Its fairly simple structure presents a montage of summary action clips, a series of longer expository clips followed by another action montage (of escape preparations) into which are inserted cast identifications, another group of expository clips, then a rapid montage of (escape) action clips culminating in what appears to be a climactic moment of escape. The trailer's straightforwardness and its shortage of hyperbolic elements demonstrate an assumption that the film "sells itself" to its audience, but the one-dimensionality of the escape story (no comic relief, no love scenes) seems to indicate that this audience was assumed to be primarily (male) action film fans, no longer a mythical "everybody."

From the outset, the trailer establishes a rhythm of images accompanied by pounding drums signifying no nonsense and no narration: trucks arrive at a prison camp in long shot, followed by a closer shot of Steve McQueen tossing a baseball into a catcher's mitt as he arrives. The montage that follows illustrates, bracket syntagma style, pre-escape life at the prison camp: someone clips a barbed wire fence, prisoners march, someone hides himself in the back of a car, men hoe garden plots outside barracks, men sneak around at night, a man climbs a fence, another knocks down a guard who tries to shoot him, and a tower guard kills the man on the fence. The inclusion of this montage appears to have been intended to show audiences what made the men want to escape, whether under the assumption that audiences might not know what conditions were like in Nazi prison camps, or perhaps (given the tameness of most of the shots) to reassure them that this film does not dwell on the horrors of war. In any event, the brief and relatively uninformative nature of the clips in this segment instantiate both transitional trailers' efforts to promote story elements without resorting to heavy-handed narration and titles and their confusion as to how to do so.

The montage is followed by an expository dialogue segment: a Nazi officer says, "Give up your hopeless attempts to escape." Men are seen planning: Richard Attenborough says, "We're gonna devote our energies to sports, gardening, all the cultural pursuits, and meanwhile, *we dig*." The trailer cuts to Steve McQueen asking someone, "How many are you taking out?" The man replies, "Two hundred and fifty." McQueen repeats the number, amazed, and the film's title is superimposed in red over the shot of the two men, accompanied by a martial-sounding musical fanfare.

Since this film's premise is aptly encapsulated by a mere three-word title, the simplicity of the minimal extracted dialogue is the only exposition required: the trailer dwells instead on the causal mechanics of escape. A montage of preparation shots ensues, to martial music: a pick-ax pounding, lifting out a square from the floor, a row of men making something, men handing bags of dirt along in the tunnel, wood being passed down a hole, a man jumping down a hole, another flat on a small trolley in the tunnel, and bags of dirt emptied out. Like the staccato lists of causal elements many transitional trailers deliver through narration, these montages signify for audiences an *accumulation* of elements and story interest, assuming that transitional-era audiences will associate quantity with quality, but will want the film, not the trailer, to connect all these dots.

As the "Great Escape" theme music begins, a shot of McQueen lingers as he slides down a wall and an identificatory title appears, naming him and his character, followed by similar (but briefer) identification shots of James Garner (he hands something through a window), Charles Bronson (he crawls along the tunnel), James Coburn (he smiles), Richard Attenborough (assigning each man a task), followed by Donald Pleasence's and James Donald's identification shots. The rhetorical convention of imparting story through characterization is glimpsed in these narratively dense clips.

The trailer cuts to a medium shot of an (unidentified) German officer shouting, "There will be no escapes from this camp," signaling a shift to another expository sequence of short clips of escape preparation scenes, this time focusing on obstacles to the escape. Someone yells, "Omigod, they found Tom!" as guards blow whistles, we see a furnace being lifted, guards with rifles running across the screen, Bronson unspooling a wire as he wheels through the tunnel, and finally, McQueen jumping down the tunnel and approaching two men: "Hold on to yourself, Bartlett, you're twenty feet short. . ." We see a long shot of the lit fence and guard towers, over which is superimposed "The Mirisch Company Presents," followed by a shot of men climbing out of a hole to escape, over which the film's title—with a barbed wire graphic motif—is superimposed. The trailer's focus on the minutiae of escape—bags of dirt, forged papers, trolleys in tunnels, "twenty feet short"—contributes to the film's promotion as a pure adventure and, compared to the big sweep of the *Casablanca* trailer's narrative of escape, seems almost reactively divorced from a sense of connection with a historical reality—the

Nazis seem like an excuse or macguffin, and the audience is assumed to want to avoid "all that political stuff" and stick to the "how-to"—a quintessential rhetoric of causality that, ironically, avoids causes.

Following this segment, yet another montage begins (of the actual escape): McQueen ties a trip wire, a German motorcyclist is tripped by it, McQueen is chased on his motorcycle, two men jump off a moving train, a man on foot is pursued, a man disguised as a German soldier takes a motorcycle, another man runs on a rooftop, a motorcycle chase is seen, a man kicks another at an airfield, then flies the plane he's commandeered, McQueen rides along a barbed wire fence on the motorcycle, a German captures an escapee, who shoots himself with the German's gun, we see Pleasence and Garner in the plane cockpit, followed by a long shot of the plane landing dangerously and having its wings clipped off by trees, and a final shot of Steve McQueen riding in a meadow: he speeds up a hill and leaps over the barbed wire fence.[26] The trailer ends abruptly, leaving a United Artists logo.

This action-driven finale, with its motorcycle-heavy texture, seems even more clearly to have been designed to target the film to a male audience assumed to be motivated to see the film by the excitement of watching vehicles in motion and guys doing stuff (mostly fighting). The trailer's action montages contribute to a rhetoric of product differentiation: the syllogism "Action is all you need to see, and action-oriented dialogue is all you need to hear," I would suggest, contains a missing, implied term: "You're sick of talky movies," telling the film's potential (male) audience that unlike many past films (as this trailer is unlike past trailers), this one will deliver an abundance of action goods.[27] Such shorthand is typical of transitional-era trailers that promote story causality. The male audience the trailer addresses is assumed to have less desire for historical knowledge (during an era of unprecedented global uncertainty following the Cuban missile crisis) than anticipation for the unfolding of the cinematic experience of the thrill ride of escape.

THE GRADUATE (Transitional Story Rhetoric)

The trailer for *The Graduate* (1967),[28] a pivotal countercultural zeitgeist, coming-of-age film, exemplifies the mismatch between promotional discourses and cinematic meaning common to trailers for many of the more innovative films of the mid- to late sixties. Thus, it displays some key contradictions prevalent within the film industry during this time. It uses a type of "minimovie" format increasingly common in the later years of the transitional era, eschewing narration for a montage that creates its own trailer narrative, and emphasizing a series of dialogue scenes presented almost completely in medium shots. These are accompanied by the film's music track, thus promoting also the Simon and Garfunkel songs "Scarborough Fair," "The Sound of Silence," and "Mrs. Robinson."

The primary convention of the rhetoric of story that this trailer utilizes is the promotion of narrative causality, although its early section seems to imply a greater focus on narrative characterization than it ultimately delivers. The assumptions it makes about what audiences want from the film's *story* result in an emphasis on the film as a "sex comedy" (i.e., highlight its *genre*) and leave many other aspects of the film's appeal and ultimate success barely visible on the screen.[29]

The first shot of the trailer is a long shot of Dustin Hoffman as Benjamin seated at a fountain on the Berkeley campus of the University of California, an American flag waving in the foreground. The shot immediately establishes a rhetorical assumption of audience recognition of both the setting (a college campus) and its import in 1967, when campuses, and particularly Berkeley's, were "ground zero" of the widespread youth-based social protest movement of the time—and of which American flags (especially their irreverent misuse) were moreover a frequent signifier in the popular media. This rhetoric places the film's story in the narrative context of college in the 1960s, building on the film's title, which metonymically links the story to that world. "Scarborough Fair" plays and the film's producer credits and then title are superimposed over the shot.

Figures 4.6. The title emerges in a shot of Dustin Hoffman
on a college campus in the trailer for *The Graduate*.

The music stops as the camera zooms back to an extreme long shot of the campus positioning the flag in the center of the frame, as we hear a sound overlap of a woman's voice: "Listen everybody, I want you all to be quiet. I've got Ben's college yearbook here, and I just want to read you some of the *wonderful* things about Ben." Here, unlike the examples of sound overlap voice-over in the *Bad Day at Black Rock* trailer, there is an obvious intradiegetic addressee, an "everybody" who belongs to the scene we have by now learned to expect the trailer to show next. But in fact the dialogue does establish that this segment of the trailer will focus on characterization, so in a way we are part of the "everybody" who is being hailed and admonished to pay attention to information about Ben. The juxtaposition of the woman's voice with the long shot of Ben on the campus jars us into an expectancy for the next scene, while the two layers of meaning create an assumption that we will read the voice, and the subsequent scene, ironically.

The trailer cuts to a shot of Benjamin sitting in his room, a sad clown painting on the wall. "Hey, there's the award-winning scholar!" A traveling close-up of Ben coming downstairs is interspersed with close shots (some from his POV) of people congratulating him, one asking, "What are you going to do now?" Benjamin replies, "I was going to go upstairs for a minute." "I meant with your future. Your *life*." "Oh. Well that's a little hard to say." Ben's face and voice, as well as the intrusive handheld shots of his party guests, fulfill our expectations of the scene's ironic tone. The trailer cuts to a shot of him sitting in front of a fish tank, as we hear "The Sound of Silence." His seatedness in both places (campus, bedroom) seems to demonstrate the same listless affect. The odd juxtaposition of the mother's party speech with the shot of Ben on campus seated under a looming flag has *almost* alluded to the film's core structuring absence—the Vietnam War (the preeminent "career" choice with which graduating men in 1968 were confronted)—but the way the trailer rushes on to the next scene leaves this idea unexplored. Ben's apathy is reconstructed as merely a causal plot element, an individual personality trait that leaves him susceptible to Mrs. Robinson's seduction.

We see him with Mrs. Robinson, followed by a shot of Mrs. Robinson in the foreground and Benjamin the background, the famous shot through her leg as he says, "Mrs. Robinson, you're trying to seduce me," (she laughs) "aren't you?" The trailer shows them in the hotel lobby, then more from the seduction scene, and girlfriend Elaine (Katharine Ross) confronting him, "Benjamin, are you having an affair with someone?" This trailer opening shorthands the story's causality ruthlessly, leaping from an apathetic Ben to the affair to the girlfriend such that the primary interest audiences are assumed to have in the film is in these sexual escapades. But the specificity of the presented scenes to this particular story (the lack of generic coding) demonstrates that it is the rhetoric of story, rather than that of genre, that dominates.

The trailer continues with a series of comedic and dramatic clips, many of which seem disjointed, cadged together only because they impart story information. Benjamin is confronted by Elaine's father. Much of their dialogue scene is presented, culminating with Benjamin's unintended punch line, "The point is, I don't love your wife, I love your daughter, sir." We see his car on a bridge, and the reconciliation scene between him and Elaine, who asks, "Why don't you just drag me off if you want to marry me so much?" These clips, and especially the last line, also present compressed story elements under the assumption that the primary audience interest is in the story's causality. The film's ending is rather awkwardly foreshadowed without imparting any character information about Elaine that might make more sense of her statement.

The trailer cuts from a clip of Benjamin confronting Mrs. Robinson to him driving, then running, the "Mrs. Robinson" song on the soundtrack; it then cuts to the final church scene, with Benjamin yelling from behind a glass partition, reaction shots of the family, and Elaine yelling "Ben!" The trailer withholds the final scene, cutting to a title crawl that includes stars, screenwriter, songs, producer and director credits, with "Scarborough Fair" playing. The trailer's near revelation of the film's ending indicates that as with the *Bad Day at Black Rock* trailer, the ways trailers present story enigma are changing in the transitional era.

Like many sixties trailers, this one seems, with hindsight, to not "get" the film. Its overriding assumption that audiences are most interested in the film's sexual plot dynamics undersells the thematic and stylistic richness that enabled the film to strike a nerve with the public as "the biggest box-office success of the late sixties."[30] In retrospect, the trailer producers seemed clueless to the fact that a film dealing with sixties cultural alienation could actually bring disaffected youth into the theater—that identifying with Ben's apathy wouldn't necessarily extend to an apathy of the pocketbook.[31] Indeed, the also clueless *Boxoffice* review of the film provided this handy "Exploitip" for exhibitors: "Hold a cap-and-gown preview with free admission to all dressed in graduation outfits," again marking the extreme mismatch between promotional strategies and the nature of this film's impact.[32]

Stylistically the trailer also underemphasizes the elements of the film that were most innovative and struck reviewers of the time: that is, the film's "switched-on cinematics,"[33] or the "sly and surprising things" Bosley Crowther felt Mike Nichols and Robert Surtees achieved with the actors and the camera such that "the overall picture has the quality of a very extensive and revealing social scan."[34] Occasional handheld camera shots and the odd angle under Anne Bancroft's leg are about all the trailer offers that hint at unconventional technique. Yet like the year's other big box-office hit, *2001: A Space Odyssey*, the film's stylistic advances were in part responsible for its popular success. Indeed, the film is remarked as one that integrates formal and narrative elements of film meaning in its critique of dominant values.[35]

The fact that the trailer for *The Graduate* is able to virtually strip the film of these aspects of its narration in order to stress the causal chain of its story not only demonstrates a resistance on the part of studio promoters to imagine that thematic and stylistic innovation might have audience appeal, but it also reveals a typical strategy utilized in this era to promote such films without calling attention to their social critique or revolutionary cinematic form: that is, story causality is reified. Such trailers contribute to naturalizing the narrative parameters of commercially oriented Hollywood storytelling as the sum total of the moviegoing experience—perhaps especially when they promote films as successful as *The Graduate*. In this case, the contradictions between the film's actual appeals and the terms in which it is promoted are thus almost concealed by the trailer's one-dimensional focus on the "sex comedy" aspect—indeed, the trailer uses story causality to promote a generic aspect of the film. The trailer's contradictions are visible only obliquely, in retrospect, in our memory of the trailer's initial image of its main character sitting on a college campus under a flag—the repressed historic that almost returns, but not quite.

CABARET (Transitional Genre Rhetoric)

In addition to reconfiguring studio-era appeals to interest in genres with the post-studio-era audience in mind, trailers from the transitional era participated in the revitalization and reinvention of flagging genres. The sample included a trailer for the musical *Cabaret* (1972),[36] which, as a rerelease trailer, has the easier job of promoting a known quantity, but as such still holds interest for an examination of trailers' audience address since it is charged with expanding the audience for an already successful film. The trailer uses the conventions of the rhetoric of genre, such as musical iconography, repetition, and equations, to display assumptions about the audience's relationship to the musical's historical era, and to its own. This example characterizes the rhetoric of genre in the transitional era because its foreshortening of the film's theatrical mise-en-scène, crosscut with a narrative that represents moments of stark historical change, figures relationships between performers, audiences and history that speak to the social space of the early seventies—in the process of revitalizing and transforming the genre of the musical.

As one review implied, the industry had about given up on the movie musical prior to the release of *Cabaret*—1972 was the height of the post–*Easy Rider* "Hollywood renaissance," in which smaller independent films, progressive content and generic innovation enjoyed new levels of success. Nonetheless, *Cabaret* surprised by cleaning up at the box office as well as at the Academy Awards and by making a star out of Liza Minnelli.[37] According to a news item in *Variety*, it was billed as a "musical-drama" prior to release, and departed from the Broadway production by relying more on the original Christopher Isherwood "Berlin Stories," on which were based both the play "I Am a Camera" and the musical.[38] By the time the rerelease trailer appeared following the 1972 Academy Awards telecast in the spring of 1973,[39] those in the industry and audiences alike were aware of the film's innovative approach to the musical, and the trailer contributes to the film's reconfiguration of the genre for new audiences.

In an echo of the vaudeville mode's promotional use of the proscenium prevalent in classical-era trailers, the trailer anchors its narrative clips from the film within the diegetic space of the cabaret stage and the song-and-dance numbers, into which the nonstage scenes are cut. Liza (Sally Bowles) is first seen onstage from behind in close-up, haloed by a spotlight: we are onstage with her. She is singing, "Everybody, they love a winner," and the narrator repeats, "Everybody loves a winner," as we see a chorus line of dancers in shorts and stockings. "Cabaret, winner of eight Academy Awards, including Liza Minnelli, best actress, and Joel Grey, best supporting actor." The repeated line (which gets repeated again by the narrator at the end of the trailer) contains an assumption that audiences will take it literally—that the narrator's emphasis on the film as a winner at the Oscars will overshadow the considerable irony with which the line is delivered in Liza's song. It also serves to underline the fact that the "winner" is a *musical*, since the narrator is highlighting and thus validating, as it were, a song lyric.

A close-up of Liza and Joel Grey (the MC) in profile, their faces moving toward each other, follows. Beginning with a close-up of Liza looking in a mirror, we then see a series of shots of Liza, Joel, and Michael York (Bob Roberts) singing "Money makes the world go around," intercut with shots of them interacting offstage. They stick their tongues out at each other. At a shot of York and Liza in a doorway, the song ends and the characters introduce themselves to each other. Another cabaret scene is shown, emphasizing shots of a happy German audience and liquor being poured. An Aryan-looking man (Helmut Griem playing Maximilian von Heune) beckons the pair to his table saying, "You are like me, adrift in Berlin. I think it's my duty to corrupt you, agreed?" Liza nods happily with a bottle at her lips; York nods too and looks at Liza. A short scene follows from a dance number with men in drag wearing Nazi helmets and using canes as rifles.

A shift in the trailer's happy tone is then marked by a "grid" (again, a parallel syntagma that crosscuts between one narratively or texturally important scene and various shorter scenes to advance exposition), here crosscutting between the drag show and increasingly ominous exterior shots. First we see one of the couple's friends (played by Marisa Berenson) saying to Griem, "Don't you see what is happening in Germany today?" We then cut back to a shot of the men goose-stepping in the drag show, followed by a medium shot of the three friends (York, Liza and Griem) embracing, and another of a child giving the Hitler salute. As they watch Nazis on parade, York asks Griem, "You still think you can control it?" The trailer cuts back to the drag show and a shot of Joel Grey in a wig holding a Nazi helmet up on a cane, laughing. Michael York knocks down a Nazi flag, then we see Grey on stage singing, "So, life is disappointing, forget it! In here" (he spins around) "life is beautiful." We then see several shots of glum audience members. Liza begins a Dietrich-esque number, which is then heard over expository clips extracted from love scenes between her and York's character, ending with her waving good-bye over her shoulder. The scene returns to the song, and the narrator returns to announce, "Everybody loves a winner. Cabaret. Winner of eight Academy Awards." The trailer ends at the end of Liza's song, as she strikes a pose on a prop chair and the other dancers punctuate the song's ending by slapping the stage.

Figure 4.7. Joel Grey spinning around in the
Cabaret trailer: "In here, life is beautiful!"

While signifiers of extracinematic spectacle are integral to the trailer's generic promotional regime by virtue of its representations of the cabaret show, gone are the wipes, the sustained cast identifications, most of the narration and the titles common to classical-era trailers' promotion of both backstage musicals and cinematic spectacle. In their place, we see inklings of some of the conventions of New Hollywood trailers, including early use of diegetic music as a de facto soundtrack virtually throughout the trailer, and an emphasis on the grid. There is also emphasis on gesture and movement rather than dialogue to express characterizations. In this case, these conventions serve also to advance the trailer's generic rhetoric, since an emphasis on gesture, rhythm, and, of course, music keep audiences aware that this is a trailer for a musical.

As historians have noted about period films, they are almost always interesting in what they communicate about historical attitudes toward the era of their production as well as the period in which the film is set. In this regard, Thomas Elsaesser has written of *Cabaret* as a "polysemic text," which, because (like other big-budget international commercial productions) it aims to address a wide audience "with very diverse entry points into its diegetic world" (and because it was such a huge success), "must in the first instance be regarded as a historical fact about 1972."[40] Such parallels are telescoped and even exaggerated in the trailer, which even more directly addresses audiences (with persuasive intent) than does the film. The rapid progression of fascist decadence in 1930s Germany and its interweaving with the genre of the backstage musical is given an intertextual and generic zing by virtue of the film starring (in her first big role) Liza Minnelli, daughter of Judy Garland. This "zing" functions perhaps even more strongly in the trailer than the film because of the way images of stars function in trailers—as was discussed, trailers inevitably display more of the star's persona *as star* than as their character in the film, since the film (at least in the ordinary trailer exhibition situation) hasn't yet been seen.[41]

That the trailer successfully telegraphs a culture's fall into decadence and fascism via the discourse of musical entertainment and the rhetoric of genre makes it an interesting counterpart to the *Yankee Doodle Dandy* trailer's promotion of showbiz and moviegoing as patriotic in the classical era.[42] Here a trailer promotes a film that problematizes and implicates its own medium and citizenry in social corruption. Given that the business of the trailer is, of course, still promotional, the interesting question becomes, How does the trailer make Germany's fall into fascism look? Fascism, according to the trailer, destroys the characters' love and breaks up their relationship, but the show goes on: "In here, life is beautiful." The generic space of the musical is thus demonstrated to be a plot element in the film (cabaret as both sanctuary and escapist self-delusion). The poignancy of the cabaret clips fits neatly into the familiar ideological construct of the sad clown, as well as with the film's declared generic reconfiguration as a "musical drama." We even love a winner who is really a loser: by the time this line is repeated at the end of the trailer, "Everybody loves a winner" has come to encompass an assumption that the audience comprehends the ironic register in Liza's lyrics but has been persuaded to see the film for the added appeal of a range of dramatic elements in addition to its musical spectacle—elements moreover assumed to be familiar to the expanded audiences for art films in this era.

The rapidity of the perceived fall of Germany into decadence and fascism is one of the more striking elements of this trailer, enabled by the musical grid. The trailer presents a neat narrative closure appropriate to a "musical drama," but in a way that figures dystopia rather than utopia.[43] The product is differentiated within a framework of generic familiarity, and in the process the trailer displays assumptions that it's addressing a broad 1972 audience with a sophisticated appreciation of cinema as art, an audience that (it is assumed) desires to see the troubling social, sexual and political contradictions of its own era resolved, and that, like the profilmic audience in the cabaret show, seeks this resolution in the safe space of the theater, perhaps preferring the experience of spectatorship to the unmediated witnessing of its own historical era.

PAPER MOON (Transitional Star Rhetoric)

The trailer for *Paper Moon* (1973)[44] is exemplary as a re-visioning of classical Hollywood conventions as well as promotional conventions. Behind-the-scenes glimpses of intergenerational star rapport mirror the trailer's and film's quotational mode (common among the "movie brat" filmmakers of the seventies), enabling the familial relationship between stars Ryan O'Neal and his young daughter Tatum to contribute to the promotion of the film's second-generation homages to early Hollywood filmmaking. The black-and-white cinematography, depression-era subject matter, and a montage of screwball comedy clips all contribute to a nostalgic trailer that strongly promotes the film's genre, while the behind-the-scenes footage of the two stars counterbalances the genre rhetoric with a star-based family narrative. The trailer's use of rapid montage and multiple grids foreshadows contemporary-era comedy trailers, while the on-set footage follows a tradition of cinema vérité more characteristic of transitional-era conventions.[45] Trailers' use of behind-the-scenes footage, as we have seen, predates the transitional era, but this trailer's incorporation of documentary conventions of its time is stylistically quite different from the earlier examples, and its sustained articulation of the film's production dynamics spotlights the contradictory impact of some of the era's innovative promotional efforts.

The trailer opens with establishing clips of Ryan and Tatum O'Neal from a cops-and-robbers chase scene. A narrator's voice-over says, "Kansas, 1936. . . . Out of the worst days of the depression comes the adventures of two unlikely con artists, Mose Pray and his companion, Addie Loggins." With this energetic introduction, the film's nostalgic mise-en-scène and its generic status (screwball buddy comedy) are immediately legible.

The trailer then switches gears, going behind the scenes, as a slate clapper enters a shot of O'Neal. The narrator continues, "Ryan O'Neal is Mose Pray." We then see O'Neal at a breakfast table fiddling with a waffle as the narrator adds jokingly, "His most challenging film role." Crew members laugh offscreen and O'Neal insists, "Keep rolling! I got it." A medium close-up of Tatum O'Neal being slated is seen as the narrator continues, "Tatum O'Neal, daughter of Ryan O'Neal, is Addie Loggins." Tatum enters the breakfast table shot and the narrator adds, "her very

Figure 4.8. Tatum O'Neal and Ryan O'Neal in an outtake
incorporated into the trailer for *Paper Moon*.

first film role." She sits and looks at O'Neal and says, "Howdy." Ryan
responds, "Howdy," and a phone rings. She starts to say something, and
he says, "Get the phone." Tatum cracks up, and we hear laughing in the
background as the phone is answered. Tatum puts her head down on the
table, and Ryan strokes her hair. The slapstick of the first clips seems to
leak "backstage" as the stars/family (seated at a meal—an archetypal
family situation) collapse in laughter at the movie set chaos.[46]

The positioning and length of this sequence demonstrate that the
producers consider the father-daughter star relationship crucial to the
film's success. While the trailer's nostalgic mode and child-star actor
have already implicitly evoked comparisons to that other pixie of
depression-era comedy, Shirley Temple, the trailer takes pains to emphasize a different approach to child actors. Unlike Temple, whose relationship to the work of filmmaking was, as Charles Eckert put it, to censor
or conceal it, Tatum's presence on the set inspires a recruiting of the
backstage production discourse for promotional purposes; in Temple's
films, Eckert argues, "both love and work are abstracted from all social
and psychological realities. They have no causes; they are unmotivated.
They appear in Shirley merely as prodigious innate capacities."[47] Tatum,
however, is securely anchored both to her father and to the film's production, serving to reassure a seventies audience, by way of depression-
era nostalgia, about the endurance of the "authentic" father/daughter
bond between the stars amid the chaos of a movie set, and thus of the
endurance of family values in a time of rapid social transformation.

We next see Tatum on a bed listening to Jack Benny on the radio as
the narrator explains, "This is the Peter Bogdanovich production, *Paper
Moon*." The trailer cuts to Bogdanovich and a policeman slating a shot of

a car, and Bogdanovich slams his fingers in the slate and mimes pain (alerting us that the efforts to construct the behind-the-scenes footage as slapstick are deliberate). We see a shot of a door being knocked on, as the narrator adds, ". . . or, as P. T. Barnum put it, 'There's a sucker born every minute.'" The Bible-selling scene is shown, interrupted at intervals by full-screen titles with period lettering: "The Director's Company Presents / A Peter Bogdanovich Production." The scene returns as the sheriff steps closer into the shot, asking, "What company you say you was from?" The trailer's juxtaposition of production footage with a clip that references P. T. Barnum and "suckers" links the con artistry of the film's protagonists to that of the production ballyhoo, overdetermining the idea of film as con job and movie stars (specifically the two O'Neals) as colorful liars. Unlike Shirley Temple, whose role was to intercede with and reform the proletarian con artist,[48] Tatum's character is seen excelling at these activities herself, more like the Dead End Kids than Shirley—and a more effective figure to promote a film in an era in which audiences are assumed to venerate road rebels, per the foregoing *Bonnie and Clyde* (1967) and *Easy Rider* (1969), prime originary films of the Hollywood renaissance.

The trailer cuts to Ryan O'Neal running down a street, and cornered by a sheriff's car. We then see the two O'Neals sitting somberly in the sheriff's office. The song "Paper Moon" begins as a title saying "Ryan O'Neal in Paper Moon" is shown, followed by a shot of the two running down a hallway. The trailer cuts to a scene with Madeleine Kahn leaving a circus, with her identificatory title superimposed, followed by a characterization clip of the three of them in the car with her maid. The trailer cuts back to the chase scene and we hear more of the song, followed by another clip from the breakfast table with O'Neal saying, "Keep rolling, I got it." Then the chase scene is back (the breakfast table behind-the-scenes footage and the chase scene serve as grids throughout the trailer) as they race away, knocking the sheriff into the mud in classic Keystone Kops slapstick.

Next to be interspersed with the chase clips is a series of clips that convey expository detail, through wisecracking screwball exchanges between the characters. O'Neal's character is revealed as not being Tatum's character's father, he protests that he won't abandon her, and Madeleine Kahn is revealed as O'Neal's love interest. The use of a slapstick grid juxtaposed with expositional elements having to do with family dynamics keeps the tone of the trailer comic, while also keeping attention focused on the star partnership as a family relationship.

At the breakfast table again, out of character, O'Neal feigns tears and looks at Tatum, "Oh, damn, I can't eat any more of this stuff!"—literally protesting the rigors of his job of creating a fictional character. We hear crew laughter and Tatum laughs too as she looks up at him in profile. The laughter overlaps into the next scene (back in the fictional world), the final one of the chase grid, with the car zooming past a pair of cops as the cops stop and turn. Music swells and the film title and director and screenplay credits are shown over the scene. The narrator concludes, "Don't miss this one! From the maker of *The Last Picture Show* and *What's Up, Doc?*" The trailer cuts to a close-up of Tatum, facing the camera, who says, "You won't be sorry!" raising her eyebrows comically à la Groucho Marx, and the trailer fades out. Tatum gets the final word, in the form of a blatant direct-address "con job."

While the work of film production is underlined, not concealed, by this trailer (of course, mostly the fun and charming parts), the role of the backstage grid is different from the promotion of the star system in classical-era trailers. By incorporating the backstage segments rhythmically rather than setting them apart as instructional, newsreel-like introductions, the "plot" of Ryan O'Neal's relationship with his daughter is available to promote the film as a melodrama of stardom even within a comic trailer. The juxtaposition of the iffy fictional relationship between the two con artists with their "real" one, an evident paragon of togetherness (in a modern, reconfigured single-parent family), creates a dynamic of distance and closeness *between* the two stars that aligns with the alternating distance from and closeness to the audience implied by the trailer's repeatedly going backstage. The alternation serves to promote the film's quality of nostalgia for family relationships, melodramatically appealing at once to daughters who long to heal relationships with fathers and fathers wishing to revisit failures with their daughters.

Tatum's final appeal functions as the ultimate sales pitch for a skeptical 1973 audience—successful because of, not in spite of, the recognition that we are being hustled. Because of the embeddedness of the behind-the-scenes narrative, the trailer assumes an audience more interested than ever in breaking the barrier between stars and audiences, and more interested in and savvy about filmmaking than ever (by now, for example, directors too are visible as stars). In the Hollywood renaissance environment, the audience has proven itself a more surprising arbiter of film content than had been thought, and this trailer's experimental blending of standard fictional clips and documentary-style behind-the-scenes footage is in keeping with the spirit of the times. Yet regardless of whether audiences are included in the backstage joke, the promotional dynamics that guarantee we are viewing stars not as authentic persons but within a "rhetoric of authenticity" are still always at work. Tatum's final direct-address Groucho imitation may be disarming, but it's also classic P. T. Barnum puffery, and is a fitting wrap-up for a trailer that displays the new levels and types of promotional effort that complemented the nostalgic tenor of the films made by Hollywood renaissance directors—some of whom were soon to dominate the blockbuster-era box office.

CHINATOWN (Transitional Story Rhetoric)

While the *Chinatown* (1974)[49] trailer has a sophisticated, contemporary look, it also helps demarcate the twilight of the precontemporary era in that it does not bear evidence of high concept marketing; rather, it emphasizes the complexities of its neo-noir detective story in the context of promoting the characterization of its main character—a characterization that doesn't quite seem to match in impact Jack Nicholson's Jake Gittes.[50] The trailer frames this characterization in terms of the centrality of Jake's search for the truth about Evelyn Mulwray (Faye Dunaway) and the case, presenting such a quest in ways that differ from the *Bad Day at Black Rock* trailer's earlier transitional-era example, yet illustrative of the trailer's and film's historical moment of the early seventies. The trailer constructs the search for the truth not so much as a straightforward feature of the narrative's enigmatic structure that trailer producers assume audiences will desire to see uncovered *for them* (by seeing the film), but more as a feature of the main character's identity, such that the revelation of the truth is constructed as a revelation *for him*. Thus, it's how the narrative enigma affects the character and his identity that the trailer assumes audiences want to see.

It opens with a graphic of the title on black, the moving image enclosed within the letters. The letters break away, revealing an image of a car in the desert, with noirish music. Over a pan to Jack Nicholson watching the desert, the voice-over narrator begins: "Los Angeles, 1937. There are lots of guys like J. J. Gittes. They're easy to find, if you want to find 'em." Nicholson steps back a bit. This narration contains the assumption that audiences will associate its hardboiled yet intimate tone with the detective conventions of film noir, at once establishing the importance of the film's revision of a familiar generic world and introducing a *narrative* world in which Gittes's character is central to the story. The narrator's use of "you" attempts to draw the trailer audience into identificatory participation not only with the character but also with the film's period setting and its world-weary attitudinal posture.

The trailer shows clips from the scene where Dunaway's and Nicholson's characters first meet, and she asserts that they've never met before, the dialogue continuing as a sound overlap while the trailer presents clips of Nicholson snooping around. After Dunaway leaves, saying, "I don't get tough with anyone, Mr. Gittes, my lawyer does," we see a car pull up and the view in the car window of Dunaway with her daughter. The narrator returns, "You do your job." (We see a reaction shot of Nicholson looking into the car.) "And sometimes you find the answers to questions that should never be asked."

The segment serves primarily to further the trailer's focus on the detective's characterization—the "you" by which the narration first assumed audiences could identify with a hypothetical person who wanted to find someone *like* Jake becomes an association of Jake himself with the audience that is now assumed to be identifying with *him*. This motif differs from the rhetoric of story's evocation of "you" in the classical era (such as "If you are looking for adventure, you'll find it in *Casablanca*"). Here there's a part of "you" that's assumed to already be *in* the film's narrative world, with the movie promoted as bringing out a preexisting affinity with this world through identification with its main character. The romantic intrigue between Nicholson and Dunaway and enigmatic elements of the detective story are also established, but in ways that are obscure by comparison to the trailer's core focus on Nicholson's character. Only in retrospect (after having seen the film) does the narrator's line as Nicholson looks into Dunaway's car make any story sense, even enigmatically—so far we have no idea what could be meant by "questions that should never be asked."

Next we see Nicholson selecting stopwatches from his glove compartment and placing two of them behind the tires of a car, as the narrator continues, "Or, you find out what happens to people who ask them." Clips are shown from the now-familiar scene in which Polanski, playing a hood, knifes Nicholson's nose. The trailer cuts to Faye Dunaway sitting at a restaurant table and Nicholson asks her questions about her affairs. The trailer cuts to Nicholson watching the dead husband being dragged out of the riverbed by police. The restaurant dialogue continues in voice-over: "Where were you when your husband died?" We return to the restaurant scene (this segment offers another example of the grid). "You were seeing someone too." The trailer cuts to Nicholson, his nose bandage revealed for the first time, then cuts back to Dunaway, who looks at it. "For very long?" "I never see anyone for very long, Mr. Gittes. It's difficult for me." The trailer's consolidation of the "nose scene" and the developing interrogatory/sexual relationship between Dunaway and Nicholson results in an emphasis on the romance element over the action (in the trailer's terms, the main outcome of the nose injury seems to be its impact on his relationship with the woman), as does the use of the Nicholson/Dunaway clips as a grid into which are intercut action clips.

The trailer cuts to a night scene, and Nicholson jumps over a fence, as John Huston's voice begins, "Mr. Gittes," then we see Huston (as Noah Cross), "You're dealing with a disturbed woman, who's just lost her husband. I don't want her taken advantage of." We next see the kissing scene with Dunaway and Nicholson, followed by a cut to him slapping her around, then grabbing her: "The truth! I said I want the truth!" He knocks her into a table, and there follows a montage of investigatory action shots from various scenes, accompanied by high tinkling piano music. The montage forms a bracket syntagma instantiating Nicholson's search for the truth. An Asian couple helps Faye Dunaway and the girl into a car as drums dominate the score, and we see an extreme close-up of a hand picking up eyeglasses in a handkerchief, followed by a shot of Nicholson leaping onto the running board of Dunaway's car at night and a man shooting at them, then by a shot of the neon lights of Chinatown seen from a moving car. This segment represents the trailer's climax, again folding the film's various action scenes (presented out of sequence) into the dynamics of the relationship between the two principals (presented sequentially), but establishing that the two aspects of the story, action and romance (formerly separated by a binary grid treatment), are beginning to merge. The chronological presentation of characterization and relationship elements privilege this aspect of the story over its suspense elements.

The trailer ends on the film's final scene: we see a policeman shoot after Dunaway's car, then we see the car in the distance, as music swells (throbbing violins). Nicholson stands with two cops, and they speak to him, culminating in the now-famous line, "Forget it, Jake, it's

Figure 4.9. Jack Nicholson's search for
the truth in the *Chinatown* trailer.

Chinatown." The line and the trailer finale's setting serve as a coda promoting the film's narrative world—one that the title neatly overdetermines as a geographically delimited space. The narrator summarizes, "You get tough. You get tender. You get close to each other. Maybe you even get close to the truth." We see the remaining crowd, then the narrator concludes, "Jack Nicholson and Faye Dunaway in a Robert Evans production of a Roman Polanski film, *Chinatown*," as the scene fades to a high shot of the street and the music throbs to a close.

This trailer makes clear the effects of a focus on characterization within the rhetoric of story, in that it frames its assumptions about what audiences want from the story within the domain of identity and relationships. The narration's continual use of the second person reinforces this by encouraging audience identification with Jake's hard-bitten detective. The emphasis on audience identification assumes a parallel between audiences of 1974 and the cynical noir detective figure revived in Jake, a parallel about which Michael Ryan and Douglas Kellner have remarked,

> *Indeed, the entire* film noir *revival of the mid-seventies can be said to instantiate the emerging reality of political liberalism—that it was powerless against the entrenched economic power blocs of the country. . . . It is in the tragic figure of the* noir *detective, determined to do right yet incapable of changing the basic realities, that the liberal ideal, with all of its well-deserved self-pity, finds its strongest expression at this point in time.*[51]

The trailer's assumptions that the film's representations of romantic tension, rather than social or political powerlessness, are what will most

THE TRANSITIONAL ERA **159**

attract audiences to *Chinatown* are exemplified by the primacy of the trailer's chronological, and thus more coherently displayed, romantic plot elements—while its political exposé elements are either withheld or veiled by being presented nonchronologically. This emphasis reasserts Hollywood moviemaking's primary narrative thrust on the formation of the couple—even though it's clear from the trailer that in this film (as in many of its noir predecessors), the couple is also destroyed. Through a focus on characterization within the rhetoric of story, *Chinatown* is generically reconfigured or assumed to be of interest more as a tragic romance than as a political thriller—demonstrating again, as did the trailer for *The Graduate*, how appealing to particular kinds of assumed audience interest in *story* information can posit a viable (in promotional terms) *genre* identity for an ambiguous or puzzling film. And as in the *Paper Moon* trailer, nostalgic elements in the film's mise-en-scène interact with the trailer's contradictory temporality such that the trailer reads as a nostalgia for a future moviegoing experience.

SUMMARY

Trailers in the transitional era seem to be searching for the configurations of the new postclassical audience. There no longer seems to be an imaginary universal, raceless (but white by omission), classless (but middle- to working-class) assumed mass of folks with basically similar (and basically conservative) values that went to the movies. While who "You!" is/are no longer seems to go without saying as it did in the classical era, this elusive audience is still addressed on the assumption that the three core rhetorical appeals are the principal means by which to bring them into the theater.

Within the rhetoric of genre, generic space is promoted in such a way that the trailers in this sample can be viewed as representations of the social space of their time. Generic space tends to be problematized to a greater degree in transitional trailers. Each still clearly utilizes the conventions of the rhetoric of genre to differentiate the product within a framework of familiarity, yet the social spaces represented in these trailers seem less readily "packaged" than before. The *War of the Worlds* trailer's evocation of a contemporary fictional social world responding to interplanetary invasion with global panic and chaos, in the process implying that it could be *non*fictional; the *Liberty Valance* trailer's figuration of the "new" Western as a space of overdetermined *author*ity; and the *Cabaret* trailer's depiction of a historical Europe where internal forces are collapsing society and entertainment is the last refuge—all instantiate how trailers of the transitional era display assumptions that audiences are no longer interested in genres in quite the same ways as before, and may not have the same values as before. Regardless of the content of the sample's many genre trailers made during this era, the rhetorical assumptions about audiences that emerge through trailers' efforts at product differentiation within generic terms map a fundamental confusion on the part of promoters about where the boundaries of appropriate or successful feature film genres are or should be drawn.

Since transitional-era films dealt with topics formerly avoided by Hollywood, first in an effort to bring audiences back to the big screen following the drop-offs in movie attendance at the close of the studio era, and later in response to broad social change, the rhetoric of story likewise faced new challenges. Trailers both promoted these shifts by calling attention to movies' newly provocative themes, and yet were confronted with promoting elements that sometimes seem to have been considered unpromotable, whether because of subject matter, style, or other kinds of innovations. What these trailers tell and what they withhold through the rhetoric of story is thus revealing about trailermakers' assumptions about the kinds of knowledge and experiences audiences desired, as well as about the ideological dictates of promotional rhetoric, during a crisis time in Hollywood (and the culture). Historical contradictions, increasingly visible within films themselves during this era, often tended to be brought into relief within the trailers not by a faithful promotion of the films' innovations but by the trailers' inability to represent new paradigms of cinematic representation, resulting in quirky mismatches and mixed messages about the film in question.

Within the rhetoric of story this is borne out by, in the case of *Bad Day at Black Rock*, the trailer's emphasis on the enigmatic aspects of its narrative in such a way that a pointed contemporary political drama resembles more an updated Western (one in which clear-cut knowledge about good and evil is no longer to be found). The trailer for *The Great Escape* boils the epic sweep of its historically specific narrative down to a no-frills "guy flick" in an early example of audience targeting. In the case of *The Graduate*, the trailer's emphasis on story causality results in a generic labeling that doesn't seem to have promoted the aspects of the film that were primarily responsible for its appeal, while in *Chinatown*, the emphasis on narrative characterization also contributes to generic reconfiguration—the trailer treats the film's resurrection of noir conventions in a way that subordinates the political to the romantic (even more than does the film itself). Regardless of which aspect of narrative these trailers promoted, the transitional era's new emphasis on provocative themes and innovative stylistic techniques tended to be recuperated into an increased focus on subjectivity and character, or a magnification of the minutiae of story causality. The sense classical-era trailers provided that films depicted an external reality that could be known (however circumscribed its representation on the screen) had shifted, and trailers began to assume less about audiences' desires for knowledge and experience of an external reality through film stories.

The rhetoric of stardom, like those of genre and story, has fewer clear-cut dimensions during the transitional era, as studios and trailer-makers experiment with how to appeal to audiences' interest in stars, now playing new roles in a rapidly changing Hollywood economy. Like *All About Eve*'s trailer, many fifties trailers emphasized the stars' performances over their "type," and new performance styles were often promoted as a way to differentiate the film.[52] The new styles were also called into service to differentiate the capacities of film in general to offer more "adult" themes than television, contributing to redefined appeals to audience interest in the star system. And like the trailer for *Paper Moon*, later sixties and early seventies trailers were seen to both experiment wildly with trailer form, attempting to use stars to hold the attention of an audience perceived as unpredictable, and to innovate more integrative features (such as clips broken up into grids) that would become dominant elements of "New Hollywood" promotional formulas—in this case also integrating appeals to audience interest in star quality, relationality, and the star system.

Transitional trailers seem to take advantage of the fact that the star system is less visibly a system—to promote stars in new and more individualized ways as embodiments of a more adult, potentially unpredictable medium. Although this increased individuality would appear to break down some of the perceived distance between stars and audiences by allowing greater visibility of quirks and qualities that make them seem even more "like us," the transitional era also saw the promotion of the newly emergent independent superstar in trailers—a figure whose ubiquity in popular culture more than anything exaggerates his or her unattainability and superhuman status.

Transitional-era trailers are all the more fascinating for the apparent lack of cohesion around questions of audience address, with the result that we can read clearly in them some of the compensatory promotional gestures that the three rhetorical appeals enable (and which carry over into the contemporary era), such as evoking nostalgia, falling back on generic familiarity and promoting spectatorship as a fulfillment of sexual desires. Yet these contradictory texts can still occasionally offer more even when they seem to offer less, such as when they invite audiences to conceive of a film, even a world, where autonomous, erudite stars warn us of their own duplicity; where old genres are refreshed by new historical realities; or where broken families find happiness in the promotional world of Hollywood.

5

The Contemporary Era: The Global Family Audience

By 1975, the watershed year for New Hollywood, the market for motion pictures had undergone a number of transformations that affected how films were conceived and perceived both within the industry and by audiences. The corporate conglomeration and increased reliance on high concept blockbuster models already mentioned, along with new levels of marketing-driven promotional regimes that maximized synergies among related products (whether ancillary to films or product placements within them), impacted the trailer industry, resulting in high concept trailer formulas that were more predictable than those for transitional trailers. While markets for "niche" films have since expanded phenomenally in conjunction with new avenues of distribution, trailers for even these films follow a promotional model heavily dictated by the rhetorical logic of the dominant blockbuster market. Thus, theatrical trailers (unlike TV spots) are still charged with drawing as large an audience as possible to *every* film. Indeed, as a result of the success of films like *The Full Monty* (1999) and *The Opposite of Sex* (1999), "major independents" such as Miramax and New Line Cinema now can always hope for a breakout hit even among smaller films, and thus gear even these promotional campaigns accordingly.[1] Moreover, "as large an audience as possible" has a different meaning in the context of New Hollywood's global reach (as do the parameters of Hollywood itself, a newly global entity no longer even remotely ascribable to a single specific geographic place).[2]

An *Entertainment Weekly* article from 1993, which surveyed trailer producers to determine the "Ten Tricky Commandments" of trailer production, lays out contemporary trailermakers' strategies succinctly:

—*Let the Stars Shine.* . . . Big surprise—name brands sell . . .

—*No Stars? Go for the Gut.*

—*Use All the Best Jokes.* . . . A few honest laughs are all a film needs to make a nice dishonest trailer . . .

—*Choose your Sex Appeal.* Don't try to sell a "woman's movie" to men, or vice versa . . .

—*Less Is More—and Least Can Be Most.*

—*Score with the Music.*

—*Get a Whole Lotta Love.*

—*Cut to the Chase.* Who needs a story line when you've got killer visuals? . . .

—*Never Say Die.* How do you promote a movie about death? Go into deep denial . . .

—*Test, Test, Test.* Even a great trailer can't save a clunker . . . "Sometimes," says [Aspect Ratio's Bob] Israel, "the truth just shines through.". . .[3]

These formulas correspond fairly accurately to prevailing popular wisdom about trailers, which audiences complain often lie by giving an overdramatized, overspectacularized or oversexed version that doesn't seem reflective of the movie at all. This popular press assessment serves to introduce a deeper consideration of the codes at work in the contemporary movie market to transform narrative films into ads for themselves. Persuasive strategies of concealment, selective positioning, emotional appeal and even dishonesty are clearly indicated. Contemporary production practices, which, as a recent *Daily Variety* article noted, are increasingly driven by marketing departments,[4] result in high concept–oriented trailers that frequently synthesize appeals to genre, story and stardom in broad strokes, delivering finely crafted yet apparently simple trailers. Graphics are streamlined, narration is punchy and there is an increased reliance on sound effects and music to heighten the sensory assault of the images.[5] Trailers moreover participate in a synergistic commercial marketplace shared by a number of other pervasively commercialized media texts, including music television, infotainment, and children's television, as well as an increase in commercial product placement within films themselves.

In part influenced by the "movie brat" or film school generation, genre formation in New Hollywood is characterized by a redoubling of the referentiality of films to other films, both through increased use of intertextual jokes and references and through a more holistic referencing

of earlier Hollywood genres and genre films, in specific as well as amor-
phously nostalgic ways. In trailers this feature of the contemporary film
market combines with the impact of the high concept–driven promotional milieu of the blockbuster era, encompassing such elements as
"the reliance on strong, reproducible images, the saturation campaign,
and widespread product tie-ins" along with an emphasis on making the
most of presold elements such as "stars, familiar stories or situations,
remakes, sequels, and series films."[6] The rhetoric of genre gains particular strength from the high-concept era's integration of preproduction
(packaging), production, and promotion, which engenders a coherent
generic identity for most films from the start.

Like those of the classical era, contemporary trailers utilizing the
rhetoric of genre privilege audience interest in the familiar over product
differentiation, but in addition to memories of classic film genres, the
familiar now encompasses a host of other cultural cues from television,
music, and other forms of entertainment. Moreover, the reach of potential audiences for whom such cues are familiar is now assumed to be
global. Much has been written about the generic hybridity of contemporary postmodern quotational popular culture, and trailers are no
exception. The inclusiveness of trailer producers' conceptions of genre
in the classical era is echoed with new energy in the image-bombarded
1980s–1990s, where generic revitalization and recombination are
standard (witness the 1999 film *Wild Wild West*, which industry buzz
jokingly began to call "Men in Black Hats" on the basis of its trailer, in
which the film's hybridization of Western and science fiction genres was
dominated by its promotion as another Will Smith vehicle along the
lines of 1997's *Men in Black*). Whereas the transitional era encompassed
two distinct periods of trailer production, the core characteristics of
contemporary trailer rhetoric had all emerged by the mid-seventies.

The rhetoric of story tends to recede as genre and star appeals gain
in prominence in contemporary trailers, as the foregoing *Entertainment
Weekly* article exemplifies, yet the conventions are still present, if more
frequently integrated with the other appeals. The trailers selected to
characterize this era's promotional challenges with regard to the rhetoric of story are all striking in the ways they demonstrate assumptions
about audience interest—or lack of it—in knowing more, both about
the film's story and the historical world. Contemporary trailers consist
less frequently of narratorial pronouncements, but even without
such hyperbolic verbal statements, strong rhetorical assumptions can be
discerned that follow the pattern of the incomplete syllogism (where

something assumed by the trailer's visual, aural or verbal argument to "go without saying" can be problematized). The assumptions these trailers offer as to audiences' desires for knowledge tend toward the reductive, as interest in film "content" is overwhelmed by audiences' assumed greater interests in dazzling new generic worlds and the ever-expanding discourse of stardom and celebrity.

Stars in the contemporary era seem never to exist anywhere *but* within the promotional world of Hollywood—now, of course, expanded to incorporate television, websites, and other media forms. While stars can control their own images to a greater extent today, those images are still circumscribed—now not by studios but by the degree to which contemporary image culture is overtaken by commercial (and therefore promotional) discourses. Perhaps the reason there are so few trailers that present both film clips and a backstage or institutional Hollywood setting in the contemporary era is that today there *is* no backstage, and stars are always already positioned overwhelmingly as commodities within a marketplace rather than as performers playing specific roles.

Within this promotional environment, the melodrama of stardom that trailers assume will draw audiences to movies is—to perhaps an even greater extent than in earlier eras—a story that transcends the individual film the trailer promotes. In the following case studies, the melodrama of stardom assumes audiences find stars and their celebrity unambiguously desirable, although the ways they are assumed to be desired can almost always be characterized as multivalent or contradictory. Contemporary trailers are addressed to audiences who are assumed to be interested in viewing star identities no longer as hyperbolic individualities so much as embedded multiplicities. Reading these cases where multivalent assumptions of audience desires for stars in contemporary trailers are foregrounded contributes to an understanding of the new melodrama of stardom in trailers as a whole.

The case studies are drawn from all segments of the contemporary era, but are weighted toward films from the 1990s in order to emphasize the state of trailer practice at the close of the twentieth century. That particular moment marked a shift in promotional discourse, as the Internet came to be utilized in ways that seemed to promise greater interactivity between producers and fans, exemplified by the much-discussed campaign for *The Blair Witch Project* (1999),[7] thus heralding major new elements in the "dialogue" between Hollywood and its audiences. By treating trailer production throughout the sound era up to the emergence of these changes, the present study emphasizes a continuity of trailer form prior to the Internet. My sense is that the apparent enrichment of communication between fans and producers enabled by Internet promotional forms is for the most part misleading, and that the current moment consists more of a continuation than a break. But the question of how audience address through theatrical movie trailers shifts as the era of Internet promotional practices unfolds is a subject for further study.

ROCKY (Contemporary Genre Rhetoric)

Along with the famous *Jaws* promotional campaign, the trailer for *Rocky* (1976)[8] is often cited as influential in the emergence of New Hollywood trailer conventions, and strikingly demonstrates an early incarnation of contemporary trailers' mission to avoid alienating any potential audience segment. Although this trailer draws on the rhetoric of story as well as that of genre, it is exemplary in its combination of the two for the purpose of expanding the audience beyond the expected male "fight film" crowd. Although at the time *Rocky* was perceived as innovative, both because its star/screenwriter had emerged out of virtual obscurity and because the main character's heroism did not reside in his abilities,[9] it belonged to a time-honored genre that, like the gangster movie, had built-in male appeal. In classical-era trailers, such films (the 1947 film *Body and Soul*, for example) were still assumed to be of interest to a universal audience that would include women, but the dynamics of the transitional era changed that. A marketing textbook tellingly characterizes contemporary trailer practice using the example of the *Rocky* trailer:

> The marketing plan sometimes calls for certain elements of the movie and the story to be played down to expand the target audience. For example, the boxing footage from Rocky turned off many women who were not interested in a movie about prize fighting. For this reason, the Rocky trailer did not use some of the most exciting footage from the movie. Although it set out to make the viewer root for a classic underdog who gets a million-to-one shot at respect and love, the trailer instead used the ice-skating sequence featuring Rocky and Clara [sic] with narration and dialogue telling about Rocky's dream and promising a simple but appealing love story. . . . It was a good example of properly positioning a film to expand what might have been a limited target audience.[10]

The *Rocky* trailer uses a series of grids[11] that alternate between ones involving Rocky's boxing world (not actual fighting scenes) and a number of scenes between Sylvester Stallone as Rocky and Talia Shire as Adrian (including the one at the ice rink). The trailer's principal rhetorical assumption is encapsulated by the tagline delivered early on by the narrator as we see Rocky kneel in a bathroom before the big fight: "His whole life was a million-to-one shot." The missing term in this enthymeme is just what exactly the odds are stacked against him *for*— the assumption is audiences will equate the fight with his only chance at success, and that audiences define success as accomplishment. While the trailer attempts to avoid pegging *Rocky* as a fight film, this line, and the subsequent scenes that serve to back up its assumption that audiences will want to see an underdog "go the distance," deliver nothing so much as they do classic boxing genre cues. The love story is incorporated but not privileged, much as romance is tied into adventure in classical-era genre trailers. In spite of the campaign's attempt to position the film as not-a-fight-film in order to appeal to women, it relies on the appeal of "presold elements" in the story: preeminently, the boxing genre convention of championing the underdog(s). This time, however, the underdog is figured as *both* members of the heterosexual—and working-class—couple.[12]

In the first clip from the ice-skating scene, Stallone explains to Shire how he became a fighter because his father told him that since he didn't have any brains he'd better use his body. We then see a training scene with Burgess Meredith, then the trailer cuts back to the ice where Shire echoes, "My mother, she said, 'You weren't born with much of a body so you better develop your brain.'" An aerial view of the boxing

Figure 5.1. Appealing to women: the skating
scene used as a grid in the *Rocky* trailer.

ring (and this trailer's profilmic audience), with the announcer speaking in voice-over, is followed by a clip from a gym scene with Stallone and Meredith in which the trainer basically tells the fighter he could have been a contender. The trailer next presents a grid comprised of clips of the couple in Rocky's dressing room as Rocky flirts with her before the fight, crosscut with clips of Burt Young (who plays Adrian's brother) telling Stallone what a loser he thinks Adrian is. We then hear cheering as we see Stallone go into the ring and the announcer says, "A 50-to-one underdog living a Cinderella story . . ."

Another grid then pairs scenes of the two fighters approaching the ring to cheers with a scene of the couple at his house for the first time, followed by a grid pairing Stallone punching sides of beef and later a punching bag, with the confrontation between Stallone, Shire and Burt Young. Intermittently, Stallone tells Shire during the crosscutting, "It really don't matter if I lose this fight, 'cause all I wanna do is go the distance. I'm gonna know for the first time in my life that I weren't just another bum from the neighborhood." And Shire tells Burt Young, "You made me feel like a loser! I'm *not* a loser!" The trailer culminates with clips from the training set piece where Stallone runs in downtown Philadelphia and pauses on the steps of a monument, raising his arms, as the soundtrack swells with the now-familiar Bill Conti "Rocky Theme."

While in this case we have evidence that the heavy use of the grid formation throughout this trailer was intended to put the focus on the film's love story and thus differentiate the product and appeal to a broader audience, it also functions to create an equation that reinforces familiar generic cues: Rocky's battle to be more than just another bum from the neighborhood (more than just a body) is visually equated with Adrian's battle to prove she's not a loser (more than just a brain). (Shire's delivery of the line, "I'm not a loser!" is the trailer's emotional climax.) Both of these battles, and the romantic plotline, are subsumed within the conventions of the boxing film, though figuring a new alliance of male and female underdogs—"I think we make a real sharp coupla coconuts, I'm dumb and you're smart, whadya think?"

At the same time, the trailer's strategy of reinforcing its identity as a boxing film without showing actual boxing does differentiate it from prior boxing films in that the use of the grid to create a visual equation implies an equality between the man and the woman in the heterosexual romance. It is hardly liberating in this case, for unlike other early seventies films that began to depict women's attempts at escape from domestic space (such as *Klute* [1971] and *Alice Doesn't Live Here Anymore*

[1974]), Adrian's escape is *into* domestic space. We might even read the equation oppositionally, as drawing attention to the circumscription of Rocky's (class) choices (all he gets to do is go the distance, not win), insofar as they parallel Adrian's, hers being both gender *and* class determined. The trailer's final tone of uplift tends to cover over any such oppositional readings, however, appearing to resolve all contradictions with Stallone's upraised fists of victory. Nonetheless, the trailer illustrates that contemporary-era trailer producers' concerns with not alienating any potential audience can lead to new forms of genre-based inclusiveness (she's a "fighter" too) that can increase the visibility of contradictions among this global audience as well as cover them up.

The working class figured more prominently in the social space of the seventies than it had in any decade since World War II. Traditional worker-based forms of struggle such as trade unionism were enjoying recession-based, and New Left–fed, visibility (on the eve, however, of the Reagan air traffic controllers union debacle that would change this). Furthermore, a new multiracial proletarian chic was visible both in urban milieus (as exemplified by the disco movement) and nationwide (with the rise in popularity of martial arts), and these trends were brought to the screen in films such as *Saturday Night Fever* (1977) and the Bruce Lee–influenced action film cycle. *Rocky* itself brought the working-class phatic "Yo!" into common parlance for a brief period of time. The *Rocky* trailer, however, with its reconfiguration of the familiar fight film thematic and the redemption of the underdog through struggle into a "simple but appealing love story" in which the million-to-one victory of the protagonist constitutes the formation of the couple, implies the maintenance of a status quo of class oppression. The trailer seems to address a global audience that sees the American working class from the outside, thus better identifying with the "simple, appealing" charms of its way of life than with its struggles.

DAYS OF HEAVEN (Contemporary Story Rhetoric)

The trailer for Terrence Malick's maverick second film *Days of Heaven* (1978), a lyrical story of a love triangle in the rural Midwest in 1916, is a striking early example of the contemporary "minimovie" mode (condensing the film's plot using a visually rich montage rather than dialogue-heavy expositional clips). The trailer's appeal to story interest is dominant, and in particular, its evocation of the film's narrative world outweighs considerations of characterization, enigma or causality. Moreover, the rhetoric of story promotes a second narrative in the process of promoting the film's narrative world, that of the American mythology of manifest destiny. It is a fascinating example of how contemporary trailers can (overtly or obliquely) comment on broader cultural narratives. The film's lyrical scenes are excerpted, accompanied by a voice-over narration that initially renders the story a history lesson. Malick had made his name in 1974 with *Badlands*, which contained an innovative nonomniscient voice-over narration featuring the diary of its fifteen-year-old female protagonist. The second film continues this tradition, employing a narration by a secondary character (also a young girl). The *trailer* backs up its selections from the film's meditative imagery with a narration (predictably male) that is at once more traditional and overtly historical than that of the film and yet itself breaks with most trailer uses of voice-over—as if the originality of the images demanded that the trailer narration also respond to the visuals on more than one register.

Demonstrating the contemporary era's more sophisticated ability to promote elements of a film's visual style compared to that of earlier eras, the trailer's opening shots are samples of the film's striking cinematography (for which Nestor Almendros won the Academy Award), constituting a bracket syntagma set to music and characterized (as is the entire trailer) by rhythmic and graceful movement, whether of the camera or its mechanical, agricultural or human subjects. This beginning sets the scene for the remainder of the trailer. We see shots of a storm-clouded sky over a prairie, a seagull flying, Richard Gere walking in a field, clouds overhead, and a group of adults and children standing on a riverbank holding period umbrellas.[13]

The narrator begins, "In 1916, America was changing." An industrial furnace door opens to its fiery innards as Gere shovels coal inside. Red-hot steel columns tumble out of their molds. In an exterior shot, a man with a megaphone in a chaotic crowd of people and horses yells, "I need stockers." We see a train as the narrator adds, "Expanding." From behind, a caravan of vehicles and huddled people is shown heading across the plains, as the narrator goes on, "Holding a promise of new prosperity." Men in suits are seen working at a table in a field of grain, followed by a lyrical shot of grain waving, as music continues. Men, women and children run to hop on a train, as the narrator continues, "People heard the call." A couple of them scramble and fight and the narrator goes on, "It made them restless."

Figure 5.2. "Holding a promise of a new prosperity."
A caravan of vehicles and huddling people heads
across the plains in the *Days of Heaven* trailer.

The choice of shots and the voice-over function to generalize the film's narrative specificity: shots that—in the film—belong to scenes integral to the construction of its narrative meanings (coal-shoveling, hiring, train-hopping) are extricated in order to serve a historical rhetoric: trailer audiences are assumed to desire knowledge of the historical backdrop of this film in order to better experience its narrative world. In extracting Almendros's lyrical images from their context and assigning them this generalizing voice-over, the trailer reduces this imagery to *National Geographic* clichés of Americana (the red-hot steel ingots, the waving wheat fields, the train . . .). This rhetorical appeal ("These are people and activities you will see in the film. They represent how it was in America in 1916.") contains a missing term, the assumption that these represented historical subjects, the "restless people" (the only ones of whom we see are itinerants and entrepreneurs), are all able to better themselves in one classless, equal-opportunity response to "America . . . changing, expanding."

A steam tractor billows smoke, seeding planes soar up and away from the moving camera and from another angle we see Sam Shepard watch them from the aforementioned table in the field as they fly up behind him, his character's house in the background. "Empires were being built in the wide-open spaces." More tractor shots are followed by a shot of Shepard gesturing by waving his arm slowly from screen left to screen right, as the narrator continues, "And so they came." Richard Gere and Brooke Adams are seen on the train, and people jump off the train, running across the field with luggage, as the narrator adds, "Each one boldly, blindly searching . . ." We see a succession of shots of the three principals (without identificatory titles): Shepard looks out at the horizon, Adams puts the back of her hand to her sweaty forehead, Gere looks out, Adams and Gere kiss in a field and play under a wagon; ". . . for the days . . ." (an extreme long shot shows Adams and Gere standing near the house on the field as she strokes his cheek) "of heaven."

In this segment, the generalized historical world of the previous section has gradually intermingled with the film's narrative world: Sam Shepard is identified as the story's "empire builder," and Richard Gere and Brooke Adams as some of the "restless people." We assume they will be working for Shepard (who wears upper-class clothing).[14] The itinerants and the agricultural entrepreneurs are merged by the narration, as images of Gere, Adams, and Shepard are all associated with the activity of "boldly, blindly searching for the days of heaven," rhetorically asserting that both capitalist and worker are looking for the same thing, and then positing that thing as personal happiness. In this section, the film's narrative world is promoted as a sort of idyll of potentiality building to an undefined happiness, collapsing at once historical and narrative specificity in apparent deference to the film's meditative visual style, which is assumed to have the power to persuade audiences, with minimal (story) information (let alone star or genre information), to see the film.

The trailer then continues its move away from the generalized shots of folks enacting manifest destiny to a more pointed focus on the three principals and their narrative situation. A man with a gun and badge points at something on a riverbed. The narrator returns, "Days of Heaven . . ." as we see Gere's apparent reaction shot; and the narrator continues, "the story of a man who had nothing," as Gere is chased by policemen on horseback. Adams sees him, horrified, and the narrator continues, "the woman who loved him . . ." and the trailer cuts to a series of romantic shots of the couple from other scenes. We then see Shepard walking along his balcony, apparently worried, as the narrator continues, "and the man who would give her everything . . ." The camera returns to the couple, seen in the distance by the house, as Adams walks away from Gere and the narrator concludes, "for a share of that love." In a reverse angle, she walks toward the house, backlit.

The shift in the trailer's narration away from the generalizations of the narrative of manifest destiny to more specific information about the film's love triangle—including its class dynamics—is visually consistent, offering the same kinds of assemblages of subtle, lyrical imagery as those brought to the service of the earlier historical segment. As in the previous section, the film's narrative details are overwhelmed by generalized visual impressions. The narrative world of the film is thus linked with the manifest destiny rhetoric in a way that creates a trailer-specific equation between the love triangle and the acquisitive thrust of westward expansion.

In the final segment, Shepard gets up from lying in the field, and says, "You know what I thought when I first saw you?" Shepard gazes at Brooke Adams as his line continues in voice-over: "I thought if only I could touch her, that everything would be all right." Adams takes off her stockings. The narrator returns, "Three people whose destinies join briefly in a dream," as the trailer cuts to Shepard turning out the light, followed by a medium close-up of Gere outdoors, looking up at the night sky in profile. The camera pans around and away from him and we see from behind that he's looking up at a lit window in the house, and the narrator concludes, "but how long could it last?" The trailer freezes on this long shot of Gere looking at the window. The music crescendos as credit titles are superimposed.

This finale asserts the preeminence of the love triangle, ending with a question ("how long could it last?") that, unlike most other questions asked in trailers, does not function enigmatically—essentially, we do know the answer to this rhetorical question. Instead, the trailer assumes we are interested in the play of "three people whose destinies join briefly in a dream," the narration reversing its earlier assumption of audience interest in the historical specificity of the film's narrative world and now positing the three principals' joining as "a dream," an idyll set outside of historical time. It thus expresses an assumption about the audience's desire to know that ultimately privileges "the 'eternal present' of Hollywood film, the appearance that everything occurs in a nonhistorical space."[15] The promotion of the film's narrative world entails addressing the troubling historical specificity of the film's images by assuming audiences prefer them boiled down to a classless "search for happiness," which is constructed as a fitting backdrop for a film that the trailer configures as a timeless rural "upstairs/downstairs" story. While the trailer is clearly at ease with positioning the film's visual artistry as a key selling point (unlike most transitional-era trailers), the images serve a story *the film itself does not tell*, here policing the boundaries of appropriate Hollywood narrative by drawing one apparently wider ("America . . . expanding") yet ultimately narrower ("three people whose destinies join briefly in a dream") than the film would appear to warrant. This trailer's striking amalgamation of story with the historical presents in high relief a rhetorical strategy common to many contemporary trailers.

CADDYSHACK
(Contemporary Star Rhetoric)

The trailer for *Caddyshack* (1980),[16] a golf comedy starring Bill Murray, wherein promotional discourses are satirized in the process of serving their nonsatirical purpose to hype the film, demonstrates the emergence of contemporary promotional satire, a more heavily ironic phenomenon than the tame trailer parodies of the transitional era. In this case the trailer satire relies primarily on the rhetoric of stardom (and to a degree, genre). It provides an example of the contemporary era's occasional use of a behind-the-scenes motif—by now almost always limited to comic trailers.[17] This trailer's very crudeness enables its film to be adequately promoted to its audience, here a segmented one assumed to want more from the stars of *Saturday Night Live*, the vastly popular satirical television show first seen in 1976, two of whose "Not Ready for Prime Time Players" are in the film's ensemble cast. Like other trailers promoting star ensembles, the accumulation of personalities here implies an accumulation of reasons to see the film. This ensemble, seen primarily in special trailer footage, moreover appears to engender a "group sensibility" of zaniness that invites its target audience to "join the club" by seeing the film. The trailer also demonstrates the increasing popularity of television stars in contemporary-era films, and a corresponding influence of televisual formats (such as the sketch comedy show) on trailers, a feature that contributes to the increasingly multivalent quality of contemporary trailers' star appeals.

The trailer opens with a crest of the Bushwood Golf Country Club. A narrator begins, "To capture the grandeur of a place like the Bushwood Country Club, to bring the dignity, power, and scope of the game of golf to the screen, it takes a special motion picture—a motion picture like—" (a golf stroke is heard, and a ball imprinted with the film's title bursts through the crest and looms into the foreground) "Caddyshack!" We then see Ted Knight (known primarily as a television comedy star) in a talking-head shot. He says, "It's the *only* funny picture that was ever made." This opening cues us to the trailer's mission (which is as much to satirize trailers as it is to promote its film) by poking fun at overblown trailer narrations, classic trailer graphics with their zooming titles and excess hyperbole.

We see the movie set and crew, and Chevy Chase leans over the back of his director's chair so that his name can be seen and says (in a tongue-twisted Lennon-esque satire of classic trailer alliteration), "This is a major motion sickness. It's a very sleazy, frontal, uh, comedy." A talking-head shot follows of a woman saying, "It's great." The narrator resumes, "It's dramatic!" as people run across a golf green. The trailer fades to a shot of Bill Murray in gopher battle paraphernalia saying, "It's a war story, y'know, men against gophers." Next the narrator adds, "It's romantic," as Murray is seen with some women, one of whom says, "I didn't tell them about us, or anything like that." This segment, which presents apparently *anti*promotional images that portray the cast and crew as slobs and womanizers, introduces an irreverence that illustrates my earlier point that stars and celebrity are unambiguously desirable in the contemporary era—they can thus afford to not "look good" to a new degree in the service of promoting a comedy.

The narrator resumes, "It's symbolic," as we see Chevy Chase doing a double-take at the camera. Ted Knight says, "Not one second in it . . . has serious under- or overtones," as he fondles two golf balls. Another woman smiles at the camera as the narrator continues, "It's got sex!" Rodney Dangerfield delivers a sex joke at the expense of Hawaiians, and the narrator resumes, "It's got song." Bill Murray sits with his shirt open, scratching behind his ear, singing a line from a silly song, injecting snorts, raspberries, and whistles. By its assumption that tasteless jokes, obvious sexual innuendoes, physical grossness, and body noises are appealing to audiences—that is, as long as they're performed by popular comedy stars—the trailer makes even clearer the film's very specific targeted demographic, the young adult male "couch potatoes" of the late seventies assumed to watch *Saturday Night Live*. At the same time, the juxtaposition of such grossness with the narration's repeated satirical repetition of the "something for everyone" variety show trailer mode ("It's got . . .") creates a more sophisticated satirical appeal to a larger variety of audiences, in essence congratulating them on their knowledge of classical trailer rhetoric. The trailer lacks the smoothness with which later trailers manage to target specific audiences while still casting wider nets, but it demonstrates an early contemporary attempt to combine appeals to various audiences.

The trailer goes on in this vein, offering up the film as "having" excitement and violence, with Murray telling the camera: "I got in a fight with this guy in the movie on the set—I pulled a knife on him. Turns out, like, he's a director or somethin', you know, big shot." This footage makes clear the trailer's conceit that the actors are desperately trying to come up with examples to justify the narrator's hyperbolic claims about the film. The bogus "behind-the-scenes" clips accumulate into the trailer's own anarchic narrative within the melodrama of stardom, a sort of Mickey-Mouse-Club-meets-*Mad*-Magazine vision of a movie set.

Murray hits a golf ball, dressed in camouflage green, wearing rubber boots and sunglasses. The narrator continues, "Spectacular costumes!" Knight is then seen, saying in a German accent, "Lots of uniforms and hitting of things!" The narrator adds: "And a musical soundtrack," as we see Murray singing a second tasteless childhood song, adding to the trailer's assumed appeal for teenage boys. The film's subsequent success demonstrates that perhaps the trailermakers' assumptions were correct: that Murray et al. could afford to alienate as many potential audience members as possible and still not deter the large target group of young males for whom such jokes were assumed to constitute a refreshing irreverence in 1980.

The trailer then winds up with a series of identificatory stills of the cast. We see a still of Murray in the camouflage hat, holding and looking at a scythe blade. The trailer reprises the opening graphic, and we hear Chevy Chase's voice: "Caddyshack! Better than Caddyshack 2!" This exit line parodies at once the contemporary era's sequel-mania and, interestingly, the anticipatory temporality of trailers noted earlier. Like the trope of "you'll love to remember . . . ," the line places the trailer's assumed audiences in a future time wherein the film—or in this case its imaginary sequel—has been seen.

The trailer's "melodrama of stardom" assumes that closeness to these stars is not something audiences desire—rather, it capitalizes on their distance. In this case it is still of course in part the celestial distance of admiring stars' "big-name" status, but even more it is a distance of excess and outrageousness, evoking the pleasures of watching stars do things that one would only enjoy seeing (if at all . . .) at the movies. Layered onto this kind of—neither romantically desirable nor identificatory—pleasure of stardom is the emergence of postmodern ironic registers (such as the supposedly newly "allowable"—because self-aware—bigotry) within promotional discourses. This is another kind of "distant" pleasure evoked by contemporary cinematic stargazing (and one that has been heavily influenced by *Saturday Night Live* and its forerunner, *The National Lampoon*). These stars contain a built-in multiplicity by virtue of almost never appealing to audience interest in their "authenticity." Both as sketch comics and as fundamentally cynical, or at least satirical, personae, stars such as Chevy Chase and Bill Murray demonstrate a prevalent contemporary mode of the postmodern star as shifting signifier.[18]

Ushering in an age of cynical comic star turns that increasingly cross generic lines in the nineties (such as in the trailer for the 1999 ensemble fantasy-comedy *Mystery Men*, starring such heirs to the postmodern cynical posture as Ben Stiller and Janeane Garofalo), the *Caddyshack* trailer exemplifies the contemporary era's assumptions, perhaps influenced by television discourses, that at least some (comedy?) audiences now desire not so much to "have" or "be" stars as to be offered by stars new attitudes to life—or perhaps, to act out new attitudes assumed to be held by audiences, in excessive ways that we can't. In contemporary commodified culture, such star promotional discourses may evidence an assumption that audiences desire to take their increasingly complex lives less seriously—while spending money to learn from stars how to do so.

RETURN OF THE JEDI
(Contemporary Genre Rhetoric)

The trailer promoting the third episode produced in the *Star Wars* saga, *Return of the Jedi* (1983),[19] is interesting in the way it calls on the rhetoric of genre to promote a prominent New Hollywood cycle, interpellating audiences in ways that are both similar to earlier trailers and create new conventions for the promotion of the "family adventure film." This trailer demonstrates how genre and story appeals can be interwoven in the contemporary trailer, while offering a culmination of many of the classical and transitional trailer practices of promoting spectacle. It should be noted that George Lucas resisted the generic appellation "science fiction" for his new saga when it first appeared in 1977, preferring the term "space fantasy."[20] Thus, while the saga has inevitably been considered critically as science fiction, Lucas's promotional efforts focused heavily on differentiating it from prior science fiction films and on emphasizing the particularities of the cycle's own characteristics, the familiarity and popularity of which are heavily referenced in the trailer for this third film of the series.

The trailer relies on the spectacular, offering a clear-cut example of the persistence of the circus mode in the contemporary era. It moves smoothly from clips of one of the film's key action set pieces to another while inserting short bits of dialogue that hint at plot points without revealing them, as well as offering a number of in-jokes that assume audiences know the first two films without insisting they do. Eschewing the film's chronological development, the trailer presents its own trajectory of narrative action (including a coherent trailer "beginning" and "ending"), privileging spectacular images and rhythmic transitions that back up the trailer's central refrain, as laid out in the first title: "Return!" This hailing assumes, of course, that audiences have seen the first films of the saga—as well they had, in record numbers.

Following the 20th Century Fox logo, the trailer shows a field of (celestial) stars as the pinpoints transform into vectored lines—the familiar visual cue for a spaceship's transition to hyperdrive, here signaling both the penetration of outer space and the start of a brand-new—science fiction—adventure. Accompanying this visual is a high-tech sound like the depressurizing hiss of the opening of a spaceship door lock, reinforcing the image of entry. A title bursts forth to the sound of an explosion: "RETURN," in the red capital letters of the *Return of the Jedi* logo. The familiar John Williams score swells, and a narrator announces, "Return! To a galaxy, far, far away." A title saying the same thing is then boxed in red, with the "Star Wars" logo at the top (a graphic configuration familiar to purchasers of *Star Wars* ancillary products). The first footage is a shot of Han Solo (Harrison Ford) at the controls, with Luke Skywalker (Mark Hamill) standing behind him, looking around the interior of a spaceship and saying, "Ready, everybody?" In quick succession the familiar characters are presented: R2-D2 answers with a techno chirp, and Han shouts "Chewy," (as we see Chewbacca) "let's see what this piece of junk can do." We then see Luke and C-3PO looking concerned, and as the music flares and the explosion sounds swell, we see several exterior space battle shots. C-3PO comments, "Here we go again!"[21]

Figure 5.3. Graphic from the trailer for
Return of the Jedi, with "Star Wars" logo border.

This opening works the imperative "Return!" into a more elaborate appeal to audiences' assumed desire to spend more time with this franchise's beloved characters (who are key to the cycle's generic appeal). The opening hyperdrive shot, which virtually sucks audiences into the film's vortex, is followed by shots of the film's characters acting as profilmic spectators (of the spectacle and adventure seen through the cockpit/screen) and offering commentary that reinforces parallels between the characters' entry into an adventure and that of the audience ("Ready, everybody?" "Here we go again!"). With the graphic logo's echoing of *Star Wars* toy packaging, audiences are moreover assumed to want to return not only to the film but to its ancillary world of products as well.

After this opening the trailer cuts to a series of action clips from the scene in Jabba's palace, as Luke (seen in full Jedi regalia for the first time) attempts to rescue his friends. The trailer cuts to Luke leaping up a diving plank (from the later scene on Jabba's barge) and the narrator reprises, "Return! To heroic adventure!" as a lightsaber shoots out of R2-D2's head and Luke flips in the air, catches the lightsaber, and leaps from one sand barge to another amid red laser fire. Han is seen in cliff-hanger fashion, dropping headfirst into the mouth of a creature buried in sand. The trailer jumps to the lightsaber battle, and the narrator reprises, "Return! to the ultimate confrontation." The opponents' lightsabers cross and the Emperor grins above, followed by a shot of C-3PO looking aghast (in a Kuleshovian kind of way . . .). The trailer cuts to a forest scene, as Leia rescues Han from storm troopers. He says, "I love you." Leia replies, "I know," offering audiences familiar with *The Empire Strikes Back* a dialogue exchange with a certain semiotic density as well as an in-joke.[22] The trailer then samples the forest battle: Ewoks swinging on vines attack storm troopers, a Scout Walker shooting Ewoks is hit from either side by two logs suspended on ropes. The narrator reprises, "Return! for the climactic chapter of the Star Wars saga."

The trailer's "climax" then begins, signaled by R2's chirp and C-3PO's editorial commentary, "Exciting is hardly the word I would choose," which serves both to communicate the character's apprehension and to summarize the film's appeal as a spectacle defying description. A speeder bike then flies through the forest, followed by a shot of Luke with Leia behind, on another bike. The narrator adds, "But most of all, return for the fun of it." They speed under a fallen log. The trailer cuts to a huge explosion on a space station, and the Millennium Falcon speeding away, followed by a reverse angle of the ship in space being pursued by an X-wing. The film's title is superimposed over this shot, leaving audiences poised in outer space, as the narrator concludes, "Return of the Jedi!" and the music comes to a crescendo.

The use of profilmic spectators as correlates to the audience's assumed spectatorial interest or vantage point, seen frequently in trailers throughout the sound era (as well as a strong genre convention of science fiction), is here institutionalized with the help of the droids' metacommentary. It is also, as has been argued, a pronounced feature of the films belonging to the genre of the "family adventure movie"— a genre that is currently "central both to the economics of the American film industry and to the moviegoing experiences of the American public."[23] Peter Krämer cites the endings of *Return of the Jedi*, *E.T. The Extra-Terrestrial* (1982), and *The Lion King* (1994) as scenes that exemplify intratextual invitations to a family audience to see itself on the screen as these "families," bidding farewell to the adventure and the film through literal farewell scenes, as they leave the theater for the reality of everyday family life. The *Return of the Jedi* trailer's various invitations and beckonings to the film's potential audience parallels this emphasis— here not on departure but on entry ("here we go again!"), thus luring spectators toward *future* participation in the film. These beckonings share qualities with such other forms of address inviting shared family adventure as advertisements for theme parks.[24]

Following the market-dominant lead of the family adventure movie (as cited above), the two points of entry Krämer cites (childish delight and adult self-awareness) are common to trailers of many New Hollywood–era genres. The ways in which and the extent to which this trailer assumes an audience "in the know" about this film cycle while appealing to the ever-repeatable novelty of childlike absorption is of interest as a feature of New Hollywood trailers as a whole (and especially those for genre films). The ease of the trailer's leaps around the film's various set pieces demonstrates assumptions that the audience cares more about the amount and dazzlement of the film's spectacle than its narrative comprehensibility. It demonstrates a primacy of appeals to interest in the familiar over product differentiation, reinforcing such appeals with reminders of repetition typical of sequel trailers ("return," "again").

The differentiation of Lucas's product had been achieved earlier in the cycle by such strategies as positioning the films as mythic space fantasies that fused archetypal storytelling ("a long time ago") with science fictional outer space settings (". . . in a galaxy far, far away"), and the work of the sequel trailers has been to promote their films through assumptions that audiences want more of the same—of *these* films that are like no others (yet still bear marks of genre). Familiarity and differentiation are redoubled by the promotion of this cycle that "wants" so much *not* to be part of a genre that it reinscribes generic appeals on a number of levels anyway. Like the *Duel in the Sun* "moments," the things for which the narration implies audiences are assumed to want to return are enumerated as hyperbolic consumable elements and structures of feeling, here combining appeals to the rhetoric of genre and that of story: "a galaxy far, far away" (a generic place), "heroic adventure" (generic action with a mythic dimension), "the ultimate confrontation" (a plot point), "the climactic chapter of the Star Wars saga" (a major plot point), and "the fun of it" (a feeling).

By privileging these familiar—and novel—elements, the *Return of the Jedi* trailer thus reinforces the boundaries of Lucas's space fantasy cycle (as at once science fiction films and something else) as well as the family adventure genre as a whole, in the process strengthening its market position. By appealing to families, and addressing (assumed) nostalgia-obsessed adults at the same time as children's (assumed) capacity for delight and absorption through these structures of feeling, the trailer also expresses the social space of the 1980s–1990s, where family structures and family dynamics were increasingly invoked in various public discourses in order to subsume social systems and social relations to private ones—and in the process to create a "kinder and gentler" capitalism in the public imaginary, masking the increasing dehumanization of the postindustrial global corporate climate.[25]

THUNDERHEART (Contemporary Story Rhetoric)

The *Thunderheart* (1992)[26] trailer, for a thriller in which an Indian FBI agent (Val Kilmer) who has denied his cultural heritage is sent to a reservation to solve a murder,[27] is a well-executed example of the way contemporary trailers privilege appeals to audience interest in story (specifically plot enigma and characterization) while integrally incorporating appeals to interest in genre and stars as well.[28] The trailer represents a familiar contemporary trailer mode (initiated, as discussed earlier, during the transitional era): the minimovie. In the minimovie, a film's narrative trajectory may be chronologically presented in sophisticated high concept terms (such as a minimal amount of extracted dialogue that succinctly states the film's clear and simple premises, interspersed with judiciously placed close-ups and action clips in rapid montages, often significantly featuring grids) usually with the aid of a voice-over narrator and/or a strong musical accompaniment, while key plot resolutions are withheld. While typical in many ways of contemporary trailers, this one goes further than many in its attempt to present issues of individual and cultural identity in the process of promoting a film, and is thus interesting to consider in relation to its assumed audiences.

The *Thunderheart* trailer begins with a prologue of evocative, silhouetted and slow-motion scenes of what appear to be Indian ritual activity (but which are actually shots of a murder taking place). This is followed by the narrator setting up the film's premise—"They sent him to a foreign land . . . in the middle of America . . . to uncover the truth"—and a dialogue scene (an FBI briefing) that is intercut with aerial shots of the southwestern landscape and clips of Kilmer driving to the reservation. This opening grid lays out expository information and samples the film's visual texture at the same time. The rest of the trailer is textured by an expanded grid (in which several scenes are reprised more than once) that alternates between a number of short action scenes and one-line dialogue scenes ("Look, it's the Washington Redskin"; "You must be the Indian FBI"; "They're not my people"; "You had yourself a vision"); one longer dialogue scene played for comic effect and to establish the relationship between Kilmer and Graham Greene (the Native American sidekick); various atmospheric shots of Native American rituals and mysteries and the main character's spiritual visions; and scenes that lay out more familiar images of detective thriller enigmas (where did the body come from, who did it, and so on).

Figures 5.4 and 5.5. Expository information and visual texture crosscut in a grid from the *Thunderheart* trailer.

The trailer privileges the identity struggle of the "Indian FBI" protagonist, who is shown being ridiculed by the people on the reservation as the narrator informs us that "Now, to find the truth, he must face the mystery within himself."[29] Such alternations shape a rhetorical appeal that links the issue of spiritual identity to the murder mystery. The enthymeme, "He's got to solve a murder; at the same time, he's got to find himself," contains a missing term: "So his quest is really not so different from yours." The rhetoric is based on the assumption that character identification interests the audience more than cultural knowledge, but that both of these can enhance audience interest in the murder plot's resolution (while prominently displaying good old murder mystery codes for those who couldn't relate to the trailer's cross-cultural appeals).

The trailer tantalizes with scenes of spiritual realities (which are often indicated to be the Kilmer character's visions) and uses sound overlaps (a staple of trailer rhetoric by the 1990s, usually for their capacity to provide a pseudonarration) to further problematize the physical reality of its images. Miragelike shots of the Indians who used to roam the canyons where police helicopters now cruise are intercut with Kilmer's multidimensional quest for truth. The drama of the juxtaposition and equation of two kinds of mystery is evoked with a sound overlap of fellow FBI man Sam Shepard speaking over a shimmering long shot of a circle of Indians in traditional costume: "We can't get suckered into that. We're here to take our man and go home." As he completes the line, the trailer cuts to a shot of him opening a Coke. This equation, drawing on shared assumptions about Coca-Cola as a signifier of both modernity (vs. tradition) and American-ness (the FBI man drinks Coke in a "foreign land . . . in the middle of America") in addition to the aforementioned Western generic conventions, presents an updated image of the lone lawman conquering the (narrative) space of the other. The trailer creates a dynamic impression of Native American spirituality (through editing in one particular series of shots, we see: a Native American leaping away from gunfire; a woman telling Kilmer that "he can shapeshift . . . into different animals,"[30] and then Kilmer whirling to see a buck leaping away into the bushes).

The relationship between the film's message of finding one's identity by following one's heart and the quest to solve a murder mystery is condensed into an attractively promoted visual drama in this trailer. Touristic images of the other and the land are counterpoised with a protagonist who is attempting to come to terms with the other within himself, amplifying the sense of mystery as a mystery of identity (in the sense of a quest for roots) that is subjectively experienced by contemporary audiences without regard to ethnicity. Hollywood's familiar ideological project of despecifying cultural histories is here turned on its head: this trailer posits cultural specificity as the key to finding identity by juxtaposing a condensed presentation of the film's fairly standard cop thriller suspense codes with Native American spiritual imagery.

This trailer's use of Western iconography, partly by its reversal of the standard Western hierarchy of cowboys and Indians, asserts that cultural roots are spatially localized and locatable within a multicultural American landscape. As Robert Burgoyne has claimed, *Thunderheart* uses the discourse of the Western to critique conventional Western ideologies and bring the "genre memory" of the Western to bear on a "war myth that can be transposed and reenacted from the perspective of the margins."[31] Burgoyne's discussion of the film explores the ways narrative and generic conventions are evoked in order to be subverted or reinscribed in a re-visioning of nationalities and community in the contemporary United States. The trailer thus participates in this reinscription, albeit in a minor way, rhetorically privileging audiences' identification with the character's search for identity, opening with juxtapositions of the Western landscape with the U.S. Capitol to dramatize the contradictions the character feels, and presenting its own narrative trajectory of the character's ethnic awakening.

Conventional Hollywood representations of Indians seem resolved or "healed" by the trailer's representation of the character's quest for identity, even as such conventions are maintained.[32] In the trailer, all these elements are couched within the principal promotional trope of withholding the solution to the film's mystery. The trailer teases the audience with the promise that the film, through Kilmer's character, will "uncover the truth," a truth that involves more the actualization of identity than it does the solving of a crime—and even less any resolution of the economic and cultural crisis of that "foreign land . . . in the middle of America" that is the source of Kilmer's disavowal.

By privileging audience identification with both aspects of Kilmer's search, this trailer assumes audience epistephilia in the form of desire for self-knowledge. This incorporates (like the *Bad Day at Black Rock* trailer) knowledge of the secrets of the other—now figured as an other within—as well as knowledge as the path to truth: here, not "the Truth," but *a* truth. With its emphasis on the equation between solving the mystery and Kilmer's internal transformation, the trailer implicitly assumes that "truth" can only be a partial one, a truth of subjectivity and identity—

not exactly a ready "hook" on which to hang a film's promotion for a mass audience. Like other examples of the rhetoric of story, the trailer calls attention to other stories than that of the film it promotes, illustrating by the desires it assumes on the part of audiences some of the values of different kinds of cultural knowledge according to the contemporary Hollywood film production industry. And although the *Thunderheart* trailer in many ways (like the film) wouldn't be considered typical, its construction of the search for knowledge as a personal quest does, in the end, typify the epistephilia contemporary trailers ascribe to audiences: one that is overwhelmingly centered on self and the individualization or privatization of social discourse.

AIR FORCE ONE (Contemporary Star Rhetoric)

In the trailer for *Air Force One* (1997),[33] Harrison Ford's star image of grim-faced patriotic righteousness, honed through a career that has moved from playfully defeating an evil empire (in the *Star Wars* series) to dolefully protecting various families from various multinational terrorists (in the Tom Clancy series), is brought to bear in promoting an action film that trumpets the satisfactions of watching the president of the United States kick ass. The quintessentially star-based trailer assumes an audience ready to ogle Ford's masculine potency in the service of American national security. It's also a typically wishful trailer for an era in which it is increasingly difficult to discern the forces that actually rule the country and the planet. In this post–Cold War fairy tale, the trailer reassures us, stars will win the war for us—even when there isn't one being fought (and unlike the star emphasis in the *Yankee Doodle Dandy* trailer, it won't be because they dance).

The trailer opens with choir music over the Columbia logo, followed by a voice-over news announcer over soft-edged small square black-and-white images framed by black within the larger film frame to make them look like TV news footage. The images (a Kennedy-at-Dallas-like montage of Ford and family departing Moscow) and a collage of news announcers' voices present exposition explaining that Air Force One and the president may be at risk. This introduction's use of smaller screen and black-and-white images, reconfigured from film footage especially for the trailer to signify television news, elides technology by slapping on the barest of conventional indicators that what we're seeing should be taken as television. Yet this works because TV as a small-screen black-and-white phenomenon (compared to film) is still a shared commonplace of cinema spectators, even though by the nineties it is usually watched in color on a big screen. References to CNN and the use of female newscasters helps to keep the paradoxically "retro" TV image anchored in the present day, allowing the segment to get a great deal of exposition out of the way rapidly. The opening is typical of contemporary trailers' frequent use of graphics to reconfigure the cinematic image. It also sets up the trailer's overdetermination of appeals to audience interest in Ford's celebrity—as he waves at his admirers regally on a small screen, his image is established as doubly watchable (we're watching a favorite star who is being watched by millions on television as a popular president).

The trailer fades to black, overlapped by Glenn Close's voice (she plays the vice president), then we see her in full frame and full color standing at a podium with the presidential seal behind her, saying, "Ladies and gentlemen, I have a statement. The president's plane, Air Force One, has been hijacked." Close's image fades to one of the plane flying toward us, and we hear jet sound effects. The film title enters the frame from the front as huge letters, which shrink as the title is positioned in the frame, followed by another, "From the director of *In the Line of Fire*."[34] As each title zooms into position we hear a thumping/slamming sound effect, a typical accompaniment to contemporary-era action trailer titles, serving to remind us that loud, dramatic, violent sounds will be heard in this film (somewhat as trailer graphics cue audiences to expect the dazzlement of visual spectacle).

The fact that the first full-screen image is of Glenn Close standing in for the missing president cues us to Close's importance to the promotion of the film within the rhetoric of stardom—which at first seems paradoxical given Ford's importance to the trailer's rhetoric. At once a "thinking woman's" star in Hollywood terms (*The Big Chill* [1983], *Dangerous Liaisons* [1988], *Reversal of Fortune* [1990], and *Hamlet* [1990]) and a genre actress (*Fatal Attraction* [1987], *101 Dalmatians* [1996], and *Mars Attacks* [1996]), Close's presence connotes *serious acting* along with a game accessibility and enables the male-oriented action trailer to offer "something for the women." Audiences are thus primed to watch themselves be governed by a hyperbolically "presidential" male-female star team that is configured as an ideal set of cultural "parents" (the trailer's figuration of Ford's fictional family notwithstanding).

The trailer's next segment is a rapid-fire montage of brief action shots on the plane that establish the danger the president is in, utilizing

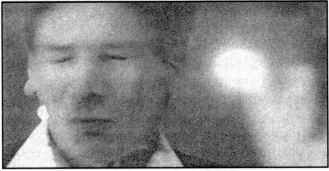

Figures 5.6 and 5.7. The *Air Force One* trailer: the vice president
(Glenn Close) announces that *Air Force One* has been hijacked (5.6);
the president (Harrison Ford) is pummeled (5.7).

the rhetorics of story (for the expository elements) and genre (the rapid
visuals and loud sounds cueing audiences to expect an action film). As
we see terrorists burst into a room, we hear a sound overlap of Ford's
voice, "You know who I am?" followed by Ford in close-up, his hands
raised in surrender. "I'm the *president* of the United States!" Gary Oldham
socks him. This clip seems to have been designed to be inserted into a
trailer, both for its shock value and as a gag: in the contradictory environment of the trailer exhibition experience it is somehow possible to
offer audiences an illicit laugh at Ford's expense without detracting from
the seriousness of his predicament—it serves to remind audiences that
"it's only a movie" (i.e., audiences might answer him, "No, you're not!
You're Harrison Ford and you get socked by bad guys all the time!").

The violence to Ford continues as a grid of clips of Oldham beating
him up and threatening his family, with Ford reacting abjectly, interspersed with scenes of the vice president meeting with other leaders to
resolve the situation. The segment ends with a close-up of his wife and

daughter, followed by a close-up of Ford's pained face as he is grabbed away from them and shoved up against an instrument panel. The shot lingers on him reacting, as a tense ambient jetlike noise is heard over, and the trailer cuts to black with Harrison Ford's identificatory title zooming into position with a swooshing thump. It lingers as Close's voice begins gravely, "I would like to ask (we then see her at the podium) *all* Americans . . . to pray for the safety of everyone (the trailer fades to black) on board Air Force One."

In this segment, any hint of humor at Ford's plight is erased by the violence of the montage and the striking powerlessness of the pummeled president. It is as if the trailer is compelled to enact the repetition of every body blow in order to convince audiences, assumed to have faith in Ford's (and in the president's) overarching might, that this superstar's character is really in danger. In this context, Glenn Close's scenes seem positioned to offer a countervailing sense of security—a vice president whose nineties career-girl femininity authoritatively, yet nurturingly, gathers the anxious profilmic audience (here "*all* Americans") for a spiritual group hug.[35] The trailer's depiction of the terrorist threat to the American way of life in the nineties is endowed with a Rocky Balboa viscerality as the president, who in the figure of Ford is a signifier at once of national identity and hyperbolic masculine potency, is put at risk in the most vivid of ways. Yet Close's vice president, the yin to Ford's yang, keeps the cultural family system together through it all. Such incorporations of assumptions about audience patriotism within action trailer dynamics are typical of nineties trailers, where male stars are often called into service to personify national might.

Sound effects of a jet engine and percussive action music accompany the trailer's final action montage, a cascade of redemptive presidential violence, paratroopers, fisticuffs, gun action, and depressurized air dangers (giving away much of the ending, as is typical of trailers by this time). The sound quiets, and the film title appears in a black field, at first as just a row of lines, then like soldiers at attention the letters turn and face front (with a swooshing sound effect), again demonstrating the extent to which contemporary trailers' graphic motifs echo classical ones (in which, as we have seen, titles turning, flipping and flopping into view were common). The letters grow, then fade to black and there is silence for a long beat, followed by a shot of Ford slamming a terrorist with a metal stool, accompanied by violent sound effects and the man's yell. Ford looks at the man. The trailer cuts to black, and a title reads "This summer."

The rhythmic following of the trailer's climactic montage with a brief violent coda is an increasingly common convention of contemporary action trailers that was probably innovated by the trailer for *Twister* (1996).[36] In that case, after the trailer seemingly concludes, displaying the final title, it resumes again with another shot of a truck hurtling at the screen, accompanied by a final loud swooshing thump. In this case, the shot is assumed to offer audiences, whom the trailer has just taken on an emotional roller-coaster ride, a satisfyingly macho closure that yet (since it is tagged on—or "trails"—after the trailer's ostensible ending) invites audiences to anticipate the *next* sensation—that is, seeing the film itself.

While the trailer takes pains to offer bigendered star turns that depict a nineties world seemingly safe for feminism (in which a woman *can* be vice president), this coda emphatically validates the ultimate primacy of the gut-punching "yang" of masculine star power. In addition to its anticipatory promotional function, the final shot structures within it a rhetorical assumption that the male audience will appreciate—and perhaps need—extra validation in order to be convinced to see a film in which the male star takes such a beating. Within this trailer's melodrama of stardom, the montages' frequent and rapid juxtaposition of shots of the (intertextually multivalent superstar) president and (intertextually multivalent superstar) vice president results in the trailer providing a sense of American government as a symbolic cultural family unit consisting of an appropriately familial (and familiar) balance of potency and nurturance.

MEN IN BLACK (Contemporary Story Rhetoric)

The trailer for *Men in Black* (1997),[37] a popular genre-bending science fiction comedy about a squad of cops who police extraterrestrial aliens, typifies the contemporary era's seamless integration of the three rhetorical appeals (to genre, story and stardom). Essentially, however, it relies more on story information than genre identity to sell the film, while promoting also Will Smith's post–*Independence Day* (1996) star turn. Like many contemporary trailers, it falls into several "acts," which in this case are structured to privilege audience interest in the film's narrative causality. It moves from teasing audiences with enigmatic images of what the "men in black" do, to addressing the question of whether Will Smith will join up with them, to watching how he joins up, to celebrating what it's like to be a "man in black," and finally, to delivering a high concept punch line stating the trailer's description of what the "men" do. It incorporates titles and other graphics as well as a narrator, in addition to a heavy use of sound overlaps and nondiegetic dialogue as de facto narration. Typical of blockbuster high concept trailers of the late nineties, it demonstrates the extent to which many such contemporary trailers have evolved into reconfigured versions of the classical era's highly layered promotional messages (and have moved away from the transitional era's attempt to downplay the hard sell with a bare-bones "slice of the movie" approach). Where once there were wipes, now there are percussive sound effects. But titles and narration have become prominent again, in reconfigured forms. Yet by combining an appeal to audience interest in narrative causality (things happen) with a quintessentially postmodern attitude of irony (nothing matters), the trailer reveals some of the contradictions of the ironic promotional dimension of contemporary popular culture.

The trailer's opening "act" begins with an unidentifiable generic trailer sound effect, like a "shoop," accompanying a light flash that leaves a white-on-black title, "MORE SECRETIVE THAN THE CIA," which then recedes. A series of clips of Tommy Lee Jones busting a van full of undocumented aliens (one of whom is revealed to be an extraterrestrial alien in human disguise) ensues. His voice is heard in voice-over, a de facto narration: "We work for a highly funded yet unofficial government agency." A big round blue and white light flash punctuates the trailer, receding and leaving another title: "MORE POWERFUL THAN THE FBI." As we see a tracking shot over a collection of alien weapons, we hear Tommy Lee Jones's voice again, "narrating" in an overly deadpan professional voice[38] that "Our mission is to monitor extraterrestrial activity on earth."

A title flashes: "AND THEY'RE LOOKING FOR A FEW GOOD MEN," inaugurating the second segment, in which Will Smith is introduced, being recruited by Jones and Rip Torn. Smith laughs at Torn's recruitment speech, and Torn asks, "What's so funny, Edwards?" Smith: "I got *no clue* why we're here." Smith's laugh and line immediately position his character as (like the audience) a bemused (entertained) outsider. Next Jones walks Smith to a coffee room where several small aliens carouse, and he converses with them briefly in jocular coworker fashion. Will Smith, watching, says, "All right, I'm in." The juxtaposition of Jones's casual cop competency with the outlandishness of the aliens is both funny and intriguing (in that they are not necessarily "bad guys"), and audiences, assumed to identify with Smith, are at this point also "in"—

that is, assumed to be recruited to see the film. Like the "Here we go again!" line in the *Return of the Jedi* trailer, such extracted lines of dialogue in contemporary trailers serve both to promote film-specific elements and to address audiences (indirectly) about spectatorship, offering contemporary variations on the earlier "See!" or "Feel!" (*direct address*) rhetoric.

Another flash is followed by a title: "THEY ARE THE MEN IN BLACK," opening the trailer's third segment. The erasure of Smith's identity is explained, and as we see an extreme close-up of sunglasses being put into a tailored jacket pocket, Jones's voice-over says, "We are the men in black." The two are seen in natty black suits, as we hear Smith's voice-over, "You know what the difference is between you and me?" Smith, in close-up with his sunglasses on, says, "I make this look good." Smith, as the *black* man in black, thus adds a cool factor to the film's characterological and star dynamics, and the moment serves as a comic aside to African-American audiences, assuming and asserting (through the rhetoric of stardom) that the film holds special appeal for them while also amusing whites (a feat of which Will Smith's prior box-office success had proved him capable). Paradoxically, the trailer asserts that all audiences can "be" the "few good men"—at the movies.[39]

In a pawnshop, a set of gun racks mechanically flips over to reveal alien weaponry. Jones: "Series four, de-atomizer." Jones hands Smith a large gun. "Now that's what I'm talkin' about." (Smith's line, with its inclusion of a hip African-American catchphrase, adds another aside to that portion of the film's assumed audience.) He then hands Smith a tiny gun, disappointing him. Smith is then seen flying through the air from the small gun's kickback. We hear Rip Torn in voice-over: "Aw, it gets better," a line of extracted dialogue that serves as a sort of aural wipe, transitioning the trailer to its fourth "act." This third segment, with its figuration of "cool" and its inclusion of the size joke, reinforces the film's eponymous masculinity as hyperbolically smooth yet paradoxically threatened (to become a "man" one must lose one's identity and be assigned a small, powerful yet destabilizing weapon), thus promoting the film's fittingly contradictory, nineties definition of manhood.

A spaceship crash-lands on a truck at night, and Rip Torn announces, "We had an unauthorized landing somewhere in upstate New York." Smith comments wryly, continuing his role in the trailer as a commentator able to step outside the narrative trajectory, "Aw, that can't be good." At the scene, Jones asks Smith, "I don't suppose you know what kind of alien leaves a green spectral trail and craves sugar water, do you?" Smith: "Uh, that was on Final Jeopardy last night." We see a very frightening alien in a pit with its jaws open menacingly and each man removes his sunglasses from his pocket and puts them on. Both Jones and Smith[40] are endowed with attitudinal postures that shift audiences' genre expectations—even large, scary aliens are funny.

A narrator begins, "This summer . . . ," as we see a side angle of both men in a car; Jones says, "Fasten your seat belt" (implicitly continuing the narrator's address to the audience). The car goes up the side of a tunnel wall to skirt around other cars. The narrator continues, "Columbia Pictures and Amblin Entertainment present . . ." Clips from a scene wherein Linda Fiorentino discovers the alien inside the man's body are shown, and she accurately guesses what the men in black are, as Smith protests, "Naw, sh——." Will Smith's wry clowning becomes a literal, if humorous, ironic disavowal of any authenticity or truth to his identity as a "man in black." Tommy Lee Jones's and Will Smith's identificatory titles accompany clips from a comical scene in which a pawnshop proprietor's head is apparently shot off by Jones, then regrows, and a clip of Smith asking a humanlike alien (whose eyes, however, blink only within the iris), "What the hell are you?" Further titles read: "In a new film / from the director of The Addams Family, and Get Shorty."

Clips from the final spaceship scene are shown, and we see a montage of shots of the men's hands reaching inside jackets for guns, then cocking their guns, and kicking a door open, becoming silhouetted in a doorway. The narrator says, "Men in Black . . . Protecting the earth from the scum of the universe"—a tagline that encapsulates the film's comic hybridization of science fiction and *Dragnet*-like police genre films. The doorway recedes and becomes a graphic "I" forming part of a larger graphic spelling "MIB." We see Smith in medium shot, low angle, holding a big gun, who (now a fully engaged "man in black") says, "Step away from your busted-ass vehicle and put your hands on your head." There is a reverse-angle shot of a large buglike alien flopping down from above, roaring, followed by a date title and logos. The music comes to a *Dragnet*-like close.

The trailer's trajectory of segments that configure the film's story as a narrative of Will Smith's "joining up" while highlighting his ironic apathy about his position right up until the final clip creates an interesting dynamic within the rhetoric of story (inflected by the rhetoric of stardom). His ironic attitude (prior to the final "busted-ass" line) is assumed to be appealing to audiences (who are assumed to want something new and sophisticated in science fiction),[41] even as the story is promoted as

Figures 5.8 and 5.9. The *Men in Black* trailer—the final transition of film image into logo: "Protecting the earth from the scum of the universe."

a process of his coming to care and to enlist. In the context of a trailer that also displays the film's hip and comic, postmodern, generic hybridity and sophisticated special effects, the character/star's attitude contributes to the trailer's articulation of some of the contradictory ideological dimensions of postmodern popular culture. While the character is shown being convinced to become a "man in black" he is simultaneously shown not to care about or believe in much of anything.

Thus, Smith's ultimate display of a hyperbolic police-state posture (coded as humorous) as he stands holding his (now big) gun and confronts an offscreen intergalactic outlaw raises the question of what, indeed, is there to believe in? And the trailer has answered this question with its tagline—"Protecting the earth from the scum of the universe," which figures an intergalactic (and multiracial) police state where questions such as How do we determine who is "scum"? are elided by the naturalization of a multiracial fascism against extraterrestrial aliens—all, of course, "in fun."[42] This trailer's contradictory address encompasses among other things an assumption that audiences (including, significantly, African-American ones) might desire a story that subtextually asserts that police states might be okay, if the job can be carried out with an appropriately arch sense of humor.[43] While the innovative film it promotes is also truly funny, the trailer demonstrates that it is always worth examining these forms of "postmodern fun" within popular promotional discourses for the ideological implications of the contradictory attitudes they assume of audiences.

PSYCHO (Contemporary Genre Rhetoric)

The trailer for the remake of Hitchcock's *Psycho* (1998)[44] is remarkable as an innovative yet typical contemporary trailer that can be seen as an apotheosis of the rhetoric of genre's core enthymeme: "You want familiarity *and* novelty." Its job is to sell a film that is a shot-for-shot reproduction of Hitchcock's classic horror film (1960), and it does so by appealing both to cinephiles (who want to see something novel done with a familiar Hitchcock film) and genre fans (who, more typically, want to see a new story that fits within a familiar genre). While the film it promotes was unsuccessful, this trailer is paradigmatic of postmodern New Hollywood's self-referentiality, incorporating assumptions of audience knowledge of Hollywood history and genres. Furthermore, the trailer is exemplary of the "new breed" of sophisticated montage artistry in the contemporary trailer industry.

As with many trailers for highly quotational postmodern films, it's clear that both sophisticated audiences (assumed to have substantial knowledge of film history as well as a strong interest in nostalgia) and younger horror fans (who may never have seen the original film) are being addressed. The combination results in the trailer's pushing a number of Hitchcock and horror buttons in the process of generating audience fear of the new Norman Bates (played by Vince Vaughn), a monster whose difference from Anthony Perkins's Norman the trailer strongly asserts.[45] Hollywood didn't know what to make of Gus Van Sant's decision to do not just a remake, but a virtual shot-for-shot reproduction of Hitchcock's master work. The buzz during production was highly skeptical, and the film was scoffed at by Hollywood pundits as the latest example of the cynical truism that there are no new stories.[46] Van Sant, a respected independent who had accelerated his Hollywood credibility enormously the previous year with the Oscar triumph of *Good Will Hunting*, was now in a prime position, having both the budget and the artistic sanction, to do something innovative within the popular film market.[47]

It is a visually striking trailer, probably containing more shots than any other trailer of its length; and at least one of its innovations, the defacement of the studio logo, has been taken up by several subsequent trailers since the film's release.[48] As the trailer opens with the Universal logo and accompanying static sounds, the globe and lettering (versions of which we associate with many past Hitchcock films, albeit not the original *Psycho*) apparently freezes and burns at the edges. Then altered images of the logo are seen, solarized, distorted and in Day-Glo colors, followed by flashes of the familiar circled numbers of Academy leader, which then appear to fly off the sprockets. This logo-defacement asserts the film's novelty, while serving somewhat like the irreverent pie throw in the classical era's *Day at the Races* trailer. The studio logo is generally perceived as an untouchable icon and reliable (contractual) "brand-identifier" of all trailers.[49] Its destruction invites audiences to

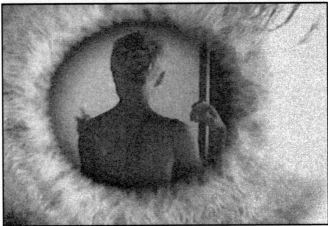

Figures 5.10 and 5.11. The Universal Studios logo distorted
(5.10) and a shot from the final trailer-specific shower
scene montage (5.11) from the *Psycho* (1998) trailer.

look at the trailer as an upending of cinematic expectations, an apparent dethronement of the promotional message that yet banks on the audience registering the striking images and the brand attachment of the logo perhaps even more for the harsh treatment it gets.

The first image of the trailer "proper" arrives, a black title with white sans serif letters at screen left reading "This is the FACE of Norman Bates." We then see Vince Vaughn as Norman in medium long shot from the film's final scene—wrapped in a blanket. The trailer cuts to a close-up of him looking up at the camera with his head bowed and smiling. The eerie static sounds have settled into droning electronic sounds, with an undercurrent of "Mother's" voice mumbling, and Norman's face freezes and "burns" away from the heat of the projector bulb. After another blackout, the title reads "This is the MIND of Norman Bates."

The radio static continues, as we see a rapid-fire montage of almost subliminal images (each gets just a couple of frames), interspersed with black-and-white TV static, sometimes colorized. The nondiegetic images of knives, screaming faces and other objectifications of murderous thoughts are each seen barely long enough to be consciously registered. The equation of this mildly disturbing montage with Norman Bates's disembodied mind encompasses an assumption that audiences believe that the contents of not only Norman's but perhaps all our minds are metaphorically comprised of a string of images, in Norman's case significantly including *media* static. Of course, the trailer's conceit is that Norman's mind consists of more disturbing images than those the rest of us might carry, enabling the trailer to assert in classic genre terms the horror monster's difference from the rest of humankind. At the same time, Norman's apparent normalcy is, as it was in the original, part of the horror, and this assumption that minds are containers for images could apply equally to the minds of both the postmodern cinephiles and the young MTV-fed audiences the trailer addresses.

Another white-on-black title appears, "On Dec. 4," after which we see Vince Vaughn's eye at a peephole, followed by another title: "Discover the world of Norman Bates." Vaughn turns to look at the camera, standing by the lake. Then begins a segment of quick-cut expository shots of no more than a couple of seconds each, most of which are familiar to viewers of the original *Psycho*, such as Julianne Moore's character walking toward the house, the close-up from above of the trysting couple in bed, and a close-up of Vaughn at the peephole. He is then seen seated in the motel room with the stuffed birds, saying, "Well, a boy's best friend is his mother." More shots of Vaughn are interspersed with generic horror images such as lightning and a black bird in flight out a window, then there is a sound overlap of Vaughn's voice: "She just, uh . . . ," as we see clips from the staircase scene, with William Macy being attacked by "Mother," and we hear his voice again, "she just goes a little mad sometimes." We see him in the motel room, followed by solarized shots of his eye at the peephole.

Each of these images from the body of the film "sells" at once the original version, Van Sant's artistry in quoting Hitchcock and a brand-new horror film. The clips appear to have been selected to integrate Hitchcock set-piece moments for the cinephiles (the lovers in bed, the POV shot walking to the house, the eye at the peephole, the overhead shot of "Mother" at the top of the stairs) with generic (indeed, clichéd) horror moments to reassure the genre fans (the lightning, the bird flying out the window) and technical wizardry such as the solarization and sound effects to signify artistry and the sheer spectacular appeal of the film. Again and still, the rhetoric of genre promotes "something for everyone." The clips also sell "the world of Norman Bates," characterizing him, "Mother," and his famous Bates Motel as more Halloween-haunted-house scary than the actual film does, the latter trading more on the terror of not knowing what's concealed beneath the placid surfaces of Norman's personality.

The punctuation of the lightning signals the trailer's "crescendo," a series of even shorter shots based on the motif of the peephole and the shower scene, a rather sophisticated sequence comprising close-ups of the eyeball and drain, where the eyeball becomes an iris through which can be seen Anne Heche's torso as Vaughn sees it through the peephole, along with other short shots from the shower scene. The segment compresses, underlines, and fetishizes the film's emphasis on eyes and looking. The camera pulls back and an eye is superimposed over the drain, the dark pupil in the place of the drain. The drain shot recedes, the pupil contracts, the eye blinks and the screen is black as Vaughn shouts, "Mother! Oh God, *Mother!*" This montage pays homage to all that's Hitchcockian[50] and at the same time evokes (for the Hitch neophytes) the pure horror of being watched and vulnerable in the shower.

With a percussive sound like a heavy metal or stone door slamming,[51] the trailer cuts to an extreme close-up of Vaughn's smiling face. The camera quickly pulls back, then cuts to a graphic of the film title in white on black (which splits horizontally like the original film's credits). More titles follow, then more shots of Vaughn's face, and the slamming noise repeats as the final date title appears.

The climactic series of clips involving the eye and the peephole joins the trailer's opening segment in offering stylistically innovative and somewhat abstract trailer set pieces that overtly promote cinematic artistry by exemplifying it—not by showing pretty images out of context, but by creating, in the first instance, a montage that includes specially shot images, and in the second, a REM-like meditation on vision and looking that belongs to the trailer alone. In combination with the rest of the trailer's emphasis on imparting knowledge of this horror film's "monster," Norman Bates (including a juxtaposition of the voice of "Mother" with Vaughn's face that gives away their fused identity), these innovations ultimately demonstrate the primacy of the trailer's appeal to audiences already in the know—the postmodern cinephiles over the first-time viewers of *Psycho*. Yet because of the makeup of the contemporary movie market, the appeal to cinephiles does not come off as an elitist ploy: *Psycho* (1998) may be a special case, but promoting its particular form of repetition also appeals to audien-ces interested in repeat viewing in general, an increasingly common phenomenon in the contemporary era even when not for a remake or re-creation of a classic film. Repeat viewing, moreover, tends to be associated with *genre* films. Even this most innovative of trailers is steeped in the rhetoric of genre's core assumption that audiences want any cinematic novelty to be couched within strongly familiar terms.

Thus, the sophistication of the trailer belies its promotional mes-sage—complex cinematic innovation is, contradictorily, packaged as a "fun ride." For all its multiple rapid-fire images, the *Psycho* (1998) trailer says basically, "Norman Bates is scary. Mother is scary. This is a hip hor-ror film," and to the repeat viewers, "You remember these great scenes." The trailer makes no attempt to enlighten audiences about the film's his-torical context or inform audiences as to why Hollywood film history is worth paying homage to or even knowing. Rather, it lays out that histo-ry as a series of intertextual visual references that appeal primarily to audience interest in seeing a film that quotes an earlier film within the same genre. Film-historical knowledge is packaged by this trailer's appeals to interest in novelty couched within familiarity as merely "value added" for *some* audiences, not celebrated as the defining component and the very condition of this film's existence as a hip generic horror film.

ENTRAPMENT
(Contemporary Star Rhetoric)

The trailer for *Entrapment* (1999),[52] an action-adventure film starring Sean Connery and Catherine Zeta-Jones, instantiates contempo-rary global trailer production practice as well-oiled machine. The trail-er's principal rhetorical appeal is to audience interest in its stars and their pairing, couched within story and genre appeals (as in most con-temporary trailers, the appeals are well integrated within one another, but stardom is still the dominant appeal here). The principal enthymeme of the trailer is introduced as we watch the 20th Century Fox and Regency logos while hearing Sean Connery's distinctive Scots accent in a voice-over pseudonarration quoting a familiar line: "Oh, what a tan-gled web we weave, when first we practice to deceive."[53] The first image after the logo is a schematized black-and-white shot of a dark tangle of wooden beams and a silhouetted male torso behind it, looking at a

Figures 5.12 and 5.13. The "perfect" graphic motif in the *Entrapment* trailer.

projection of an indecipherable text or formula. This image fades to a graphic of the word "PERFECT" in large soft-edged letters, over which a smaller line of white-on-black text is then superimposed: "Then again, practice makes perfect." This audiovisual amalgam of call-and-response truisms forms an enthymeme ("Deception messes everything up; but not if we do it well") that contains a missing term: the assumption that for movie audiences eager to watch a caper film, expertise transcends ethics. This rhetoric, like the remainder of the trailer, assumes audiences will find the deceptive relationship between the two principal stars the most appealing aspect of the adventure.

By 1999, typical contemporary trailers are able to utilize spoken dialogue from a film so efficiently as de facto narration that this film's terse extracted lines seem almost written for the trailer. The spoken words in the trailer following Connery's opening quote consist exclusively of the following lines of dialogue: "This was seventy stories up with smart glass windows." "This is classic Mac." "He's a wealthy guy. Doesn't have to steal anymore." "Do you think this guy steals because he has to?" "We sent a couple of guys after him." "They were both *men*." "Why are you following me?" "I've got a proposition for you." "Rule Number One: How do I know that you're not a cop?" "I'm a thief." "Rule Number Two: Never trust a naked woman." "You *are* keeping it strictly business, right Mac?" "What is this 'stuff' we are downloading?" "The loot, my dear, is right in there." "First we try." "Then we trust." "Yes!!!" "Has there ever been anyone you couldn't seduce?" "No." "Did he take the bait?" "You're the most beautiful crook I've ever seen!" "You change partners, you change the rules." "Nice try." "Mac does the job." "The job was a cover." "You were playing both sides!" "I watch Mac's back." "This is called entrapment!" "No, actually it's called blackmail. Entrapment is what cops do to thieves. You coming?" "AAAAAAAA!" "HOLD ON!!!"

The trailer's visual structure relies almost equally on clips of the two principals (along with a few of Zeta-Jones's police colleague Will Patton and Connery's sidekick Ving Rhames) and action images of the high-tech, corporate skyscraper environment in which the caper takes place. The lines are largely spoken by seen characters, in clips from dialogue scenes that are interwoven with the many quick-cut action shots by utilizing sound overlaps. The graphics return three more times to continue the "perfect" motif: letters form out of numbers (ones and zeros, communicating through the rhetoric of genre that the caper is a computer-based, high-tech one) in a narrow horizontal line that bisects the screen in pseudowipes three times, reading: "perfect partners" (after the line "They were both *men*"), then "perfect crime" (after Rhames's "strictly business" line) and finally "perfect trap" (after a shot of twin skyscrapers connected by a narrow bridge, accompanied by Catherine Zeta-Jones's line "The loot, my dear, is right in there"). The same typeface and wipelike structure is used for the subsequent cast identification titles, which do not form out of numbers but explode, leaving chunks of graphic debris before they fade, consistent with the rhetoric of stardom's convention of identifying the pairing of stars as explosive events (and implying through the rhetoric of genre that explosions will be involved).[54]

On two occasions in this brief trailer we see several shots from a scene in which Connery surprises a naked Zeta-Jones in her room, wherein he is in a classic voyeuristic positioning (seated in darkness by her bed) while she is supine (she then sits up and covers herself with a sheet). Subsequent clips that juxtapose images of Connery looking at something (once through a telephoto lens) with eroticized

Figure 5.14. Catherine Zeta-Jones's
identification title in the *Entrapment* trailer.

images of an athletic Zeta-Jones (such as one of her elevated rear end deftly descending in order to dodge a laser simulation of an "electric eye" alarm) reinforce the voyeuristic aspect of the appeal to interest in the stars' relationship. Indeed, the crosscutting between Connery at the telephoto and Zeta-Jones's rump goes back and forth four times (with each clip being no more than three or four frames).

Audiences are thus invited to identify with either the looker or the object of the look, depending on their assumed gender, and to desire the other one—their obvious age differences notwithstanding.[55] The fact that the trailer sustains the enigma of just how romantically involved the two get, emphasizing this more distanced, visual aspect of their sexual chemistry along with the enigmatic dimension of their partnership in crime, results in a teasing "melodrama of stardom" rooted in the desirability, yet improbability of finding the "perfection" the trailer holds out.

The integration of the romantic and voyeuristic clips with quick-cut clips of the two apparently engaged in a high-tech robbery of a multinational corporate edifice (one image shows a financial "situation room" dominated by an interactive global map) serves to merge the trailer's appeals to interest in the stars' sexuality with the idea of infiltration. The assumption of interest in the pair's deception and the caper's "perfect trap" combines with the rhetoric of genre's appeals to audience interest in the "perfect crime," here an infiltration by outsiders of a corporate space of high finance. The appeal of this generic space is not that of joining the corporate world but of subverting it—of breaking into it and circumventing its laws. The trailer emphasizes the gleaming glass walls and sterile white hallways of this world being repeatedly violated, as brief shots depict Connery and Zeta-Jones climbing their exteriors and being chased through their interiors.

The infiltration, however, is inevitably a double one since, as the trailer and film title make fairly clear, one of the pair is an undercover cop. This rhetorical appeal thus offers a global audience an updated notion of the rhetoric of stardom's ideology of relationships as events: in today's corporate capitalist world, the trailer's rhetoric implies, such "events" are never not enmeshed within money, the law and the state, even when we expertly try to circumvent those institutions. The ideological complement of corporate infiltration and romance-as-deception well suit a market-driven global popular culture in which acquiring money for self is naturalized as the only reason left for defying corporate capitalism. Promoting stars' pairings as explosive events thus can encompass both the exciting and the seedier aspects of such explosions,

Figure 5.15. "The loot, my dear, is right in there": the *Entrapment* trailer.

and the contradictions inherent to stardom's appeal can be seen to enhance the promotion of contemporary "event movies" just as they were enlisted to promote films in the classical era.[56]

SUMMARY

The contemporary era's charge to avoid alienating any potential audience in the new global marketplace produces a body of trailers in the eighties and nineties exemplifying the rhetoric of genre that express the increasingly homogeneous cultural economy and social space of their time. New trailer conventions also become prevalent, such as a greater numbers of shots, a heavy use of grids, and (as begun in the transitional era) reliance on gestures in addition to dialogue to communicate characterization. Furthermore, contemporary trailers trumpet the pleasures of generic spectacle even more than did earlier trailers, often consciously appealing to audiences in terms that evoke nostalgia for the simpler generic conventions and cinematic forms of the classical era. Following the confusions and false starts of the transitional era's problematic genres, generic space in the contemporary era has a seamless quality in part attributable to its production within a high concept–dominated market.

The genre trailers, representing some of the more deliberate or overt examples of audience address within the contemporary promotional market, often address their assumed global audience on registers that seem on some level to be centered on family dynamics, a characteristic that holds true for much of the rest of this era's sample even when the film's content is not obviously about family. The assumptions generated by the *Rocky* trailer within the rhetoric of genre are that making the couple is the primary appeal of a fight film; the *Return of the Jedi* trailer emphasizes its space fantasy cycle as an intergalactically stepped-up family outing; while in the new *Psycho* trailer, the core of the film's appeal for horror fans is the terrorizing dysfunctionality of a mother-son relationship (in ways that mark the trailer, like the film, as a 1990s text in spite of the film's fidelity to Hitchcock's 1960 version). Contemporary trailer production practice often appears to want to reduce the enormous, multicultural global audience for Hollywood films to the simpler, more manageable tropes of a giant family system, assuming that, like a family, it possesses a shared set of values. More than in the transitional era, which in the process of chasing its dwindling audience tended to acknowledge difference by default, or even than in the classical era, when a universal audience was assumed to want to go to all films, contemporary trailers—for all their global reach—often assume their audiences live in a limited and circumscribed world that is experienced much like the "inner circle" of a family. Trailers utilizing the rhetoric of genre thus promote the allures of generic space(s) that audiences are assumed to want to "go to" when seeing a film by way of a guiding assumption that audiences want cinematic novelty to be couched in strongly familiar (and often familial) terms. Many of these assumptions about what kinds of generic space audiences want are suggestive of the contemporary social space of "Global Hollywood," a nongeographically limited entity at once more vast and more circumscribed than any earlier social world.

The contemporary examples demonstrate that the rhetoric of story in the high-concept era has moved away from the classical era's problem of promoting stories that couldn't quite be told, as well as the transitional era's problem of promoting cinematic innovations that weren't yet understood. There is more leeway in cinematic storytelling in the contemporary movie market than in the classical era, and in spite of the stylish repetitiveness of much studio product, overall there is arguably more stylistic experimentation within the current generation of Hollywood filmmakers (which now, as was stated earlier, must be said to include most of the "independents") than there was even in the "Hollywood renaissance" of the early seventies.

But this examination of studios' textual assumptions about audience desires for story knowledge, and thus other kinds of knowledge and experiences, within these trailers points to another kind of problem or lack within the promotional discourse of the high-concept era: a paucity of faith in the audience's desire to know anything in particular. In an era of apparent cinematic abundance, as these trailers hint, the things audiences are assumed to want from films have dwindled to: an evocation of a historical world that reverberates back to an "eternal present" (as in *Days of Heaven*), a search for truth that can only ultimately inform about the self (as in *Thunderheart*); and an institutionalization of apathy and of simplistic political solutions (as in *Men in Black*). Here I am being polemical, ignoring other aspects of these contradictory texts, in order to point out the nevertheless often reductive aspects of contemporary trailers' appeals to audiences' interest in film stories, a factor worth examining as we watch contemporary trailers. In the process of *advertising* stories, trailers *tell* stories about what trailer producers think audiences want. These stories, the domain of ideology, selectively display and withhold elements or aspects of film narratives, textually demonstrating some indications of Hollywood's image of its audiences' desires for knowledge and experience in the social world.

Trailers appealing to audience interest in stars in the contemporary era demonstrate a return to formula in the context of a Hollywood economy dominated by high concept marketing. Star appeals are increasingly integrated with those of story and genre in high-tech contemporary trailers that fluidly weave these appeals together using multiple grids and sophisticated applications of music, sound effects and dialogue overlaps, along with graphics and text that cue viewers to the key art of the overall campaign. Yet stars still sell movies, and as these examples suggest, marketers have found newer and subtler ways to enlist stars— who in the contemporary market are always already promoting themselves—to promote even "niche" films to a wide range of audiences. More often than not, contemporary trailers that operate primarily within the rhetoric of stardom ensure that their stars are recognized by audiences (segmented and mass ones alike) as multiplicitous entities— whether by way of a multiplicity within their primary identities as stars, multivalent relationships with other star/characters within the trailer or the increasingly multivalent intertextual echoes of their presence in other films and their positioning as celebrities within the contemporary media marketplace.

Thus, we can see in the *Caddyshack* trailer a sense of its star ensemble as shifting signifiers whose satirically couched promotions of the film evoke a playful lack of any secure identity either as characters or stars; in the *Air Force One* trailer a countervalent positioning of two kinds of gendered star power in order to promote its film, and figure national governance, as both aggressive and nurturing; and in the *Entrapment* trailer's promotion of an intergenerational (and extratextually controversial) star pairing by assuming audience interest more in the romance's deceptive subtext than its fulfillment. Such appeals to audience interest in stardom thus increase trailers' reach not only to the film being promoted, but to any number of other star texts. And by assuming audiences want multiplicity in their stars, such appeals naturalize an attitude toward identity that might be familiar to contemporary audiences accustomed to the commodification of identity for purchase within commercial discourses, as well as to their own multitasking, reinvention and relocation according to the needs of the corporate marketplace.

Trailers in the contemporary era appeal to the newly global yet contradictorily segmented audience in terms that seem to aim to simplify generic space, and thus social space, along the familiar lines of family dynamics; that treat story knowledge, and thus historical knowledge, within the implicitly narrow boundaries of an assumed diminishment of curiosity; and that at the same time promote stars, and thus conceive of social identity, as more shifting and multivalent than ever. This ideological combination well suits the social and economic demands the broader culture placed on contemporary consumer-producers in the late twentieth century. Still, contemporary trailers are a site where hopeful moments are figured: in the yearnings of a woman to "go the distance" to her own kind of (nonboxing) victory, in the representation of a quest for a marginal cultural identity as heroic, in a magnificence of pure cinematic imagery that celebrates a historically specific (and auteur-specific) pleasure of looking, in a transgressing of the walls of corporate high finance. Even in the twenty-first century, trailer spectatorship can still be enjoyed, not only as a "blackboard"[57] for awakening us to an awareness of Hollywood's implied audiences and their assigned consumer identities, but as an anticipatory site where Hollywood can occasionally, vividly remind us of the reality of our fondest dreams.

6

Conclusion. The Cinema Is Dead: Long Live the Cinema of (Coming) Attractions

n the digital environment, the proclamation of the "death of cinema" advanced (however ironically) by Jean-Luc Godard and others has new purchase, as the technology, production and distribution systems, reception practices and the very matter from which movies are made are all in the process of being irrevocably transformed.[1] The ability of trailers, a cinematic form displaying (reconfigured versions of) rhetorical conventions that date back to the early sound era, to pour themselves seamlessly into these new technologies and systems like *Terminator 2*'s morphing man, speaks to their existence as a unique form of cinema. It is interesting that the filmmaker famous for declaring the death of cinema also expressed a desire to make trailers instead of films.[2] While the death-of-cinema conceit is misleading, in that all new media forms (and their "content") are deeply embedded in the extensive wealth of cinematic traditions and conventions developed over the past century, the profound changes in cinema's institutional structures make now an ideal time to consider the place of trailers in its evolving (signifying and economic) systems.

These case studies of trailers throughout the sound era and their rhetorical appeals point to many commonalities within the "genre" of trailers across the three eras. As early as the 1930s, classical trailers embodied such features, often considered by cultural critics as more characteristic of the postmodern cultural forms of the postindustrial West, as their presentation of highly glossed, referential and quotational texts, or their intensified hybridization of commercial and narrative discourses. We can also see formal continuities between early promotional cinematic address and contemporary trailers, even given their vastly different technological capabilities: today's trailers still use (reconfigured versions of) classical titles, fades and wipes—albeit with bigger and sparser words and an emphasis on sound "wipes" over visual ones—for the same reasons earlier ones did: to make sure audiences know they aren't just watching a (very short) film, but are being told and sold *to* watch a film: they are being *addressed*.

This continuity of trailer rhetoric is comforting on one level, in that the sophistication with which marketing rhetoric is interwoven with popular media can be seen to predate our own heavily commercialized historical era, implying that the presence or prevalence of promotional narratives such as trailers doesn't in itself define popular culture as irrevocably commodified. Looking back, it's easy to see that trailers' coexistence on the screen with an abundance of less blatantly commercial film texts in the classical era comprised a heritage of American popular cinema that was rich and varied, even as the classical film bill as a whole solidified the perception of a commodification of the visible.[3] Indeed, as Miriam Hansen's discussion of the classical era's "vernacular reflexivity" makes clear, the era's popular films could even engage "processes of mimetic identification that are more often than not partial and excessive in relation to narrative comprehension," and "allow their viewers to confront the constitutive ambivalence of modernity."[4] Classical trailers, already a fundamentally contradictory "cinema of (coming) attractions," could obviously fit this description as well.

Through principal rhetorical appeals to audience interest in film genres, stories and stars, trailers reconfigure the generic worlds, the narrative trajectories and the stars of their films into new kinds of cinematic signifiers. Removed from the plenitude of their films' generic environments, the conventional causality and temporal sense of their stories and the fully available/desirable identificatory nuances of their star performances, these signifiers contribute to spatially discontinuous, narratively reconfigured, figurally schematized film texts (trailers) that are the cinematic expression par excellence of Tom Gunning's thesis that "the system of attraction remains an essential part of popular filmmaking."[5] As nostalgic texts that paradoxically appeal to audiences' idealized memories of films they haven't seen yet, they attract audiences not only to themselves (as attractions), nor even only to the attractions within the individual films they promote, but to an ever renewed and renewable desire for cinematic attraction per se. Like magnets, they attract (or occasionally, repel) in an attempt to draw bodies to a center, assembling their assumed audiences in a suspended state of present-tense readiness for a future that is always deferred. The center to which they attempt to draw audiences—the narrative and promotional world of "Hollywood"— is all the more compelling for the degree to which its lures are repeated and reconfigured, in ever novel yet ever familiar ways, within the trailer exhibition experience (itself currently in the process of being reconfigured and renewed by the Internet and a general expansion of promotional venues).

Trailers thus often manage within their brief 90 seconds (give or take) to inscribe an ever renewable hope for good films, and film scholars and lay audiences alike continue to flock to their seats for them, as well as enjoying their new level of visibility in the new media age, on DVDs and on the Internet. In the face of the diminishing returns of a global film economy, and a historical moment of arguably bleaker than ever prospects for long-term planetary survival, the increasingly wide reach of trailers is a phenomenon worth examining in relation not only to the global spread of commercial regimes of signification but also to the textual manifestations of contemporary utopian consciousness within commercial culture.

This unique form of cinema, or "cinema of (coming) attractions," can be viewed as a form of contract that trailermakers offer audiences that expresses the promise of the cinematic experience, inviting the "act of faith" that Thomas Elsaesser characterizes as contemporary moviegoing:

> When buying a movie ticket, we are effectively taking out a contract, by which in exchange for our money, we are guaranteed (temporary access to) a normative, quality-controlled product. Conversely, our part of the deal is to be prepared to pay: not for the product itself and not even for the commodified experience it represents, but simply for the possibility that such a transubstantiation of experience into commodity might "take place." Neither the term "product" nor "service," neither the idea of "consumption" nor the concept of "leisure" quite capture the nature of this act of faith.[6]

Trailer spectatorship is likewise an amorphous contractual arrangement to which audiences bring their hopes for the possibility of this transubstantiation.[7] As a recent *New York Times Magazine* article on contemporary trailers put it, "A trailer is a studio's prayer, one that is answered on opening weekend. And everyone wants the answer to be yes."[8]

Trailers exaggerate this ineffable act of faith that constitutes the cinematic experience as a whole, the utopian consciousness that stirs in the hearts of moviegoers every time the lights go down and the show begins, for it is at this hopeful moment of beginning that trailers are experienced. I have thus treated them as fundamentally contradictory texts, which assume we want to go to known yet new cinematic spaces; while there experiencing narratives that offer at once secure, familiar story types and endless open possibilities; and doing all this through the agency of stars whose myriad promotional identities both embrace us with the intimacy of their resemblance to us and exclude us by reminding us of their celestial distance. These contradictory appeals, designed to keep a range of audiences wanting more and continually coming back to the theater, enable trailers to perpetually hover in the consciousness of the viewer as incomplete, unformed "ideas" of movies rather than as samples of particular movies or merely ads for movies.

For all the reductiveness of the ideological assumptions trailers tend to display about audiences in each era, like the sculptor's partially carved block of marble or Mallarmée's blank page, trailers are what we imagine—and hope—the films to become; the films they promote are thus ever richer in the imagined interstices of the paradoxical trailer montage than they can ever be in their narrative "fullness" on the screen. Jane Gaines's discussion of Ernst Bloch and utopian hope in relation to the doubleness of the "dream product" of popular film sees the "mirrorings of Hollywood realism" as an imagistic realm that "cannot help but bring us more at the same time that it restricts us to less."[9] With regard to trailers, this hopeful dimension lies in that present tense yet simultaneously future zone evoked by their unique montage structure, enabling them to be seen as quintessential expressions of Bloch's "anticipatory consciousness." Perhaps more heavily than any other kind of montage, trailers privilege the spaces *between* the excerpted images— in which audiences place their memories of and desires for Hollywood's capacity to help us "imagin[e] beyond things as they are."[10]

In contemporary culture, the irrevocably promotional mode of global capitalism results in a pervasive sense of satisfaction endlessly deferred, even as the perpetual present of the contemporary social world offers an illusion that cultural forms are satisfying. There is always a newer, better movie, a new Game Boy cartridge, a next level to master; and one of the few promises on which global capitalism does deliver is the provision of those kinds of "nexts," thus perpetuating the cycle. As this increasingly market-driven culture evolves, ontological shifts occur that are not always immediately visible. "Globalization," as Toby Miller et al. express, *stands for something real, a sense from across time, space and nation that those very categories are in peril. . . . Time is manipulated in concert with the interests of global capital, space is torn asunder, and traditional social bonds are compromised by ownership based on profit rather than township.*[11]

Trailers' unique temporal status as cinematic forms embodying a heightened present tense in which is imbricated a future potentiality is emblematic of the zeitgeist of globalization, while demonstrating that the cinematic expression of this zeitgeist is again, in some ways, nothing new. Such textual features as looking forward to the same-as-it-ever-was, the reconfiguration of imagination into commodity and the expression of social identities and relations as monadic, consumable events are all present in trailer rhetoric as early as the 1930s. This continuity has implications for thinking about the choices we make when positioning ourselves as spectators of popular media in the twenty-first century. If classical Hollywood trailers participated in a vernacular reflexivity that, like the films of the era, "engaged the contradictions of modernity at the level of the senses,"[12] perhaps spectators of today's trailers (which display rhetorical forms consistent with their classical counterparts) can learn from historical trailers ways of consciously reading contemporary ones, better to experience sensorially the contradictions of our own era's cultural surround.

Viewing American sound-era trailers as a continuously consistent cinematic form, while viewing the ways they reconfigure films into promotional texts as being emblematic of the pervasively commercial zeitgeist of global capitalism, might also serve to remind us that just as trailers are not movies, the cultural experience of space, time and nation under globalization is not the only reality. The anticipatory consciousness experienced during trailer spectatorship, or "ontology of the Not-Yet,"[13] is based on real hopes that lie *outside* trailers, and indeed, outside cinema and other media texts as well.

READING TRAILERS DIALECTICALLY

The imminent awakening is poised, like the wooden horse of the Greeks, in the Troy of dreams.

—Walter Benjamin

The new levels of penetration of marketing discourses in the environment of "global Hollywood," characterized by "the coordinated efforts of large entertainment-information conglomerates to annex cultural consumption and elevate market criteria over other ways of interpreting culture's value,"[14] thus require new approaches to critical spectatorship. Consumers/spectators need to be able to engage with texts such as trailers in ways that facilitate distinguishing the assumptions of marketing rhetoric from the socially shared pleasures of popular cultural forms. Calling for this distinction is not in itself new, and indeed questions surrounding the contradictory experience of commercial visual or media culture have heightened the recent appeal of the cultural theorist who perhaps most provocatively addressed the complexities of modern mass cultural imagery, Walter Benjamin. For Benjamin, the value of such imagery lay in part as raw material for the historian's quest to come to terms with modernity, as the juxtapositions enabled by mechanical reproduction and modern urban spaces threw tradition up against innovation in provocative and potentially dialectical ways.[15]

Benjamin's notion of "dialectical images," capable through montage of facilitating an "imminent awakening" from the dream world of mass culture, and the *Arcades Project* from which the above epigraph is drawn, are influential in contemporary American cultural studies,[16] although Benjamin's elaboration of the dialectical image was somewhat fragmentary. The argument that mystified texts can themselves contribute to a demystification of the systems and structures that produce them (to which the epigraph alludes), is worth attempting to apply to trailers. As with all attempts to find liberatory or consciousness-raising kernels within the behemoth of today's commercial media culture (a far cry from Benjamin's arcades), however, a rigorous awareness of the capacities of corporate capitalism to recuperate and remystify is required. We have seen that contemporary trailers (like other commercial texts) ably use montage, irony, and reflexivity in the service of their promotional agendas.

By exploring trailer rhetoric principally for the ways in which it can offer information about the implied audiences to whom trailers are addressed, the case studies serve more than anything as ideological critique, as attempts to contribute to a cognitive mapping of commercial capitalism's shifting notions of space, history, and identity.[17] In this sense, I hope the analyses facilitate a certain degree of "awakening" on the part of readers interested in experiencing trailers more critically. Although this critical dimension does not in itself constitute viewing trailers dialectically (or as dialectical montages), it is worth summarizing the historically specific rhetorics I have discussed.

While trailers demonstrate a continuity in their rhetoric, the three principal appeals—to audience interest in genres, stories and stars—yield a number of typical assumptions that trailers make about audiences that are specific to each of the three eras I treat, some of which are made visible by reading trailers' rhetoric in each era. This summary of the shifts in typical trailer rhetoric is meant to read as exploratory rather than conclusive, in hopes of demonstrating the ongoing value of rhetorical analysis to enhance a critical trailer spectatorship.

Through the rhetoric of *genre*, trailers "produce" their own kinds of generic space(s) through conventional means such as iconography, hyperbole, generalization and equations, designed to differentiate the film within a rubric of generic similarity, at times participating in the reconfiguration or designation of genres. Such representations of generic space also assume things about audiences' interests and participation in the social space of their time.

In classical-era trailers, generic space was a comfort zone of familiarity spiced with differentiation. Trailers invited mythic universal American audiences into the spaces of cinematic genres, promising them that within their boundaries, they could experience safe levels of diversity and innovation, perhaps as the nation as a whole still appeared to keep democracy safe through economic recovery and a world war.

In the transitional era, generic space was now more a remembered zone of familiarity. Trailers either promoted the sameness of tried-and-true genres beyond their relevance, or assumed audiences longed for familiar genres when the films that trailers promoted charted unknown territories of story or style. As the case studies pointed out, trailers often recuperated confusing innovation within outmoded generic boundaries, echoing commercial culture's responses to other innovative or difficult features of the social space of this tumultuous era.

Contemporary trailers offer new formulas for promoting generic space, echoing and referencing, yet transforming the classical forms. They assume that the newly globalized audience desires, for example, to "Return!" to the simpler, yet increasingly quotational and intertextual generic spaces of popular film franchises. Generic space in the contemporary film industry thus appears to have complex and entrenched parameters and impermeable boundaries even as it seems to provide the global audience with a simple, direct, accessible land of fun. The complexity of the social space of multinational capitalism in the millennial era (e.g., the information superhighway, global economic and environmental interdependencies) is likewise at times glossed within public discourse through a rhetorical fantasy land populated by good guys and evildoers.

Within the rubric of these generic spaces, trailers make assumptions about audiences' interests in movements of *story* and narrative, usually in relation to the story's characterizations, causality, enigmatic structures, or narrative worlds; they assume certain kinds of desire for knowledge and experience. They often assume as well the relative importance to audiences in each era of more general desires for knowledge of the historical world and of social narratives and outcomes beyond a film's individual story.

In the classical era, film story dimensions were withheld to a large degree, so as not to "give away the product." The sample and case studies show ways in which stories were thus characterized in broad, enigmatic terms. Trailers often integrated appeals to interest in all four aspects of narrative in the context of fairly formulaic and narration-driven texts, which promoted stories that under the Production Code had circumscribed limits. Trailermakers assumed audiences desired knowledge and experience through movies that would enhance their participation in the social world and in history, implying a broader assumption that the individual still had the capacity to participate in the unfolding of history.

Transitional-era trailers simplified their films' increasingly innovative story features, often using the rhetoric of story to emphasize a *generic* identity for the film. There was also a pronounced emphasis on the convention of promoting story causality through narrations that summed up story trajectories into dramatic lists, reminding audiences of the regularity and rhythms of the passage of narrative time. Such strategies could be seen as stabilizing features in an era when the films being promoted, like the kinds of knowledge and experience they figured in the sociocultural environment, were undergoing a profound period of questioning and destabilization.

Contemporary trailers more successfully fold story appeals into genre appeals, formularizing assumptions about audiences' desires to know and experience narrative features in ways that tend to simplify stories, often reading as expanded taglines or high concept statements for the films. They frequently utilize the convention of promoting the film's narrative world, assuming audiences' desires to experience the unfolding of the contemporary event film more as a surrounding environment than as a causal chain of activity. In an era in which popular

culture figures the capacity for individual agency as increasingly delimited to the various realms of consumption, *being* "in a world . . ." replaces
making one.

Within these assumed parameters of audience desires for genres
and stories, most trailers make assumptions about the audience's interest in the *stars* who people the narratives and inhabit the
generic spaces of Hollywood films. Whether through promoting a star's
inherent qualities, his or her past or current relationships or capacity for
relationships or his or her position within a star system or celebrity culture, trailers assume audiences want imaginatively to be or to possess
(sexually/romantically) certain kinds of people, and more broadly, they
make assumptions about identity and social relations. Of the three, the
rhetorical appeal to interest in stardom is the lowest logical type (stars
are components of film narratives, which fall within genres), and thus
possesses the highest level of organization and semiotic density (such
as the complexity that stars' indexical connection to the external world
brings with it) of the three appeals. Trailers' rhetorical appeals are
all thus built on the foundation of star appeals and cannot function
unless peopled with (famous or emerging) stars, just as contemporary
Hollywood wisdom considers casting as the most crucial feature in
packaging a film.

Classical-era trailers assumed audiences desired to participate in
the "melodrama of stardom," and so invited audiences to consider
themselves a part of the promotional world of Hollywood, giving them
credit as "the makers of stars." Whether promoting star quality, relationality or the star system as a whole, classical trailers displayed the
contradictory features of stars' simultaneous closeness and inaccessibil-
ity to audiences in terms that clearly articulated their status as commodities. In the days when stars seemed to have a well-defined place in
the studio economies, the culture appeared to be peopled by individuals in clear-cut social roles, even if some roles (such as the housewife
imperative) were temporarily suspended during wartime.

In the transitional era, stars' commodification became less clear-cut,
in line both with their shifting stature within reconfigured studio
economies and with trailermakers' greater insecurity about the types of
stars desired by Hollywood's smaller, more segmented audiences.
Trailers in this period often responded by hyperbolically emphasizing
the star's consumability, such as promoting films on the basis of the
era's newly acceptable levels of sex appeal or other controversial film

features. Other trailers took the opposite tack, misreading the marketability of new stars and emphasizing instead other appeals. The parameters of social identity were likewise undergoing experimentation, misreadings and shifts during this era, as exemplified by postwar suburbanization, the sexual revolution, the feminist movement and "the generation gap."

Contemporary trailers offer stars as multivalent intertextual entities, at times no longer recognizable as individual human beings so much as promoted across film texts as franchises (even, increasingly, "nonhuman" franchises, such as the *RoboCop* and *Terminator* series). Stars "become" genres, as these formerly unified textual categories of trailer rhetoric become increasingly synergistically interwoven within the high concept promotional environment. Social identity likewise becomes a locus of fluidity and multivalence, as technology affords individuals new "addresses," introduces new forms of reproducibility and raises new privacy questions.[18] The nature and availability of work also changes, with those in the workforce required to respond to new demands for flexibility, taking on multiple social roles and obligations in order to make ends meet.

These rhetorical features coexist with the anticipatory, utopian dimension of trailers, which as mentioned previously, resides more in the "spaces between" the images of the trailer montage than in their rhetoric per se. In other words, trailers' expression of an anticipatory consciousness (beyond the anticipation that we will see the film) relies not on the *implied* audience I have sought through the looking glass of trailer rhetoric, but on the affective and subjective ways their rhetoric is received by real, gendered, class-specific, multiethnic, historically embodied audiences. I have offered my own examples of how this dimension can be experienced with regard to the case studies in the chapter summaries, but further exploration of the reception of trailers by audiences is needed. The unique form of cinema that comprises trailer montage is nevertheless still tempting to mine for its capacities to embody a "dialectical image" within the belly of the beast of movie marketing. Positing the ways in which interactions between trailer rhetoric and trailers' evocations of anticipatory consciousness might make possible a spectatorial experience that breaks out of the promotional dimension and into deeper critical and (film-)historical awareness is a goal that this book can only begin to address.

If the dialectical image is accessible through trailer spectatorship, I suggest that it consists neither in ideological critiques of their rhetorical appeals (such as the foregoing) alone, nor even in combining such critique with the subjective experience of their "ontology of the Not-Yet" that the spectacle of their promotional montages enables (although this combination is a prerequisite for critical trailer spectatorship). Rather, trailers operate most effectively as dialectical images when a contemporary critical trailer spectatorship is informed by and juxtaposed with viewings and readings of historical ones. Vivian Sobchack argues that the effectiveness for Walter Benjamin of montage's capacity to destroy the "ideological fusion of nature and history" lies in its "temporal field that dialectically relates the abstracted and emblematic 'decayed fragments' of the past to the naturalized conditions of the lived historical present."[19] Trailer montage, however, by offering not decayed but *embryonic* fragments of a (textual) *future* (a not-yet-seen film), comprises a different kind of temporal field with respect to the lived historical present, as we have seen. Such montage tends to serve more readily to naturalize an ideological relationship to the future than to rupture it.

But the increased visibility of trailers from all eras, on movie channels, DVDs, in stores and on the Internet, results in an enhanced spectatorial juxtaposition of old and new trailers in an environment in which the boundaries between marketing and commemorating cinema have become blurred. Indeed, the marketing of films and film history through these and other venues is currently expanding in unforeseen ways.[20] Thus, our experiences of contemporary trailers are, increasingly, inevitably overlaid with afterimages of trailers from other times through the vicissitudes of contemporary televisual and cybernetic "flow." The unique features of this "cinema of (coming) attractions" are in this way thickened historically and can at times be experienced dialectically, as our media spectatorship layers in frequent looks back on "decayed fragments" of Hollywood's hopes for "attractions" that have already "gone." Our readings of the ways *current* trailers provide expressions of the historical contradictions of the contemporary moment can thus be enriched, and a conscious critical trailer spectatorship becomes possible.

o textual analysis of a trailer can communicate "the whole story" of where and how it sits as a promotional text and a snapshot of Hollywood's ideas about films and audiences. For that one would need additionally to interrogate (in greater detail than is possible here) the promotional and production history of the film itself, the institutional history of the studio that made it, the economic system in which it operated and the cultural system within which it was originally seen. Given access to industry files, for example, further work might be pursued to determine whether the actual market research that went into the campaigns for the trailers I have examined backs up these analyses.

Nonetheless, the degree to which trailers incorporate rhetorical assumptions as integral components of their persuasive regimes points to their unique capacity to allow readings of some of the ways Hollywood sees its audiences. In part, my goal in performing these analyses has been to revitalize textual analysis as a nontotalizing tool for film historiography, by demonstrating that methods such as classical rhetoric can enable us to explore strictly textual features of trailers that make specific, legible contributions to the operations of ideology as they play out in cinematic persuasion.

Trailers' paradoxical nature as simultaneously reductive and expansive is crucial to my purpose in writing about them as cinematic texts that can potentially contribute to the "marriage of semiotic and commodity theories" alluded to by Barbara Klinger in her call to study the epiphenomena of commercial films.[21] Trailers are one of the more pervasive vehicles through which Hollywood has kept and keeps in the forefront of audience awareness the centrality of "the system of attraction" to its significatory practices. As such, they demonstrate that the key to sustaining the magnetic force, or *attractiveness* to the attractions that constitute popular film, has been to keep as many oscillations and paradoxes as possible in play with regard to how (and whom) attractions attract.

This exploration of oscillations, poles, paradoxes and contradictions, boundaries and the imaginary interstices between them within trailers has called inevitably upon the languages of both semiotic and commodity theories to treat not only the meaning-producing characteristics of trailers but their money-producing ones as well. It is offered as an opening, which other scholars with access to other kinds of readings and knowledge (such as studies of trailer audience reception or cross-cultural analyses) will no doubt expand and perhaps contest. My hope is that such explorations of trailers can point to a greater potential for the analysis of popular film to contribute to our efforts to make sense of our increasingly fragmented and contradictory lives as historical subjects in the twenty-first century.

Filmography
of Trailers Viewed

This list represents most of the trailers viewed for the purposes of the project. It does not include contemporary trailers viewed during the normal course of moviegoing, and I have omitted trailers that did not fit the scope of the project (such as non-U.S. trailers or teasers) unless they were significant for some reason. The majority of these were from the collection of the UCLA Film and Television Archive, although some were viewed on cable television, and some were viewed on laser discs and DVDs of the films.

SILENT AND CLASSICAL ERA
1920
Shore Acres

1924
Beau Brummel

1925
Capital Punishment
Cyclone Cavalier
Girl Who Wouldn't Work, The
Goat Getter
Lost World, The
Pride of the Force, The
Re-Creation of Brian Kent, The
Silent Sheldon

1926
Heart of a Coward, The
High Flyer, The
Tentacles of the North
Last Alarm, The
Out of the Storm
Speed Cop
West of the Law

1927
Jazz Singer, The
King of Kings, The
Scorcher, The
Show Girl, The

1929
Dangerous Woman, A
Marriage Playground, The
Sunny Side Up

1930
Feet First
Hell's Angels
Sky Hawk, The

1931
Dirigible
Fanny Foley Herself
Forbidden Adventure
Spider, The

1932
Devil and the Deep
Movie Crazy
Night after Night
One Hour with You
Service for Ladies
Trouble in Paradise
Under-Cover Man

1933
Alice in Wonderland
Cradle Song
Dinner at Eight
Jungle Bride
Power and the Glory, The
Sign of the Cross, The
Take a Chance
This Day and Age

1934
Cleopatra
Four Frightened People
High School Girl
Six of a Kind

1935
Anna Karenina
Brewster's Millions

Call of the Wild, The
Drunkard, The
Last Outpost, The
Midsummer Night's Dream, A
Mutiny on the Bounty
Ruggles of Red Gap

1936
Black Legion
Fury
Gambling with Souls
Marihuana
Swing Time

1937
Alcatraz Island
Assassin of Youth
Day at the Races, A
Double or Nothing
History Is Made at Night
Live, Love and Learn
Nothing Sacred
She Married an Artist
Slaves in Bondage

1938
Alexander's Ragtime Band
Army Girl
Boys Town
City Streets
Drums
God's Step Children
Hold That Co-Ed
Kidnapped
Mad About Music
Service de Luxe
Sing, You Sinners
Straight, Place, and Show
Vivacious Lady

1939

Four Wives
Gone with the Wind
Goodbye, Mr. Chips
Housekeeper's Daughter, The
It's a Wonderful World
King of the Turf
Made for Each Other
Man in the Iron Mask, The
Oklahoma Kid, The
Only Angels Have Wings
Second Fiddle
Stand Up and Sing
Wizard of Oz, The

1940

All This, and Heaven Too
Bitter Sweet
City for Conquest
Fighting 69th, The
Go West
Grapes of Wrath, The
Kit Carson
Kitty Foyle
Letter, The
Phantom Rancher
Rebecca
Secrets of a Model
Souls in Pawn
They Drive by Night

1941

Chocolate Soldier, The
Citizen Kane
Corsican Brothers, The
Four Mothers
Lady Eve, The
Nice Girl?
Son of Monte Cristo, The
Sullivan's Travels

1942

Bambi
Casablanca
Cat People
Devil's Harvest
Flying Tigers
Glass Key, The
Iceland
Kings Row
Lady for a Night
Larceny Inc.
Lone Star Ranger
Reap the Wild Wind
Song of the Islands
Undercover Man
Yankee Doodle Dandy

1943

China
Coney Island
Gang's All Here, The
I Walked with a Zombie
Lady of Burlesque
Leopard Man, The
Tender Comrade
What a Woman!

1944

Cobra Woman
Double Indemnity
I'll Be Seeing You
In Society
Lifeboat
My Buddy
Show Business
Song of the Open Road
Step Lively
Story of Dr. Wassell, The

1945

Blood on the Sun
Incendiary Blonde
Isle of the Dead
Leave Her to Heaven
Northwest Trail
Phantom Speaks, The
Picture of Dorian Gray, The
Rhapsody in Blue
Roughly Speaking
Royal Scandal, A
Strange Affair of Uncle Harry, The
White Gorilla, The

1946

Big Sleep, The
Caesar and Cleopatra
Canyon Passage
Devil Bat's Daughter
Devil Monster
Duel in the Sun
Humoresque
It's a Wonderful Life
I've Always Loved You
Kid from Brooklyn, The
Killers, The
Monsieur Beaucaire
Night in Paradise
Renegades
Smoky
Strangler of the Swamp
Wife of Monte Cristo, The
Yearling, The

1947

Life with Father
Ramrod
Unconquered
Voice of the Turtle, The

1948

Arch of Triumph
Emperor Waltz, The
Force of Evil
Key Largo
Miracle in Harlem
One Touch of Venus
Paleface, The
Plunderers, The
Romance on the High Seas
Rope
Saigon
Sitting Pretty
When My Baby Smiles at Me

1949

Criss Cross
House Across the Street, The
Jolson Sings Again
Kiss in the Dark, A
Lady Gambles, The
Look for the Silver Lining

TRANSITIONAL ERA
1950

All About Eve
Backfire
Bright Leaf
Destination Moon
Father of the Bride
50 Years Before Your Eyes
Jolson Sings Again
Riding High

1951

African Queen, The
American in Paris, An
Day the Earth Stood Still, The

Pandora and the Flying Dutchman
Storm Warning
When Worlds Collide

1952

High Noon
Ivanhoe
Never Wave at a WAC
Quiet Man, The
Singin' in the Rain

1953

Appointment in Honduras
Band Wagon, The
Knights of the Round Table
Phantom from Space
Robe, The
Salt of the Earth
Shane
War of the Worlds, The

1954

Anatahan
Athena
Atomic Kid, The
Brigadoon
Cat Women of the Moon
Rear Window
Red Garters
River of No Return
Seven Brides for Seven Brothers
Them!
This Is My Love
20,000 Leagues Under the Sea
Wild One, The

1955

Bad Day at Black Rock
Blackboard Jungle
East of Eden

I'll Cry Tomorrow
It Came from Beneath the Sea
My Sister Eileen
Oklahoma!
Rebel Without a Cause
Tarantula

1956

Around the World in Eighty Days
Carousel
Earth vs. the Flying Saucers
Gaby
Giant
High Society
Invasion of the Body Snatchers
Julie
Killing, The
Man Who Knew Too Much, The
Tea and Sympathy
Violent Years, The

1957

Band of Angels
Bridge on the River Kwai, The
Designing Woman
Interlude
Jailhouse Rock
Jet Pilot
Kettles on Old MacDonald's Farm, The
Loving You
Man of a Thousand Faces
Man on Fire
Night the World Exploded, The
Paths of Glory
Peyton Place
Silk Stockings
Three Faces of Eve, The
Tip on a Dead Jockey
20 Million Miles to Earth
Voodoo Woman

1958

Bell Book and Candle
Big Country, The
Day the Sky Exploded, The
I Married a Monster from Outer Space
I Want to Live!
Man of the West
My World Dies Screaming
Screaming Skull, The
7th Voyage of Sinbad, The
South Pacific
Vertigo
Vikings, The
White Wilderness

1959

Ben-Hur
Big Fisherman, The
Missile to the Moon
Mouse That Roared, The
Mummy, The
North By Northwest
Pillow Talk
Plan 9 from Outer Space
Porgy and Bess
Some Like It Hot
That Kind of Woman
Warlock

1960

Amazing Transparent Man, The
Can-Can
Cinderfella
Elmer Gantry
Entertainer, The
Flaming Star
Let's Make Love
Millionairess, The
Never on Sunday
North to Alaska

Pollyanna
Psycho
Sex Kittens Go to College
Spartacus

1961

Absent Minded Professor, The
Blood and Roses
Breakfast at Tiffany's
El Cid
Guns of Navarone, The
Misfits, The
One-Eyed Jacks
Two Rode Together
West Side Story

1962

Burn, Witch, Burn!
Cape Fear
Day Mars Invaded Earth, The
Days of Wine and Roses
Dr. No
Geronimo
Hands of a Stranger
Hatari!
Horizontal Lieutenant, The
Kid Galahad
L-Shaped Room, The
Lawrence of Arabia
Lion, The
Lolita
Man Who Shot Liberty Valance, The
Miracle Worker, The
Night Creatures
Phaedra
Premature Burial, The

1963

Atom Age Vampire
Captain Newman, M.D.

Cleopatra

Diamond Head

55 Days at Peking

From Russia with Love

Gidget Goes to Rome

Great Escape, The

Hud

I Could Go on Singing

Irma la Douce

Jason and the Argonauts

Just for Fun

Marilyn

Mary, Mary

Mouse on the Moon, The

Move Over, Darling

My Six Loves

Three Lives of Thomasina, The

Thrill of It All, The

Tom Jones

Under the Yum Yum Tree

Wheeler Dealers, The

1964

Becket

Carpetbaggers, The

Curse of the Mummy's Tomb, The

Dead Ringer

Dear Heart

Dr. Strangelove or: How I Learned to Stop
Worrying and Love the Bomb

Father Goose

Fistful of Dollars, A

Goldfinger

Good Neighbor Sam

Gorgon, The

Hard Day's Night, A

Long Ships, The

Mary Poppins

Robin and the 7 Hoods

7 Faces of Dr. Lao

Sex and the Single Girl

Shot in the Dark, A

What a Way to Go!

Wild and Wonderful

World of Henry Orient, The

1965

Art of Love, The

Battle of the Villa Fiorita, The

Doctor Zhivago

Go Go Mania

Greatest Story Ever Told, The

Hallelujah Trail, The

Help!

Lord Jim

None But the Brave

Pawnbroker, The

Rounders, The

Satan Bug, The

Sound of Music, The

1966

After the Fox

Destination Inner Space

Dimension 5

Follow Me, Boys!

Georgy Girl

Good, The Bad, and The Ugly, The

John F. Kennedy: Years of Lightning,
Day of Drums

Poppy Is Also a Flower, The

Psychopath, The

That Man in Istanbul

This Property Is Condemned

1967

Africa—Texas Style!

Camelot

Don't Look Back

Frankenstein Created Woman

Graduate, The
Happening, The
More than a Miracle
Point Blank
Riot on Sunset Strip
Rough Night in Jericho
She Freak
Trip, The
Valley of the Dolls

1968

Barbarella
Candy
Destructors, The
Funny Girl
Guns for San Sebastian
Hour of the Wolf
Lion in Winter, The
Night of the Living Dead
Oliver!
Pretty Poison
Psych-Out
Rosemary's Baby
Skidoo
Vengeance of She, The
Wild in the Streets

1969

Dream of Kings, A
Easy Rider
Gay Deceivers, The
Goodbye, Mr. Chips
Marooned
Viva Max!
Wild Bunch, The
Women in Love

1970

Act of the Heart
Airport

Baby Maker, The
Borsalino
Boys in the Band, The
Catch-22
Diary of a Mad Housewife
First Love
Hawaiians, The
Kremlin Letter, The
Song of Norway
Twelve Chairs, The
Zabriskie Point

1971

Banana Monster
Billy Jack (teaser and trailer)
Black Beauty
Clockwork Orange, A
$ (Dollars)
Fiddler on the Roof
Hospital, The
Last Picture Show, The
Le Mans
Summer of '42
Sunday, Bloody Sunday
Trojan Women, The
Who Slew Auntie Roo?

1972

Cabaret
Candidate, The
César and Rosalie
Deliverance
Duck, You Sucker
Fritz The Cat
King of Marvin Gardens, The
Lady Sings the Blues
Magnificent Seven Ride!, The
Man, The
Oh! Calcutta!
Play It Again, Sam

Poseidon Adventure, The
Pulp
1776
What's Up, Doc?

1973

American Graffiti
Arena, The
Bang the Drum Slowly
Black Caesar
Class of '44
Day of the Jackal, The
Extreme Close-Up
Legend of Boggy Creek, The
Magnum Force
Mean Streets
Paper Moon
Papillon
Scarecrow
Serpico
Seven-Ups, The
Spook Who Sat by the Door, The
Summer Wishes, Winter Dreams
Thief Who Came to Dinner, The

1974

Blazing Saddles
Chinatown
Claudine
Conversation, The
Gambler, The
Godfather: Part II, The
Golden Voyage of Sinbad, The
Harry and Tonto
Ladies and Gentlemen: The Rolling Stones
Lenny
Mysterious Island of Captain Nemo, The
Queen Boxer
Rape Squad
Sugarland Express, The

Taking of Pelham One Two Three, The
That's Entertainment!
They Call Her One Eye
Three Musketeers, The
Thunderbolt and Lightfoot
Towering Inferno, The
Where the Lilies Bloom
Young Frankenstein

CONTEMPORARY ERA
1975

Aloha, Bobby and Rose
Barry Lyndon
Bite the Bullet
Death Race 2000
Dersu Uzala
Devil Is a Woman, The
Eiger Sanction, The
Hennessy
Jaws
Killer Elite, The
Killer Force
Lepke
Monty Python and the Holy Grail
One Flew Over the Cuckoo's Nest
Reincarnation of Peter Proud, The
Rollerball
Royal Flash
Sheba, Baby
Yakuza, The

1976

Bound for Glory
Car Wash
Casanova
Embryo
Futureworld
Leadbelly

Logan's Run
Murder by Death
Nickelodeon
Rocky
Sky Riders
Song Remains the Same, The
Star Is Born, A
Stay Hungry
St. Ives
Treasure of Matecumbe
Two Minute Warning

1977

Cassandra Crossing, The
Chatterbox
Crash!
Demon Seed
Greatest, The
I Never Promised You a Rose Garden
Julia
Mansion of the Doomed
Mr. Billion
New York, New York
Rollercoaster
Saturday Night Fever
Sorcerer
Star Wars
Young Lady Chatterley

1978

Coma
Days of Heaven
F.I.S.T.
Girlfriends
Goin' Coconuts
Same Time, Next Year
Slow Dancing in the Big City

1979

Apocalypse Now

Rocky II
Running
10
Wanderers, The
Warriors, The
Yanks

1980

Bronco Billy
Caddyshack
Dressed to Kill
Foxes
Friday the 13th
Great White
Idolmaker, The
Incredible Shrinking Woman, The
Nine to Five
Smokey and the Bandit II
Stardust Memories
Superman II
Times Square
Used Cars
Xanadu

1981

Arthur
Body Heat
Escape from New York
Excalibur
Eye for an Eye, An
Eyewitness
For Your Eyes Only
Four Seasons, The
Fox and the Hound, The
Friday the 13th Part 2
Heavy Metal
Night Crossing
Night the Lights Went Out in Georgia, The
Pennies from Heaven
Prince of the City

Rollover

Scanners

Sharky's Machine

So Fine

Sphinx

This Is Elvis

True Confessions

1982

Blade Runner

Deathtrap

Firefox

Hanky Panky

Night Shift

Officer and a Gentleman, An

One from the Heart

Paradise

Pink Floyd The Wall

Return of the Soldier, The

Split Image

Tag: The Assassination Game

Tempest

Tron

Victor/Victoria

World According to Garp, The

Zapped!

1983

Big Chill, The

Breathless

El Norte

Man with Two Brains, The

Night in Heaven, A

Return of the Jedi

Scarface

Staying Alive

1984

Blood Simple

City Heat

Cotton Club, The

Dune

Ghostbusters

Mrs. Soffel

Once Upon a Time in America

Places in the Heart

Pope of Greenwich Village, The

1985

Creator

Fletch

Invasion U.S.A.

Lost in America

Man with One Red Shoe, The

Mask

Runaway Train

Silverado

1986

Big Trouble in Little China

Crocodile Dundee

Flight of the Navigator

Great Mouse Detective, The

Heartbreak Ridge

Karate Kid, Part II, The

Manhattan Project, The

Money Pit, The

Mosquito Coast, The

Never Too Young to Die

Off Beat

Out of Bounds

Raw Deal

Ruthless People

Tough Guys

1987

*batteries not included

Good Morning, Vietnam

Moonstruck

Roxanne

Throw Momma from the Train
Who's That Girl?

1988
Bagdad Cafe
Cry in the Dark, A
Die Hard
Mississippi Burning
Moon Over Parador
Talk Radio

1989
Abyss, The
Adventures of Baron Munchausen, The
Blaze
Do the Right Thing
Fabulous Baker Boys, The
Field of Dreams
Mystery Train
Romero
Sea of Love
War of the Roses, The
When Harry Met Sally . . .

1990
Arachnophobia
Awakenings
Betsy's Wedding
Eating
Freshman, The
Havana
Home Alone
Longtime Companion
Mr. and Mrs. Bridge
Pacific Heights
Postcards from the Edge
Texasville
Two Jakes, The
White Palace

1991
Barton Fink
Eve of Destruction
Father of the Bride
Iron & Silk
Naked Lunch
Rambling Rose
Regarding Henry
Sleeping with the Enemy
Super, The
Terminator 2: Judgment Day
Thousand Pieces of Gold
Young Soul Rebels

1992
Bodyguard, The
Crying Game, The
Dracula
Incident at Oglala
Last of the Mohicans, The
League of Their Own, A
Malcolm X
Power of One, The
Raising Cain
Rapid Fire
Reservoir Dogs
Single White Female
Thunderheart
Toys
Unlawful Entry
White Men Can't Jump

1993
Alive
Amos & Andrew
Army of Darkness
Calendar Girl
Dragon: The Bruce Lee Story
Hard Target

Mrs. Doubtfire

Sliver

1994

Angie

Black Beauty

Cabin Boy

Hoop Dreams

I.Q.

Mask, The

North

Pontiac Moon

Ready to Wear

War, The

When a Man Loves a Woman

1995

Braveheart

Congo

Crossing Guard, The

Dangerous Minds

Four Rooms

Perez Family, The

Welcome to the Dollhouse

1996

Basquiat

Bound

Fled

Get on the Bus

Independence Day

Mission: Impossible

Spitfire Grill, The

Twister

1997

Air Force One

Austin Powers: International Man of Mystery

Batman & Robin

Contact

Cop Land

Face/Off

Godzilla

How to Be a Player

Men in Black

Mimic

My Best Friend's Wedding

Paradise Road

She's So Lovely

Speed 2: Cruise Control

Titanic

Wild America

1998

Babe: Pig in the City

Gods and Monsters

Home Fries

Jack Frost

Meet Joe Black

Patch Adams

Prince of Egypt, The

Psycho

Shakespeare in Love

Siege, The

Stepmom

You've Got Mail

1999

American Pie

Any Given Sunday

Astronaut's Wife, The

Austin Powers: The Spy Who Shagged Me

Blue Streak

Bringing Out the Dead

Bowfinger

Cider House Rules, The

Deuce Bigalow: Male Gigolo

Drop Dead Gorgeous

Entrapment

Eyes Wide Shut

Girl, Interrupted

Green Mile, The

Hurricane, The

Ideal Husband, An

Lake Placid

Man on the Moon

Mystery Men

Outside Providence

Red Violin, The

Snow Falling on Cedars

Stuart Little

Talented Mr. Ripley, The

Wild Wild West

Notes

CHAPTER 1

1. Among the more significant of the articles written specifically about trailers are probably the following: Mary Beth Haralovich and Cathy Klaprat, "*Marked Woman* and *Jezebel:* The Spectator-in-the-Trailer," *Enclitic* 5–6, nos. 1–2 (1981–1982): 66–74; Gregory Lukow and Steven Ricci, "The 'Audience' Goes 'Public': Intertextuality, Genre, and the Responsibilities of Film Literacy," *On Film* 12 (1984): 28–36; Paolo Lughi, "When Saying Is Getting Somebody to Do Something: Manipulation and Speech Acts in the Verbal Language of the Trailer," *Semiotic Inquiry/Recherches Semiotiques* 4, nos. 3–4 (Sept.–Dec. 1984): 356–371; S. T. Eastman et al., "Influences of Previews on Movie Viewers' Expectations," *Current Research in Film* 1 (1985): 51–57; Anat Zanger, "Next on Your Screen: The Double Identity of the Trailer," *Semiotica* 120, nos. 1–2 (1998): 207–230; Andy Medhurst, "The Big Tease," *Sight and Sound* 8, no. 7 (July 1998): 24–26; and Marshall Sella, "The 150-Second Sell, Take 34," *New York Times Magazine,* July 28, 2002, 32–37. These range from semiotic approaches (Haralovich and Klaprat, Lukow and Ricci, Lughi, Zanger) to communication studies–oriented audience analyses (Eastman) to more popular commentaries (Medhurst, Sella). Jenni Olson's various "Homo Promo" programmings at gay and lesbian film festivals and on video are also noteworthy. Current research by Vinzenz Hediger and Drehli Robnik will be addressed below. I should also point to two films: *The Politics of Perception* by Kirk Tougas (1973, 33 minutes), which presents a trailer for a Hollywood film, then denaturalizes it by displaying a print of the print, followed by a print of that print and so forth until the images disintegrate (thanks to Philippe-Alain Michaud for telling me about this film); and *The C Files: Tell Saga* (2000) by the Swiss artist duo COM & COM (Johannes M. Hedinger and Marcus Gossolt), which is an artwork comprising the promotional campaign for an unmade film, including a 3 1/2 minute trailer (thanks to Johannes Hedinger for showing me the trailer). The website "Movie Trailer Trash" contains a historical section, "A Brief History of the Trailer," that draws on some of the present research: <http://www.movietrailertrash.com/views/history.html>.

2. Jane M. Gaines, "Fabricating the Female Body," in Jane Gaines and Charlotte Herzog, eds., *Fabrications: Costume and the Female Body* (New York: Routledge, 1990), 15.

3. See Toby Miller et al., *Global Hollywood* (London: British Film Institute, 2001).

4. My study treats American film trailers from the sound era only, but a cross-cultural study of trailers from different countries and different kinds of film markets would be a valuable subject for further research.

5. A useful review of the foundational principles and analyses of film semiotics is found in Robert Stam, Robert Burgoyne and Sandy Flitterman-Lewis, *New Vocabularies in Film Semiotics: Structuralism, Post-Structuralism and Beyond* (London: Routledge, 1992).

6. A series of anthologies comprising recent research on audiences offers rich evidence of both the industry's shifting discourses about its audiences and actual audience behaviors throughout Hollywood history. My work on trailers as textual evidence of Hollywood's conceptions of its audiences can be viewed as providing another piece of the puzzle, particularly as explored in the second volume. See Melvyn Stokes and Richard Maltby, eds., *American Movie Audiences: From the Turn of the Century to the Early Sound Era* (London: British Film Institute, 1999); *Identifying Hollywood's Audiences: Cultural Identity and the Movies* (London: British Film Institute, 1999); and *Hollywood Spectatorship: Changing Perceptions of Cinema Audiences* (London: British Film Institute, 2001).

7. Defending phenomenology, Frank Tomasulo has similarly characterized the discarding of film studies' founding methodologies as "throwing out *the parent* with the bath water," in "The Text-in-the-Spectator: The Role of Phenomenology in an Eclectic Theoretical Methodology," *Journal of Film and Video* 40, no. 2 (summer 1988): 20.

8. In Burke's words, "Not only does the nature of our terms affect the nature of our observations, in the sense that the terms direct the attention to one field rather than to another. Also, many of the 'observations' are but implications of the particular terminology in terms of which the observations are made." Kenneth Burke, *Language as Symbolic Action: Essays on Life, Literature, and Method* (Berkeley: University of California Press, 1966), 46, quoted in *The Terministic Screen: Rhetorical Perspectives on Film*, ed. David Blakesley (Carbondale: Southern Illinois University, 2003), 2.

9. Blakesley, 2, 9.

10. Ibid., 17.

11. For example, Miriam Hansen's study of spectatorship in American silent film asks of its subject matter virtually the same question I ask of mine: "When, how, and to what effect does the cinema conceive of the spectator as a textual term, as the hypothetical point of address of filmic discourse? And once such strategies have been codified, what happens to the viewer as a member of a plural, social audience?" *Babel and Babylon: Spectatorship in American Silent Film* (Cambridge: Harvard University Press, 1991), 2.

12. See, for example, Walter Benjamin's *Arcades Project*, cited in Susan Buck-Morss, *The Dialectics of Seeing: Walter Benjamin and the Arcades Project* (Cambridge: MIT Press, 1989); Charles Eckert, "The Carole Lombard in Macy's Window," *Quarterly Review of Film Studies* 3, no. 1 (winter 1978): 1–22; Anne Friedberg, *Window Shopping: Cinema and the Postmodern* (Berkeley: University of California Press, 1993); Mary Ann Doane, *The Desire to Desire* (Bloomington: Indiana University Press, 1987); Jeanne Allen, "The Film Viewer as Consumer," *Quarterly Review of Film Studies* 5, no. 4 (fall 1980): 481–499; and Miriam Hansen's study cited in note 11.

13. Friedberg, 67–68.

14. Susan Stewart, *On Longing: Narratives of the Miniature, the Gigantic, the Souvenir, the Collection* (Durham: Duke University Press, 1993), 20.

15. Tom Gunning, "The Cinema of Attractions: Early Film, Its Spectator and the Avant-Garde," *Wide Angle* 8, nos. 3–4 (1986), reprinted in *Early Cinema: Space, Frame, Narrative*, ed. Thomas Elsaesser (London: British Film Institute, 1990), 57.

16. Genette defines the epitext as "any paratextual element not materially appended to the text within the same volume but circulating, as it were, freely, in a virtually limitless physical and social space." Trailers correspond to what Genette calls the "publisher's epitext," encompassing "posters, advertisements, press releases and other prospectuses . . . , periodical bulletins addressed to booksellers, and 'promotional dossiers' for the use of sales reps." Gérard Genette, *Paratexts: Thresholds of Interpretation* (New York: Cambridge University Press, 1997), 344, 347.

17. Anthony Wilden, *System and Structure* (London: Tavistock, 1972), 238.

18. This is not only a contemporary phenomenon; there is a substantial body of writing on Hollywood cinema's role in the promotion of specific values and/or trappings of capitalism during the classical era. See in particular Hansen's study cited in note 11; Eckert, "Carole Lombard"; Gaines, "Fabricating the Female Body"; Mary Beth Haralovich, "Advertising Heterosexuality," *Screen* 23, no. 2 (July–Aug. 1982): 50–60; Eric Smoodin, *Animating Culture: Hollywood Cartoons from the Sound Era* (New Brunswick: Rutgers University Press, 1993); and Susan Ohmer, "Female Spectatorship and Women's Magazines: Hollywood, *Good Housekeeping*, and World War II," *Velvet Light Trap* 25 (spring 1990): 53–68.

19. This awareness encompasses such qualities as detailed by Peter Wollen in his influential article on Godard that outlined the "seven cardinal virtues" of "counter cinema" that became the premiere critical commandments of structuralist-era film studies. ("Godard and Counter Cinema: Vent d'Est," in *Movies and Methods*, vol. 2, ed. Bill Nichols [Berkeley: University of California Press, 1985], 501–507).

20. Vinzenz Hediger's formulation of a "nostalgia for the coming attraction" is considered below.

21. Transferring the meaning of one sign to another (from a person, situation, thing or feeling to a commodity), Judith Williamson argues, ads work through us— we complete their meaning by making the connections the ad doesn't make explicit ("I can be like Lindsey Wagner if I buy this car she's showing me"), yet the ads enable this connection-making through their form. We are drawn "into the transformational space between the units of the ad. Its meaning only exists in this space: the field of transaction; and it is here that we operate—*we are this space. . . .*" "[I]f the signified exists in the transformational space and we, as subjects, are constituted in it too . . . this is placing *us* in the space of the signified." This is in part a more nuanced way of stating the widely recognized fact that in advertising, the audience is the ultimate commodity. But, in addition, the audience's meaning-making capacities are a part of the text of the ad. Judith Williamson, *Decoding Advertisements: Ideology and Meaning in Advertising* (New York: Marion Boyars, 1978), 44–45.

22. Advertising scholar Michael Schudson's view of advertising as "capitalist realism" helps illuminate the visual commonalities of trailers. Capitalist realism "glorifies the pleasures and freedoms of consumer choice in defense of the virtues of private life and material ambitions." The aesthetic modes that capitalist realism can encompass (not just the aesthetic of realism per se) include surrealism, comedy or farce, which are all "set out of time and out of space[.] . . . [T]hey present simplified social scenes that show the world 'as it should be,' they picture people as representatives of larger social categories, and they seek an accommodation with whatever is new or newly marketable." "The surface is 'overaccented.'" Michael Schudson, *Advertising: The Uneasy Persuasion* (New York: Basic Books, 1984), 232.

23. Peter Wollen characterizes this aspect of Bazin's work thus: "Bazin emphasized the importance of physiognomy, upon which—as in the films of Dreyer—the interior spiritual life was etched and printed." *Signs and Meaning in the Cinema* (Bloomington: Indiana University Press, 1969), 132. See also Roland Barthes, "The Face of Garbo," in *Mythologies*, trans. Annette Lavers (New York: Hill and Wang, 1972), 56–57.

24. Soviet filmmaker Lev Kuleshov's experiments with editing in the 1910s included juxtaposing shots of a variety of subjects with a single reaction shot of actor Ivan Mozhukhin, with the result that the identical facial expression appeared to signify different emotions depending on what sort of image it followed. Ephraim Katz, *The Film Encyclopedia* (New York: HarperCollins, 1994), 768.

25. The higher decibel level of trailers compared to that of the films they precede has been well documented. See, for example, Bill Desowitz, "The Loud Debate over Trailers," *Los Angeles Times Calendar*, July 6, 1997, 1; and Paul Farhi, "Blockbusters That Thrill You to Deaf," *Washington Post*, July 5, 1998, A1.

26. This trope has been satirized by comics (notably Janeane Garofalo) and indeed by trailers themselves—often the first to satirize their own conventions.

27. In the bracket syntagma, "among the occurrences that it groups together, there is the same kind of relationship as that between the words in a typographical bracket. In the bracket syntagma it is frequently the case that different successive evocations are strung together through optical effects (dissolves, wipes, pan shots, and, less commonly, fades)." Christian Metz, *Film Language: A Semiotics of the Cinema* (New York: Oxford University Press, 1974), 126. See also a recent article that revisits Metz's *Grande Syntagmatique* to assess its usefulness for rhetorical film studies, in which implications of Metz's various emphases on film as rhetoric, as grammar, or as an "indiscernible mixture between grammar and rhetoric" (41) are considered. Ann Chisholm, "Rhetoric and the Early Work of Christian Metz: Augmenting Ideological Inquiry in Rhetorical Film Theory and Criticism," in Blakesley, *The Terministic Screen*, 37–54.

28. Christian Metz, "Problems of Denotation in the Fiction Film," in *Film Language*, 108–146.

29. Interview with Smitty, owner of In Sync Advertising, 1994.

30. This process is interesting to think about in relation to suture theory. Trailers enable an odd sort of "hyper-suture" in which the "absent one" does not represent an ideal spectator position, but a film we haven't yet seen, for which we can construct an imaginary full-length plot cued by the trailer's images of attraction.

31. Williamson, *Decoding Advertisements*.

32. Iser argues, with regard to reading: "The reader must be made to feel for himself the new meaning of the novel. To do this he must actively participate in bringing out the meaning and this participation is an essential precondition for communication between the author and the reader. Rhetoric, then, may be a guiding influence to help the reader produce the meaning of the text, but his participation is something that goes far beyond the scope of this influence." Specifically, in Fielding's *Joseph Andrews*: "Is the conflict to be resolved? If so, how, and why? The answers are not given us. They are the gaps in the text. They give the reader the motivation and the opportunity to bring the two poles meaningfully together for himself." *The Implied Reader: Patterns of Communication in Prose Fiction from Bunyan to Beckett* (Baltimore: Johns Hopkins University Press, 1974), 30, 34.

33. See, for example: Fred Goldberg, *Motion Picture Marketing and Distribution* (Boston: Focal Press, 1991); Aljean Harmetz, "Movie Trailers: Fine Art or Artful Finesse?" *New York Times*, Apr. 20, 1981, C13; David Lees and Stan Berkowitz, "The True Story behind Those 'Coming Attractions' (You'll Laugh! You'll Cry!)," *Los Angeles Magazine*, Jan. 1979, 96; John Wilson, "Man with a Trailer: Impresario of the Movie Teaser," *Los Angeles Times*, June 20, 1977, 10.

34. Market research is still typically taken with a grain of salt by studios, however. As recently as 1998, marketing executives questioned the validity of trailer tests for accurately gauging viewer responses: "There are so many variables that affect the retention of trailers after one sees a film." Kirk Honeycutt, "Audience in Projection Booth: Filmgoers' Reaction to Trailers Being Used to Predict B.O. Bows," *Hollywood Reporter*, May 8, 1998, 3. See also Janet Harbord's discussion of contemporary "lifestyle marketing." *Film Cultures* (London: Sage Publications, 2002), 84–91.

35. Freud's concept of the "navel" of a dream, "the spot where it reaches down into the unknown," is suggestive both of the trailer's centrifugal concatenation of an unseen film's most provocative imagery, and the way it promotes audiences' desires for an ideal film. *The Interpretation of Dreams*, ed. and trans. James Strachey (New York: Basic Books, 1965), 564. (Thank you to Colin Gardner.)

36. Some trailers for rereleases are treated, when they utilize the footage and rhetoric of the original trailer. It should also be noted that while the rule is still a single trailer produced per film, this can be misleading in that earlier and later versions of trailers, produced for different phases in a film's ad campaign, often coexist. The trailers I viewed offered no reliable version documentation, and information on sequential trailer versions is a worthy subject for further research.

37. Smoodin, 45.

38. Ibid., 60.

39. Ibid.

40. I am indebted to Vinzenz Hediger's discussion of the anticipatory dimension of trailers in relation to their source films as a "futurum exactum," which he posits in psychoanalytic terms as a compensation for lack (of knowledge of the future). "Trailer: Demnächst in diesem Theater; Zur Mediengeschichte eines amerikanischen Filmwerbemittels" (master's thesis, University of Zurich, 1995). I am also indebted to Lutz Nitsche for his précis of the thesis and for calling my attention to this concept. Hediger's integration of historical and psychoanalytic resources in defining the cultural status of trailers as nostalgic objects has great value. While drawing on many psychoanalytic concepts, my study rather privileges social-historical formulations such as Raymond Williams's (see note 41 below) over psychoanalytic ones, in search of an audience-centered primer for critical spectatorship.

41. Raymond Williams characterizes the "structures of feeling" that constitute bourgeois ideology's reification of the past, the false "conversion of experience into finished products." *Marxism and Literature* (Oxford: Oxford University Press, 1977), 128–129.

42. Bloch argues, "Expectation, hope, intention towards possibility that has still not become: this is not only a basic feature of human consciousness, but, concretely corrected and grasped, a basic determination within objective reality as a whole."

The Principle of Hope (London: Basil Blackwell, 1959), 7, 13. I am indebted to Doug Kellner's analysis of Bloch's opus, "Ernst Bloch, Utopia and Ideology Critique," in the *Illuminations* website: <http://www.uta.edu/english/dab/illuminations>.

43. I borrow the term from Nick Browne's characterization of the flow of TV watching that includes programs but also ads, station IDs and public service announcements, in his article "The Political Economy of the Television (Super)Text," *Quarterly Review of Film and Video* 9, no. 3 (1984): 174–182, reprinted in *Television: The Critical View*, 4th ed., ed. Horace Newcomb (New York: Oxford University Press, 1987).

44. The broader implications of contemporary trailer supertexts will not be addressed here but deserve further treatment.

45. Tom Gunning, "The Whole Town's Gawking: Early Cinema and the Visual Experience of Modernity," *Yale Journal of Criticism* 7, no. 2 (1994): 191.

46. Charles Musser, "Rethinking Early Cinema: Cinema of Attractions and Narrativity," *Yale Journal of Criticism* 7, no. 2 (1994): 227.

47. Tom Gunning, "'Now You See It, Now You Don't': The Temporality of the Cinema of Attractions," *Velvet Light Trap* 32 (fall 1993): 6.

48. Ibid., 7.

49. While unique, the temporal mode of trailers is nonetheless an intensification of a temporality that Thomas Elsaesser argues is experienced in blockbuster cinema: "The same as different: genre cinema and the norms of story construction involve the self in remembered pleasure and anticipated memory, both of which lock the spectator into a kind of repetition compulsion that ties the cinema experience to recollection and expectation. These shifting structures of temporality and the moment, of place and space not only constitute key aspects of human subjectivity, they generate a subjectivity (in the form of 'desire' or 'fantasy') that can be attached to objects and products. This is what we understand by 'commodity fetishism,' because what defines the commodity in this context is precisely the ability of an object to attract and fix a desire or a fantasy." "The Blockbuster: Everything Connects, but Not Everything Goes," in *The End of Cinema as We Know It: American Film in the Nineties*, ed. Jon Lewis (New York: New York University Press, 2001), 15–16.

50. Interestingly, I found evidence that at least one "trailer man" actually came from a circus background. According to Vinzenz Hediger, Frank Whitbeck, head of the trailer department at MGM from 1934 through 1957, started his career as a circus barker for Barnum and Bailey in the late 1890s, and used his vocal talents for MGM trailers and featurettes up until the 1950s. Moreover, his approach, far from being seen as a throwback, was considered innovative in cinematic promotional terms: Hediger notes that David O. Selznick said of him in 1943, "Whitbeck has always been years ahead of the rest of the business in his conception and

production of trailers." This would tend both to back up my argument about trailers' circus roots and speak to a continuity of circus-influenced discourse in trailers well into the classical era. *Verführung zum Film: Der amerikanische Kinotrailer seit 1912*, Zürcher Filmstudien 5 (Zurich: Schüren, 2001).

51. "While many . . . films, especially before 1903, were modeled on familiar acts and vernacular iconography, the transposition of these into a new medium emphasized distinctions between genres. . . . Fictional genres were derived largely from vaudeville acts, such as comic skits and sight gags, dances, erotic scenes, highlights from popular plays and operas, and melodramatic episodes; they were also reenactments of historical events and tall tales of the Wild West, tableaux from Passion Plays, and trick films in the tradition of the magic shows." Hansen, *Babel and Babylon*, 30.

52. Numerous other examples for various conventions of the vaudeville and circus modes in trailers are detailed in my dissertation, "A Cinema of (Coming) Attractions: American Movie Trailer Rhetoric" (Ph.D. diss., University of California, Los Angeles, 2000).

53. Rick Altman's thesis that classical-era promotional discourses tended to promote multiple genres bears mentioning here. As will be discussed, trailers tend to take a more inclusive view of promoting genres than do the posters in Altman's example. See his *Film/Genre* (London: British Film Institute, 1999).

54. Jane M. Gaines, "From Elephants to Lux Soap: The Programming and 'Flow' of Early Motion Picture Exploitation," *Velvet Light Trap* 25 (spring 1990): 35.

55. Ibid., 35–36.

56. Trailers' presentation of a variety of songs in musicals, presented here as an example of the circus mode, has much in common with the vaudeville mode's "variety show" motif, indicating the impossibility of fully separating the circus and vaudeville influences in trailers. While it is useful to distinguish the democratic impulse to promote "something for everyone" from the hyperbolic impulse to promote "everything for everyone," it should be noted that hyperbole and generalization are not mutually exclusive and that in most trailers the modes tend to work together.

57. Thomas Elsaesser, "Digital Cinema: Delivery, Event, Time," in Elsaesser and Kay Hoffmann, eds., *Cinema Futures: Cain, Abel, or Cable?* (Amsterdam: Amsterdam University Press, 1998), 212.

58. Drehli Robnik, "I Can Hardly Wait: Preview and Anticipation in the Multi-Media Film Experience," presented at "You Can Have It: Kinorituale," Vienna, Nov. 1999.

59. Robnik here quotes Thomas Elsaesser's comments about the contemporary blockbuster film's "carefully orchestrated marketing campaign [which] involves a build-up and an intensification, followed by a media-blitz whose nearest analogy

is the weather. It is much like a hurricane gathering force in mid-Atlantic, as it were, showing first signs of turbulence in toy shops or on MTV, before moving inland." Elsaesser, "Digital Cinema," 214.

60. Robnik, "I Can Hardly Wait." My apologies to Robnik for any misrepresentations of his paper: I am citing my notes, which were taken on the basis of a simultaneous translation of his lecture presented in German at the conference. Many thanks to Julia Ezergailis for the translation.

61. If we play with the sexual overtones of Robnik's "attraction of coming" formulation in relation specifically to trailers, the attraction, I would argue, is one of "not coming—yet."

62. Jane M. Gaines, "Dream/Factory," in Christine Gledhill and Linda Williams, eds., *Reinventing Film Studies* (London: Edward Arnold, 2000), 107.

63. As Noël Burch, Dana Polan and others pointed out years ago, contemporary advertising "would make a Godard green with envy" (Noël Burch, "Narrative/Diegesis —Thresholds, Limits," *Screen* 23, no. 2 [July–Aug. 1982]: 32. See also Dana Polan, "A Brechtian Cinema? Towards a Politics of Self-Reflexive Film," in *Movies and Methods*, vol. 2, ed. Bill Nichols [Berkeley: University of California Press, 1985]). Ironic, formalist or abstract distance no longer offers automatic protection from advertising's manipulations. In fact, ironic positionings are often integral to the development of consumer identities for "Generation X" (and Y) audiences, as articulated by a "Gen-X" scholar with a knack for titles: Bill Salzmann, "Reality Bites, so Buy a Big Gulp," *Bad Subjects*, no. 19 (Mar. 1995); <http://eserver.org/bs/19/Salzmann.html>.

64. Gaines, "Dream/Factory," 110.

65. Factual details in this brief trailer history are drawn largely from the Cerone article cited in note 66 below, but various articles in *Variety*, *Motion Picture Herald*, *Los Angeles Times*, and other trades in the Academy of Motion Picture Arts and Sciences clipping file, as well as Swiss scholar Vinzenz Hediger's important research also informed my understanding of this history. The history of trailers per se is really another book, and is well covered by Hediger's 2001 book based on his dissertation: *Verführung zum Film*.

66. Daniel Cerone, "The Great Movie Come-On," *Los Angeles Times*, Aug. 5, 1989, VI-1.

67. Mary Beth Haralovich, "Motion Picture Advertising: Industrial and Social Forces and Effects, 1930–1948" (Ph.D. diss., University of Wisconsin–Madison, 1984), 226–227.

68. Smitty interview, 1994.

69. "Reading Up: Assessing the Impact of Newspaper Movie Ads and Content," *Hollywood Reporter*, May 11–17, 1999, *Movies and the Media Special Issue*, M24.

70. Smitty interview, 1994.

71. Kevin Thomas, "Movie Trailers Have Long Run," *Los Angeles Times*, Oct. 25, 1966, 10.

72. Ibid.

73. Personal communication with Vinzenz Hediger, Nov. 11, 1998.

74. Miriam Hansen, "The Mass Production of the Senses: Classical Cinema as Vernacular Modernism," in Gledhill and Williams, *Reinventing Film Studies*, 340.

75. Justin Wyatt, *High Concept: Movies and Marketing in Hollywood* (Austin: University of Texas Press, 1994), 156.

76. Douglas Gomery summarizes the postclassical shift in audience thus: "Weekly attendance in movie theatres in the United States peaked in 1946 and then began to drop, so that by the early 1960s it was half of what it had been in the glory days of the Second World War." "Hollywood as Industry," in John Hill and Pamela Church Gibson, eds., *American Cinema and Hollywood: Critical Approaches* (New York: Oxford University Press, 2000), 21.

77. Personal communication with Hediger.

78. Lees and Berkowitz, 96.

79. Wyatt, *High Concept*, 72.

80. This confusion is often seen in cases where trailers for smaller-scale "art films" attempt to appeal to broader audiences, as in the trailer for *Act of the Heart* (1969). And Wyatt details confusions in the promotional campaign for *Billy Jack* (1971) in Wyatt, *High Concept*, 110–111.

81. The phrase is Gerald Mast's from *A Short History of the Movies* (Indianapolis: Bobbs-Merrill Educational Publishing, 1981), 430, quoted in Wyatt, *High Concept*, 73.

82. These practices were in turn influenced by *Billy Jack*'s pioneering of "four-walling," or saturation distribution, in 1973, according to Wyatt, *High Concept*, 110.

83. Thomas Schatz, "The New Hollywood," in Jim Collins, Hilary Radner and Ava Preacher Collins, eds., *Film Theory Goes to the Movies* (New York: Routledge, 1993), 17.

84. Ibid., 19–22.

85. Timothy Corrigan, "Auteurs and the New Hollywood," in *The New American Cinema*, ed. Jon Lewis (Durham: Duke University Press, 1998), 47.

86. Wyatt, *High Concept*, 20.

87. Contemporary trailer campaigns usually start with a "teaser," produced early in the film's production, which is shorter and contains less footage than the trailer. The main theatrical trailer, of which there may occasionally be more than one version, is usually 90 seconds to three minutes long. The case studies I treat here are all theatrical trailers, but my research as a whole encompasses selected teasers. (I do not treat television spots, which are a different facet of the film promotional campaign.)

88. Vinzenz Hediger, "The Narrative Turn in Film Advertising: On the Physiognomy of Contemporary Trailers," presented at "You Can Have It: Kinorituale," Vienna, Nov. 1999.

89. Clearly, however, the shifts and "eras" I identify are hermeneutic constructs, useful primarily as pointers to articulate some differences amid the continuities of promotional history, and as such, they can be seen as somewhat arbitrary. Some would argue that the "New Hollywood" began with the "Hollywood renaissance" of the late sixties, for example. See Michael Ryan and Douglas Kellner, *Camera Politica: The Politics and Ideology of Contemporary Hollywood Film* (Bloomington: Indiana University Press, 1990).

90. This sampling strategy is influenced by the late George Custen's use of the "purposive sample" in his *Bio/Pics* (New Brunswick: Rutgers University Press, 1992), where a necessarily smaller corpus of more readily available films was selected out of a larger group, with the goal of reproducing the range of the larger group's relevant characteristics. In my case the coded parameters were: whether the trailer was representative (of the broader group of trailers viewed from its era generally, or of rhetorical features of audience address within the broader group); whether it was exemplary of rhetorical appeals to audience interest in genre, story, stardom or a combination of these elements; and the genre, year and studio of origin (and budget level) of the trailer. The smaller sample of eighty or so is proportionally similar to the larger sample of the UCLA collection in these features, although there are so many gray areas in some of these categories the process of maintaining proportional similarity during selection was more intuitive than systematic.

CHAPTER 2

1. An empirical "who," or a determination of actual trailer audience reception practices, would moreover be inaccessible for most of the period I am treating.

2. See, for example, a *Variety* article that demonstrates the extent to which studio marketing departments determine which films are greenlit: Christian Moerk and Claude Brodesser, "The 'OK' Corral: Admen, Exex Shoot It Out over Greenlights," *Daily Variety*, Sept. 29, 1999, 1.

3. The explorations into semiotics that have taken place in film studies in the past thirty years appear to have obviated or subsumed Aristotelian rhetoric. Indeed, semiotic analysis and cultural studies are often considered rhetorical criticism, as in Barry Brummett's discussions of cultural studies, along with Marxist, psychoanalytic and feminist criticism, as "varieties of rhetorical criticism," and Renato Barilli's consideration of Barthes, Genette and Todorov as partaking of a "contemporary revival of rhetoric." Brummett, *Rhetoric in Popular Culture* (New York: St. Martin's Press, 1994), 110–154; Barilli, *Rhetoric*, trans. Giuliana Menozzi (Minneapolis: University of Minnesota Press, 1989), 121–122. Roland Barthes's *S/Z*

(cited in note 51 below) offered a model for reading texts based on five codes of signification that bear resemblances to the rhetorical tropes I will discuss (although they serve to illuminate the texts more than the audience in the texts), and semiotic models and vocabulary contribute to these textual analyses as well as rhetoric proper.

4. David Blakesley, ed., *The Terministic Screen: Rhetorical Perspectives on Film* (Carbondale: Southern Illinois University, 2003), 17, 1.

5. Bill Nichols, "Film Theory and the Revolt against Master Narratives," in Christine Gledhill and Linda Williams, eds., *Reinventing Film Studies* (London: Edward Arnold, 2000), 38.

6. Mary Beth Haralovich and Cathy Klaprat, "*Marked Woman* and *Jezebel:* The Spectator-in-the-Trailer," *Enclitic* 5–6, nos. 1–2 (1981–1982): 66–74.

7. Jacques Lacan's elaboration of the acquisition of language as a progression from a prelinguistic real through the Imaginary of the "mirror stage," to the Symbolic realm wherein differences beyond the simple opposition "I/not I" can be discerned is a model that many film theorists have found fruitful to extend to discussions of the film spectator's apprehension of cinematic language(s). Although this is not a Freudian or Lacanian study per se, I use the term "imaginary" in its Lacanian sense. See Jacques Lacan, *The Language of the Self: The Function of Language in Psychoanalysis*, translation and commentary by Anthony Wilden (Baltimore: Johns Hopkins University Press, 1968).

8. Pam Cook, *The Cinema Book* (London: British Film Institute, 1985), 241.

9. Anthony Wilden's reading of the respective realms of the Symbolic and Imaginary orders of signification is useful here: "The Symbolic is the domain of similarity and difference; the Imaginary that of opposition and identity. The Symbolic is the category of displaced reciprocity and mediated relationships; the Imaginary that of mirror-relationships, specialization in symmetry or pseudo-symmetry, duality, complementarity, and short circuits. . . . The Symbolic function is collective and the domain of the Law; the Imaginary creates the illusion of subjective autonomy. . . . The separation of the organism from the environment is Imaginary; the ecosystem is Symbolic. . . . The being of the Imaginary is either/or; the being of the Symbolic is both-and." *System and Structure: Essays in Communication and Exchange* (London: Tavistock, 1972), 264–265 (in most recent scholarship the terms are no longer capitalized).

10. This process is moreover potentially sped up and made more accessible by the presence of theatrical trailers on DVDs.

11. In my experience (based on acquaintances' complaints about trailers over the several years that I have been writing about them), audiences seem to mind differently when trailers "lie" than they do with other types of advertising.

12. For example, Barbara Klinger discusses trailers and other such film epiphe-nomena as "digressive modalities of reading" and argues that "we need to recog-nize the effect that the film industry has on viewing—how industrial practices constitute an inter-textual network which pluralizes the classic text during its cir-culation as a commodity." Moreover, in order "to examine the role that promotion-al texts play in reception, existing formulations must be reconsidered and revised, to better effect the marriage of semiotic and commodity theories." "Digressions at the Cinema: Commodification and Reception in Mass Culture," in James Naremore and Patrick Brantlinger, eds., *Modernity and Mass Culture* (Bloomington: Indiana University Press, 1991), 119, 125, 120. Toby Miller et al. further this call, noting that "there is only a fragmentary screen studies address of the expansion of mar-keting in global Hollywood," wherein "the distribution oligopoly necessitates the enrichment and legitimacy of marketing and . . . ensures a preponderance of com-mercialized texts in the cultural curriculum and exposure to commercial signs in the social space produced around the film-marketing environment." *Global Hollywood* (London: British Film Institute, 2001), 165, 170. And Janet Harbord con-siders film advertising and promotional discourses as components of a range of "intermediary networks" in which "the 'value' of a film is produced relationally. . . . The relational discourse of value operates across discursive domains where film as culture is produced—in marketing and journalism, the texts of advertising, promo-tion, reviews and features." *Film Cultures* (London: Sage Publications, 2002), 2–3.

13. Rhetoric's scarcity in film studies until recently was probably largely based on its association early on with communication studies as a social science, while film studies has institutionally aligned itself with the humanities. Moreover, rhetori-cal studies tended to develop within communication studies along nonhermeneutic lines generally viewed by film scholars as having limited value for critical analysis.

14. Even for Terry Eagleton, one of rhetoric's champions, a characteristic of "a post-structuralist or postmodernist perspective [is] to see all discourse as traced through by the play of power and desire, and thus to view all language as ineradi-cably . . . a rhetorical performance within which questions of truth or cognition are strictly subordinate. If this is so, then all language is 'ideological,' and the category of ideology, expanded to breaking-point, . . . collapses." *Ideology: An Introduction* (London: Verso, 1991), 201. For Mas Ud Zavarzadeh, a leading voice in contempo-rary political film theory, "[r]hetoric in postmodern film theory is understood not as the 'outside' of film and writing, but in fact, as the logic of 'textuality,' which is the film itself, and textuality, as the movement of 'difference,' is a resistance to the idea of the political that argues for global transformative practices." *Seeing Films Politically* (Albany: State University of New York Press, 1991), 54.

15. Bill Nichols makes precisely this point in *Ideology and the Image* (Bloomington: Indiana University Press, 1981), 178.

16. "Rhetoric, like wisdom and ideology, dream-work and desire, has roots in the unconscious. It, too, works performatively to enforce or evade the censorship of disciplinary norms and customary practice. Rhetoric must move us. Its *actio* is to dispose us toward attitudes or actions of our own. Such actions, like changes of attitude, carry transformative power. In fact, rhetoric possesses the power to render the self, or subject of its address, contingent. . . . Rhetoric provides a means of embodying relationality and the contingency it entails." Bill Nichols, "Film and the Uses of Rhetoric," presented at Society for Cinema Studies, San Diego, 1998, 6, 9.

17. Ibid.

18. Blakesley, 2.

19. Aristotle's other categories of rhetoric are deliberative (dealing with counsel or advice) and judicial (dealing with prosecution and defense). Lane Cooper, *The Rhetoric of Aristotle* (New York: D. Appleton–Century Company, 1932), 17.

20. Where a formal syllogism would state "All graduates of Harvard are well educated. Elaine is a Harvard graduate. Therefore, she must be well educated"; its enthymeme counterpart would be "Elaine must be well educated since she graduated from Harvard," leaving the statement "All graduates of Harvard are well educated" as an implied commonplace assumed to be shared by listeners. Maxine C. Hairston, "Bringing Aristotle's Enthymeme into the Composition Classroom," in *Rhetoric and Praxis: The Contribution of Classical Rhetoric to Practical Reasoning*, ed. Jean Dietz Moss (Washington, D.C.: Catholic University Press, 1986), 60–61.

21. According to Lloyd Bitzer, Aristotle considered the enthymeme the "substance of rhetorical persuasion." As Bitzer argues, this is because "enthymemes occur only when speaker and audience jointly produce them. Because they are jointly produced, enthymemes intimately unite speaker and audience and provide the strongest possible proofs. The aim of rhetorical discourse is persuasion; since rhetorical arguments, or enthymemes, are formed out of premises supplied by the audience, they have the virtue of being self-persuasive. Owing to the skill of the speaker, *the audience itself helps construct the proofs by which it is persuaded*." "Aristotle's Enthymeme Revisited," *Quarterly Journal of Speech* 45 (Dec. 1959): 408; emphasis in original. Hairston also emphasizes the value of the enthymeme as a dialogical process between speaker and audience, and refers to it as an embodiment of "situational and pragmatic thinking. . . . Basing an argument on an enthymeme necessarily involves drawing the audience's attitudes, beliefs, and experience into the structure of the argument. Those attitudes, beliefs, and experience form the groundwork for the argument; the very fact that the rhetor does not need to articulate them establishes a bond of intimacy and trust between speaker and listener. . . . So an enthymeme really represents a *process*, a dynamic activity— the listener or reader contributes to his own persuasion . . . [yet] it cannot be

developed out of context or by formula. The person arguing cannot set up the argument before knowing the audience because it holds the key to the appropriate strategy." Hairston, 63, 65 (emphasis in original).

22. As one contemporary trailer producer put it, "Market research can be helpful if you use it simply as a tool. But if you rely too heavily on it, it can kill you. It's a mistake to think this is a science. Making trailers is part magic, part voodoo, part experience." Frank Thompson, "Drawing a Crowd: 100 Years of Movie Marketing," *The 25th Annual Key Art Awards Exhibition Catalog* (Los Angeles: Hollywood Reporter, 1996), 24.

23. Janet Staiger, "Announcing Wares, Winning Patrons, Voicing Ideals: Thinking about the History and Theory of Film Advertising," *Cinema Journal* 29, no. 3 (spring 1990): 6.

24. However, these elements are not necessarily uncontested, as exemplified by the multifaceted ways in which genres can be codified and compounded (see Rick Altman's work on genres, cited in note 34 below).

25. I thank Jim Friedman for the question.

26. Bill Nichols provides answers to questions such as these for documentary film in his detailed analysis of the various ways documentaries construct rhetorical arguments in *Representing Reality: Issues and Concepts in Documentary* (Bloomington: Indiana University Press, 1991).

27. Sergei Eisenstein, *Film Form: Essays in Film Theory* (New York: Harcourt Brace Jovanovich, 1949), 57.

28. Eisenstein, 82.

29. Vivian Sobchack, "'Happy New Year/Auld Lang Syne': On Televisual Montage and Historical Consciousness," in *Reality²*, ed. James Friedman (New Brunswick: Rutgers University Press, 2002), 113.

30. In Aristotelian terms, the associative structures of fictional films would fall within the domain of poetics.

31. Judith Williamson, *Decoding Advertisements: Ideology and Meaning in Advertising* (New York: Marion Boyars, 1978), 44.

32. Bertrand Russell's theory of logical types, an important component of communication theory, states that "there is a discontinuity between a class and its members," such that "[t]he class cannot be a member of itself, because the term used for the class is of a different level of abstraction or logical type from the terms used for the members of the class." As described by Anthony Wilden within the framework of an analysis of communication theory, in his *System and Structure: Essays in Communication and Exchange* (London: Tavistock, 1972), 117.

33. The narration for the *Casablanca* trailer, one of the case studies in Chapter 3, is a good example of one of the ways the appeals are imbricated in the classical era. The trailer opens with a generalized genre appeal ("If you are looking for

adventure, you'll find it in Casablanca"), moving into greater specificity as the story is characterized ("Against this fascinating background is woven the story of an imperishable love. And the enthralling saga of six desperate people, each in Casablanca to keep an appointment with destiny"), followed by cast identifications that highlight the ways in which the specific star personae fit into the formula. The appeal to interest in the film's story is this trailer's dominant rhetoric, however.

34. See, for example, Rick Altman, *Film/Genre* (London: British Film Institute, 1999); Janet Staiger, "Announcing Wares, Winning Patrons, Voicing Ideals: Thinking about the History and Theory of Film Advertising," *Cinema Journal* 29, no. 3 (spring 1990): 3–31; Mark Stuart Miller, "Promoting Movies in the Late 1930s: Pressbooks at Warner Bros." (Ph.D. diss., University of Texas, Austin, 1994); Mary Beth Haralovich, "Motion Picture Advertising: Industrial and Social Forces and Effects, 1930–1948" (Ph.D. diss., University of Wisconsin-Madison, 1984).

35. Some video rental stores reinforce the prominence of genre and stardom as selection parameters in spectatorial decision making, often disguising the familiarity aspect of genre by fragmenting categories as much as possible, offering the consumer a seemingly vast range of selections and emphasizing the centrality of the consumer's role as selector (disguising also the limitations of choices). See Robert Eberwein, "Ideology and Video Rental Stores," presented at Society for Cinema Studies, Pittsburgh, 1992.

36. As Steve Neale characterizes, the function of genres is "to institutionalize a set of expectations which [the industry] will be able, within the limits of its economic and ideological practices, to fulfill. . . . Genres . . . provide a means of regulating memory and expectation, a means of containing the possibilities of reading. Overall, they offer the industry a means of controlling demand, and the institution a means of containing coherently the effects that its products produce." Stephen Neale, *Genre* (London: British Film Institute, 1980), 54–55.

37. The interaction between audiences' experiential knowledge of generic cinematic space and the industry's impulses to police the boundaries of cinematic meaning in trailers can be illuminated by reference to Henri Lefebvre's concept of "representations of space." Lefebvre's monumental reconceptualization of spatiality in human imagination and experience, *The Production of Space*, addresses the quest for an antimetaphoric "science of space," which attempts to express the relationship between space, social organization and modes of production. He argues that each mode of production "offers up its own peculiar space, as it were, as an 'object' for analysis and overall theoretical explication" (31). Within Lefebvre's schema, cinema would be considered a "representation of space," or social space as "conceived" (as opposed to space as "perceived" or space as "lived," both categories of experience rather than represented experience) (40). *The Production of Space*, trans. Donald Nicholson-Smith (Oxford: Basil Blackwell, 1991).

38. Janet Harbord, *Film Cultures* (London: Sage Publications, 2002), 79.

39. Neale cites an article by Charles Musser showing that *The Great Train Robbery* (1903), which critics have come to canonize as the first Western, was perceived within the industry at the time as pertaining to the crime genre. Charles Musser, "The Travel Genre in 1903–04: Moving toward Fictional Narratives," *Iris* 2, no. 1 (1984): 56–57, cited in Steve Neale, "Questions of Genre," *Screen* 31, no. 1 (1990): 55.

40. Rick Altman, "Reusable Packaging: Generic Products and the Recycling Process," in *Refiguring American Film Genres: Theory and History*, ed. Nick Browne (Berkeley: University of California Press, 1998), 9.

41. My discussions of the three rhetorical conventions have omitted, for reasons of length, many of the examples from which I constructed these arguments, but they are detailed in the dissertation from which this book is drawn. See my "A Cinema of (Coming) Attractions: American Movie Trailer Rhetoric" (Ph.D. diss., University of California, Los Angeles, 2000).

42. Vivian Sobchack calls attention to the function of repetition as a promotional strategy specifically within the historical epic film in her essay "'Surge and Splendor': A Phenomenology of the Hollywood Historical Epic," *Representations*, no. 29 (winter 1990): 24–49.

43. Fredric Jameson, "Reification and Utopia in Mass Culture," *Social Text* 1, no. 1 (winter 1979): 137.

44. This example also demonstrates how studio branding can be interwoven with, yet subordinated to, rhetorical appeals.

45. Since trailers are generally produced before the film's music is completed, they often use music from the soundtracks of other films. In this case, the trailer also reinforces the film's identity as a Sharon Stone vehicle.

46. This convention is also utilized within the rhetoric of story.

47. Altman, *Film/Genre*, 60.

48. David Finkle, "Sleek Previews: Tales behind the Trailers," *Village Voice*, Apr. 7, 1998.

49. Vinzenz Hediger, "The Narrative Turn in Film Advertising: On the Physiognomy of Contemporary Trailers," presented at "You Can Have It: Kinorituale," Vienna, Nov. 1999.

50. Responding to the question "who tells" a film story, Gunning identifies three constituent levels of filmic discourse: the profilmic (or everything in front of the camera), the enframed image and editing. "Taken together, they constitute the filmic narrator." This narrator, while "not a flesh-and-blood entity[,] . . . embodies the design organizing narrative discourse, the intentions which unify its effects." And while such organizing entities "do not exist outside the text but are evident in the rhetorical arrangement of its devices," the image of a narrator "does

provide . . . the image of the author within the text[,] . . . the sense of an interven-
ing figure who has arranged the images on the screen in a particular manner with
specific social consequences. The concept of the filmic narrator helps us relate
filmic form to broader contexts." Tom Gunning, *D. W. Griffith and the Origins of
American Narrative Film: The Early Years at Biograph* (Urbana: University of Illinois
Press, 1991), 18–21.

51. Roland Barthes, *S/Z: An Essay*, trans. Richard Miller (New York: Hill and
Wang, 1974). I am indebted again to Tom Gunning, who highlights the primacy of
these four "basic données" of filmic narrative in his article "The Whole Town's
Gawking: Early Cinema and the Visual Experience of Modernity," *Yale Journal of
Criticism* 7, no. 2 (1994): 190.

52. For Nichols epistephilia replaces scopophilia as the principal psychic
motor of documentary film, but while trailers are the domain of fiction and do
evoke the realm of scopophilia, I find epistephilia a useful concept to discuss in
relation to their persuasive arguments that we should see the film they promote—
at the least, trailers allude to this "pleasure in knowing" by oscillating between
withholding and satisfying audience desire for story knowledge. Perhaps we can
see trailers as in some sense a documentary mode, in that they do make truth
claims about their source films (for example, while we expect other sorts of advertisements to lie, we protest when trailers mislead us). See Bill Nichols, *Representing
Reality: Issues and Concepts in Documentary* (Bloomington: Indiana University Press,
1991), 31, 178.

53. For more on the discourse of "Hollywood" and its articulations in film
paratexts, see my "Consuming Production: Documentaries about the Making of
Movies" (master's thesis, San Francisco State University, 1991).

54. The rhetoric of stardom also invites audiences to participate in the glamour of cinematic celebrity, and various ways in which the promotional world of
Hollywood is specifically evoked via stars will be considered below. Here,
Hollywood is promoted as a narrative world—where the *story* (in addition to the
film's story) is that of the making of the film, and/or the "narrative" world of which
filmmaking is a part.

55. Richard Dyer, *Stars*, rev. ed. (London: British Film Institute, 1998), 62.

56. I am referring here, respectively, to Andrew Britton, "Stars and Genre," in
Stardom: Industry of Desire, ed. Christine Gledhill (London: Routledge, 1991), 198,
205; Cathy Klaprat, "The Star as Market Strategy," in *The American Film Industry*,
rev. ed., ed. Tino Balio (Madison: University of Wisconsin Press, 1985), 368–370;
Virginia Wright Wexman, *Creating the Couple: Love, Marriage, and Hollywood
Performance* (Princeton: Princeton University Press, 1993), 23; Hortense

Powdermaker, *Hollywood the Dream Factory* (Boston: Little, Brown, 1950), 251–252; and Justin Wyatt, *High Concept: Movies and Marketing in Hollywood* (Austin: University of Texas Press, 1994), 53–55. Quotes are from Wexman and Wyatt, respectively.

57. Anthony Wilden, *System and Structure: Essays in Communication and Exchange* (London: Tavistock, 1972), 238.

58. For example, for viewers of the trailer for *The Crossing Guard* (1995) who know that Jack Nicholson and Angelica Huston were lovers in real life, the representations of their fictional romance in the trailer are endowed with enhanced appeal.

59. Wilden, *System and Structure*, 238–239.

60. Of course, such contradictions are not unique to *trailers'* promotion of stars. As Allen and Gomery note, "Nearly every scholar who has investigated the phenomenon has commented on the set of paradoxes that lie at the basis of stardom. The star is powerless, yet powerful; different from 'ordinary' people, yet at one time was 'just like us.' Stars make huge salaries, yet the work for which they are handsomely paid does not appear to be work on the screen. . . . The star's private life has little if anything to do with his or her 'job' of acting in the movies, yet a large portion of a star's image is constructed on the basis of 'private' matters: romance, marriage, tastes in fashion, and home life." Robert C. Allen and Douglas Gomery, *Film History: Theory and Practice* (New York: Alfred A. Knopf, 1985), 174.

61. Christine Gledhill, "Signs of Melodrama," in Gledhill, *Stardom*, 207.

62. Ibid., 213.

63. Ibid., 226.

64. Richard Dyer, "*A Star Is Born* and the Construction of Authenticity," in Gledhill, *Stardom*, 137; emphasis added.

65. Nichols continues, "When we recognize a star appearing in a new role, we take it less as documentary evidence of how he or she occupies a historical space and more as an anchor and reference point from which we depart, moving into the specificities of this narrative and its imaginary world. The indexical bond remains, but its evidentiary value is sharply discounted. . . . Our attention flows inward, to comprehend and interpret a story set in *a* world rather than outward, to understand and assess an argument about *the* world." *Representing Reality*, 150.

66. Danae Clark approaches stardom precisely in order to redress such avoidances, which she sees as replicated by most film studies treatments due to their focus on the star-text relation, which she considers "reinscribe[s] the inequities that exist behind the image by refusing to examine the material conditions out of which this signification is produced." Clark opens up an important consideration of the labor history of Hollywood actors, one that as she argues, most text-centered film histories tend to obfuscate. My *audience*-centered textual study, however, seeks to uncover the rhetorical significance of stars as promotional "hooks," and by doing so, to facilitate audience detachment from the assigned identities implied by

their address to audiences. In such an approach, the star-text relation is crucial, because many of the ways promotional discourses are used by producers to conceal the material conditions of actors' labor from audiences can be read in promotional texts themselves. My focus on the star-text relation is thus not incompatible with Clark's focus on the star-labor relation. Counter to current trends among film historians, I believe that a focus on the text does not doom an approach to textual determinism. Danae Clark, *Negotiating Hollywood: The Cultural Politics of Actors' Labor* (Minneapolis: University of Minnesota Press, 1995), 4.

67. Gledhill, "Signs of Melodrama," 219.

68. Using the Greimasian semiotic rectangle ("the representation of a binary opposition or of two contraries . . . , along with the simple negations or contradictories of both terms . . .") in the manner suggested by Fredric Jameson (as a model for ideological closure, wherein the semiotic rectangle "becomes powerfully restructured into a relationship of tension between presence and absence," able to "interrogate the ideological organization of texts and identify the ways ideological contradictions are represented or disguised in textual features"), the rhetoric of stardom in trailers can be examined for the ways in which it promotes stars along the two axes of desire and identification. See Fredric Jameson, *The Political Unconscious: Narrative as a Socially Symbolic Act* (Ithaca: Cornell University Press, 1981), 166; Teresa L. Ebert, "The Romance of Patriarchy: Ideology, Subjectivity, and Postmodern Feminist Cultural Theory," *Cultural Critique*, no. 10 (fall 1988): 29.

69. In her study of the Marilyn Monroe phenomenon in mass culture, Baty characterizes the icon as a more institutionalized unit of mass-cultural signification than the familiar Peircian definition of it solely in terms of resemblance: "Icons are culturally resonant units that convey a familiar set of 'original' meanings and images." She differentiates icons from these more frequent mass-cultural units of signification that are "quick encapsulations; once a story, person, or event is translated into mediapheme form, it ricochets through the channels of mass mediation with ease. Mediaphemes may become icons, but they rarely do; they tend to last as long as a story, issue, or person is 'hot.'" For example, in Baty's terms, familiar film "bytes" such as Arnold Schwarzenegger saying "hasta la vista, baby" in *The Terminator* or Sharon Stone crossing her legs in *Basic Instinct* would be considered mediaphemes that participate in the potential construction of Schwarzenegger and Stone as icons. Trailers and key art for Hollywood films are prime sites where these mediaphemes are offered up and through which they circulate, ever hopeful of helping to confer iconic status on the stars they figure. And such mediaphemes, like icons, refer not only to their "object," a historical and historicized identity, but also to "the economy within which [that object] is produced and circulated." S. Paige Baty, *American Monroe: The Making of a Body Politic* (Berkeley: University of California Press, 1995), 60.

70. The alternations between narrative and musical segments in musical films themselves, of course, highlight the oppositions between spectacle and the everyday as well, as Richard Dyer's article "Entertainment and Utopia" explores. But the effects of such juxtapositions are amplified and foreshortened in trailers. "Entertainment and Utopia," in *Movies and Methods*, vol. 2, ed. Bill Nichols (Berkeley: University of California Press, 1985), 220–232.

71. One trailer literalizes this invitation as a wedding invitation: in the trailer for *My Best Friend's Wedding* (1997), titles interspersed with clips read: "This summer you're invited to witness / A realization / A revelation / And a romance . . ."

72. Intermittent reinforcement, the technique of arbitrarily selective rewarding of behaviors, results in lab rats consistently performing the desired behavior regardless of whether they are rewarded.

CHAPTER 3

1. Richard Maltby, "Introduction," in Richard Maltby and Melvyn Stokes, eds., *Identifying Hollywood's Audiences: Cultural Identity and the Movies* (London: British Film Institute, 1999), 4.

2. Richard Maltby, "Sticks, Hicks and Flaps: Classical Hollywood's Generic Conception of Its Audiences," in Maltby and Stokes, *Identifying Hollywood's Audiences*, 38.

3. The phrase is used by Thomas Cripps in *Hollywood's High Noon: Moviemaking and Society before Television* (Baltimore: Johns Hopkins University Press, 1997), 67.

4. These strictures are cited in Leonard J. Leff and Jerold L. Simmons, *The Dame in the Kimono: Hollywood, Censorship, and the Production Code from the 1920s to the 1960s* (New York: Grove Weidenfeld, 1990), 281–292.

5. Robert Sklar, *Movie-Made America: A Cultural History of American Movies* (New York: Vintage Books, 1975), 74.

6. *Variety*'s reviewer (Aug. 29, 1933) and the *New York Times* review (Mordaunt Hall, Aug. 24, 1933), respectively.

7. Ibid.

8. John Barrymore's offscreen persona, for example, was commonly understood by this time to be that of a drunken egomaniac.

9. It was thus termed in the headline for a review in *Newsweek* (June 13, 1936), which praised the film's honesty, arguing that MGM "dropped all the formulas" and that the film "not only condemns lynching, visibly proving that the wrong man can be the victim of mob hysteria, but completely indicts the clannishness of communities where lynchings have occurred." The review concludes, "Because of the integrity with which it presents the subject, *Fury* is one of the most praiseworthy films ever produced. Unmistakably, it shows the effectiveness of the motion picture for educational propaganda."

10. Ruth Vasey notes, "The PCA [Production Code Administration] had a policy of not approving stories that dealt with ethnic bigotry, on the basis that such treatments were 'provocative and inflammatory.'. . . The PCA would have perceived a story featuring the persecution of African Americans as 'inflammatory' to the point of being unthinkable, and indeed, such subjects were simply not on the studios' agenda." *The World According to Hollywood, 1918–1939* (Madison: University of Wisconsin Press, 1997), 137–139.

11. Lang's director credit in the trailer was somewhat unusual for thirties trailers, evidencing the fact that his "imported artist" cachet was already of value with his first American film.

12. This genre-based trailer does hint at the film's happy ending, but because the rhetoric of story is minimized, we don't gain detailed knowledge of its narrative.

13. Cripps, 64.

14. Sklar, *Movie-Made America*, 182. Sklar notes, "More than any other movie comedians, before or since, [the Marxes and Mae West] turned traditional culture on its head," although "[a]fter 1934, the Production Code and changing audience tastes forced them to set the old values right side up again."

15. In order to present quotations accurately, I italicize film or book titles named within trailer titles only if the trailer title itself does so. Trailers are not usually sticklers for bibliographic form.

16. *Variety*, Mar. 31, 1937, and the *New York Times* (Frank S. Nugent), Mar. 29, 1937, respectively.

17. This film follows Arthur's appearance in *Mr. Deeds Goes to Town* (1936). According to Ephraim Katz, it falls in the wake of the main turning point of her career, her appearance in John Ford's film *The Whole Town's Talking* (1935), after which she "went on to play a succession of fetching, vivacious, often oddball, unpretentious heroines," but she had yet to reach the "peak of her popularity in Frank Capra's social comedies of the late '30s." Ephraim Katz, *The Film Encyclopedia* (New York: HarperCollins, 1994), 53.

18. The comparison highlights the difference between the promotional mandate of classical-era trailers, or in Vinzenz Hediger's terms, "showing as announcing," and that of the contemporary era, "storytelling as selling." Hediger, "The Narrative Turn in Film Advertising: On the Physiognomy of Contemporary Trailers," presented at "You Can Have It: Kinorituale," Vienna, Nov. 1999.

19. Peter Roffman and Jim Purdy, *The Hollywood Social Problem Film: Madness, Despair and Politics from the Depression to the Fifties* (Bloomington: Indiana University Press, 1981), 130.

20. Again, this somewhat atypical trailer was selected along with more typical ones in order to vivify the unique operations of trailer address, which are seen here in high relief.

21. The film earned $4.75 million in U.S. theater rentals (booking fees paid by exhibitors to distributors). Where available, I annotate each trailer case study with the film's rental figures (and later, box-office receipts) from *Variety*'s annual lists of the top 100 films of the year. Film rentals and box-office receipts are not equivalent, but according to reference librarians at the Margaret Herrick Library, at least up to the early 1990s one could roughly compare the two by considering box-office receipts as about double the amount of an equivalent film rental figure (since exhibitors received about 40–50 percent of the box-office take). While I make no specific claims about the influence of these trailers on their films' box-office performance, the figures nonetheless inform us about the film's place in the culture of its time.

22. Actually the trailer, a fairly standard formulaic NSS prerelease handling of the film, pales in relation to the film release's impact on its historical moment, which has been explored in at least one article: Richard Raskin, "*Casablanca* and United States Foreign Policy," *Film History* 4, no. 2 (1990): 153–164.

23. The film earned $4.8 million in U.S. theater rentals.

24. I included two films from the same director (Michael Curtiz), studio (Warner Bros.) and year because their trailers point up so clearly the differences between two distinct rhetorical strategies employed in the classical era to promote films on the basis of story or genre.

25. Thomas Schatz, "World War II and the Hollywood 'War Film,'" in *Refiguring American Film Genres: Theory and History*, ed. Nick Browne (Berkeley: University of California Press, 1998), 111.

26. Schatz, "World War II," 108–109, citing Dana Polan, *Power and Paranoia: History, Narrative, and the American Cinema, 1940–1950* (New York: Columbia University Press, 1986).

27. George F. Custen, *Bio/Pics: How Hollywood Constructed Public History* (New Brunswick: Rutgers University Press, 1992), 212.

28. The 2nd earning film of 1947 with $10.75 million in U.S. theater rentals.

29. Laura Mulvey, for example, notes, "While the film remains visibly a 'Western,' the generic space seems to shift. The landscape of action, although present, is not the dramatic core of the film's story, rather it is the interior drama of a girl caught between two conflicting desires." "Afterthoughts on 'Visual Pleasure and Narrative Cinema' inspired by King Vidor's *Duel in the Sun* (1946)." *Visual and Other Pleasures* (Bloomington: Indiana University Press, 1989), 35.

30. The complexity of the film's generic identity, which the trailer attempts to corral within a Western framework, was noted in at least one review, which remarked on the film's "crossing of strains so long dealt with separately by producers," i.e., "mating of Western melodrama with the sex theme," in the process emphasizing the film as "a very big picture, star-studded as an exploitation man's

dream and scenically beautiful as a sunset over the Grand Canyon; and . . . also, not so anticipatedly, very, very hot stuff." William R. Weaver, *Motion Picture Herald*, Jan. 11, 1947, 3409.

31. The studio pressbook reinforces this rhetoric with a page highlighting "The Making of *Duel in the Sun*" that cites not only Selznick's involvement with *Gone with the Wind*, but that of *Duel*'s film editor, production designer and costume designer as well. Studio pressbooks collection, Margaret Herrick Library, Academy of Motion Picture Arts and Sciences.

32. "A fresh cycle may be initiated by attaching a new adjective to an existing noun genre, with the adjective standing for some recognizable location, plot type, or other differentiation factor." Rick Altman, "Reusable Packaging: Generic Products and the Recycling Process," in Browne, *Refiguring American Film Genres*, 19–20.

33. Vivian Sobchack calls attention to this linking in "'Surge and Splendor': A Phenomenology of the Hollywood Historical Epic," *Representations*, no. 29 (winter 1990): 24–49.

34. The extratextual knowledge of Jones's status as Selznick's lover and "discovery" may contribute additional purchase for this interpretation, through the rhetoric of stardom, inasmuch as Selznick can be seen as strongly motivated to "sell" the star.

35. The 56th earning film for 1948, with $2.2 million in U.S. theater rentals.

36. Hitchcock was reputed to have had creative control of most of his trailers, and although this trailer was made by the Warner Bros. trailer department (which after 1940 had a contract with NSS as well but still produced trailers), we can assume that for the most part, Hitchcock made it. About the later Universal ones, we know that Robert Faber was heavily involved, but even in those cases, as Hitchcock's assistant for twenty years, Peggy Robertson, put it, "You have to remember that every Hitchcock picture was 99 9/10 Hitchcock. It was always Hitch, and the trailers worked the same way." Michael Goodwin, "The Lost Films of Alfred Hitchcock," *New West*, Apr. 1981, 87.

37. The effect of this extra piece of footage (which I experienced, of course, differently than was intended, since I saw this trailer *after* having seen *Rope*) was striking: it was as if the extra scene, which was visually compatible with the rest of the film (except for its setting), pointed to the fragmentary character of the film itself, or indeed of any film. We are reminded that a film is a selective set of shots and scenes that tell a story, yet that the story is a thing unto itself that could have included other shots and scenes: the trailer teaches audiences to distinguish between a film's narrative discourse and its plot. I have since come across evidence that Hitchcock deliberately used his trailers to teach audiences more about his films. At the Hitchcock centennial celebration at the Academy of Motion Picture Arts and Sciences, the host of "From the Hitchcock Collection," Peter Bogdanovich,

introduced the trailer for *Psycho* by recounting his confession to "Hitch" in 1961 that it was not his favorite Hitchcock film, and Hitchcock's response. Hitchcock told Bogdanovich, "You didn't see the humor in it," and insisted that Peggy Robertson show Bogdanovich the long trailer for the film, which is narrated by Hitchcock in a very tongue-in-cheek way as he strolls around the set, and is accompanied by a playful television sitcom-style music score.

38. D. A. Miller, who writes from a gay perspective about the curious absence (even in critical discourse) of discussion of this aspect of the film, while the lesser transgression of the conceit of the "one-shot film" is considered the film's big rule-breaker, notes, "Though by their cursory mention of it critics seem to imply that the protagonists' homosexuality is as plain to see as its proofs may go without saying, homosexuality is in fact extensively prevented from enjoying any such obviousness not only, of course, by the famously hardass Production Code in force at the time of the film's making, which strictly forbade the display and even denomination of homosexuality, but also, more diffusely, by the cultural surround of legal, social, psychic, and aesthetic practices (the last including those of specta-torship) that tolerate homosexuality only on condition that it be kept out of sight." D. A. Miller, "Anal *Rope*," in *Inside Out: Lesbian Theories, Gay Theories*, ed. Diana Fuss (New York: Routledge, 1991), 123.

39. The *Variety* review notes, "It's definitely not for the kiddies," and recom-mends marketing it to "key situations where large groups of the morbidly curious can be attracted." The review makes a note of the film's backdrop of the Leopold-Loeb case on which Patrick Hamilton's play was based, remarking that the "theme of a thrill murder . . . is in questionable taste" (Sept. 1, 1948). Bosley Crowther's *New York Times* review also dances around the film's transgressive elements, chid-ing Hitchcock in his opening, "The fondness of Alfred Hitchcock for cinematic tours de force is admirable evidence of the agility and aggressiveness of his mind. But it is also a disposition which sometimes leads him to stick out his neck and place it, professionally speaking, in positions of evident peril. It is in such a deli-cate position that his neck now appears to be lodged as the consequence of his having stretched it in his new film, an item called 'Rope.'" Crowther also notes that "the emphasis on the macabre in this small story is frightfully intense," and calls Stewart's performance "limp and mopish" (*New York Times*, Aug. 27, 1948, 12).

CHAPTER 4

1. See Toby Miller et al., *Global Hollywood* (London: British Film Institute, 2001); and Justin Wyatt, *High Concept: Movies and Marketing in Hollywood* (Austin: University of Texas Press, 1994).

2. See, for example, Ronald L. Davis, *Celluloid Mirrors: Hollywood and American Society since 1945* (New York: Harcourt Brace and Co., 1997); and Thomas Doherty, *Teenagers and Teenpics: The Juvenilization of American Movies in the 1950s* (Boston: Unwin Hyman, 1988).

3. Hortense Powdermaker, *Hollywood the Dream Factory* (Boston: Little, Brown, 1950), 251–252.

4. The 11th earning film of 1950, with $2.9 million in U.S. theater rentals.

5. It is interesting that such an "edge" is evoked in this trailer, which promotes Davis's first film outside her long tenure at Warner Bros., the studio with whom she had butted heads (and made headlines) in a bid for greater control of her contract.

6. Interestingly, while the trailer assumes audience interest in Davis as an authoritative star, reviews of the time painted a different picture. Martin Shingler's study of the reception of *All About Eve* treats the film's reception in the light of postwar popular discourse surrounding women's domestication, positing a "structuring absence in the way that mainstream reviews shifted the meanings of the film away from those indicated by its narrative, title and original publicity. Despite the fact that the film was promoted as being 'all about women—and their men,' the majority of the reviewers in 1950 avoided such a contentious and divisive topic . . ." Thus, in this instance, the trailer's rhetoric of stardom results in a more feminist reading of the film than was apparent in its actual reception. "Interpreting *All About Eve*: A Study in Historical Reception," in Melvyn Stokes and Richard Maltby, eds., *Hollywood Spectatorship: Changing Perceptions of Cinema Audiences* (London: British Film Institute, 2001), 58–59.

7. The Committee for the First Amendment's assembly of filmmakers and stars made their famous trip to Washington more than two years prior to the release of *All About Eve*.

8. Indeed, during the production of *The War of the Worlds*, Frank Scully notes in "Scully's Scrapbook" in *Variety* that the achievements of Pal's special effects "bunch" outrival the atomic bomb for sheer spectacle. "Having caught three disappointing atomic explosions to date," as Scully puts it, he witnessed a simulated atomic bomb on the set of *The War of the Worlds*, concluding, "These special effects, incidentally, are the stars of the picture. Of course, there are actors in it . . . but the stars are really stars." *Variety*, May 5, 1952, 61.

9. Gregory Bateson, *Steps to an Ecology of Mind* (New York: Ballantine Books, 1972), 327.

10. However, reviewers remembered it: "'The War of the Worlds' is . . . as fearsome as a film as was the Orson Welles 1938 radio interpretation. . . . Its exploitation and word-of-mouth potentials are tremendous and the box-office possibilities big. Just as listeners willingly mesmerized themselves into being

scared half-to-death by the broadcast, so will viewers take vicarious pleasure in the terror loosed in the film—and then walk out of theatres relieved to find the world still as it was." *Variety*, Mar. 2, 1953, in *Variety Film Reviews* (Hollywood: Hollywood Film Archive, 1907–1996).

11. The withholding or rationing of special effects shots of spaceships and creatures in trailers is sometimes a feature of production schedules (live-action footage is available for promotional use sooner than are effects scenes), and sometimes a deliberate withholding, as was true of the promotional campaigns for *E.T. The Extra-Terrestrial* (1982) and *Godzilla* (1997).

12. As Vivian Sobchack notes, "[T]he dull and flat language of reality is often used to create credibility and lend a documentary quality to SF cinema." *Screening Space: The American Science Fiction Film* (New Brunswick: Rutgers University Press, 1997), 154.

13. Sobchack points out that "the language of science and technology is antiromantic and thus anti-individualistic," its intonations "exceedingly democratic in their reductive capacity, their ability to efface personality," lending to the generic creation of a "corporate consciousness, a group protagonist, . . . quite appropriate to the *public* concerns of science fiction." Sobchack, *Screening Space*, 154–155; emphasis in original.

14. The 57th earning film of 1955, with $2 million in U.S. theater rentals.

15. The trailer's emphasis on Tracy's entrance into town is cemented in the film's pressbook by print ads and other exploitation elements (such as a coloring contest using the picture of Tracy with his suitcase on the train tracks). Interestingly, the pressbook and ads also feature the fact that Tracy's character has one arm, which the trailer virtually conceals by using shots that deemphasize it. Studio pressbooks collection, Margaret Herrick Library, Academy of Motion Picture Arts and Sciences.

16. The hinted denouement makes the trailer a fitting transitional precursor to the contemporary trailer practice of privileging revelation over enigma. Indeed Hediger has offered this trailer as an example that combines the classical "showing as announcing" and contemporary "storytelling as selling" modes. Vinzenz Hediger, "The Narrative Turn in Film Advertising: On the Physiognomy of Contemporary Trailers," presented at "You Can Have It: Kinorituale," Vienna, Nov. 1999.

17. Edward Buscombe, *The BFI Companion to the Western* (New York: Atheneum, 1988), 44.

18. The trailer for *High Noon*, the quintessential fifties revisionist Western to which *Bad Day* is compared in at least one review (*New York Times*, Feb. 6, 1955), similarly refrains from characterizing its story in ways that might hint at the film's allegorical thematic of the Blacklist.

19. One review indicates that the film itself was not seen as a Western: "While the story has a western setting, it is not of the oater school, being a gripping drama in modern dress with a 1945 dateline for the action. Besides telling a yarn of tense suspense, the smoothly valued Schary production is concerned with a social message on civic complacency." *Variety*, Dec. 15, 1954.

20. The 26th earning film of 1962, with $3.9 million in U.S. theater rentals.

21. Thomas Schatz, *Hollywood Genres: Formulas, Filmmaking, and the Studio System* (Philadelphia: Temple University Press, 1981), 77.

22. Buscombe, 44.

23. Trailers for other transitional-era Westerns, such as William Wyler's *The Big Country* (1958) and George Stevens's *Shane* (1953), also pointed to their directors' names as draws. The trailer for *The Big Country* also hypermonumentalizes familiar Western tropes while citing its director's name to cement its status as a major A picture and thus rehabilitate the Western. In an earlier trailer for *Shane*, where the film is similarly monumentalized as "the greatest Western ever filmed," the director is also flagged to enhance the film's (and the genre's) legitimacy for a newly art-conscious (assumed) audience, and the trailer notes other "masterpieces" directed by Stevens.

24. The 16th earning film of 1963, with $4.6 million in U.S. theater rentals.

25. Concurrent with the "roadshow" era was the emergence of new kinds of cinematic innovations available for popular audiences, in part inspired by the "British invasion" and Richard Lester's Beatles films, as well as more American forms of dark humor such as Kubrick's *Dr. Strangelove*. Although I do not present these as case studies, trailers for these films likewise served as an important innovative "other" simultaneous to the more staid roadshow productions, exemplifying more playful uses of montage and specially shot trailer footage.

26. Other than McQueen, Garner and Pleasence, the escapees are generally seen in long shots where their faces are not identifiable—probably to preserve an element of suspense so that moviegoers will be less sure which of the principals survives the escape.

27. Indeed, the fact that the film was made a year after the successful World War II epic *The Longest Day*, which elongates (even within its title) the action of D-Day, may have been an element of the trailer's product differentiation efforts.

28. The top earning film of 1967, with $39 million in U.S. theater rentals.

29. The trailer's focus on story, in conjunction with the film's and characters' embeddedness in late-twentieth-century culture, results in my using characters' names in descriptions this time.

30. Michael Ryan and Douglas Kellner, *Camera Politica: The Politics and Ideology of Contemporary Hollywood Film* (Bloomington: Indiana University Press, 1990), 20.

31. The trailer for *The Grapes of Wrath* similarly downplayed the film's treatment of the Great Depression.

32. *Boxoffice*, Jan. 1, 1968, from *Boxoffice Online Reviews:* <http://www.boxoffice.com/classic.html>.

33. *Variety*, Dec. 20, 1967, in *Variety Film Reviews* (Hollywood: Hollywood Film Archive, 1907–1996).

34. *New York Times*, Dec. 22, 1967, 44.

35. In a discussion of the new narrative strategies of a number of films from the late sixties, Michael Ryan and Douglas Kellner note, "The frequent use of discontinuous, reflexive, and interrupted narratives . . . is . . . not only a playful formal device. It gets at the heart of the American imaginary, inasmuch as that is based in narratives (of individual success, of American history, and so on). The fact that the American imaginary is inseparable from cultural representations implies that its critique is inseparable from formal and generic revisions. Consequently, that critique is frequently carried out at the level of image construction, camera technique, editing, generic mixing, and so on. . . . *The Graduate* was . . . innovative in style, relying on imported French New Wave techniques—jump cuts, long takes with hand-held cameras, tight close-ups—to render the experience of alienation from the American ideal of material success." Ryan and Kellner, 19, 20.

36. The 8th earning film of 1972, with $10,885,000 in U.S. theater rentals.

37. "If the movie musical died, as was rumored last year, its reincarnation is 'Cabaret,' a smash hit featuring next year's Academy Award winner, Liza Minnelli." Guy H. Giampapa, WNAC-TV, Boston, cited in Mary Jo Gorman, "Allied Artists' 'Cabaret' Is Selected Blue Ribbon Award Winner for March," *Boxoffice*, Apr. 24, 1972, 9.

38. "'Cabaret' Follows Book More Closely than Legituner," *Variety*, July 12, 1971.

39. This rerelease trailer adds award information in its narration but (again like most from the classical and transitional eras) is structurally the same as the original trailer.

40. Elsaesser continues, "As such, it records a number of (transgressive) cultural shifts (about popular music, gender, and sexuality) which have now become commonplaces, but which at the time perhaps needed to articulate themselves in the context of a referential world—Germany in the 1930s—which itself connoted transgression, danger, ambiguity. . . . *Cabaret* represented its diegetic universe as a blend of youth, the politics of the street, impending apocalypse, and sexual adventure, suggesting a number of *Zeitgeist* parallels between the 1930s and the 1970s." "Subject Positions, Speaking Positions: From *Holocaust, Our Hitler*, and *Heimat* to *Shoah* and *Schindler's List*," in *The Persistence of History: Cinema, Television, and the Modern Event*, ed. Vivian Sobchack (New York: Routledge, 1996), 152–153.

41. Elsaesser also argues that Liza Minnelli's literally "addressing an audience" in the film emerges from an unusually multivocal speaking position compared to other commercial films. This multivocal aspect of her performance is less directly seen in the trailer, which, like many other trailers for commercial films with homosexual content, plays down this aspect (we glimpse the homosexual relationship between the two male characters and see Liza's Marlene-esque drag, but her speaking position is decidedly less multivocal in the trailer).

42. The linkage of entertainment and corruption is also interesting in relation to the rhetoric of stardom's promotions of the seedier aspects of Hollywood stardom.

43. Richard Dyer's influential article on musicals emphasizes them as a utopian genre, in which social contradictions are resolved narratively and musically through figurations of utopian moments. The *Cabaret* trailer similarly resolves the contradictions of promoting dystopic entertainment via generic cues. Richard Dyer, "Entertainment and Utopia," in *Movies and Methods*, vol. 2, ed. Bill Nichols (Berkeley: University of California Press, 1985), 220–232.

44. The 5th earning film of 1973, with $13 million in U.S. theater rentals.

45. "Movie-brat" directors (the first generation of postclassical, television-raised, and film school–educated filmmakers) had already demonstrated a facility for this with George Lucas's 1969 documentary featurette, *Filmmaker*, about the making of Francis Ford Coppola's film *The Rain People*.

46. Such scenes have become commonplace in contemporary entertainment media, as numerous TV sitcoms (*Fresh Prince of Bel Air*, *Home Improvement*) and feature films (*A Bug's Life*, *Toy Story 2*) have displayed comic flubs or staged "outtakes" over end credits. This trailer appears to have innovated the use of "gag reel" footage to promote a film, which, along with the vérité style of its behind-the-scenes segments, indicates it as indeed *transitional* in this specific sense, between classical and contemporary behind-the-scenes modes.

47. Charles Eckert, "Shirley Temple and the House of Rockefeller," in *Stardom: Industry of Desire*, ed. Christine Gledhill (London: Routledge, 1991), 72.

48. Ibid., 67.

49. The 21st earning film of 1974, with $8,433,000 in U.S. theater rentals.

50. This mismatch is interesting—of course, the extent of the cult appeal of Nicholson's character could not have been known before the film came out, yet contemporary trailers rarely "undersell" heroic or star-making characterizations in the way this transitional-era trailer does, perhaps because of the greater melding of star image and characterization in the contemporary era, a subject that will be explored in the following chapter.

51. Ryan and Kellner, 83.

52. A more specific example of this latter point would be the trailer for the era's other big "Eve" film, *The Three Faces of Eve* (1957).

CHAPTER 5

1. Since the acquisition of October Films by Universal in 1997, major studios also dominate independent film distribution. See Justin Wyatt, "The Formation of the Major Independent," and James Schamus, "To the Rear of the Back End: The Economics of Independent Cinema," in Steve Neale and Murray Smith, eds., *Contemporary Hollywood Cinema* (New York: Routledge, 1998), 74–106.

2. See Tino Balio, "'A Major Presence in All of the World's Important Markets': The Globalization of Hollywood in the 1990s," in Neale and Smith, 58–73.

3. Bronwen Hruska, "The Trailer Hitch: Movie Marketers' Ten Tricky Commandments," *Entertainment Weekly*, Dec. 3, 1993, 40–41.

4. "With shrinking margins and rising production costs, studios are losing their appetite for making movies. And getting approval to make them is harder—and increasingly in the hands of marketing and exhibition execs." Christian Moerk and Claude Brodesser, "The 'OK' Corral: Admen, Exex Shoot It Out over Greenlights," *Daily Variety*, Sept. 29, 1999, 1.

5. As a number of recent articles have noted (and my own experience backs up), trailers have become increasingly loud in recent years. See, for example, Bill Desowitz, "The Loud Debate over Trailers," *Los Angeles Times Calendar*, July 6, 1997, 1; and Paul Farhi, "Blockbusters That Thrill You to Deaf," *Washington Post*, July 5, 1998, A1; both articles cite loud trailers as significant contributors to (if not scapegoats for, according to Desowitz) the trend toward louder movies.

6. Justin Wyatt, *High Concept: Movies and Marketing in Hollywood* (Austin: University of Texas Press, 1994), 117, 129.

7. This campaign is treated at length in Mary Paulette Adeline Johnson, "Online, Onscreen: Motion Picture Promotion Via the Internet" (master's thesis, Carleton University [Ann Arbor: UMI Dissertation Services, 2001]).

8. The 2nd earning film of 1976, with $54 million in U.S. theater rentals.

9. The *Box Office* review of Nov. 22, 1976, states, "Fight pictures being rare, 'Rocky' succeeds as an offbeat entry by combining a Cinderella story with a rich character study of a man who boxes because he doesn't know much else. Sylvester Stallone, who stars in his own original screenplay and choreographed the bouts, is being named for Oscar consideration."

10. Fred Goldberg, *Motion Picture Marketing and Distribution* (Boston: Focal Press, 1991), 42–43.

11. This contemporary trailer technique emerged in transitional trailers, and again, *grid* is a common industry term for trailer sequences that (akin to Metz's "parallel syntagmas") crosscut between segments of one scene and those of another (or a variety of clips).

12. Working-class heroes were enjoying new prominence in the mid-seventies, inspired in part by the liberal post-Watergate climate. *Rocky* follows such films of working-class rebellion as 1975's *Dog Day Afternoon* and *White Line Fever*.

13. One indication that visual style and its sensory appeal were indeed key features of this film's promotional campaign is the tagline attributed to the film on the Internet Movie Database (source unknown): "Your eyes . . . Your ears . . . Your senses . . . will be overwhelmed."

14. Unlike the *Casablanca* trailer, which while eliding historical knowledge and story knowledge does signal the break from historical to story-specific information via narration ("Against this fascinating background is woven the story of an imperishable love"), this trailer never really attempts to separate the two.

15. Michael Ryan and Douglas Kellner, *Camera Politica: The Politics and Ideology of Contemporary Hollywood Film* (Bloomington: Indiana University Press, 1990), 83–84.

16. The 17th earning film of 1980, with $20 million in U.S. theater rentals.

17. Other examples are teasers for *Toys* (1992) and *The Muse* (1999).

18. Murray's crossover to dramatic roles alters this dynamic in his particular case toward the late nineties.

19. The top earning film of 1983, with $165.5 million in U.S. theater rentals.

20. Lucas's early insistence on this generic retooling was for the most part effective in the popular imaginary, judging by the number of interviews and news articles that use "space fantasy" as a genre descriptor for the cycle (33 were located on a Lexis-Nexis search of entertainment news dating from 1985). However, critical studies of the science fiction genre such as Sobchack's *Screening Space* and Annette Kuhn's anthology, *Alien Zone: Cultural Theory and Contemporary Science Fiction Cinema* (New York: Verso, 1990), include the *Star Wars* films under the science fiction umbrella.

21. I have reversed my usual practice of privileging stars' names over those of the characters because the rhetoric of stardom is muted in this trailer, which partly because it's a sequel in a known cycle (audiences are assumed to be already familiar with the characters, not just their star personae), and partly because of the intermixing of human with alien and robot characters (who effectively don't have star personae), reinforces the primacy of characterization over star identity.

22. In the earlier film the identical lines were spoken but by the opposite characters, and Han's saying "I know" (instead of "I love you, too") served as a telling bit of characterization. Here, Leia "gets him back."

23. Peter Krämer, "Would You Take Your Child to See This Film? The Cultural and Social Work of the Family-Adventure Movie," in Neale and Smith, 306.

24. Krämer characterizes the films in this genre (including about three-quarters of the top 20 films in *Variety*'s list of all-time top grossers) as follows: "[A]ll share certain basic characteristics. They are intended, and manage, to appeal to all age groups, especially children and their parents, by combining spectacular, often fantastic or magical action with a highly emotional concern with familial relationships, and also by offering two distinct points of entry into the cinematic experiences they provide (childish delight and absorption on the one hand, adult self-awareness and nostalgia on the other hand)." Krämer, 305.

25. George Lucas's corporate identity is an example of this trend—borrowing from Japanese management styles, during the seventies and eighties he fashioned his company Lucasfilm into a California ranch-style home away from home, offering employees a small-town familial structure in the workplace (in a new twist on old paternalistic studio regimes), complete with pets, sports teams, and ski trips. See my "Consuming Production: Documentaries about the Making of Movies" (master's thesis, San Francisco State University, 1991), 32. Spielberg et al. have perpetuated the paternal pattern at Dreamworks SKG, where free gourmet meals and ample snacks are offered, perhaps to compensate for the enforced intensity of the pace of production work.

26. The 66th earning film of 1992, with $9 million in U.S. theater rentals.

27. While making *Thunderheart*, director Michael Apted also completed a documentary about Indian activist Leonard Peltier called *Incident at Oglala*, textually manifesting the political dimensions of the kind of institutional frame-up of Native Americans that the fictional film presents less overtly in its privileging of the suspense narrative. The trailer for the documentary evokes a drama of the truth revealed—and is less compelling than that for *Thunderheart*.

28. Interestingly, like *Bad Day at Black Rock*, the other primary case study of the rhetoric of story's appeals to audience interest in enigma, the *Thunderheart* trailer deals with conflicts that arise when a male outsider attempts to enforce the law in a community not his own. Also like the other trailer, it treats the issue of race or racism as well as the issue of American-ness. Since both films were made during significant times of national redefinition (the Cold War and the multiculturalism debates of the nineties), and appear to be liberal interventions in these contemporary issues or debates, it's useful to compare the ways their trailers' respective promotions of story enigma assume audiences' desires for various kinds of knowledge.

29. Here the trailer exemplifies the trope of "Now" described previously as a convention of contemporary trailer rhetoric of story causality.

30. Interestingly, in the film, however, we see that she is pulling his leg—the trailer audience learns only after seeing the film that it, like Kilmer, has been suckered by its own willingness to believe the stereotypes, and that the trailer has traded on these audience-held stereotypes of Native Americans.

31. Robert Burgoyne, *Film Nation: Hollywood Looks at U.S. History* (Minneapolis: University of Minnesota Press, 1997), 47.

32. Conventional representation is maintained in the comic relief "helper" figure of Graham Greene as tribal police officer, for example, whose charm is real but whose role as sidekick is generically familiar in its desubjectivization.

33. The 5th earning film of 1997, with approximately $171.9 million in box-office receipts.

34. For auteurists in the know, this reference to Wolfgang Petersen increases the film's artistic cachet, since Petersen's *Das Boot* (1981) worked such visual wonders with another cramped military space. Yet by citing not the director's name but his most popular film (starring Clint Eastwood), the trailer also offers intertextual juice to Eastwood fans (and action movie fans) who aren't aware of directors.

35. Contradictorily, Close's presence also might heighten anxiety for those (male) audiences assumed to worry about the fate of the nation if the (male) president is killed.

36. The shock-value coda also echoes *The Great Train Robbery*'s final shot of a gun aimed at the audience.

37. The 2nd earning film of 1997, with more than $250 million in box-office receipts.

38. This is a genre cue, which backs up Vivian Sobchack's comments about "the dull and flat language of reality . . . often used to create credibility and lend a documentary quality to SF cinema." *Screening Space: The American Science Fiction Film* (New Brunswick: Rutgers University Press, 1997), 154.

39. I would argue that this also includes women in an identificatory capacity, not just as those who *desire* the "men." The very generality of the film's concept of "men in black" seems to paradoxically allow, rather than exclude, women's identification, a notion the film itself backs up by including at the end a woman as one of the "men."

40. It is perhaps an interesting footnote (albeit for the rhetoric of stardom) that the two stars' last names are almost as generic as the virtually nameless characters they play, since it reminds us that a significant element of stars' promotion, especially in the classical era, was a reassignment of names and erasure of former identities that at times resembled this film's narrative erasure of identity.

41. In this regard the studio may be deliberately attempting to follow in the footsteps of the successful *Mars Attacks* (1996).

42. The tagline and trailer also essentially elide the film's differentiation between law-abiding and outlaw aliens.

43. Walter Benjamin's point about fascism representing an aestheticization of politics might thus perhaps be reconfigured for the postmodern era, wherein the emphasis is not so much on aestheticization as on an overlay of ironic "fun" as a way that texts such as this trailer can veil their potentially reactionary aspects. See Walter Benjamin, "The Work of Art in the Age of Mechanical Reproduction," in *Illuminations*, ed. Hannah Arendt, trans. Harry Zohn (New York: Schocken, 1968), 242.

44. The 86th earning film of 1998, with some $20.4 million in box-office receipts.

45. The trailer for Hitchcock's original *Psycho*, a long chatty walk through the set with Hitch wherein he describes in a bemused tone what happens where, is a far cry from this one, which while reverential to Hitchcock by virtue of highlighting the film's key quotational set pieces, clearly demonstrates a high concept sensibility, simplifying the promotional message within stylistically complex terms.

46. For example, *Variety* editor Peter Bart, in a "Memo to Gus Van Sant," wrote, "To be honest, Gus, while I think the billboards are cool, I can't decide about the movie. I realize everything is being recycled these days, but a re-creation? Shot-by-shot? . . . It's one thing to look to the past for inspiration, Gus, but you're taking the process a step further. Implicit in your exercise is the admission that we cannot, in fact, improve on previous work, so let's just re-constitute it." "Inside Moves: Putting Our Pop Culture on Rewind," *Variety*, Nov. 2–8, 1998, 2.

47. Indeed, one critic, citing the expectant prerelease "buzz," noted, "It's not the full-on 'queer *Psycho*' that Van Sant fans predicted, but it is an extraordinary drag act." Jonathan Romney, "Horror without a Hitch," *Manchester Guardian Weekly*, Jan. 17, 1999.

48. The Paramount and Columbia logos, respectively, are defaced in the openings of trailers for *Bringing Out the Dead* and *Blue Streak* (1999), while the *Mission: Impossible 2* (2000) trailer opens with a pan around the Paramount logo mountain to begin its narrative on a mountain face.

49. While I'm reasonably sure there may have been earlier logo displacements or defacements in trailers, I believe this is the first one to influence significantly subsequent trailer practice. Of course, logos are tampered with or spoofed frequently during their appearances in actual films, such as the Paramount logo morphing into the film diegesis in the Indiana Jones films, and on television, where Mary Tyler Moore's "MTM" logo replaces the MGM lion with a mewing kitten. Furthermore, the logos themselves have been transformed and modernized before our eyes over time by the studios themselves.

50. If any Hollywood auteur can be said to have achieved the stature of the generic, it would be him—the adjectival form of his name can actually be found in some dictionaries.

51. The slamming is both a contemporary trailer convention, as has been discussed, and a Hitchcockian sound motif, such as the prison cell door in *Frenzy*.

52. The 23rd earning film of 1999, with approximately $87.7 million in box-office receipts.

53. The quotation is from Sir Walter Scott's poem *Marmion* (1808), canto 6, stanza 17.

54. Perhaps this was also thought to be a needed generic touchstone because the trailer's actual visuals don't contain any explosions (a common visual motif in contemporary action-adventure films).

55. Discomfort with their age difference was an extra- (and inter)textual component of the pairing of these two stars. On the heels of other films that paired older men with younger women, reviewers felt this film seemed to serve as the straw that broke the camel's back. "When producer-star Sean Connery . . . handpicked his co-star for *Entrapment*, he emulated last year's popular Hollywood trend that paired Michael Douglas with Gwyneth Paltrow in 'A Perfect Murder,' Warren Beatty with Halle Berry in 'Bulworth' and Harrison Ford with Anne Heche in 'Six Days Seven Nights.' Nearly 40 years her senior, Connery chose the fresh-faced Catherine Zeta-Jones. . . . The old gent doesn't seem comfortable with the fact that he could be his new love interest's grandfather, however, and the resulting uneven relationship jars the whole film." *Boxoffice Online Reviews:* <http://www. boxoffice.com>.

56. Interestingly, in a review that characterizes the film as "the very embodiment of a star vehicle," Roger Ebert describes its hypothetical trailer, which, juxtaposed to this description of the actual one, might help us recall both similarities and contrasts between classical and contemporary trailer rhetoric. "Watching the film, I imagined the trailer. Not the movie's real trailer, which I haven't seen, but one of those great 1950s trailers where big words in fancy type-faces come spinning out of the screen, asking us to Thrill! to risks atop the world's tallest building, and Gasp! at a daring bank robbery, and Cheer! as towering adventure takes us from New York to Scotland to Malaysia. A trailer like that would be telling only the simple truth. It also would perhaps include a few tantalizing shots of Zeta-Jones lifting her leather-clad legs in an athletic ballet designed to avoid the invisible beams of security systems. And shots of a thief hanging upside-down from a 70-story building. And an audacious raid through an underwater tunnel. And a priceless Rembrandt. And a way to steal $8 billion because of the Y2K bug. And so on." "*Entrapment*," *Chicago Sun-Times Online:* <http://www.suntimes.com/ebert/ebert_reviews/1999/04/043003.html>.

57. Jean-Luc Godard's metaphor of the screen as blackboard is irresistible to reference here in spite of the resultant mixed metaphor—interestingly, Godard once expressed a desire to make trailers instead of films. He also made a number of beautiful ones for his own films. See Vinzenz Hediger, "A Cinema of Memory in the Future Tense: Godard, Trailers and Godard Trailers," in James Williams, Michael Temple and Michael Witt, eds., *Forever Godard: The Work of Jean-Luc Godard, 1950 to the Present* (London: Black Dog Publishing, 2003); see also Colin MacCabe, *Godard: Images, Sounds, Politics* (Bloomington: Indiana University Press, 1980).

CHAPTER 6

1. See Wheeler Winston Dixon, "Twenty-five Reasons Why It's All Over," in *The End of Cinema as We Know It: American Film in the Nineties*, ed. Jon Lewis (New York: New York University Press, 2001), 356–366.

2. Vinzenz Hediger has explored the implications of this for Godard's body of films: "[T]o the extent that Godard's work represents a critique of mainstream cinema it does so by virtue of its resembling mainstream trailers rather than by virtue of its not resembling mainstream films. In short, Godard films represent less a radical alternative to mainstream cinema than its continuation by its own means, albeit in a different direction: in the direction of a cinema where trailers no longer announce films, but dis- and replace them." "A Cinema of Memory in the Future Tense: Godard, Trailers and Godard Trailers," presented at Godard conference, London, 2000, 2; in James Williams, Michael Temple and Michael Witt, eds., *Forever Godard: The Work of Jean-Luc Godard, 1950 to the Present* (London: Black Dog Publishing, 2003).

3. Eric Smoodin, *Animating Culture: Hollywood Cartoons from the Sound Era* (New Brunswick: Rutgers University Press, 1993), 45.

4. Miriam Hansen, "The Mass Production of the Senses: Classical Cinema as Vernacular Modernism," in Christine Gledhill and Linda Williams, eds., *Reinventing Film Studies* (London: Edward Arnold, 2000), 343.

5. Tom Gunning, "The Cinema of Attractions: Early Film, Its Spectator and the Avant-Garde," *Wide Angle* 8, nos. 3–4 (1986), reprinted in *Early Cinema: Space, Frame, Narrative*, ed. Thomas Elsaesser (London: British Film Institute, 1990), 60.

6. Thomas Elsaesser, "The Blockbuster: Everything Connects, but Not Everything Goes," in Lewis, *End of Cinema*, 16.

7. For trailer audiences, I would argue, it is more a transubstantiation of commodity into experience.

8. Marshall Sella, "The 150-Second Sell, Take 34," *New York Times Magazine*, July 28, 2002, 34.

9. Jane Gaines, "Dream/Factory," in Gledhill and Williams, *Reinventing Film Studies*, 108, 109.

10. Ibid.

11. Toby Miller et al., *Global Hollywood* (London: British Film Institute, 2001), 197.

12. Hansen, "Mass Production of the Senses," 342.

13. Ernst Bloch, *The Principle of Hope* (London: Basil Blackwell, 1959), 13.

14. Miller et al., 167.

15. For a productive analysis of the implications of the "Benjamin revival" in relation to the role of modern visual culture in historiography, see James Tweedie, *Moving Pictures, Still Lives: Neobaroque Cinema, Visual Culture, Theory* (Ph.D. diss., University of Iowa, [Ann Arbor: UMI Dissertation Services, 2002]).

16. Walter Benjamin, *The Arcades Project*, trans. Howard Eiland and Kevin McLaughlin (Cambridge: The Belknap Press of Harvard University Press, 1999), 392. The influence predates this recent translation, however, generated in particular by Susan Buck-Morss's rich exploration, *The Dialectics of Seeing: Walter Benjamin and the Arcades Project* (Cambridge: MIT Press, 1989). See also Margaret Cohen, *Profane Illumination: Walter Benjamin and the Paris of Surrealist Revolution* (Berkeley: University of California Press, 1993).

17. Again, this aspect of my ideological critique of trailers draws on Michael Schudson's characterization of advertising as a whole as "capitalist realism."

18. On these points, see Donna Haraway, *Modest Witness@Second Millennium.FemaleMan© Meets Oncomouse™: Feminism and Technoscience* (London: Routledge, 1997).

19. Vivian Sobchack, "'Happy New Year/Auld Lang Syne': On Televisual Montage and Historical Consciousness," in *Reality²*, ed. James Friedman (New Brunswick: Rutgers University Press, 2002), 110, quoting Buck-Morss, "Dialectics of Seeing."

20. My suspicion given the current marketing environment is that, in the future, the autonomous, discrete theatrical trailer will be increasingly replaced by multiplicitous and interchangeable trailer segments or modules (more akin to the model of television advertising for films), as the tropes of trailer rhetoric become increasingly embedded in public and virtual spaces.

21. Barbara Klinger, "Digressions at the Cinema: Commodification and Reception in Mass Culture," in James Naremore and Patrick Brantlinger, eds., *Modernity and Mass Culture* (Bloomington: Indiana University Press, 1991), 120.

Selected Bibliography

BOOKS, JOURNAL ARTICLES, AND PRESENTATIONS

Allen, Jeanne. "The Film Viewer as Consumer." *Quarterly Review of Film Studies* 5, no. 4 (fall 1980): 481–499.

Allen, Robert C., and Douglas Gomery. *Film History: Theory and Practice*. New York: Alfred A. Knopf, 1985.

Altman, Rick. *Film/Genre*. London: British Film Institute, 1999.

Anderson, Christopher. *Hollywood TV: The Studio System in the Fifties*. Austin: University of Texas Press, 1994.

Aune, James Arnt. *Rhetoric and Marxism*. Boulder, CO: Westview Press, 1994.

Austin, Bruce A. *Immediate Seatings: A Look at Movie Audiences*. Belmont, CA: Wadsworth, 1989.

Austin, Bruce A., and Thomas F. Gordon. "Movie Genres: Toward a Conceptualized Model and Standardized Definitions." *Current Research in Film* 3 (1987): 12–33.

Balio, Tino. "'A Major Presence in All of the World's Important Markets': The Globalization of Hollywood in the 1990s." In *Contemporary Hollywood Cinema*, edited by Steve Neale and Murray Smith, 58–73. New York: Routledge, 1998.

———, ed. *The Hollywood Film Industry*. Madison: University of Wisconsin Press, 1985.

———. *Hollywood in the Age of Television*. Boston: Unwin Hyman, 1990.

Barilli, Renato. *Rhetoric*. Translated by Giuliana Menozzi. Minneapolis: University of Minnesota Press, 1989.

Barthes, Roland. *Image/Music/Text*. Translated by Stephen Heath. New York: Hill and Wang, 1977.

———. *Mythologies*. Translated by Annette Lavers. New York: Hill and Wang, 1972.

———. *S/Z: An Essay*. Translated by Richard Miller. New York: Hill and Wang, 1974.

Bateson, Gregory. *Steps to an Ecology of Mind*. New York: Ballantine Books, 1972.

Baty, S. Paige. *American Monroe: The Making of a Body Politic*. Berkeley: University of California Press, 1995.

Bazin, André. *What Is Cinema?* Vol. 1. Translated by Hugh Gray. Berkeley: University of California Press, 1967.

Benjamin, Walter. *The Arcades Project*. Translated by Howard Eiland and Kevin McLaughlin. Cambridge: The Belknap Press of Harvard University Press, 1999.

———. "The Work of Art in the Age of Mechanical Reproduction." In *Illuminations*, edited by Hannah Arendt. Translated by Harry Zohn. New York: Schocken Books, 1968.

Bitzer, Lloyd F. "Aristotle's Enthymeme Revisited." *Quarterly Journal of Speech* 45 (Dec. 1959).

Blakesley, David, ed. *The Terministic Screen: Rhetorical Perspectives on Film*. Carbondale: Southern Illinois University, 2003.

Bloch, Ernst. *The Principle of Hope*. London: Basil Blackwell, 1959.

Bordwell, David. *Narration in the Fiction Film*. Madison: University of Wisconsin Press, 1985.

Bottéon, Christophe. "Ces Petits Films qui Dopent les Grands." *Cinéma* 72, no. 558 (Aug. 1995): 6–7.

Brenkman, John. "Mass Media: From Collective Experience to the Culture of Privatization." *Social Text* 1, no. 1 (winter 1979): 94–109.

Britton, Andrew. "Stars and Genre." In *Stardom: Industry of Desire*, edited by Christine Gledhill, 198–206. London: Routledge, 1991.

Browne, Nick. "The Political Economy of the Television (Super)Text." In *Television: The Critical View*, edited by Horace Newcomb. 4th ed. New York: Oxford University Press, 1987.

———. "The Spectator-in-the-Text: The Rhetoric of *Stagecoach*." In *Movies and Methods*, vol. 2, edited by Bill Nichols, 458–475. Berkeley: University of California Press, 1985.

———, ed. *Refiguring American Film Genres: Theory and History*. Berkeley: University of California Press, 1998.

Brummett, Barry. *Rhetoric in Popular Culture*. New York: St. Martin's Press, 1994.

Buck-Morss, Susan. *The Dialectics of Seeing: Walter Benjamin and the Arcades Project*. Cambridge: MIT Press, 1989.

Burch, Noël. "Narrative/Diegesis—Thresholds, Limits." *Screen* 23, no. 2 (July–Aug. 1982): 16–33.

Burgoyne, Robert. *Film Nation: Hollywood Looks at U.S. History*. Minneapolis: University of Minnesota Press, 1997.

Buscombe, Edward. *The BFI Companion to the Western*. New York: Atheneum, 1988.

Chisholm, Ann. "Rhetoric and the Early Work of Christian Metz: Augmenting Ideological Inquiry in Rhetorical Film Theory and Criticism." In *The Terministic Screen: Rhetorical Perspectives on Film*, edited by David Blakesley, 37–54. Carbondale: Southern Illinois University, 2003.

Clark, Danae. *Negotiating Hollywood: The Cultural Politics of Actors' Labor*. Minneapolis: University of Minnesota Press, 1995.

Cochrane, Robert H. "Advertising Motion Pictures." In *The Story of Films*, edited by Joseph P. Kennedy, 237–241. Chicago: A. W. Shaw Co., 1927.

Cohen, Margaret. *Profane Illumination: Walter Benjamin and the Paris of Surrealist Revolution*. Berkeley: University of California Press, 1993.

Cooper, Lane. *The Rhetoric of Aristotle: An Expanded Translation with Supplementary Examples for Students of Composition and Public Speaking*. New York: D. Appleton–Century Co., 1932.

Cormack, Mike. *Ideology and Cinematography in Hollywood, 1930–39*. New York: St. Martin's Press, 1994.

Corrigan, Timothy. *A Cinema without Walls*. New Brunswick: Rutgers University Press, 1991.

Cripps, Thomas. *Hollywood's High Noon: Moviemaking and Society before Television*. Baltimore: Johns Hopkins University Press, 1997.

Custen, George. *Bio/Pics: How Hollywood Constructed Public History*. New Brunswick: Rutgers University Press, 1992.

Davis, Ronald L. *Celluloid Mirrors: Hollywood and American Society since 1945*. New York: Harcourt Brace and Co., 1997.

DeCordova, Richard. *Picture Personalities: The Emergence of the Star System in America*. Champaign: University of Illinois Press, 1990.

Dixon, Wheeler Winston. "Twenty-five Reasons Why It's All Over." In *The End of Cinema as We Know It: American Film in the Nineties*, edited by Jon Lewis, 356–366. New York: New York University Press, 2001.

Doane, Mary Ann. *The Desire to Desire*. Bloomington: Indiana University Press, 1987.

Doherty, Thomas. *Teenagers and Teenpics: The Juvenilization of American Movies in the 1950s*. Boston: Unwin Hyman, 1988.

Dyer, Richard. "Entertainment and Utopia." In *Movies and Methods*, vol. 2, edited by Bill Nichols, 220–232. Berkeley: University of California Press, 1985.

———. *Heavenly Bodies*. London: Macmillan Education Ltd., 1986.

———. "*A Star Is Born* and the Construction of Authenticity." In *Stardom: Industry of Desire*, edited by Christine Gledhill, 132–140. London: Routledge, 1991.

———. *Stars*. London: British Film Institute, 1998.

Eagleton, Terry. *Ideology: An Introduction*. London: Verso, 1991.

Earnest, Olen J. "*Star Wars*: A Case Study of Motion Picture Marketing." *Current Research in Film* 1 (1985): 1–18.

Eastman, S. T., et al. "Influences of Previews on Movie Viewers' Expectations." *Current Research in Film* 1 (1985): 51–57.

Ebert, Teresa L. "The Romance of Patriarchy: Ideology, Subjectivity, and Postmodern Feminist Cultural Theory." *Cultural Critique*, no. 10 (fall 1988): 19–58.

Eberwein, Robert. "Ideology and Video Rental Stores." Presented at Society for Cinema Studies, Pittsburgh, 1992.

Eckert, Charles. "The Carole Lombard in Macy's Window." *Quarterly Review of Film Studies* 3, no. 1 (winter 1978): 1–22.

———. "Shirley Temple and the House of Rockefeller." In *Stardom: Industry of Desire*, edited by Christine Gledhill, 60–73. London: Routledge, 1991.

Eisenstein, Sergei. *Film Form: Essays in Film Theory*. Edited and translated by Jay Leyda. New York: Harcourt Brace Jovanovich, 1949.

Elsaesser, Thomas. "The Blockbuster: Everything Connects, But Not Everything Goes." In *The End of Cinema as We Know It: American Film in the Nineties*, edited by Jon Lewis. New York: New York University Press, 2001.

———. "Digital Cinema: Delivery, Event, Time." In *Cinema Futures: Cain, Abel, or Cable?* edited by Thomas Elsaesser and Kay Hoffmann, 201–222. Amsterdam: Amsterdam University Press, 1998.

———. "Subject Positions, Speaking Positions: From *Holocaust*, *Our Hitler*, and *Heimat* to *Shoah* and *Schindler's List*." In *The Persistence of History: Cinema, Television, and the Modern Event*, edited by Vivian Sobchack, 145–183. New York: Routledge, 1996.

Freud, Sigmund. *The Interpretation of Dreams*. Edited and translated by James Strachey. New York: Basic Books, 1965.

Friedberg, Anne. *Window Shopping: Cinema and the Postmodern*. Berkeley: University of California Press, 1993.

Gaines, Jane M. "Dream/Factory." In *Reinventing Film Studies*, edited by Christine Gledhill and Linda Williams, 100–113. London: Edward Arnold, 2000.

———. "From Elephants to Lux Soap: The Programming and 'Flow' of Early Motion Picture Exploitation." *Velvet Light Trap*, no. 25 (spring 1990): 29–43.

Gaines, Jane M., and Charlotte Herzog, eds. *Fabrications: Costume and the Female Body*. New York: Routledge, 1990.

Gamson, Joshua. *Claims to Fame: Celebrity in Contemporary America*. Berkeley: University of California Press, 1994.

Gaudreaut, André. "Narration and Monstration in the Cinema." *Journal of Film and Video* 39, no. 1 (spring 1987): 29–37.

Genette, Gérard. *Narrative Discourse: An Essay in Method*. Translated by Jane E. Lewin. Ithaca: Cornell University Press, 1980.

———. *Narrative Discourse Revisited*. Translated by Jane E. Lewin. Ithaca: Cornell University Press, 1988.

————. *Paratexts: Thresholds of Interpretation.* Translated by Jane E. Lewin. New York: Cambridge University Press, 1997.

Gledhill, Christine, ed. "Signs of Melodrama." In *Stardom: Industry of Desire*, edited by Christine Gledhill, 207–229. London: Routledge, 1991.

————, ed. *Home Is Where the Heart Is.* London: British Film Institute, 1987.

————. *Stardom: Industry of Desire.* London: Routledge, 1991.

Gledhill, Christine, and Linda Williams, eds. *Reinventing Film Studies.* London: Edward Arnold, 2000.

Goldberg, Fred. *Motion Picture Marketing and Distribution.* Boston: Focal Press, 1991.

Gomery, Douglas. "Hollywood as Industry." In *American Cinema and Hollywood: Critical Approaches*, edited by John Hill and Pamela Church Gibson, 19–28. New York: Oxford University Press, 2000.

————. *The Hollywood Studio System.* New York: St. Martin's Press, 1986.

————. *Shared Pleasures.* Madison: University of Wisconsin Press, 1992.

Grant, Barry Keith, ed. *Film Genre Reader.* Austin: University of Texas Press, 1986.

Gunning, Tom. "The Cinema of Attractions: Early Film, Its Spectator and the Avant-Garde." *Wide Angle* 8, nos. 3–4 (1986): 63–70. Reprinted in *Early Cinema: Space, Frame, Narrative*, edited by Thomas Elsaesser. London: British Film Institute, 1990.

————. *D. W. Griffith and the Origins of American Narrative Film: The Early Years at Biograph.* Urbana: University of Illinois Press, 1991.

————. "'Now You See It, Now You Don't': The Temporality of the Cinema of Attractions." *Velvet Light Trap*, no. 32 (fall 1993): 3–12.

————. "The Whole Town's Gawking: Early Cinema and the Visual Experience of Modernity." *Yale Journal of Criticism* 7, no. 2 (1994): 189–201.

Hairston, Maxine C. "Bringing Aristotle's Enthymeme into the Composition Classroom." In *Rhetoric and Praxis: The Contribution of Classical Rhetoric to Practical Reasoning*, edited by Jean Dietz Moss, 59–78. Washington, D.C.: Catholic University Press, 1986.

Handel, Leo A. *Hollywood Looks at Its Audience: A Report of Film Audience Research.* Urbana: University of Illinois Press, 1950.

Hansen, Miriam. *Babel and Babylon: Spectatorship in American Silent Film.* Cambridge: Harvard University Press, 1991.

————. "Benjamin, Cinema and Experience: 'The Blue Flower in the Land of Technology.'" *New German Critique* 40 (winter 1987): 179–224.

————. "The Mass Production of the Senses: Classical Cinema as Vernacular Modernism." In *Reinventing Film Studies*, edited by Christine Gledhill and Linda Williams. London: Edward Arnold, 2000.

Haralovich, Mary Beth. "Advertising Heterosexuality." *Screen* 23, no. 2 (July–Aug. 1982): 50–60.

————. "Film Advertising: The Film Industry and the Pin-up: The Industry's Accommodations to Social Forces in the 1940s." *Current Research in Film* 1 (1985): 127–164.

————. "Motion Picture Advertising: Industrial and Social Forces and Effects, 1930–1948." Ph.D. diss. University of Wisconsin–Madison, 1984.

Haralovich, Mary Beth, and Cathy Klaprat. "*Marked Woman* and *Jezebel:* The Spectator-in-the-Trailer." *Enclitic* 5–6, nos. 1–2 (1981–1982): 66–74.

Haraway, Donna. *Modest Witness@Second Millennium.FemaleMan© Meets Oncomouse™: Feminism and Technoscience.* London: Routledge, 1997.

Harbord, Janet. *Film Cultures.* London: Sage Publications, 2002.

Harms, John, and Douglas Kellner. "Toward a Critical Theory of Advertising." *Illuminations* website: <http://www.uta.edu/huma/illuminations/kell6.htm>.

Haug, W. F. *Critique of Commodity Aesthetics: Appearance, Sexuality and Advertising in Capitalist Society.* Minneapolis: University of Minnesota Press, 1986.

Heath, Stephen. "*Jaws*, Ideology, and Film Theory." In *Movies and Methods*, vol. 2, edited by Bill Nichols, 509–514. Berkeley: University of California Press, 1985.

————. "Narrative Space." In *Questions of Cinema.* Bloomington: Indiana University Press, 1981.

Hediger, Vinzenz. "A Cinema of Memory in the Future Tense: Godard, Trailers and Godard Trailers." In *Forever Godard: The Work of Jean-Luc Godard, 1950 to the Present*, edited by James Williams, Michael Temple and Michael Witt. London: Black Dog Publishing, 2003.

————. "The Narrative Turn in Film Advertising: On the Physiognomy of Contemporary Trailers." Presented at "You Can Have It: Kinorituale," Vienna, Nov. 1999.

————. "Trailer: Demnächst in diesem Theater; Zur Mediengeschichte eines amerikanischen Filmwerbemittels." Master's thesis, University of Zurich, 1995.

————. *Verführung zum Film: Der amerikanische Kinotrailer seit 1912.* Zürcher Filmstudien 5. Zurich: Schüren, 2001.

Hendrix, Jerry, and James A. Wood. "The Rhetoric of Film: Toward a Critical Methodology." *The Southern Speech Communication Journal* 39 (winter 1973): 105–122.

Horner, Winifred Bryan, ed. *The Present State of Scholarship in Historical and Contemporary Rhetoric.* Columbia: University of Missouri Press, 1983.

Iser, Wolfgang. *The Implied Reader: Patterns of Communication in Prose Fiction from Bunyan to Beckett.* Baltimore: Johns Hopkins University Press, 1974.

Jakobson, Roman. "Linguistics and Poetics." In *Style in Language*, edited by T. A. Sebeok, 350–377. New York: 1960.

Jameson, Fredric. "Nostalgia for the Present." *South Atlantic Quarterly* 88, no. 2 (spring 1989): 53–64.

————. *The Political Unconscious: Narrative as a Socially Symbolic Act*. Ithaca: Cornell University Press, 1981.

————. "Postmodernism, or The Cultural Logic of Late Capitalism." *New Left Review*, no. 146 (July–Aug. 1984): 53–92.

————. "Reification and Utopia in Mass Culture." *Social Text* 1, no. 1 (winter 1979): 130–148.

Jauss, Hans Robert. *Toward an Aesthetic of Reception*. Translated by Timothy Bahti. Minneapolis: University of Minnesota Press, 1982.

Jhally, Sut. *The Codes of Advertising: Fetishism and the Political Economy of Meaning in the Consumer Society*. New York: Routledge, 1990.

Jowett, Garth S. "Giving Them What They Want: Movie Audience Research before 1950." *Current Research in Film* 1 (1985): 19–35.

Kahn, Richard. "Motion Picture Marketing." In *The Movie Business Book*, edited by Jason E. Squire, 263–272. Englewood Cliffs, NJ: Prentice-Hall, 1983.

Kellner, Douglas. "Advertising and Consumer Culture." In *Questioning the Media: A Critical Introduction*, edited by John Downing, Ali Mohammadi and Annabelle Sreberny-Mohammadi, 329–344. Thousand Oaks, CA: Sage Publications, 1995.

————. "Critical Theory, Commodities and the Consumer Society." *Theory, Culture and Society* 1 (1983): 66–81.

Kernan, Lisa Devereux. "A Cinema of (Coming) Attractions: American Movie Trailer Rhetoric." Ph.D. diss., University of California, Los Angeles. Ann Arbor: UMI Dissertation Services, 2000.

————. "Consuming Production: Documentaries about the Making of Movies." Master's thesis, San Francisco State University, 1991.

Klaprat, Cathy. "The Star as Market Strategy." In *The American Film Industry*, revised edition, edited by Tino Balio, 351–376. Madison: University of Wisconsin Press, 1985.

Klenotic, Jeffrey F. "The Place of Rhetoric in 'New' Film Historiography: The Discourse of Corrective Revisionism." *Film History* 6, no. 1 (1994): 45–58.

Klinger, Barbara. "Cinema and Social Process: A Contextual Theory of the Cinema and its Spectators." Ph.D. diss., University of Iowa, 1986.

————. "Digressions at the Cinema: Commodification and Reception in Mass Culture." In *Modernity and Mass Culture*, edited by James Naremore and Patrick Brantlinger, 117–134. Bloomington: Indiana University Press, 1991.

————. *Melodrama and Meaning: History, Culture, and the Films of Douglas Sirk*. Bloomington: Indiana University Press, 1994.

Krämer, Peter. "Would You Take Your Child to See This Film? The Cultural and Social Work of the Family-Adventure Movie." In *Contemporary Hollywood Cinema*, edited by Steve Neale and Murray Smith, 294–311. New York: Routledge, 1998.

Kuhn, Annette. *Alien Zone: Cultural Theory and Contemporary Science Fiction Cinema*. New York: Verso, 1990.

Lacan, Jacques. *The Language of the Self: The Function of Language in Psychoanalysis*. Translation and commentary by Anthony Wilden. Baltimore: Johns Hopkins University Press, 1968.

Lefebvre, Henri. *The Production of Space*. Translated by Donald Nicholson-Smith. Oxford: Basil Blackwell, 1991.

Leff, Leonard J., and Jerold L. Simmons. *The Dame in the Kimono: Hollywood, Censorship, and the Production Code from the 1920s to the 1960s*. New York: Grove Weidenfeld, 1990.

Leiss, William, Stephen Kline and Sut Jhally. *Social Communication in Advertising: Persons, Products, and Images of Well-Being*. New York: Methuen, 1986.

Leitch, T. M. "Twice-Told Tales: The Rhetoric of the Remake." *Literature Film Quarterly* 18, no. 3 (1990): 138–149.

Lewis, Jon, ed. *The End of Cinema as We Know It: American Film in the Nineties*. New York: New York University Press, 2001.

———. *The New American Cinema*. Durham: Duke University Press, 1998.

Lughi, Paolo. "When Saying Is Getting Somebody to Do Something: Manipulation and Speech Acts in the Verbal Language of the Trailer." *Semiotic Inquiry/Recherches Semiotiques* 4, nos. 3–4 (Sept.–Dec. 1984): 356–371.

Lukk, Tiiu. *Movie Marketing: Opening the Picture and Giving It Legs*. Los Angeles: Silman-James Press, 1997.

Lukow, Gregory, and Steven Ricci. "The 'Audience' Goes 'Public': Intertextuality, Genre, and the Responsibilities of Film Literacy." *On Film* 12 (1984): 28–36.

MacCabe, Colin. *Godard: Images, Sounds, Politics*. Bloomington: Indiana University Press, 1980.

Maltby, Richard. "Sticks, Hicks and Flaps: Classical Hollywood's Generic Conception of Its Audiences." In *Identifying Hollywood's Audiences: Cultural Identity and the Movies*, edited by Melvyn Stokes and Richard Maltby, 23–41. London: British Film Institute, 1999.

McGee, Mark Thomas. *Beyond Ballyhoo: Motion Picture Promotion and Gimmicks*. Jefferson, NC: McFarland, 1989.

Medhurst, Andy. "The Big Tease." *Sight and Sound* 8, no. 7 (July 1998): 24–26.

Messaris, P. "Reports: The Film Audience's Awareness of the Production Process." *Journal of the University Film Association* 33, no. 4 (1981): 53–56.

Metz, Christian. *The Imaginary Signifier*. Bloomington: Indiana University Press, 1977.

———. "Problems of Denotation in the Fiction Film." In *Film Language: A Semiotics of the Cinema*, 108–146. New York: Oxford University Press, 1974.

Miller, D. A. "Anal *Rope*." In *Inside Out: Lesbian Theories, Gay Theories*, edited by Diana Fuss, 119–41. New York: Routledge, 1991.

Miller, Mark Crispin. "Hollywood: The Ad." *The Atlantic* 265, no. 4 (Apr. 1990): 41–54.

Miller, Mark Stuart. "Promoting Movies in the Late 1930s: Pressbooks at Warner Bros." Ph.D. diss., University of Texas, Austin, 1994.

Miller, Toby, Nitin Govil, John McMurria and Richard Maxwell. *Global Hollywood*. London: British Film Institute, 2001.

Morin, Edgar. *The Stars*. New York: Grove Press, 1960.

Mudd, Charles S. "The Enthymeme and Logical Validity." *Quarterly Journal of Speech* 45 (Dec. 1959), 409–414.

Musser, Charles. "Rethinking Early Cinema: Cinema of Attractions and Narrativity." *Yale Journal of Criticism* 7, no. 2 (1994): 203–232.

———. "The Travel Genre in 1903–04: Moving toward Fictional Narratives." *Iris* 2, no. 1 (1984): 56–57.

Neale, Steve. *Genre*. London: British Film Institute, 1980.

———. "Questions of Genre." *Screen* 31, no. 1 (1990): 45–66.

Neale, Steve, and Murray Smith, eds. *Contemporary Hollywood Cinema*. New York: Routledge, 1998.

Negt, Oskar, and Alexander Kluge. *Public Sphere and Experience: Toward an Analysis of the Bourgeois and Proletarian Public Sphere*. Minneapolis: University of Minnesota Press, 1993.

Nichols, Bill. *Blurred Boundaries: Questions of Meaning in Contemporary Culture*. Bloomington: Indiana University Press, 1994.

———. "Film and the Uses of Rhetoric." Presented at Society for Cinema Studies, San Diego, 1998.

———. "Film Theory and the Revolt against Master Narratives." In *Reinventing Film Studies*, edited by Christine Gledhill and Linda Williams, 34–52. London: Edward Arnold, 2000.

———. *Ideology and the Image*. Bloomington: Indiana University Press, 1981.

———. *Representing Reality: Issues and Concepts in Documentary*. Bloomington: Indiana University Press, 1991.

Ohmer, Susan. "Female Spectatorship and Women's Magazines: Hollywood, *Good Housekeeping*, and World War II." *Velvet Light Trap*, no. 25 (spring 1990): 53–68.

———. "The Science of Pleasure: George Gallup and Audience Research in Hollywood." In *Identifying Hollywood's Audiences: Cultural Identity and the Movies*, edited by Melvyn Stokes and Richard Maltby, 61–80. London: British Film Institute, 1999.

Öhner, Vrääth. "Happy Trails: The Trailer as Trace of a Future Impression." Presented at "You Can Have It: Kinorituale," Vienna, Nov. 1999.

Opinion Research Corporation. "The Public Appraises Movies: A Survey for Motion Picture Association of America." Princeton, 1957.

Perelman, Chaim, and L. Olbrechts-Tyteca. *The New Rhetoric: A Treatise on Argumentation*. Notre Dame, IN: University of Notre Dame Press, 1969.

Perez, Gilberto. "Toward a Rhetoric of Film: Identification and the Spectator." Presented at Society for Cinema Studies, Chicago, Mar. 2000.

Polan, Dana. "Above All Else to Make You See: Cinema and the Ideology of Spectacle." *Boundary*, no. 2 (1982–1983): 129–144.

———. "A Brechtian Cinema? Towards a Politics of Self-Reflexive Film." In *Movies and Methods*, vol. 2, edited by Bill Nichols, 661–672. Berkeley: University of California Press, 1985.

———. *Power and Paranoia: History, Narrative, and the American Cinema, 1940–1950*. New York: Columbia University Press, 1986.

Powdermaker, Hortense. *Hollywood the Dream Factory*. Boston: Little, Brown, 1950.

Quart, Leonard, and Albert Auster. *American Film and Society since 1945*. New York: Praeger Publishers, 1984.

Raskin, Richard. "*Casablanca* and United States Foreign Policy." *Film History* 4, no. 2 (1990): 153–164.

Ray, Robert B. *A Certain Tendency of the Hollywood Cinema, 1930–1980*. Princeton: Princeton University Press, 1985.

Reichenbach, Harry. *Phantom Fame: An Anatomy of Ballyhoo*. New York: Simon and Schuster, 1931.

Renov, Michael. "Advertising/Photojournalism/Cinema: The Shifting Rhetoric of Forties Female Representation." *Quarterly Review of Film and Video* 11, no. 1 (1989): 1–21.

Robnik, Drehli. "I Can Hardly Wait: Preview and Anticipation in the Multi-Media Film Experience." Presented at "You Can Have It: Kinorituale." Vienna, Nov. 1999.

Roffman, Peter, and Jim Purdy. *The Hollywood Social Problem Film: Madness, Despair and Politics from the Depression to the Fifties*. Bloomington: Indiana University Press, 1981.

Rosen, Philip, ed. *Narrative, Apparatus, Ideology*. Oxford: Oxford University Press, 1986.

Rosten, Thomas. *At the Intersection: Cultural Studies and Rhetorical Studies*. New York: Guilford Press, 1999.

Ryan, Michael, and Douglas Kellner. *Camera Politica: The Politics and Ideology of Contemporary Hollywood Film*. Bloomington: Indiana University Press, 1990.

Saba, Cosetta G. "Pubblicità: Interferenze Autoriali. *Bianco e Nero* 63, no. 1 (Jan.–Feb. 2002): 31–51.

Salzmann, Bill. "Reality Bites, so Buy a Big Gulp." *Bad Subjects*, no. 19 (Mar. 1995).

Sant'Agata, Charles Ronald. "Motion Picture Advertising in the United States: A Study to Determine its Changes." Ph.D. diss., University of California, Los Angeles, 1966.

Sargent, Epes Winthrop. *Picture Theater Advertising*. New York: Moving Picture World/Chalmers Publishing Co., 1915.

Schamus, James. "To the Rear of the Back End: The Economics of Independent Cinema." In *Contemporary Hollywood Cinema*, edited by Steve Neale and Murray Smith, 91–106. New York: Routledge, 1998.

Schatz, Thomas. *Hollywood Genres: Formulas, Filmmaking, and the Studio System*. Philadelphia: Temple University Press, 1981.

———. "The New Hollywood." In *Film Theory Goes to the Movies*, edited by Jim Collins, Hilary Radner and Ava Preacher Collins, 8–36. New York: Routledge, 1993.

Schudson, Michael. *Advertising: The Uneasy Persuasion*. New York: Basic Books, 1984.

Shapiro, M. E., and T. Biggers. "Emotion-Eliciting Qualities in the Motion Picture Viewing Situation and Audience Evaluations." *Current Research in Film* 3 (1987): 1–11.

Shingler, Martin. "Interpreting *All About Eve*: A Study in Historical Reception." In *Hollywood Spectatorship: Changing Perceptions of Cinema Audiences*, edited by Melvyn Stokes and Richard Maltby. London: British Film Institute, 2001: 46–62.

Simonet, Thomas. "Conglomerates and Content: Remakes, Sequels, and Series in the New Hollywood." *Current Research in Film* 3 (1987): 152–164.

Simons, Herbert W., ed. *The Rhetorical Turn*. Chicago: University of Chicago Press, 1990.

Sklar, Robert. *Movie-Made America: A Cultural History of American Movies*. New York: Vintage, 1975.

Smoodin, Eric. *Animating Culture: Hollywood Cartoons from the Sound Era*. New Brunswick: Rutgers University Press, 1993.

———. "'Compulsory' Viewing for Every Citizen: *Mr. Smith* and the Rhetoric of Reception." *Cinema Journal* 35, no. 2 (1996): 3–23.

Sobchack, Vivian. "'Happy New Year/Auld Lang Syne': On Televisual Montage and Historical Consciousness." In *Reality²*, edited by James Friedman. New Brunswick: Rutgers University Press, 2002.

———. *Screening Space: The American Science Fiction Film*. New Brunswick: Rutgers University Press, 1997.

———. "'Surge and Splendor': A Phenomenology of the Hollywood Historical Epic." *Representations*, no. 29 (winter 1990): 24–49.

Stacey, Jackie. *Star Gazing: Hollywood Cinema and Female Spectatorship*. New York: Routledge, 1994.

Staiger, Janet. "Announcing Wares, Winning Patrons, Voicing Ideals: Thinking about the History and Theory of Film Advertising." *Cinema Journal* 29, no. 3 (spring 1990): 3–31.

———. "The Old in the New: A Couple of Contemporary Twists of Film Advertising Practices." Presented at "You Can Have It: Kinorituale." Vienna, Nov. 1999.

———, ed. *The Studio System*. New Brunswick: Rutgers University Press, 1995.

Stalter, K. "Explosive Close-ups Trigger 'Blown Away.'" *American Cinematographer* 76, no. 2 (Feb. 1995): 72–74.

Stam, Robert, Robert Burgoyne and Sandy Flitterman-Lewis. *New Vocabularies in Film Semiotics: Structuralism, Post-Structuralism and Beyond*. London: Routledge, 1992.

Stewart, Susan. *On Longing: Narratives of the Miniature, the Gigantic, the Souvenir, the Collection*. Durham: Duke University Press, 1993.

Stokes, Melvyn, and Richard Maltby, eds. *American Movie Audiences: From the Turn of the Century to the Early Sound Era*. London: British Film Institute, 1999.

———. *Hollywood Spectatorship: Changing Perceptions of Cinema Audiences*. London: British Film Institute, 2001.

———. *Identifying Hollywood's Audiences: Cultural Identity and the Movies*. London: British Film Institute, 1999.

Suleiman, Susan, and Inge Crosman, eds. *The Reader in the Text: Essays on Audience and Interpretation*. Princeton: Princeton University Press, 1980.

Tomasulo, Frank. "The Text-in-the-Spectator: The Role of Phenomenology in an Eclectic Theoretical Methodology." *Journal of Film and Video* 40, no. 2 (summer 1988): 20–32.

Turim, Maureen. "Gentlemen Consume Blondes." In *Movies and Methods*, vol. 2, edited by Bill Nichols, 369–378. Berkeley: University of California Press, 1985.

Tweedie, James. *Moving Pictures, Still Lives: Neobaroque Cinema, Visual Culture, Theory*. Ph.D. diss., University of Iowa. Ann Arbor: UMI Dissertation Services, 2002.

Vasey, Ruth. *The World According to Hollywood, 1918–1939*. Madison: University of Wisconsin Press, 1997.

Wasko, Janet. *Hollywood in the Information Age*. Austin: University of Texas Press, 1994.

Wexman, Virginia Wright. *Creating the Couple: Love, Marriage, and Hollywood Performance*. Princeton: Princeton University Press, 1993.

White, Hayden. *The Content of the Form: Narrative Discourse and Historical Representation*. Baltimore: Johns Hopkins University Press, 1987.

Wilden, Anthony. *The Rules Are No Game*. London: Routledge and Kegan Paul, 1987.

———. *System and Structure: Essays in Communication and Exchange*. London: Tavistock, 1972.

Williams, Linda. "Visual Culture and Spectatorial Discipline: 'The Care and Handling of *Psycho*.'" Presented at "Scary Women: The Symposium," University of California at Los Angeles, Jan. 29, 1994. (A revised version appeared as "Discipline and Fun: *Psycho* and Postmodern Cinema." In *Reinventing Film Studies*, edited by Christine Gledhill and Linda Williams, 351–378. London: Edward Arnold, 2000.)

Williams, Raymond. *Marxism and Literature*. Oxford: Oxford University Press, 1977.

———. *Problems in Materialism and Culture*. London: Verso, 1980.

———. *Television: Technology and Cultural Form*. New York: Schocken Books, 1975.

Williamson, Judith. *Consuming Passions: The Dynamics of Popular Culture*. New York: Marion Boyars, 1986.

———. *Decoding Advertisements: Ideology and Meaning in Advertising*. New York: Marion Boyars, 1978.

Wolfe, Charles. "The Return of Jimmy Stewart: The Publicity Photograph as Text." *Wide Angle* 6, no. 4 (1984): 44–52. Reprinted in *Stardom: Industry of Desire*, edited by Christine Gledhill, 92–106. London: Routledge, 1991.

Wollen, Peter. "Godard and Counter Cinema: Vent d'Est." In *Movies and Methods*, vol. 2, edited by Bill Nichols, 501–507. Berkeley: University of California Press, 1985.

———. *Signs and Meaning in the Cinema*. Bloomington: Indiana University Press, 1969.

Wyatt, Justin. "The Formation of the Major Independent." In *Contemporary Hollywood Cinema*, edited by Steve Neale and Murray Smith, 74–90. New York: Routledge, 1998.

———. *High Concept: Movies and Marketing in Hollywood*. Austin: University of Texas Press, 1994.

Wyatt, Justin, and R. L. Rutsky. "High Concept: Abstracting the Postmodern." *Wide Angle* 10, no. 4 (1988): 42–49.

Zanger, Anat. "Next on Your Screen: The Double Identity of the Trailer." *Semiotica* 120, nos. 1–2 (1998): 207–230.

Zavarzadeh, Mas Ud. *Seeing Films Politically*. Albany: State University of New York Press, 1991.

TRADE JOURNAL AND POPULAR MAGAZINE ARTICLES

Bart, Peter. "Inside Moves: Putting Our Pop Culture on Rewind." *Variety*, Nov. 2–8, 1998, 2.

Beaupre, Lee. "Deny Trailers Reaching Trail's End: Some Chains Abandon Their Use." *Variety*, Aug. 2, 1967, 4.

Burr, Ty. "Our Next Attraction." *Entertainment Weekly*, Dec. 8, 1995, 72–73.

———. "The Studios' Net Worth." *Entertainment Weekly*, May 31, 1996, 62–63.

"'Cabaret' Follows Book More Closely than Legituner." *Variety*, July 12, 1971.

Cerone, Daniel. "The Great Movie Come-On." *Los Angeles Times*, Aug. 5, 1989, 1, 7.

Desowitz, Bill. "The Loud Debate over Trailers." *Los Angeles Times Calendar*, July 6, 1997, 1.

Dutka, Elaine. "Trailer Camp: How Many Toys in His Attic?" *Los Angeles Times Calendar*, Aug. 23, 1992, 26.

Ebert, Roger. "*Entrapment*." *Chicago Sun-Times Online*:
<http://www.suntimes.com/ebert/ebert_reviews/1999/04/043003.html>.

Entrapment. Boxoffice Online Reviews: <http://www.boxoffice.com>.

Fadden, James. "Trailers: Hollywood's Recreational Vehicle to Box Office Heaven." *Back Stage*, Aug. 19, 1983, 5.

Farhi, Paul. "Blockbusters That Thrill You to Deaf." *Washington Post*, July 5, 1998, A1.

Fierman, Daniel, and Jeff Jensen. "A Star Is Reborn." *Entertainment Weekly*, Nov. 27, 1998, 8–9.

Finkle, David. "Sleek Previews: Tales behind the Trailers." *Village Voice*, Apr. 7, 1998.

"For Whom Are We Making Pix?" *Variety*, Sept. 27, 1950, 3, 24.

Francis, Barbara. "Movie Trailers: The Lure of the Filmstrip Tease." *Los Angeles Times Calendar*, Oct. 7, 1979, 7.

Goldstein, Patrick. "Reel Masters of the Two-Minute Drill." *Los Angeles Times Calendar*, Aug. 27, 1991, 1.

Goodwin, Michael. "The Lost Films of Alfred Hitchcock." *New West*, Apr. 1981, 84–87.

Gorman, Mary Jo. "Allied Artists' 'Cabaret' Is Selected Blue Ribbon Award Winner for March." *Boxoffice*, Apr. 24, 1972, 9.

Greenberg, James. "Theatrical Trailers Enter the Realm of Big Business." *Variety*, Mar. 6, 1986, 10.

Harmetz, Aljean. "Movie Trailers: Fine Art or Artful Finesse?" *New York Times*, Apr. 20, 1981, C13.

Honeycutt, Kirk. "Audience in Projection Booth: Filmgoers' Reaction to Trailers Being Used to Predict B.O. Bows." *Hollywood Reporter*, May 8, 1998.

Hruska, Bronwen. "The Trailer Hitch: Movie Marketers' Ten Tricky Commandments." *Entertainment Weekly*, Dec. 3, 1993, 40–41.

Karger, Dave. "Trailer Trash." *Entertainment Weekly*, July 10, 1998, 10–11.

Klady, Leonard. "Truth about Trailers: They Work." *Variety*, Nov. 28, 1994, 13.

———. "TV Still Tops at Luring Pic Auds." *Daily Variety*, June 27, 1994, 1.

Lees, David, and Stan Berkowitz. "The True Story behind Those 'Coming Attractions' (You'll Laugh! You'll Cry!)." *Los Angeles Magazine*, Jan. 1979, 96.

Lydgate, William. "Hollywood Listens to the Audience." *Reader's Digest*, Apr. 1944, 83–85.

Manna, Sal. "Coming Attractions." *American Way*, Sept. 2, 1986, 56–59.

Moerk, Christian, and Claude Brodesser, "The 'OK' Corral: Admen, Exex Shoot It Out over Greenlights," *Daily Variety*, Sept. 29, 1999, 1.

Montesano, Anthony P. "Things to Come: Trailers Whet Viewer Appetites, Leave Them Wanting More." *Back Stage*, Feb. 2, 1990, 30.

Morgan, Laura. "Same Old Song," *Entertainment Weekly* (the "Biz" column), Nov. 19, 1999, 29.

"The 'Prize Baby' Remembers: Four Decades of Progress in the Making of Trailers by National Screen Service." *Motion Picture Herald*, Nov. 7, 1959, 16–17.

"Reading Up: Assessing the Impact of Newspaper Movie Ads and Content." *Hollywood Reporter*, May 11–17, 1999, *Movies and the Media Special Issue*, M24.

Rehm, John. "Inside Pitches: Sexy Movie Advertising Morally Wrong and Misleading." *Advertising Agency and Advertising & Selling* 43, no. 4 (Apr. 1950): 70.

Robbins, Jim. "Biz Realities Force NSS into Per-Use Trailer Deals." *Daily Variety*, Nov. 3, 1982. In Margaret Herrick Library clipping file, Academy of Motion Picture Arts and Sciences.

"Robert Faber: The Trailer Maker." *The Cinemaphile*, Apr. 1976, 4, 76.

Romney, Jonathan. "Horror without a Hitch," *Manchester Guardian Weekly*, Jan. 17, 1999.

Sargent, Epes Winthrop. "Development of Exploitation." *Variety*, Dec. 29, 1931, 12.

———. "Exploitation: Its Beginning and Its Advance." *Moving Picture World* 85, no. 4 (Mar. 1927): 286.

Scully, Frank. "Scully's Scrapbook." *Variety*, May 5, 1952, 61.

Seguin, Denis. "Follow the Leader." *Screen International*, July 10, 1998, 11.

Sella, Marshall. "The 150-Second Sell, Take 34." *New York Times Magazine*, July 28, 2002, 32–37.

Sennett, Ted. "'Coming Attractions' Must Be a Good Movie, It's Playing at All the Local Theatres." *Variety*, Jan. 3, 1968, 39.

Skenazy, Lenore. "Coming to a Theater Near You: Trailers are Kanew's Medium." *Advertising Age*, June 23, 1986, 38.

Thompson, Frank. "Drawing a Crowd: 100 Years of Movie Marketing." *The 25th Annual Key Art Awards Exhibition Catalog*. Los Angeles: Hollywood Reporter, 1996.

Turan, Kenneth. "The Lure of Trailers." *American Film*, Oct. 1982, 51–55.

Wadsley, Pat. "Mini Masterpieces: Teasers, Trailers and Spots before Your Eyes." *Theatre Crafts*, Jan. 1987, 70–72.

Weaver, William R. "Studios Use Audience Research to Learn What Pleases Customers." *Motion Picture Herald*, July 20, 1946, 37.

Wells, Jeffrey. "Thrills! Chills! Laffs!: And These Are Just the Previews!" *Los Angeles Times Calendar*, May 16, 1993, 22–23.

Whiteside, Thomas. "Zooming Up from a Pinpoint." *New Republic*, Sept. 22, 1947, 25–27.

Wilson, John. "Man with a Trailer: Impresario of the Movie Teaser." *Los Angeles Times*, June 20, 1977, 10.

Index

CPSIA information can be obtained at www.ICGtesting.com
Printed in the USA
LVOW131246300812

296636LV00001B/25/P